W9-BYM-220

SAP MM—Functionality and Technical Configuration

SAP PRESS is issued by
Bernhard Hochlehnert, SAP AG

SAP PRESS is a joint initiative of SAP and Galileo Press. The know-how offered by SAP specialists combined with the expertise of the publishing house Galileo Press offers the reader expert books in the field. SAP PRESS features first-hand information and expert advice, and provides useful skills for professional decision-making.

SAP PRESS offers a variety of books on technical and business related topics for the SAP user. For further information, please visit our website: *www.sap-press.com*.

G. Hartmann/U. Schmidt
Product Lifecycle Management with SAP
2005, 620 pp.
ISBN 1-59229-036-1

H. Hölzer/M. Schramm
Quality Management with SAP
2005, 538 pp.
ISBN 1-59229-030-2

S. Karch, L. Heilig, C. Bernhardt, A. Hardt, F. Heidfeld, R. Pfennig
SAP NetWeaver Roadmap
2005, 312 pp.
ISBN 1-59229-041-8

F. Forndron/T. Liebermann/M. Thurner/P. Widmayer
mySAP ERP Roadmap
2006, 293 pp.
ISBN 1-59229-071-X

A. Goebel, D. Ritthaler
SAP Enterprise Portal
2005, 310 pp., with CD
ISBN 1-59229-018-3

Martin Murray

SAP MM— Functionality and Technical Configuration

Editor Jawahara Saidullah
Copy Editor John Parker, UCG, Inc., Boston, MA
Cover Design Silke Braun
Printed in Germany

ISBN 1-59229-072-8
ISBN 13 978-1-59229-072-7
1st edition 2006

Contents

24 Balance Sheet Valuation 411

25 Material Ledger 425

26 Classification System 433

1 Materials Management Overview

The Materials Management module (MM) is a core component of the SAP software. The functionality within MM is the engine that drives the Supply Chain. In this chapter, we shall describe the elements that make MM such an important part of SAP and the Logistics function.

In this book we will describe importance of the Materials Management module as it relates to the overall functionality within the SAP software and as a part of the supply chain.

MM contains many aspects of SAP functionality, including purchasing, goods receiving, material storage, consumption-based planning, and inventory. It is highly integrated with other modules such as Finance (FI), Controlling (CO), Production Planning (PP), Sales and Distribution (SD), Quality Management (QM), Plant Maintenance (PM), and Warehouse Management (WM).

1.1 Materials Management as a Part of SAP

1.1.1 SAP History

SAP was founded in 1972 and is now a market and technology leader in client/server enterprise application software. It provides comprehensive solutions for companies of all sizes and all industry sectors. SAP is the number-one vendor of standard business-application software and the third largest software supplier in the world. SAP delivers scalable solutions that enable its customers to further advance industry best practices. SAP is constantly developing new products that allow their customers to respond to dynamic market conditions and help them maintain competitive advantage.

In 1979, SAP released its mainframe product called R/2. Materials Management (then called RM) was a core module of this release. SAP dominated the German market, and in the 1980s SAP developed a broader market in the rest of Europe. In 1992, SAP developed the client/server application we all know now as R/3. This allowed SAP to bring the software to the U.S. market and within a few years SAP became the gold standard for ERP software.

When businesses chose SAP as their enterprise application software, they identified the integration of the modules as a key advantage. Many other software companies used a best-of-breed approach and developed highly complex interfaces to integrate the separate software packages. Supporting and maintaining just one system rather than several systems with different hardware platforms has yielded a significant cost saving for companies.

1.1.2 Core SAP Functionality

SAP was originally developed as an enterprise application-software package that was attractive to very large manufacturing companies. As the number of companies adopting SAP began to grow, a number of smaller companies in many different industries came to believe that SAP was the product that could give them a competitive advantage.

Many of these companies required just the core SAP functionality. That usually comprises FI, MM, SD, and PP. Often companies would start their implementations with this core functionality and then on the second and third phases of their implementations they would introduce functionality such as CO, WM, Human Resources (HR), etc.

In Release 4.7 Enterprise of SAP R/3, the company introduced the concept of the Enterprise Core. This included all of the R/3 4.6 functionality. It did include some limited functional enhancements and developments to the existing 4.6 functionality. SAP announced that, going forward, all legal changes and support packs, including stabilization and performance enhancements, would be applied at the Enterprise Core level.

For Release 4.7 Enterprise, several core areas are included. These are Finance (FI, CO), Human Resources (HR), Product Lifecycle Management (PP, AM, QM), and Supply Chain Management (WM, PP, MM).

SAP has now introduced mySAP ERP, which is the next level of SAP R/3 evolution. This new software suite includes four core functional areas. These are mySAP ERP Financials (FI, CO), mySAP ERP Human Capital Management (HR), mySAP ERP Corporate Services (QM, EH&S), and mySAP ERP Operations (PP, WM and MM).

As SAP develops more extensive solutions and tools for its customers, Materials Management continues to be an important part of the foundation on which subsequent functionality is built.

1.2 Materials Management as Part of Logistics

1.2.1 Definition of Logistics and Supply Chain

Logistics can be defined as the management of business operations, including the acquisition, storage, transportation, and delivery of goods along the supply chain. The supply chain can be defined as a network of retailers, distributors, transporters, storage facilities, and suppliers that participate in the sale, delivery, and production of a particular product.

1.2.2 Management of the Supply Chain

From these definitions it is clear that materials management is an integral part of the Logistics function within SAP. There are three flows that are important when we look at MM in the supply chain. These are:

- The material flow
- The information flow
- The financial flow

The material flow describes the movement of materials from the vendor to the company and then on to the customer (and, potentially, customer returns). Today companies are integrating with suppliers and customers, not just interfacing. Therefore any improvements companies can provide to the visibility of their material flow will allow them to be flexible and responsive to their customers. Customers will want to do business with companies who are responsive. Those companies will also be able to gain a competitive advantage and increase market share by being more flexible, quicker, more dependable.

The information flow includes the transmitting of orders (including EDI, fax, etc.) and updating the status of all deliveries. Companies that can show customers and vendors viability by using real time information have a distinct competitive advantage over others.

The financial flow includes the financial documents that are created at each material movement.

1.2.3 SAP and Logistics

We have defined the Logistics function and the flows within the supply chain. So how does SAP help clients to manage this supply chain to gain a competitive advantage?

SAP R/3 software provides a company with the ability to have the correct materials at the correct location at the correct time, with the correct quantity and at the most competitive cost. The competitive advantage is achieved when the company can manage the process. This involves managing the company's relationships with its vendors and customers. It also, involves controlling their inventory, forecasting customer demand, and receiving timely information with regards to all aspects of the supply-chain transactions.

When we break this down and look at the modules involved in the management of the supply chain, we can see that although materials management is an integral part of Logistics, it is only part of the big picture.

The Logistics function in SAP includes the following:

- ▶ Materials Management (MM)
- ▶ Sales and Distribution (SD)
- ▶ Quality Management (QM)
- ▶ Plant Maintenance (PM)
- ▶ Production Planning (PP)
- ▶ Project Systems (PS)
- ▶ Finance (FI)
- ▶ Warehouse Management (WM)
- ▶ Logistics Information System (LIS)

There is additional functionality in the Logistics area, such as Batch Management, Handling Unit Management, Variant Configuration, Engineering Change Management, and Environmental, Health, and Safety (EHS). These can be important in the Logistics area, depending on the individual customer requirements.

1.3 MM Integration with Other Modules

MM is thus one of many modules that are important in the Logistics function of SAP. Looking at the supply chain we can see where MM integrates with the other modules to create an efficient product for managing the supply chain.

1.3.1 The Material Flow of the Supply Chain

As defined already, the material flow is the movement of the material from the vendor to the customer. To instigate a flow, a material need would be have to be created by either the Production Planning module (PP) via a materials requirements planning (MRP) system or by a sales order created in Sales and Distribution (SD). The need is created, and a Purchase Requirement is sent to the vendor, relating to instructions on delivery date, quantity and price.

The vendor sends the material, and it is received and may be subject to a quality inspection in Quality Management (QM). Once approved, the material can be stored and may be stored in a warehouse using Warehouse Management (WM).

The material could be required in a Production Order in Production Planning (PP) or be part of a larger project defined in Project System (PS).

Once a final material is available for the customer, it can be picked from the warehouse and shipped to the customer using the SD module.

From the description of this simple flow it is easy to see that MM is highly integrated with the other SAP modules.

1.3.2 The Information Flow of the Supply Chain

Using the simple example described in the next paragraph, the information flow can be easily understood.

Initially, there may be an order from a customer. This order could be transmitted via electronic data interchange (EDI) to the SAP system. The information on SAP will communicate whether the item is in stock, and if not the information is sent to the MRP tool. Information is sent back to the customer giving the delivery date.

The MRP tool takes all the information regarding the production schedules, capacity of the production facility, and the available materials involved in production to create production orders and material requests that appear as information in the procurement system.

The information in the procurement system creates orders with required delivery dates, which are transmitted to vendors. The return information from the vendor will confirm the date of delivery of the material.

The vendor can send EDI transmissions informing the company of the status of the delivery.

Upon receipt of the material, information is passed from the receiving documents to the warehousing system (WM), in order to store the material correctly. The information is passed to the production systems (PP) to calculate if the production order is ready to commence.

Once the material is ready to ship, SAP produces information for shipping (SD) and can send that information to the customer.

At all of the touch points with SAP, information has been recorded and are available to be reviewed and analysed. The more information that is shared across the total supply chain, the more cost benefits can be achieved with improvements based on the analytical data. The Logistics Information System (LIS) and other standard reports in SAP can give the supply-chain management team invaluable insights into how their logistics function operates.

1.3.3 The Financial Flow of the Supply Chain

The typical flow of financial information in the supply chain includes the invoices received by the company from their vendors, the payments to the vendors, the billing of the customers for the materials, and the incoming payments.

The vendor supplies material to the company and sends an invoice to be paid against. The company has choices within SAP on how to pay the vendor: either pay on receipt of the materials (two-way match), or more often, on receipt on the vendor invoice (three-way match). The accounts payable department carries out this function. The invoice-verification process within SAP is an excellent example of the integration between the MM and Finance modules.

The financial flow of the supply chain has not changed in magnitude, as did the information and material flows. However, the current SAP R/3 system allows the supply chain users to analyse the financial key performance indicators (KPI) that are part of the overall supply chain. These can include Inventory Turns, Days of Working Capital, Days of Inventory, Days Sales Outstanding and Days Payables Outstanding. The integration of MM and the other key modules within the Logistics function combine to provide this important information in an accurate and timely fashion.

Developments in the financial flow of the supply chain have direct impacts on the MM module. The imaging of invoices is an important development that allows companies to scan the incoming invoices (either internally or using a third party) and create a Workflow (WF) to speed approval. A message is sent to the purchaser, and approval time is shortened.

Companies now use Procurement cards (P-cards) to reduce costs and speed up the financial flow. Purchasing with a P-card ties purchasers into an approved vendor list and allows companies to focus on obtaining discounts and favourable rates with certain vendors. The other benefit is that the P-card reduces the invoice processing by the accounts payable department. The individual purchases are managed by spending limits associated with each p-card user and payment is made directly to the vendor by the P-card company. The use of P-cards is an example of how developments in the supply-chain management outside of SAP influence the integration between SAP modules, in this case FI and MM.

In this chapter we have seen that the Materials Management module of SAP is a core component of any SAP implementation. MM can be described as the engine that drives the supply-chain functionality within SAP. It also integrates with most other SAP modules in some way. The aim of the following chapters is to focus the reader on the functionality and configuration of MM and its complex integration with other SAP modules.

2 MM Organizational Structure

Correctly defining the Materials Management organizational structure is the foundation for a successful SAP implementation. It is extremely important to make accurate decisions about entities such as company codes, plants, and storage locations.

In any new SAP implementation, there are a number of decisions that need to be made in order to ensure a successful project. Decisions regarding the client structure, company codes, plants, and warehouses are all important to the project and require knowledge of the objects to be decided upon and consensus between the customer and the project-implementation team.

2.1 Client Structure

2.1.1 What is a Client?

A company that purchases SAP software will install it on its servers, which is then configured for its specific needs. This is called an instance. Companies can have more than one SAP instance, but they will exist on different SAP systems. Within one SAP instance, a number of clients will be created. We define a client as an organizational and legal entity in the SAP system. The master data is protected within the client, as it cannot be accessed from outside. The master data in a client is only visible within that client and cannot be displayed or changed from another client. There will be multiple clients in a SAP system. Each of these clients can have a different objective and each client represents a unique environment. A client has its own set of tables and user data. Objects can be either client dependent or client independent. When SAP objects are used by only one client, they are defined as client dependent. There are objects, such as ABAP/4 programs, that are used by all the clients in a SAP system. These objects are called client independent.

SAP delivers the software with three clients: 000, 001, and 066, which are discussed below.

Client 000

This is the SAP reference client, and it contains tables with default settings but no master data. Client 000 can be copied, using the client copy function, to create the clients that will be used in the implementation. For important configuration work, you will need to log on to SAP Client 000. For configuration of the Correction and Transport System (CTS), this client must be used. Client 000 also plays an important role in upgrade processes. Each time an SAP customer upgrades its system, client-dependent changes automatically will be upgraded in Client 001, and the changes then can be copied to other clients. Client 001 should not be changed or deleted from the system.

Client 001

This is delivered as the preparation production client. It is initially identical to Client 000. After any upgrades, Client 001 will not be identical to Client 000. Customizing can be done in this client but it cannot be used as the production client. SAP customers can choose whether to use or not to use this client.

Client 066

This is the client used by SAP for its SAP Early Watch service. This client enables SAP to remotely access the customer system. SAP provides this service to the customer to improve system performance and for system support. SAP recommends having an Early Watch session before a customer's implementation goes live and another after the go-live date.

2.1.2 Creating the Client Landscape

Once the SAP software has been installed with the three delivered clients, the technical team will need to create a number of clients that reflect the customer needs. The general client structure for a SAP implementation would include a development client, training client, quality client, and production client.

The development client is where all development work should take place. There may be more than one development client created. For example, there may be a *sandbox client*, for general users to practice and test configuration. In addition, there may also be a *clean* or *golden* development client where the specific configuration is made and from which it is then transported to the quality client for review before moving to the production client.

The training client usually reflects the current production system and is used primarily for the training of project staff and end users. When configuration is transported to the production client, it is transported to the training client at the same time. The training client is useful for training, but is not a necessity for implementation.

Other clients may be needed for Business Information Warehouse (BW) and other components such as Enterprise Buyer Professional (EBP) and Customer Relationship Management (CRM).

To successfully manage this client environment, there should be strict procedures and security so that the integrity of the clients is maintained.

2.1.3 Defining a Client

There are four aspects to be considered when defining a client. These are described below.

Organizational Structure

The customer should define a client as the highest organizational unit in its organizational structure. The client is the basis for the construction and configuration of other organizational units.

Business Environment

A client should be a representation of a holding company or group of companies in the physical business world.

Technical Environment

The client defines the boundary of the master data. The information can only be accessed inside the client.

Work Environment

The client is the work area that end users interact with the system. Ninety percent of the tables in the client are client dependent.

2.1.4 Correction and Transport System (CTS)

Changes created in the development client must be moved, or transported, to the quality client for testing and then to the production client. The CTS is the vehicle by which you can move objects such as programs, screens, configurations, or security settings from one client to another. The CTS provides consistency between the clients by maintaining log entries. The CTS provides a standardized procedure for managing and recording changes made to a client.

When you are configuring functionality in the development client that has been designated as the client to migrate from, you will find that saving the configuration will require extra steps.

On saving, there will be an **Enter change request** dialog screen. This will require you to either add this configuration step to an existing Customizing request or to create a new request. If you opt to create a new request, another pop-up screen will appear that requires a short description of the change you are making and that may default the other information, such as your user ID, source client, category, and target client. If the target client is blank, ensure that you enter the correct target client for your change request.

On saving this change request, the system will display the change-request number. The system will have saved the configuration change you have made and logged that change in the change request.

The change request can be viewed by using transaction code SE01. On the initial screen, enter the change request number, or press F4 to find your request. Click on the display button and the request will be displayed. By expanding the view it is possible to see the changes that have been made to the tables in the current client and that will be migrated to the target client. If you have authorization, you may also release the change request so that it can be migrated. If you do not have authorization, the change request will need to be released by a designated resource.

By using transaction code SE10, you are able to see all requests and repairs that are owned by a user ID. It is important to note that a change request cannot be released if it is empty, if the objects are not locked properly, or if the objects are not locked in another task or change request. The next section will explain the functionality of company codes, creating and assigning a client.

2.2 Company Code

2.2.1 What is a Company?

The U.S. Census Bureau (2002) defines a company as follows:

"A company comprises all the establishments that operate under the ownership or control of a single organization. A company may be a business, service, or membership organization; it may consist of one or several establishments and operate at one or several locations. It includes all subsidiary organizations, all establishments that are majority-owned by the company or any subsidiary, and all the establishments that can be directed or managed by the company or any subsidiary."

SAP defines a company and a company code separately. SAP defines a company as the smallest organizational unit for which legal financial statements can be prepared. A company can contain one or more company codes, but they must use the same chart of accounts and the same fiscal-year breakdown.

SAP defines a company code as the smallest organizational unit for which a complete self-contained set of accounts can be drawn up. You will be able provide data for generating balance sheets and profit-loss statements. The company code will represent legally independent companies. Using more than one company code allows a customer to manage financial data for different independent companies at the same time.

For example, when a customer is deciding on its organizational structure, the customer can use one or many company codes. Thus, if a U.S. company has components of its organization in Canada and in Mexico, it may decide that it should use three company codes. The company-code currencies can be different for each component, but they would be required to use the same chart of accounts.

2.2.2 Creating a Company Code

The creation of a company and company codes is usually part of the Financials configuration, but you may need to create these on occasion.

The company field is defined in transaction OX15. It is defined as a six- character alphanumeric string. The navigation path is **IMG • Enterprise Structure • Definition • Financial Accounting • Maintain Company**.

The company code can be created using transaction OX02. The navigation path is **IMG • Enterprise Structure • Definition • Financial Accounting • Define, Copy, Delete, Check Company Code**. The field is defined as a four-character alphanumeric string. In transaction OX02, it is possible to copy from an existing company code and change the name, city, and country to your company details. This transaction will update table T001.

After creating the company code, you will need to maintain the company- code address. To do this you need to use transaction OBY6. This transaction will update table SADR.

2.2.3 Assigning a Company Code

Once a company code has been defined, it must be assigned to a number of objects. In the IMG, there are a number of financial configuration steps that need to be carried out. The company code can be assigned to the following:

- Credit Control Area
- Financial Management Area
- Company

The next section follows on from the SAP structure of a company to the structure, creation and assignment of a plant.

2.3 Plants

2.3.1 What is a Plant?

The definition of a plant depends on its use. From a materials-management view, a plant can be defined as a location that holds valuated stock. A production-planning view defines a plant as an organizational unit that is central to production planning. A plant also can be defined as a location that contains service or maintenance facilities. The definition of a plant will vary depending on the need of the customer.

2.3.2 Prerequisites for a Plant

Before setting up a plant, certain other settings need to be defined. These are described below.

Factory Calendar

A factory calendar identifies the workdays, public holidays, and company holidays. The SAP system is delivered with some factory calendars, but a new factory calendars can be configured based on a company's schedule.

Country Key

A country key is required to define a plant. The system is delivered with country keys, and new country codes need to be configured if they are not in the system.

Region Keys

A region code is required along with the country code. The region is defined as a state or province associated with a country.

2.3.3 Defining a Plant

A four-character string defines the plant field. It can be configured using transaction OX10. The navigation path is **IMG • Enterprise Structure • Definition • Logistics—General • Define, Copy, Delete, Check Plant**.

Figures 2.1 and 2.2 show, respectively, the program screen for entering initial plant information and the screen for entering secondary information once the initial information is entered.

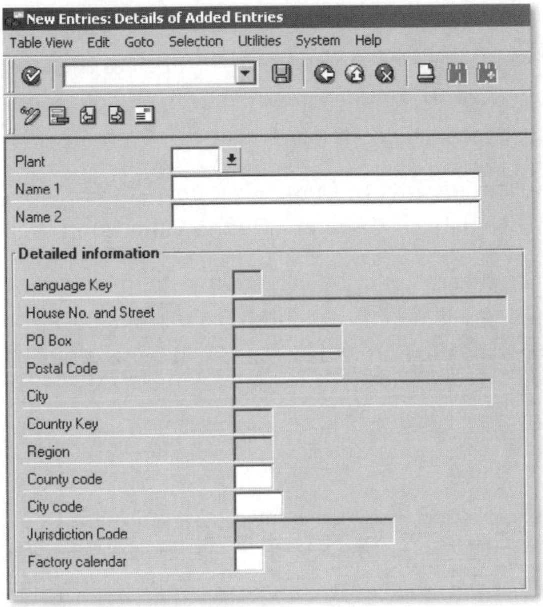

New Entries: Details of Added Entries

Table View Edit Goto Selection Utilities System Help

Plant

Name 1

Name 2

Detailed information

Language Key

House No. and Street

PO Box

Postal Code

City

Country Key

Region

County code

City code

Jurisdiction Code

Factory calendar

Figure 2.1 Initial Screen for Entering a Plant

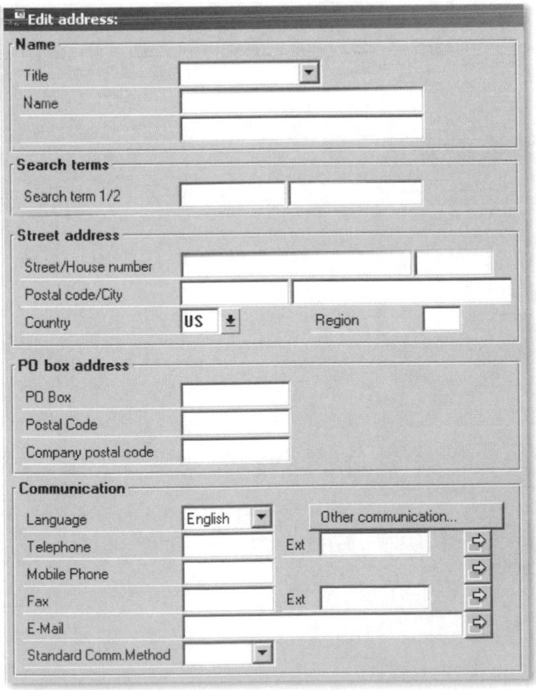

Edit address:

Name

Title

Name

Search terms

Search term 1/2

Street address

Street/House number

Postal code/City

Country US Region

PO box address

PO Box

Postal Code

Company postal code

Communication

Language English Other communication...

Telephone Ext

Mobile Phone

Fax Ext

E-Mail

Standard Comm.Method

Figure 2.2 Screen for Entering Secondary Information

2.3.4 Valuation Level

The valuation level is an important configuration step because it specifies the level at which material stocks are valuated for the whole client. There are two options for the valuation level: plant level or company code level.

The valuation level can be defined using OX14. The navigation path is **IMG • Enterprise Structure • Definition • Logistics—General • Define Valuation Level**.

There are several situations in which there should be valuation at the plant level, e.g., if Production Planning or Costing will be implemented, or if the application is using the SAP retail system. Once a valuation is determined, it should not be changed.

2.3.5 Assigning a Plant

Once a valuation level has been established, it is possible to assign a plant to an existing company code. This assignment is performed so that all plant transactions can be attributed to a single legal entity; that is, a company code. This can be achieved in OX18. The path for this transaction is **IMG • Enterprise Structure • Assignment • Logistics—General • Assign Plant to Company Code**.

Figure 2.3 illustrates the assignment of plants to company codes. A plant is assigned to one company code, but a company code can have more than one plant assigned to it.

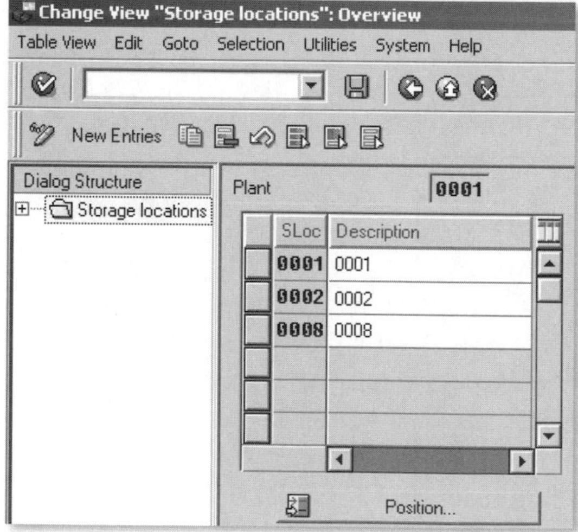

Figure 2.3 Assignment of Plants to Company Codes

This section has described the importance of the plant within the organizational structure and now in the next section, the storage location functionality is explained.

2.4 Storage Locations

2.4.1 What is a Storage Location?

In its systems, SAP traditionally defines a storage location as a place where stock is physically kept within a plant. There will always be at least one storage location defined for one plant. It is the lowest level of location definition within the Materials Management module.

When we look at a physical storage location, there are no set rules on how a storage location should look. Some SAP customers may have a highly developed inventory-monitoring system that uniquely defines a physical location, storage bin, tank, tote, tray, draw, cabinet, etc., as a location that contains inventory separated from other inventory. Depending on the physical size of the materials involved, this may be as small as a 5cm square bin or as large as a whole building.

Some customers may not have sophisticated inventory systems, and you may be presented by a location with no obvious storage definitions. Materials may not be stored in individual locations and may be mixed without procedural picking or placement strategies. In this case, an assessment of the current state and proposals on how to re-engineer the storage facility would be appropriate before trying to define storage locations.

Although the storage location is the lowest location level in Materials Management, it is not the lowest level in the SAP system. Depending on the requirements of the SAP customer, the number of materials that are stored, the number of unique locations, and the sophistication of the customer's current inventory system, there may be a need to implement the Warehouse Management module. This provides the opportunity to manage inventory at a bin level.

When Warehouse Management (WM) is implemented in an SAP system, there is a need to tie the Warehouse Management functionality to Materials Management. This is achieved by assigning a warehouse to a storage location or number of storage locations.

2.4.2 Defining a Storage Location

A four-character string defines the storage location. It can be configured using transaction OX09. The navigation path is **IMG • Enterprise Structure • Definition • Materials Management • Maintain Storage Location**.

Enter the plant number in the initial screen of OX09 (see Figure 2.4). This will then direct you to the screen shown in Figure 2.4. Press the **New Entries** button and then you can add the storage location number and a description. Then highlight your new storage location and click on the addresses of storage location in the dialog structure.

Click on the **New Entries** field to enter a number for the storage location address (see Figure 2.5). This can be up to three characters. Once entered you will be directed to another screen for the entry of secondary information such as address and telephone number. This screen is shown in Figure 2.2.

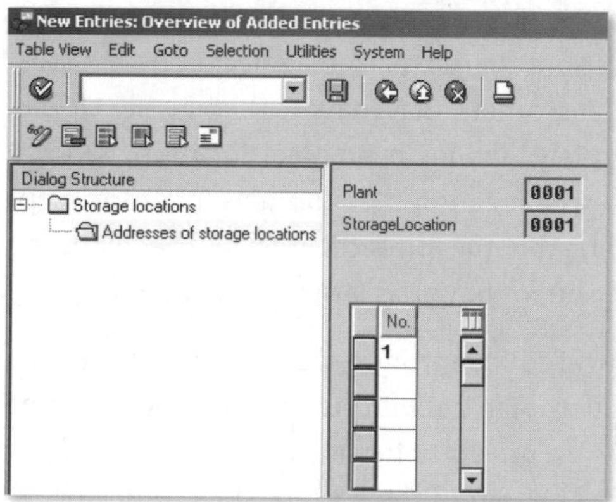

Figure 2.4 Initial Screen of OX09

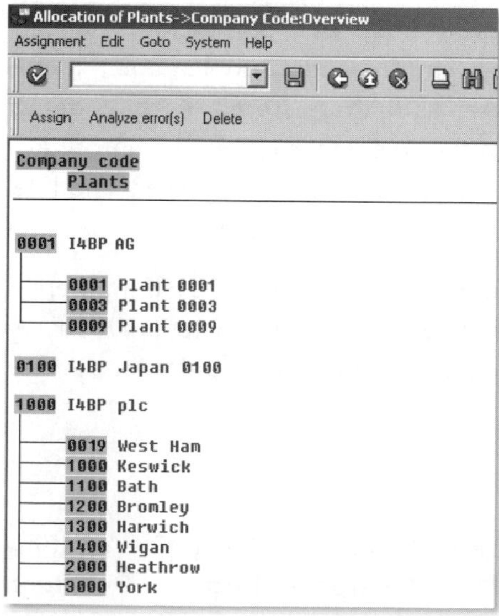

Figure 2.5 Entering a Number for the Storage Location Address

2.4.3 Automatic Creation of Storage Locations

It is possible to create storage locations automatically when an inward goods movement for a material is performed. The configuration needs the plant and/or the type of movement to be defined to allow the automatic creation of storage locations.

This configuration can reduce storage-location data maintenance. The automatic storage location will only be activated is the movement is for normal stock, not special stock.

This configuration can be entered using transaction OMB3. The navigation path is **IMG • Materials Management • Inventory Management and Physical Inventory • Goods Receipt • Create Storage Location Automatically**.

Automatic creation of storage locations can be set for each plant where this functionality is needed (see Figure 2.6) or for a particular goods movement (see Figure 2.7).

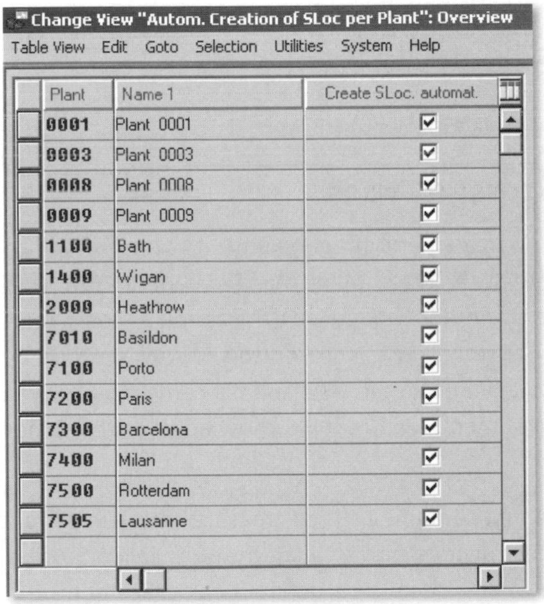

Change View "Autom. Creation of SLoc per Plant": Overview

Table View Edit Goto Selection Utilities System Help

Plant	Name 1	Create SLoc. automat.
0001	Plant 0001	☑
0003	Plant 0003	☑
0008	Plant 0008	☑
0009	Plant 0009	☑
1100	Bath	☑
1400	Wigan	☑
2000	Heathrow	☑
7010	Basildon	☑
7100	Porto	☑
7200	Paris	☑
7300	Barcelona	☑
7400	Milan	☑
7500	Rotterdam	☑
7505	Lausanne	☑

Figure 2.6 Automatic Storage-Location Creation by Plant

The storage location is the lowest level of the organizational structure of the MM module. However, in the next section we will examine how the Warehouse Management module interfaces with the MM module.

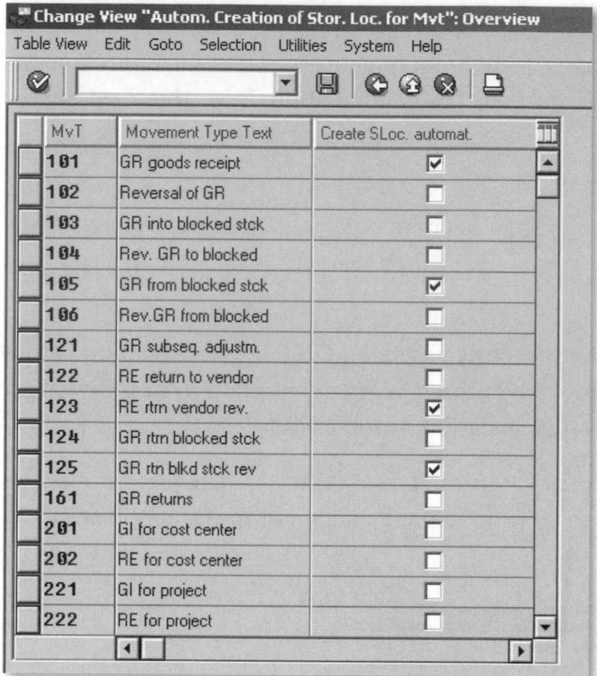

MvT	Movement Type Text	Create SLoc. automat.
101	GR goods receipt	X
102	Reversal of GR	
103	GR into blocked stck	
104	Rev. GR to blocked	
105	GR from blocked stck	X
106	Rev.GR from blocked	
121	GR subseq. adjustm.	
122	RE return to vendor	
123	RE rtrn vendor rev.	X
124	GR rtrn blocked stck	
125	GR rtn blkd stck rev	X
161	GR returns	
201	GI for cost center	
202	RE for cost center	
221	GI for project	
222	RE for project	

Figure 2.7 Automatic Storage-Location Creation by Movement Type

2.5 Warehouse and Storage Types

Although not part of Materials Management functionality, it is important to understand the integration points with Warehouse Management (WM). It is important for MM users to have some knowledge of WM as many companies implement both MM and WM. The warehouse is linked to the MM module by assigning the warehouse to the storage location in MM and if a company has WM and MM activated, the goods movements will require knowledge of the major elements of WM.

A warehouse is a physical location that contains defined areas that are called Storage Types, and these are then further divided into smaller locations called Storage Bins. In Warehouse Management, it is possible to define stock placement and picking strategies based on material location and sequence.

To create a warehouse, use the following path **IMG • Enterprise Structure • Definition • Logistics Execution • Define, Copy, Delete, Check Warehouse**.

The warehouse is defined by a three-character string (see Figure 2.8). There are no address details associated with a warehouse.

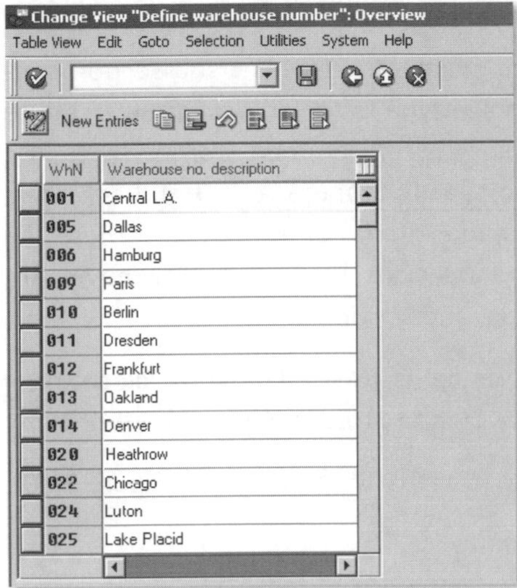

WhN	Warehouse no. description
001	Central L.A.
005	Dallas
006	Hamburg
009	Paris
010	Berlin
011	Dresden
012	Frankfurt
013	Oakland
014	Denver
020	Heathrow
022	Chicago
024	Luton
025	Lake Placid

Figure 2.8 Defining the Warehouse

2.5.1 Assign a Warehouse to Plant and Storage Location

The way to ensure that the SAP identifies that certain storage locations are controlled by the functionality in Warehouse Management is to assign a warehouse to a storage location. The navigation path for assigning a warehouse to a plant and storage location is **IMG · Enterprise Structure · Assignment · Logistics Execution · Assign Warehouse Number to Plant/Storage Location**. Figure 2.9 shows the display view.

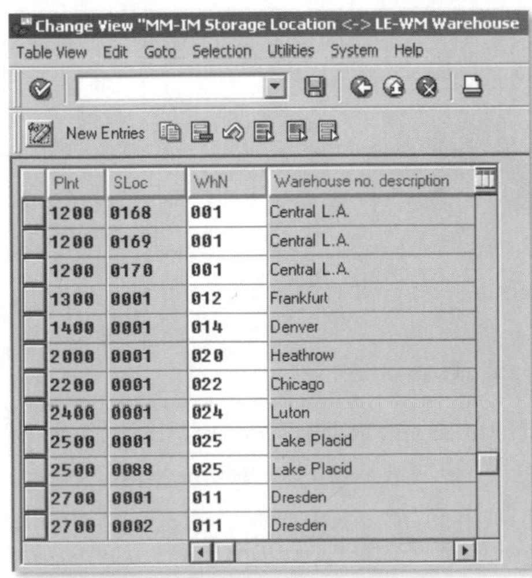

Plnt	SLoc	WhN	Warehouse no. description
1200	0168	001	Central L.A.
1200	0169	001	Central L.A.
1200	0170	001	Central L.A.
1300	0001	012	Frankfurt
1400	0001	014	Denver
2000	0001	020	Heathrow
2200	0001	022	Chicago
2400	0001	024	Luton
2500	0001	025	Lake Placid
2500	0088	025	Lake Placid
2700	0001	011	Dresden
2700	0002	011	Dresden

Figure 2.9 Assigning a Warehouse to a Plant/Storage Location Combination.

2.5.2 Storage Type

A storage type is defined as an area of the warehouse that is a sub-section containing a number of storage bins. The storage type is available to the warehouse user for creating searches based on storage types. Common storage types in a warehouse will be areas such as **Cold Room**, **Bulk Storage**, and **High Rack Area**. Storage types pre-defined by SAP are called interim storage types. These are defined numerically from 900 to 999. The areas are used by SAP for movement postings such as goods receipt, goods issue, and posting differences.

The navigation path for creating storage types is **IMG • Logistics Execution • Warehouse Management • Master Data • Define Storage Type**.

Each warehouse can have any number of storage types defined (see Figure 2.10).

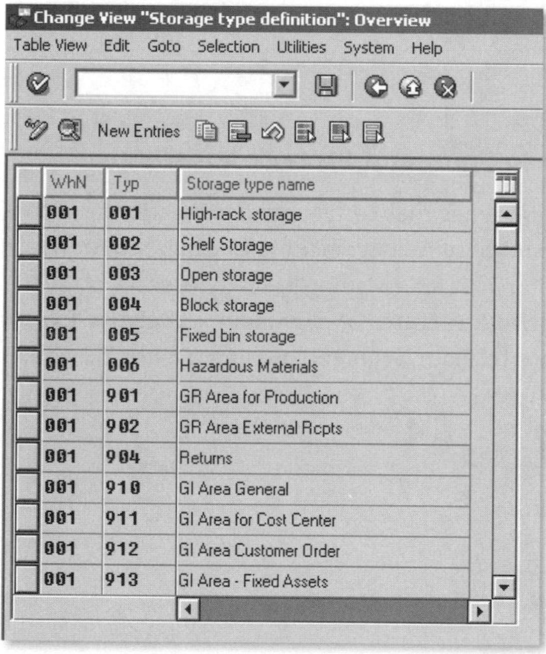

WhN	Typ	Storage type name
001	001	High-rack storage
001	002	Shelf Storage
001	003	Open storage
001	004	Block storage
001	005	Fixed bin storage
001	006	Hazardous Materials
001	901	GR Area for Production
001	902	GR Area External Rcpts
001	904	Returns
001	910	GI Area General
001	911	GI Area for Cost Center
001	912	GI Area Customer Order
001	913	GI Area - Fixed Assets

Figure 2.10 Warehouse with Storage Types Defined

2.5.3 Storage Sections and Storage Bins

A subdivision of the storage type is the storage section. This is simply a group of similar storage bins. Even if the customer does not want to define storage sections, one storage section must be defined per storage type. This is normally defined as 001 in the IMG. The navigation path is **IMG • Logistics Execution • Warehouse Management • Master Data • Define Storage Section**.

Storage bins are the lowest level of storage. Storage bins are not defined in the IMG. Authorized warehouse staff can quickly and frequently change these. Storage bins can be defined manually using transaction LS01N or automatically by using transaction LS10.

Now that the structural organization of Materials Management is defined for the physical elements, the next section goes on to explain an important logical aspect of MM, the Purchasing and the Purchasing Organization.

2.6 Purchasing Organization

2.6.1 What is a Purchasing Organization?

The purchasing function within SAP customers can range from simple to very complex. The largest SAP customers may spend hundreds of millions of dollars in purchasing each year and have a sophisticated purchasing department that works at many different levels, from strategic global procurement to low-level vendor relationships. SAP can be defined to allow all purchasing departments to be accurately reflected.

A purchasing organization is simply defined as a group of purchasing activity that is associated with all or a specific part of the enterprise.

2.6.2 Types of Purchasing Organizations

Purchasing at an Enterprise Level

Purchasing for a SAP customer may take place at the highest level within an organization. If a customer has a central purchasing department that co-ordinates purchasing for all companies within the enterprise, then the purchasing organization can be configured in that manner. The purchasing organization is defined in SAP and then assigned to all companies.

Purchasing at the Company Level

If a SAP customer does not have a single enterprise wide purchasing function, it may have purchasing centralized for each company. This may be appropriate for customers with companies in various countries, in which case an enterprise purchasing department may not be possible. In this scenario the purchasing organization is created and assigned for each company code. Even with this scenario, a purchasing organization may cover several companies. For example, a purchasing organization for Latvia may be assigned as the purchasing organization for the companies based in the countries of Latvia, Lithuania, and Estonia.

The purchasing organization can be assigned to a company code by using transaction OX01. The navigation path is **IMG • Enterprise Structure • Assignment • Materials Management • Assign Purchasing Organization to Company Code**.

Purchasing at the Plant Level

In an enterprise that has companies with large autonomous plants the purchasing decisions may be made at a local level. The SAP customer may decide that assigning one purchasing organization to one company is not appropriate, and it would be a better business decision to assign a purchasing organization at the plant. This scenario has an advantage when the vendors are at a local level and few vendors supply materials or services to more than one plant.

The purchasing organization can be assigned to a plant transaction OX17. The navigation path is **IMG • Enterprise Structure • Assignment • Materials Management • Assign Purchasing Organization to Plant**.

Reference Purchasing Organization

One purchasing organization can be defined as a reference purchasing organization. This is a purchasing organization that can be set up as a strategic purchasing department. In large companies, the strategic purchasing function analyses purchasing data and works to negotiate the best prices for material and services from global vendors. This strategic purchasing department can obtain prices and special conditions that can be used by purchasing organizations across the enterprise.

Often this reference purchasing organization is not assigned to any company code, as it is a function of the whole enterprise. A purchasing organization must be assigned to this reference purchasing organization to have access to the information on the system.

To assign a purchasing organization that will reference another purchasing organization, the navigation path is **IMG • Enterprise Structure • Assignment • Materials Management • Assign Purchasing Organization to Reference Purchasing Organization**.

2.6.3 Create a Purchasing Organization

The navigation path to create a purchasing organization is **IMG • Enterprise Structure • Definition • Materials Management • Maintain Purchasing Organization**.

Figure 2.11 shows the screen for creating a purchasing organization.

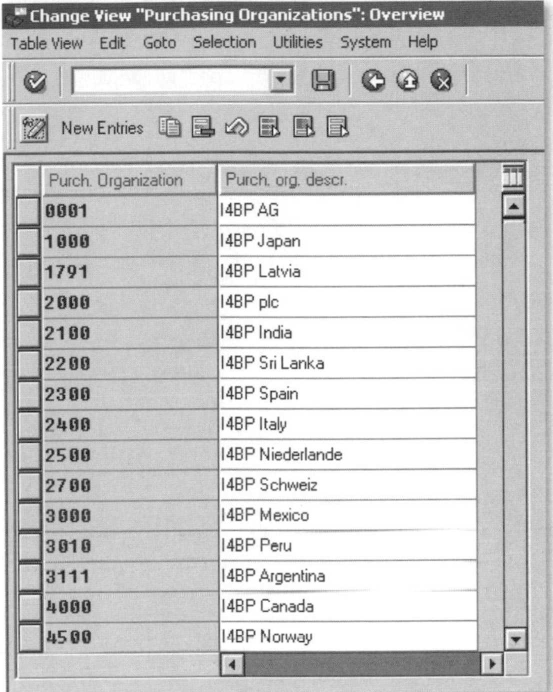

Figure 2.11 Creating a Purchasing Organization

2.6.4 Purchasing Groups

An SAP customer has the opportunity to define its purchasing department below the level of purchasing organization. The purchasing group can be defined as a person or group of people dealing with a certain material or group of materials purchased by through the purchasing organization.

The purchasing group is defined in configuration. The navigation path is **IMG • Materials Management • Purchasing • Create Purchasing Groups**.

The purchasing group is a three-character alphanumeric field and is entered along with a description, telephone and fax number.

In this chapter we have seen that knowledge of the SAP organizational structure is important to anyone working on an SAP implementation. Each company will create its own version of the SAP landscape, correction and transport and other technical elements. It is important that you understand what these are and how your company adopts them. Understanding the principle of the Materials Management structure is important to anybody working with the module, whether as a configurator or while advising a company on the organizational structure.

3 Master Data in MM

The Materials Management functionality includes a number of important master data files. The Material Master and Vendor Master files are at the core of Procurement, Inventory Management, and Invoice Verification.

A number of master data files in Materials Management require a significant amount of understanding, not only on the part of the SAP consultant but also on the part of the SAP customer. When implementing SAP, customers are generally transitioning from one or more legacy systems. A key aspect of any implementation is the conversion of data to the master data files in SAP.

A fundamental indicator of a successful implementation is the level to which the data has been correctly converted into the SAP master data files. In this chapter, we shall examine the master data files that are integral to the practice of materials management.

3.1 Material Master

3.1.1 Material Master Overview

When customers implement SAP, they are often overwhelmed by the information contained in the Material Master file. When customers examine their existing systems, such as BPICS, JDEdwards, or Lawson, they find that their product or material files contain a fraction of the data contained in the SAP Material Master.

3.1.2 Material Master Tables

The Material Master transaction allows the users to enter all the information relevant to a particular item of material into the correct tables. There is not one Material Master file, but a number of tables that contain information that combined reflect all the information for that material.

Many tables are updated when information is entered into the Material Master transaction. The Material Master transaction is structured so that there are entry screens for different functional information such as Purchasing, Sales, or Accounting, but there is also an organizational dimension to data entry. The material information can be entered at each level of the organization, e.g., at the levels of plant, storage location, or sales organization.

3.1.3 Material Numbering

An issue that SAP customers can face when converting their item files over to the Material Master is whether or not to keep their legacy numbering scheme. This would mean that they would continue entering their own material numbers. They have the option of allowing SAP to automatically assign material numbers.

Often, legacy systems have meaningful material numbering. This numbering has usually been in place for some time and staff is familiar with the numbering. For the simplicity of maintenance, automatic assignment of material number is the best choice. When working with your client, be aware that there are arguments to use and not to use a meaningful numbering scheme in SAP.

The material number field is defined in configuration. Using the transaction OMSL or the navigation path **IMG • Logistics—General • Material Master • Basic Settings • Define Output Format for Material Numbers**.

Figure 3.1 shows the configuration screen for defining the output format for material numbers.

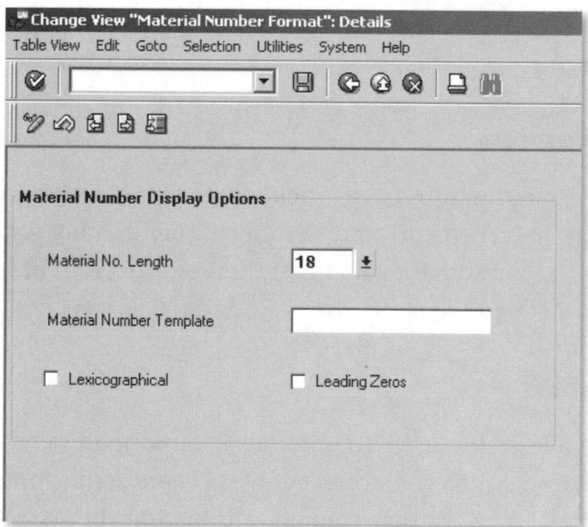

Figure 3.1 Configuration Screen for Defining Output Format

This configuration screen does not have many input fields but is extremely important when initially defining the Material Master. Once your customer has decided upon the Material Master numbering scheme you can first enter the length of the material number.

Then the customer may decide that it needs the automatically assigned material numbers in a certain format that can be defined. In this case, you can define the template and the special characters required. Figure 3.2 shows the template defined for internally assigned material numbers.

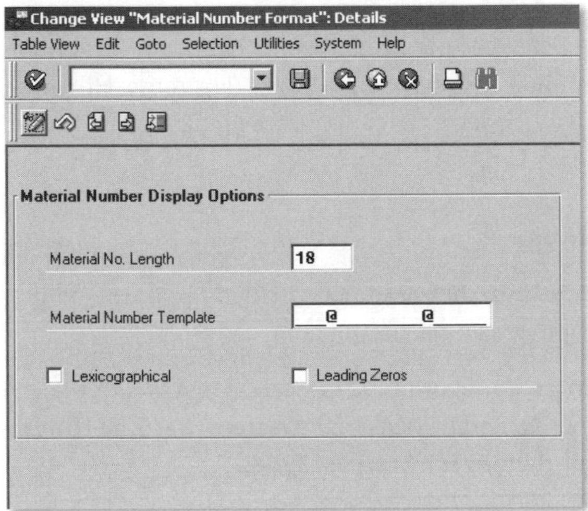

Figure 3.2 Template for Internally Assigned Material Numbers

In this case, the customer requires the material numbers to appear as this example, 123@45678901@23456. The only character that cannot be used in the template is the underscore, as that is used to signify a non-template field.

The two other fields in the OMSL transaction have to do with how the material number is stored and how SAP determines what the number is.

The lexicographical indicator is only relevant for numeric material numbers, either internally or externally defined. In the case shown in Figure 3.2, the indicator is not set. This means that the numbers are stored with leading zeros are right-justified. For instance, if a user enters the number 12345678, that number will be stored as 000000000012345678, i.e., with 10 leading zeros.

If the indicator is set, then the numeric number is not right-justified and not padded with zeros. The field acts more like a character string, where a leading zero becomes as valid character.

In the following example, the indicator is now set. A user entering material 12345678 would find that the material number would be stored as 12345678, with no padding. If the user then entered 0012345678, it would be stored in that way, and this would be a different material number in SAP. However, an internally assigned material number would be padded with the leading zeros, 000000000012345678. Therefore, there would be three separate material numbers.

Remember that this indicator cannot be changed once there are numeric material numbers in the system, so it must be defined before any tests are run in the system.

The other field in the transaction OMSL is the leading-zeros indicator. If this indicator is set, then the material number is shown with the leading zeros. However, if the lexicographical indicator is set, then the leading-zeros indicator is ignored by the system.

3.1.4 Material Number Range

When the definition of the material number has been decided upon, the configuration for the material number range can be completed.

The material number ranges can be configured in transaction MMNR or via the navigation path **IMG • Logistics—General • Material Master • Basic Settings • Material Types • Define Number Ranges for Material Types**.

The transaction allows a range of numbers to be entered and the option to make that range either external or internally assigned. Figure 3.3 shows the number ranges defined for internal and external number assignment

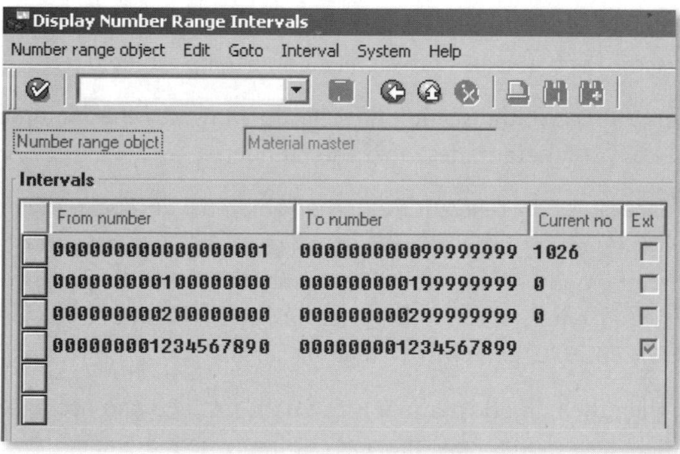

Figure 3.3 Defined Internal and External Number Ranges

3.1.5 Material Type

A material type is a definition of a group of materials with similar attributes. A material type must be assigned to each material record entered into the Material Master.

The transaction for the material type definition is OMS2. The navigation path is **IMG • Logistics—General • Material Master • Basic Settings • Material Types • Define Attributes of Material Types**.

The material type is configured so that fields in the Material Master are pre-defined for the materials assigned to that material group (See Figure 3.4). So you can configure the price control for a material type to be Standard Price, and all materials assigned to that material type will be standard price.

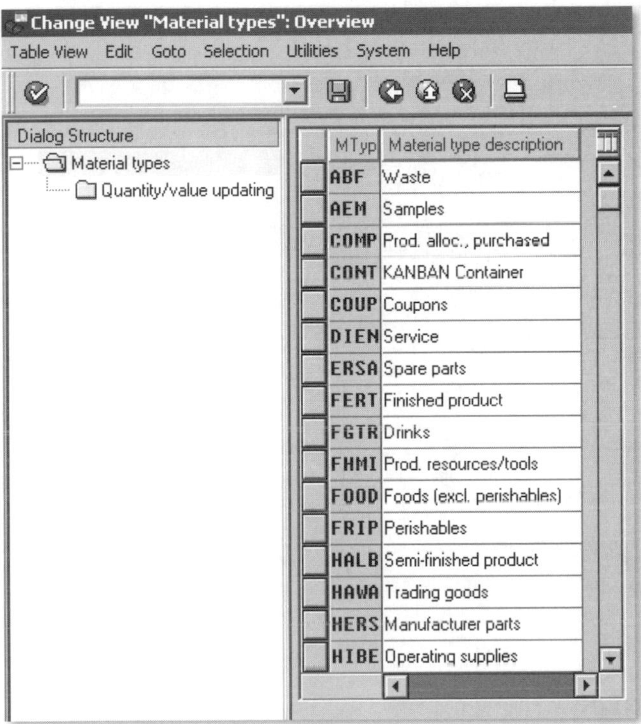

Figure 3.4 Material Types and Descriptions

Once the material type has been created, the attributes can be defined. Figure 3.5 shows the attributes that can be assigned to each material type. Once the material type has been defined, then the number range can be assigned.

Now we have looked at the details that go into making up the material master. The next section will go on to explain the functionality of another important element in the Materials Management module, the vendor master.

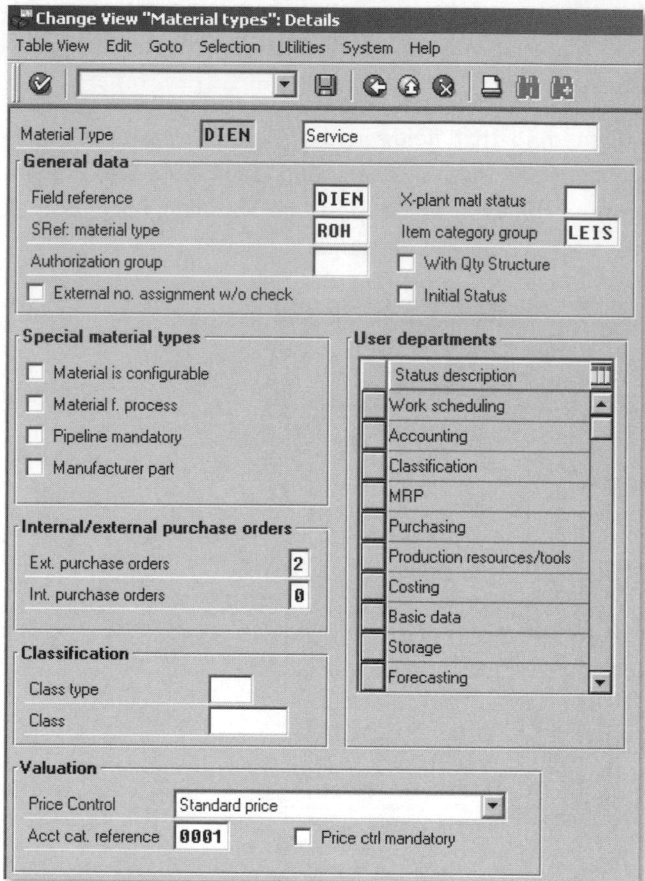

Figure 3.5 Attributes Assigned to Material Types

3.2 Vendor Master

3.2.1 Definition of a Vendor

We define a vendor as a person or company who supplies materials or services to the person or company requiring those materials or services. For SAP customers, every supplier that they need to convert from their legacy systems will require a vendor master record in SAP.

3.2.2 Vendor Master in SAP

The vendor master in SAP holds details about each vendor used by the customer. The vendor master has three distinct sections. These are discussed in some detail below.

General Data

The general data is, as the name suggests, general information about the vendor that can be entered into the system by the group identified to create vendor records. The basic date entered at this level includes name, search terms, address, telephone, and fax. Once this data is entered then further information can be added to the vendor master record by Accounting and Purchasing. This data can be entered using transaction code XK01.

Accounting Data

The accounting data is the financial data that is entered at the company code level. This data includes tax information, bank details, reconciliation account, payment terms, payment methods, and dunning information. The transaction used in financial accounting to enter this information is FK01.

Purchasing Data

The purchasing data is the data entered for the vendor at a purchasing organizational level. We shall discuss the purchasing organization later in the book. The data entered is relevant for one purchasing organization and may be different between purchasing organizations. The data entered includes control data required in purchasing, partner functions, purchasing default fields, and invoice verification indicators. This data can be entered using transaction MK01.

3.2.3 Vendor Account Groups

When you create a vendor, you must assign an account group to that vendor. Therefore, these account groups must be defined in configuration before vendor creation.

The account group is defined via the navigation path **IMG • Financial Accounting • Vendor Accounts • Master Data • Preparations for Creating Vendor Master Data • Define Account Groups with Screen Layout**.

In Figure 3.6, you can see the existing account groups. If you need to define another account group, click on the **New Entries** button. The screen shown in Figure 3.7 will appear.

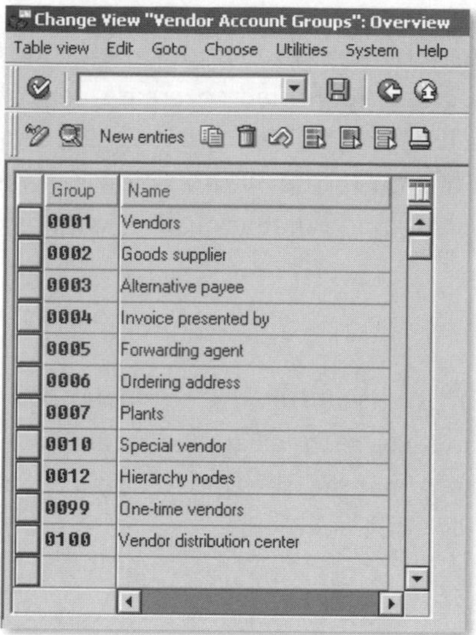

Figure 3.6 Account Group with Description

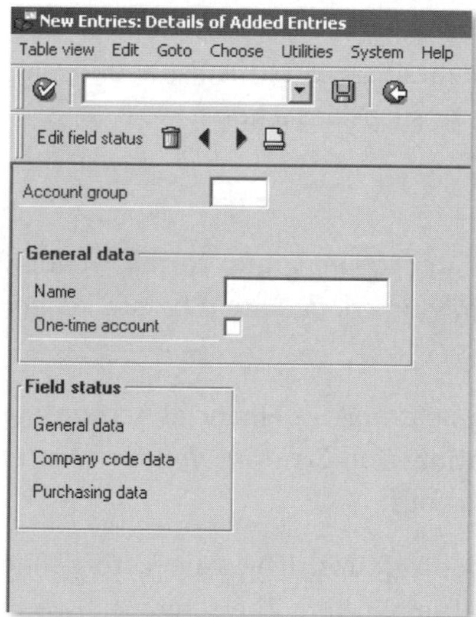

Figure 3.7 Field Entry for Account Group and Description

On this screen you can specify if an account group is just for one-time vendors. For vendors that you only deal with once, their data is entered into the document and not as master data. Once you have entered the account group and description, you can then modify the field status as needed. This transaction allows you to configure the system to show or to not allow users to enter information into certain fields. Highlight the field status for the general, company code, or purchasing data and then click on the **Edit Field Status** button.

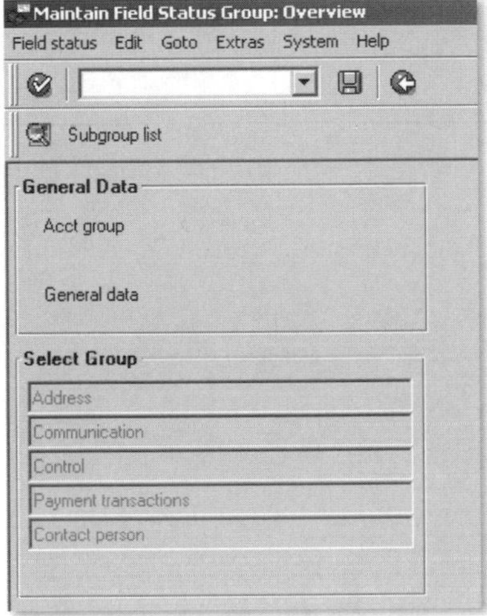

Figure 3.8 Field Groups for General Data Screen

Figure 3.8 shows the specific field groups that are available to configure. For the general data screen these are the **Address**, **Communication**, **Control**, **Payment transactions**, and **Contact person** groups. Double-click on the group you want to configure.

This configuration screen, shown in Figure 3.9, allows you to make certain fields as either a required entry or an optional entry (as they all are in this figure); display only, or suppressed. This configuration becomes specific to the account group that is entered when a vendor master record is created.

The screen layouts can also be modified for company code using the navigation path **IMG · Financial Accounting · Vendor Accounts · Master Data · Preparations for Creating Vendor Master Data · Define Screen Layout per Company Code**.

The screen layout can also be modified by the particular activity. In other words, the screen for creating a vendor can be modified to appear different from the screen for modifying a vendor. The navigation path, **IMG · Financial Accounting · Vendor Accounts · Master Data · Preparations for Creating Vendor Master Data · Define Screen Layout per Activity**.

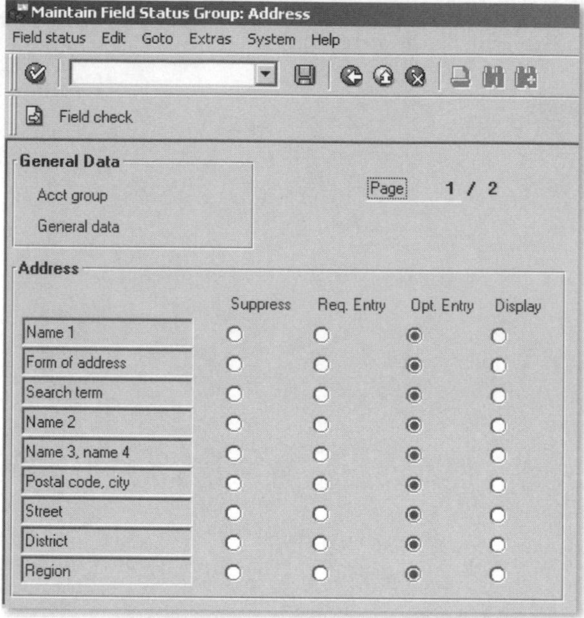

Figure 3.9 Some Fields Used to Configure Address Field Group

3.2.4 Vendor Number Range

When defining the vendor number range it is important to remember that vendor numbers, like material numbers, can be externally or internally assigned. Many SAP customers decide to create different number ranges for each of their account groups. This requires careful consideration when defining number ranges to prevent the number ranges from overlapping.

The transaction to create vendor number ranges is XKN1. The navigation path is **IMG • Financial Accounting • Vendor Accounts • Master Data • Preparations for Creating Vendor Master Data • Create Number Ranges for Vendor Accounts**.

Figure 3.10 shows the configuration for vendor number ranges.

For this transaction you should enter a unique number for the range (a two- character field) and then the range for the numbers for your defined number range. The current number field allows you to define the current number. The Ext. field allows you to define whether the number range is externally (user) defined.

Once the number range is defined, it can be assigned to a vendor account group. The navigation path is **IMG • Financial Accounting • Vendor Accounts • Master Data • Preparations for Creating Vendor Master Data • Assign Number Ranges to Vendor Account Groups**.

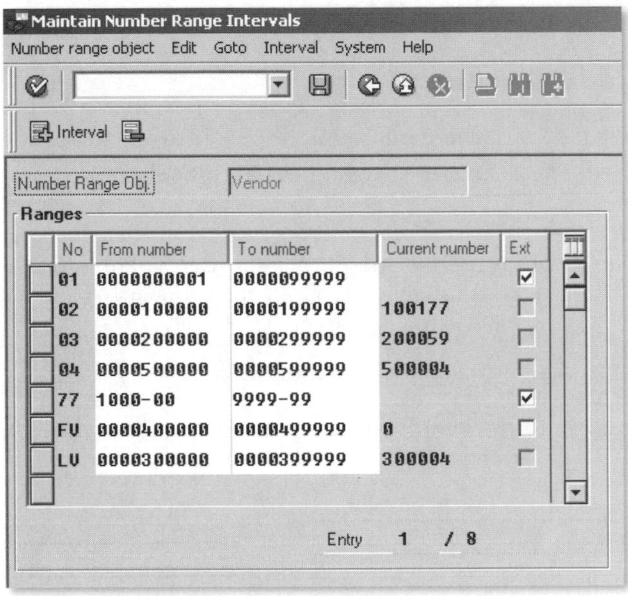

Maintain Number Range Intervals

Number range object Edit Goto Interval System Help

Number Range Obj. Vendor

Ranges

No	From number	To number	Current number	Ext
01	0000000001	0000099999		☑
02	0000100000	0000199999	100177	☐
03	0000200000	0000299999	200059	☐
04	0000500000	0000599999	500004	☐
77	1000-00	9999-99		☑
FV	0000400000	0000499999	0	☐
LV	0000300000	0000399999	300004	☐

Entry 1 / 8

Figure 3.10 Configuration for Vendor Number Ranges

Change View "Assign Vendor Account Groups->Number Range":

Table View Edit Goto Selection Utilities System Help

Group	Name	Number range
0001	Vendors	01
0002	Goods supplier	XX
0003	Alternative payee	XX
0004	Invoice presented by	XX
0005	Forwarding agent	XX
0006	Ordering address	XX
0007	Plants	XX
0010	Special vendor	02
0012	Hierarchy nodes	01
0099	One-time vendors	01

Figure 3.11 Vendor Account Groups and Assigned Number Ranges

The number range can be assigned to many vendor account groups, as shown in Figure 3.11. Therefore, if your SAP customer decides to use just one number range for all the vendors, the configuration would show one number range assigned to all account groups.

3.3 Purchasing Information Data

3.3.1 Purchasing Information Record

The purchasing information record is where information specific to a material and a vendor is held. This can then be further specified for a particular purchasing organization.

The purchasing information record is used in the purchase order where information from the record is defaulted into the purchase order (PO). Information such as purchasing group, net price, invoice verification indicators, and delivery tolerances all can be entered into the purchasing information record.

Four categories of purchasing information records can be created. These are:

- Standard
- Pipeline
- Consignment
- Subcontracting

It is important to identify the correct category before creating a purchasing information record.

3.3.2 Purchasing Information Record for a Non-Stock Material

The purchasing information record usually applies to a vendor and a specific material that it supplies. However, the vendor occasionally may be supplying a service to a non-stock material. For example, there may be an operation in a production order where material is sent out for a treatment. There is no material number at that point for the material in the production order, but there is a purchase information record for a group of materials, that is a specific material group such as certain raw materials or semi-finished non-stock items. In the system, it is possible to create a purchasing information record for a vendor and a material group. This contains the same information that a vendor/material purchasing information record would have.

3.3.3 Purchasing Information Record Numbering

The fact that there are different types of purchase information record makes number ranges necessary. The number ranges for the purchase information record can be assigned either externally or internally.

The number ranges for the purchase information records can be pre-defined in SAP, and SAP recommends that the customer accept the given number ranges. The system does allow the number ranges to be changed if the customer requires it.

The transaction to define the purchasing information record number ranges is OMEO. The navigation path is **IMG • Materials Management • Purchasing • Purchasing Information Record • Define Number Ranges**.

The pre-defined number ranges for the purchase information records are:

- Stock Material—internally assigned 5300000000 to 5399999999
- Stock Material—externally assigned 5400000000 to 5499999999
- Non-Stock Material—internally assigned 5500000000 to 5599999999
- Non-Stock Material—externally assigned 5600000000 to 5699999999

3.3.4 Purchasing Information Record-Screen Layout

The screens in the purchasing information record transactions can be modified to allow field changes. The path for this transaction is **IMG • Materials Management • Purchasing • Purchasing Information Record • Define Screen Layout**.

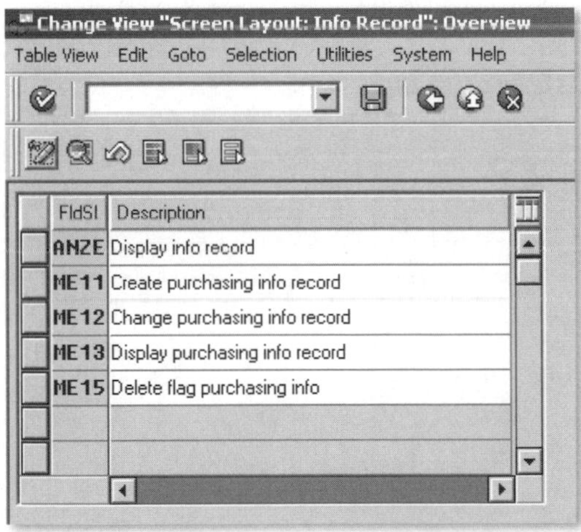

Figure 3.12 Record Transactions and Screen-Layout Modifications

The screen shown in Figure 3.12 allows you to choose the modifications for each transaction. To select a transaction, double-click on the transaction will take you to a screen where you can modify the screen layout (Table T162). You then can select one of the field-selection groups in order to modify the individual fields.

Figure 3.13 shows the Field Selection Groups available to select from for the Purchasing Information Record transaction. Figure 3.14 shows the individual fields of the Quantities field selection group for transaction ANZE.

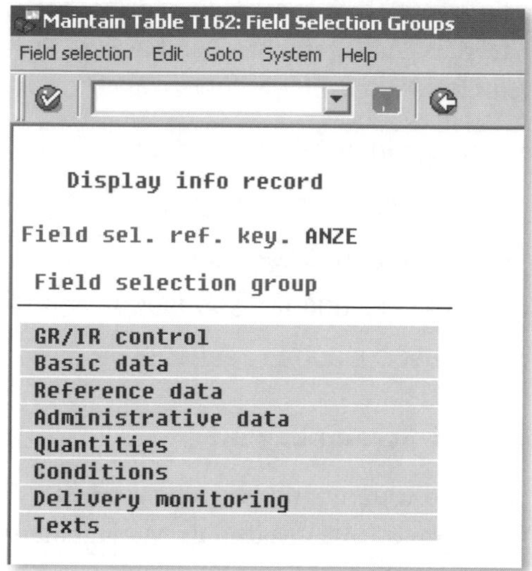

Figure 3.13 Field Selection Groups Available for Purchasing Information Record Transaction

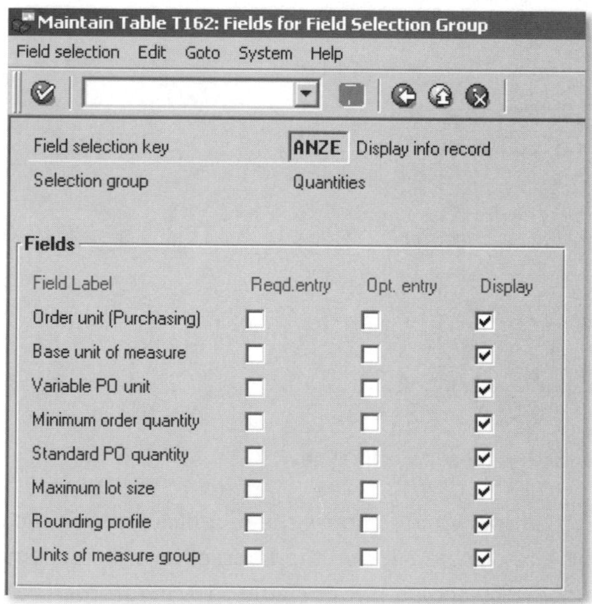

Figure 3.14 Quantities Field-Selection Group for Transaction ANZE

3.4 Batch Management Data

3.4.1 What is a Batch?

A batch is a quantity of material grouped together for various reasons. It is often determined that the materials have the same characteristics and values. For instance, in the chemical industry a certain number of containers of a certain product may be considered a batch because they were produced at the same time and have the same physical and chemical characteristics. These characteristics may differ from those of another batch of material produced on the same day.

The pharmaceutical industry is one sector where material batches are extremely important. Each batch of material is recorded throughout the product and distribution process. In the case of product recall; the batch number stamped on the pack or bottle of material is the identification that is needed.

To understand how important batch recording has become, consider the regulations within the European Union. The EU requires that each batch of pharmaceutical material imported into the EU must be accompanied with a batch certificate. This must contain the testing specifications of the product, analytical methods and test results, statements that indicate that it conforms to cGMP (current Good Manufacturing Procedures), and sign-off by a company official.

3.4.2 Batch Level

In SAP, the batch number can be determined at different levels. This determination needs to made early in any implementation project. Batches can be determined at client level, plant level, and material level.

Client Level

If the batch level is configured at the client level, then the batch number can only be assigned once throughout the whole client. One batch number will exist for one batch regardless of material or location. There is no issue when batches are moved from plant to plant, as the batch number would not exist in the receiving plant. This is a level where, in some countries, batch numbers are unique to a company and not to a material.

Plant Level

Batch level at the plant level is the SAP default. This means that the batch is unique to a plant and material but not applicable across the company. Therefore, a batch of material at a different plant within the company could have the same batch number with different characteristics. When transferring batch material from one plant to another, the batch information is not transferred, and the batch information needs to be re-entered at the receiving plant.

Material Level

Batch level at the material level means that the batch number is unique to a material across all plants. Therefore, if a batch of material is transferred to another plant, the batch information will be adopted in the new plant without re-entering the batch information, as that batch number could not have been duplicated for that material in the receiving plant.

3.4.3 Changing the Batch Level

Choosing the batch level should be done early in any implementation. However, due to unforeseen circumstances, you may need to change the level at which batches are set.

The batch level can be changed using the transaction OMCE. The navigation path is **IMG • Logistics—General • Batch Management • Specify Batch Level and Activate Status Management • Batch Level**.

In this transaction, the level can be changed between client, plant, and material. When changing batch level, and prior to configuration, be aware of the following:

- To change the batch level from plant level to material level, the material has to be batch-managed in all plants
- Any change in batch level requires significant testing before transporting the change to a production system
- Batch-level configuration affects batch-status management functionality

3.4.4 Batch-Status Management

Batch-status management is simply the ability to make a batch either restricted or unrestricted. The transaction code for this configuration is OMCS and the navigation path is **IMG • Logistics—General • Batch Management • Specify Batch Level and Activate Status Management • Batch Status Management**.

The configuration is simply an option to make batch status management active or not active. However, the batch-level configuration does affect the way in which batch-status management works, as seen below:

- If the batch-level configuration occurs at the material or client level, then the batch status management is effective for all plants in the client

- If the batch-level configuration is at the plant level, then you can configure the system to determine at which plant you require batch status management to be active. The transaction to configure this is OMCU and the navigation path is **IMG • Logistics—General • Batch Management • Specify Batch Level and Activate Status Management • Plants with Batch Status Management**.

3.4.5 Initial Batch Status

After defining the batch-status management, there is additional configuration that may be important to a SAP customer. If you have configured that batch-status management is active and that each batch will have a restricted or an unrestricted status, it is possible to configure the system to set the initial status when a batch is created.

This transaction code to set the initial status of a batch to restricted or unrestricted status is OMAB. The navigation path is **IMG • Logistics—General • Batch Management • Specify Batch Level and Activate Status Management • Initial Status of New Batch**.

The configuration for this is based on the material type. For example, it is possible to configure for all semi-finished goods, material type HALB, to have a batch status of restricted when the batches are created for materials with that material type.

3.4.6 Batch-Number Assignment

The batch number range is predefined in SAP. The predefined range 01 is defined as 0000000001 to 9999999999. The number range object for this is BATCH_CLT. This can be changed in configuration using transaction OMAD or via the navigation path **IMG • Logistics—General • Batch Management • Batch Number Assignment • Maintain Internal Batch Number Assignment Range**.

There are two configuration steps that can be carried out if the customer requires it. First, there is the ability to allow batch number to be assigned internally using the internal number range. To configure this use transaction OMCZ or navigation path **IMG • Logistics—General • Batch Management • Batch Number Assignment • Activate Internal Batch Number Assignment • Activate Batch Number Assignment**.

Second, there is the ability to configure the system to allow the automatic numbering of batches on a goods receipt with account assignment. This navigation path **IMG • Logistics—General • Batch Management • Batch Number Assignment • Activate Internal Batch Number Assignment • Internal Batch Number Assignment for Assigned Goods Receipt**.

3.5 Serial Number Data

3.5.1 What is a Serial Number?

A serial number is given to a unique item to identify it and to record information about it. The serial number is different from a batch number. While, a batch number is given to a number of items, a serial number is unique to one. The serial number is most often found to refer to equipment, such as motors, lathes, drills, or vacuums. For the SAP customer, there may be many areas where serial numbers need to be addressed. If the SAP customer produces items that should be uniquely defined, then serial numbers may be used. If that customer uses machines in production, it may regularly purchase maintenance items that are serialized. Plant maintenance is an area of high use of serial numbers, as the functionality includes user data for equipment that is most often serialized.

3.5.2 Serial Number Profile

The serial number profile is created to define attributes for the serial number. The serial number profile is a four-character alphanumeric field defined in transaction code OIS2. The navigation path is **IMG • Plant Maintenance and Customer Service • Master Data in Plant Maintenance and Customer Service • Technical Objects • Serial Number Management • Define Serial Number Profiles • Serial Number Profile**.

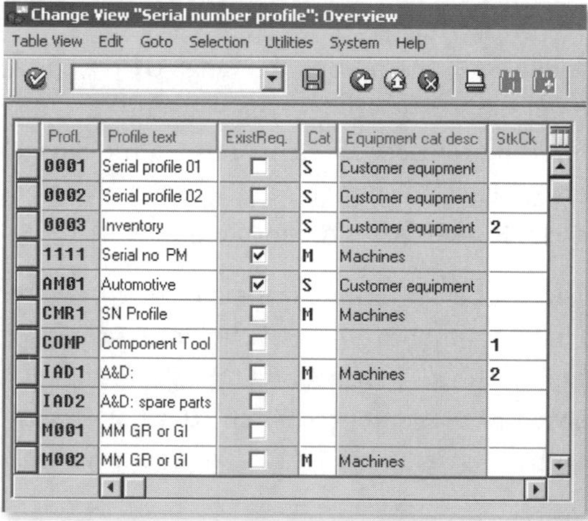

Profl.	Profile text	ExistReq.	Cat	Equipment cat desc	StkCk
0001	Serial profile 01	☐	S	Customer equipment	
0002	Serial profile 02	☐	S	Customer equipment	
0003	Inventory	☐	S	Customer equipment	2
1111	Serial no PM	☑	M	Machines	
AM01	Automotive	☑	S	Customer equipment	
CMR1	SN Profile	☐	M	Machines	
COMP	Component Tool	☐			1
IAD1	A&D:	☐	M	Machines	2
IAD2	A&D: spare parts	☐			
M001	MM GR or GI	☐			
M002	MM GR or GI	☐	M	Machines	

Figure 3.15 Configuration Screen for Serial Number Profiles

The fields in Figure 3.15 show what is needed for configuring serial number profiles. The first field is the profile, the four-character field, followed by a profile description. The field titled **ExistReq** is an indicator that when not set allows the user to create the serial number master record during a business transaction. If the indicator is set, the serial number master record must exist before the transaction can take place.

The **Cat** field is for the equipment category, a Plant Maintenance item, which defines the type of equipment for which this serial number profile is used. For example, **A** is for machines, while **S** for customer equipment.

The **StkChk** field is used to indicate whether the system should perform a stock check when the serial number is assigned.

The configuration of the serial number profile should be performed with the aid of a Plant Maintenance consultant, who will ensure that the customer's requirements for Plant Maintenance are taken into account.

3.5.3 Serializing Procedures

Serial numbers are used in many different areas of SAP, not just in Materials Management. In each of these areas, the procedure of assigning serial numbers can be different. Using the transaction OIS2, you can define whether a serial number is optional, required, or automatic for a number of serializing procedures. The navigation path for this transaction is **IMG · Plant Maintenance and Customer Service · Master Data in Plant Maintenance and Customer Service · Technical Objects · Serial Number management · Define Serial Number Profiles · Serializing Procedures**.

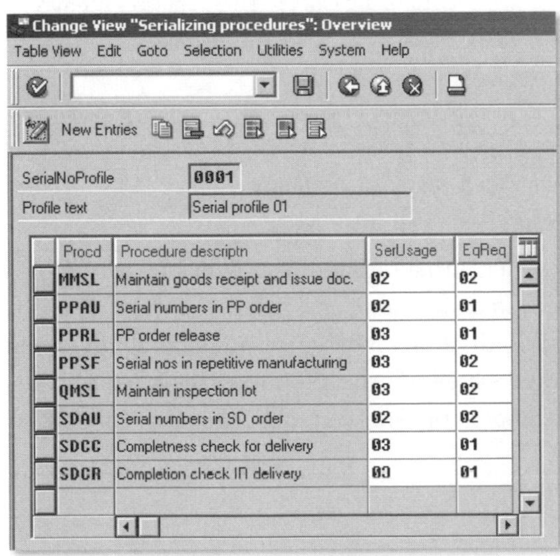

Figure 3.16 Serializing Procedures for Serial Number Profile 0001

In Figure 3.16, the serial number profile 0001 is assigned a number of procedures. For each of these procedures, there are configuration items for serial number usage. The **SerUsage** field can be configured to be none, optional, obligatory, and automatic. The other field, **EqReq**, is to allow serial numbers to be allowed with or without Plant Maintenance equipment.

The procedures that can be assigned to each serial number profile are defined in SAP. Table 3.1 identifies the procedure and its business meaning with relation to Serial Numbers (SN).

Procedure	Business Meaning
HUSL	Enables SN to be assigned in Handling Unit Management
MMSL	Enables SN to be assigned in Goods Receipt, Goods Issue, Stock Transfers, Stock Transport Orders and Physical Inventory
PPAU	Enables SN to be assigned in Production & Refurbishment orders
PPRL	Enables SN to be assigned in Production & Refurbishment orders when they are released
QMSL	Enables SN to be assigned when entering the original value in an QM Inspection Lot
SDAU	Enables SN to be assigned in Sales Orders, Inquires and Quotations
SDCC	Enables SN to be assigned when performing completeness checks for deliveries
SDCR	Enables SN to be assigned when performing completeness checks for return deliveries
SDLS	Enables SN to be assigned for deliveries
SDRE	Enables SN to be assigned for return deliveries

Table 3.1 Business Procedures and Meanings for Serial Number Profiles

This chapter described the major elements that define the master files of the MM module. Many companies use batch management and serial numbers and it is important that if you are involved with these that you understand how each works. Both batches and serial numbers are important to industries such as pharmaceutical and chemical where each batch or serial number may have very different characteristics.

4 Material Master Data

Data entered into the Material Master is extremely important to an SAP implementation. Incorrect or missing data can cause companies to halt operations. Understanding how to enter correct data into the Material Master is vital for all SAP modules.

In this chapter, we will look at the data entry screens for the Material Master file. It is important that you understand what a field in the Material Master means and how it relates to the data in a customer's legacy system.

Data conversion is not often treated with the importance that it deserves. The earlier in the implementation the team works on understanding the data in the SAP master files, the more time there will be to correctly convert legacy data and create data that is not in the customer's legacy files.

Prior to the start of any implementation, it is a good idea for customers to start parallel projects on cleansing their legacy data and eradicating duplicate and redundant records. Often companies have many duplicate records for one vendor, and that should be identified and corrected before any data is loaded into SAP.

The customer may have more than one legacy system and may be combining master data from several systems to be loaded into SAP. The more complicated the data-rationalization task, the earlier this would need to begin to ensure a successful loading of data into SAP before an implementation goes live.

Before entering the first material into the SAP Material Master, there is a certain amount of configuration to be completed. First, we shall look at the industry sector assignment.

4.1 Industry Sector

The industry sector has to be assigned for each Material Master record added. In general, SAP customers use just one industry sector for all their Material Master records, but this is not mandatory.

To configure the industry sectors, use transaction code OMS3 or the path **IMG • Logistics—General • Material Master • Field Selection • Define Industry Sectors and Industry Sector-Specific Screen Selection**.

The SAP system has four pre-defined industry sectors:

- P for the Pharmaceutical Sector
- C for the Chemical Industry Sector
- M for the Mechanical Engineering Sector
- A for Plant Engineering and Construction

Defining a new industry sector requires the choice of a single character for the industry sector and a description. The new industry sector needs to be linked to a field reference. This field reference is defined in transaction OMS9 or navigation path **IMG • Logistics—General • Material Master • Field Selection • Maintain Field Selection for Data Screens**.

The field reference is a list made up of Material Master fields and the individual fields can be **Hidden**, **Displayed**, **Optional Entry**, or **Required Entry**. Careful consideration needs to be exercised when configuring a new field reference.

4.2 Material Type

Simply put, a material type is group of materials with similar attributes. The material type allows the management of different materials in a uniform manner.

4.2.1 Standard Material Types

A number of SAP delivered material types can be used without having to configure any new material types.

CONT—KANBAN Container

This is a material type delivered by SAP to use for creating KANBAN containers. These materials only have the basic data view.

DIEN—Services

Services are either internally supplied or externally supplied by a vendor. Service Material Master records will not have storage information. The services can involve activities such as consulting, garbage collection, or legal services.

ERSA—Spare Parts

Spare parts are materials used for equipment maintenance in the plant. The material is purchased and stored like any other purchased item, but a spare part is not sold and therefore does not contain sales information. If a maintenance item is sold, then this should use a different material type such as a trading good.

FERT—Finished Good

A finished good is a material that has been manufactured by some form of production from items, such as raw materials. The finished good is not purchased, so it does not contain any purchasing information.

FHMI—Production Resources/Tools (PRT)

PRTs are purchased and used by the plant maintenance department. This material type is assigned to items used in the maintenance of plant equipment, such as test machines, drill bits, or calibrating tools. The material type for PRTs does not contain sales information, as the PRTs are not purchased to sell. In addition, PRTs are only managed on a quantity basis.

HALB—Semi-Finished Goods

Semi-finished products are often purchased and then completed and sold as finished goods. The semi-finished products could come from another part of the company or from a vendor. The semi-finished material type allows for purchasing and work scheduling, but not sales.

HAWA—Trading Goods

Trading goods are generally materials that are purchased from vendors and sold. This kind of material type only allows purchasing and sales information, as there are no internal operations carried out on these materials.

HERS—Manufacturer Parts

Manufacturer parts are materials that can be supplied by different vendors who use different part numbers to identify the material.

HIBE—Operating Supplies

Operating supplies are vendor-purchased and used in the production process. This HIBE material type can contain purchasing data, but not sales information. This type of product includes lubricants, compressed air, or solder.

IBAU—Maintenance Assembly

Maintenance assembly is not an individual object, but a set of logical elements to separate technical objects into clearly defined units for plant maintenance. For example, a car can be a technical object; the engine, transmission, axles, etc. are the maintenance assemblies. An IBAU material type contains basic data and classification data.

KMAT—Configurable Material

Configurable materials form the basis for variant configuration. The KMAT material type is used for all materials that are variant configuration materials. A material of this type can have variables that are determined by the user during the sales process. For example, automotive equipment produced by a manufacturer may have variable attributes that each car manufacturer needs to be different for each car, such as length of chain, or height of belt.

LEER—Empties

Empties are materials consisting of returnable transport packaging and can be subject to a nominal deposit. Empties can be made from several materials grouped together in a bill of material that is assigned to a finished material. An example of an empty can be a crate, drum, bottle, or pallet..

LEIH—Returnable Packaging

Reusable packaging material is used to pack finished goods to send to the customer. When the finished good is unpacked, the customer is obliged to return the returnable packaging material to the vendor.

NLAG—Non-Stock Material

Non-stock material type is used for materials that are not held in stock and are not inventoried. These materials can be called consumables and include items such as maintenance gloves, safety glasses, or grease. Items like this are purchased when needed.

PIPE—Pipeline Material

The pipeline material type is assigned to materials that are brought into the production facility by pipeline. Materials like this are not planned for because they are always at hand. This type of material type is used, e.g., for oil, water, electricity, or natural gas.

ROH—Raw Materials

Raw material is purchased material that is fed into the production process and may result in a finished good. There is no sales data for a raw material, as it is not sold. If the company wanted to classify a material that would normally be a raw material, then it should be considered a trading good.

UNBW—Non-Valuated Material

Non-valuated material type is similar to the NLAG (non-stock material) except that the non-valuated material is held by quantity and not by value. Examples of this are often seen in plant maintenance, where there are materials that are extremely important to the plant equipment but of little or no other value. Therefore, the plant maintenance department will monitor inventory to allow for planned purchases.

VERP—Packaging Material

Unlike LEER (Empties), the packaging material type is for materials that are packaging but that are free of charge to the customer in the delivery process. This does not mean that the packaging material has no value; often, the packaging material has a value and a physical inventory is recorded.

WETT—Competitive Products

Used by the sales department to monitor competitor's goods. The material type is to identify these types of products. Only basic data is held for these materials.

In addition to these material types, there are a number of additional material types used for SAP Retail customers. These types include FRIP (perishables), NOF1 (non-food items), FOOD (food except perishables), FGTR (beverages), MODE (apparel), VKHM (additional items, such as clothes labels) and WERB (advertising material).

4.2.2 Configuring Material Types

The material type can be configured in the transaction OMS2 using the navigation path **IMG · Logistics—General · Material Master · Basic Settings · Material Types · Define Attributes for Material Type**.

The method for creating a new material type is to select an existing material type and copy to a new one. Copying from an existing material type reduces the amount of configuration required. Figure 4.1, shows the configurable fields for the material type. The four-character material type should always start with a **Z** for a user defined material type.

Once a new material type has been configured, the valuation areas defined for that material type can be configured. The valuation area is the level at which material is valuated, and plant or company code. A number of valuation areas can be defined for a material type, as seen in Figure 4.2.

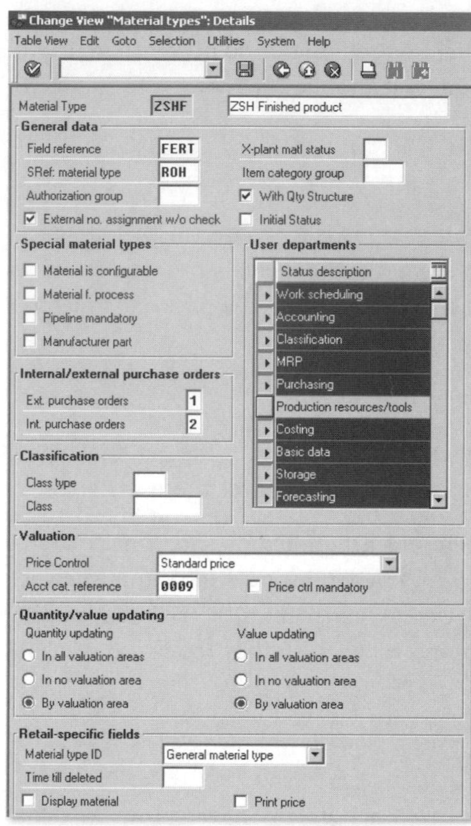

Figure 4.1 Configurable Fields for Material Type

Change View "Quantity/value updating": Overview

Table View Edit Goto Selection Utilities System Help

Val. are	Matl type	Qty updating	Value updating	Pipe.mand.	PipeAllowd
0001	ZSHF	☐	☐	☐	☐
0099	ZSHF	☑	☑	☐	☐
1000	ZSHF	☑	☑	☐	☐
1002	ZSHF	☐	☐	☐	☐
1003	ZSHF	☐	☐	☐	☐
1030	ZSHF	☐	☐	☐	☐
1040	ZSHF	☐	☐	☐	☐
1100	ZSHF	☑	☑	☐	☐
1111	ZSHF	☐	☐	☐	☐
1200	ZSHF	☑	☑	☐	☐
1300	ZSHF	☑	☑	☐	☐
1400	ZSHF	☑	☑	☐	☐
1973	ZSHF	☐	☐	☐	☐
2000	ZSHF	☑	☑	☐	☐
2001	ZSHF	☐	☐	☐	☐

Figure 4.2 Valuation Areas for Material

The four fields that can be configured for the valuation area/material type combination are:

- ▶ Qty Updating—This field can specify whether a material assigned this material type can be managed on a quantity basis for this valuation area.
- ▶ Value updating—This field can specify whether a material assigned this material type can be managed on a value basis for this valuation area.
- ▶ Pipe.mand.—This field can specify whether a material assigned this material type is subject to mandatory pipeline handling for this valuation area.
- ▶ PipeAllowd—This field can specify whether a material assigned this material type is allowed to be subject to pipeline handling for this valuation area.

4.2.3 Changing a Material Type

The material type of a material may need to be changed. For example, if a raw material that has only been used for in-house production has a requirement to be sold, the material type may need to be changed from ROH to HAWA (Trading Good).

There are a number of caveats regarding unrestricted material type changes as can be seen in Tables 4.1 and 4.2.

Material with Old Material Type	Material with New Material Type
No price control specification	Can only allow standard price
PRT view maintained	PRT view must be maintained
Not a configurable material	Must not be a configurable material
Allows inspection plans	Must allow inspection plans
Material for process indicator	Must be the same setting
Manufacturer part indicator	Must be the same setting

Table 4.1 Changing a Material Type—Scenario 1

In addition, there are a number of caveats if the material has any stock, reservations, or purchasing documents against it.

Material with Old Material Type	Material with New Material Type
Stock value updated in G/L account	Must be the same G/L account
Quantity and value updating	Must be the same as previously
WM transfer request open	WM view must be maintained
Batch managed	Must be batch-managed

Table 4.2 Changing a Material Type—Scenario 2

4.3 Basic Data

4.3.1 Creating a Material Master Record—Immediately

The Material Master record can be created in a number of different ways. The most common way for a Material Master record to be created is via transaction MM01, or via the navigation path **SAP Menu · Logistics · Materials Management · Material Master · Material · Create (General) · immediately**.

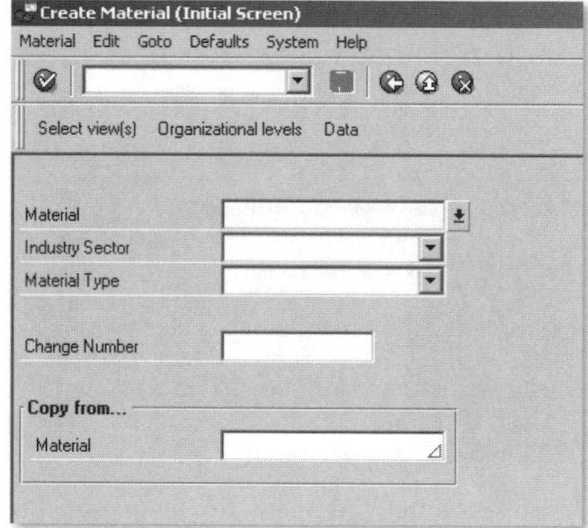

Figure 4.3 Initial Fields Required to Create Material Master Record

Figure 4.3 shows the fields needed to initially create the record. These are:

- **Material**—Leave blank for internal numbering or enter a material number
- **Industry sector**—Enter the selected industry sector
- **Material type**—Enter a defined material type or a user-defined material type
- **Change number** (optional)—Enter a change number if the customer is using Engineering Change Management
- **Copy from Material** (optional)—Enter a material number of a material that provides the information required for the new material.

4.3.2 Creating a Material Master Record—Schedule

If you decide to schedule the creation of the Material Master, you can use transaction code MM11 or the navigation path **SAP Menu • Logistics • Materials Management • Material Master • Material • Create (General) • Schedule**.

This has the same entry fields as MM01 (see Figure 4.3), but it also has a field that requires the material user to enter a date on which the material can be scheduled to be created.

4.3.3 Creating a Material Master Record—Special

This particular way of creating the Material Master record needs to have the material type already defined. For example, if you want to create a Material Master record for a ROH material type (raw material), then you can use transaction MMR1 or the navigation path **SAP Menu • Logistics • Materials Management • Material Master • Material • Create (Special) • Raw Material**.

Table 4.3 shows the transactions for creating Material Master for the various material types

Material Type	Transaction
Raw Materials (ROH)	MMR1
Semi-Finished Materials (HALB)	MMB1
Finished Products (FERT)	MMF1
Operating Supplies (HIBE)	MMI1
Trading Goods (HAWA)	MMH1
Non-Valuated Material (UNBW)	MMU1
Non-Stock Material (NLAG)	MMN1
Packaging (VERP)	MMV1
Empties (LEER)	MML1
Services (DIEN)	MMS1
Configurable Material (KMAT)	MMK1
Maintenance Assembly (IBAU)	MMP1
Competitor Product (WETT)	MMW1
Returnable Packaging (LEIH)	MMG1

Table 4.3 Transactions for Creating Materials by Material Type

4.3.4 Organizational Levels

Once the material type, industry sector, and external material number are entered (if applicable), a dialog box will show the views applicable to the particular material type. Users then can choose for which views they wish to enter information.

Once the views have been selected, a dialog box will appear with the organizational levels required for this Material Master record (See Figure 4.4).

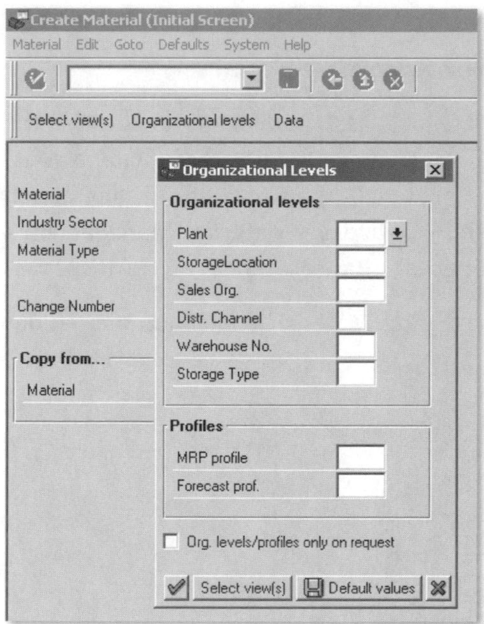

Figure 4.4 Organizational Levels for Creating Material Master Record

The organizational levels relate to the level at which Material Master information is held. Distribution Channel is required for Sales and Distribution screens, Warehouse Number for Warehouse Management screens, and other items.

Figure 4.4 shows that the data entry user can enter the plant, storage location, sales organization, distribution channel, warehouse number, and storage type. The other two fields on the screen are profiles, one for materials requirements planning (MRP) and one for forecasting.

MRP Profile

The MRP profile is a key that provides a set of field values for MRP screens that save having to make data entry decisions.

The MRP profile is not part of configuration and can be defined by authorized end users via transaction MMD1 or through the navigation path **SAP Menu • Logistics • Materials Management • Material Master • Profile • MRP Profile • Create**.

Figure 4.5 shows some of the fields that can be defaulted for the MRP profile.

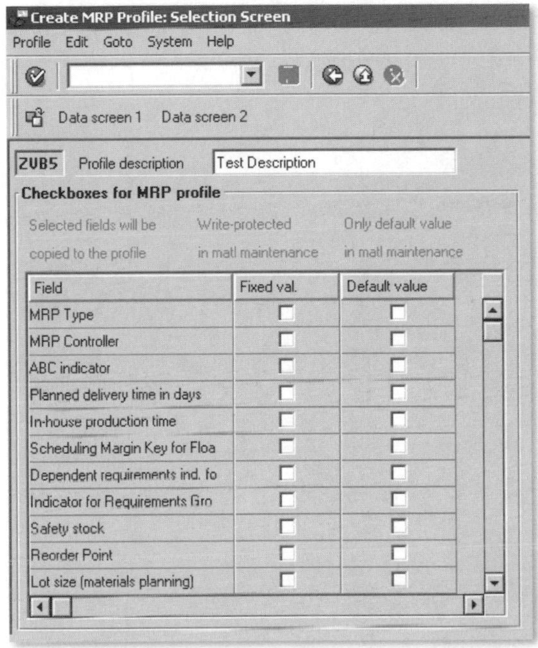

Figure 4.5 Possible Default Fields for the MRP Profile

The MRP profile allows you to highlight a field from the list of fields on the MRP screens. You can choose one of two options. Either the data from the field is entered into the Material Master as a fixed value that cannot be overwritten or as a default value that can be changed. Once the fields that are going to be part of the MRP key have been decided upon, the values need to be entered. The MRP profile can be changed, using transaction MMD2, or deleted.

Forecast Profile

The forecast profile is very similar to the MRP profile, as it is a key that provides a set of field values for the forecasting screen.

The forecast profile can be defined by authorized end users via transaction MP80 or through the navigation path **SAP Menu • Logistics • Materials Management • Material Master • Profile • Forecast Profile • Create**.

4.3.5 Basic Data Screen

After the views have been selected and the organizational levels entered, the first screen that is viewed is the basic data screen (see Figure 4.6).

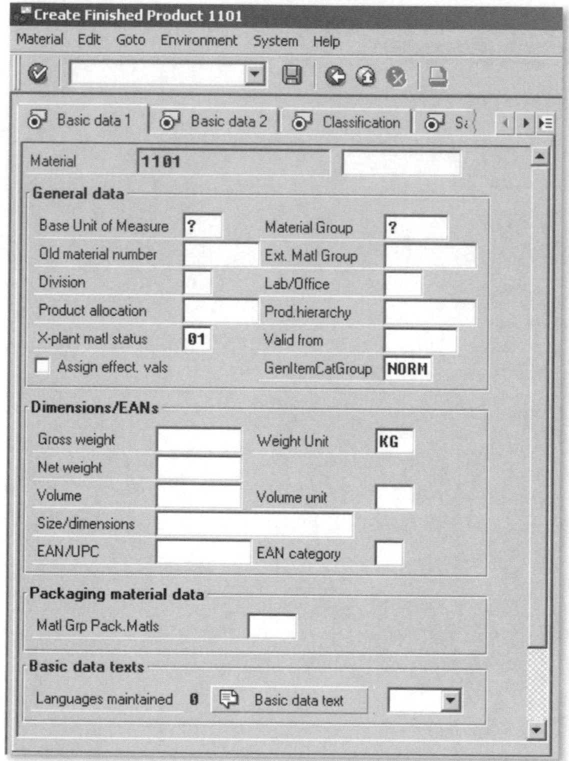

Figure 4.6 Fields for Basic Data Screen for Material Master

The basic data screen allows data entry for non-organizational level fields. This screen does not require a plant or sales organization to be defined, but allows the data entry user to enter basic information about the material. These mandatory fields on this screen, as defined by configuration, are the minimum information that can be added to create a Material Master. If the complete Material Master is created by a number of different departments, each entering its own information, then this basic data is used to enter material at the client level.

Material Description

The first field to be entered is the material description. We can add different descriptions of the material based on the language, with **EN** as English, **DA** as Danish, or **NL** as Dutch, for instance. The material description is only 40 characters long, so it is good practice to define a material-description policy. Abbreviations and standard wording should be used where possible.

Base Unit of Measure

The base unit of measure is the unit of measure, which is the lowest level for the material. For instance, a material that is sheet metal may be sold in single sheets, stored in pallets of sheets, and purchased by the truck load, but the base unit of measure may a square foot. In Figure 4.6, you will see a base unit of measure button that allows the conversion factors to be entered. Figure 4.7 shows the unit of measure conversions that relate back to the base unit of measure.

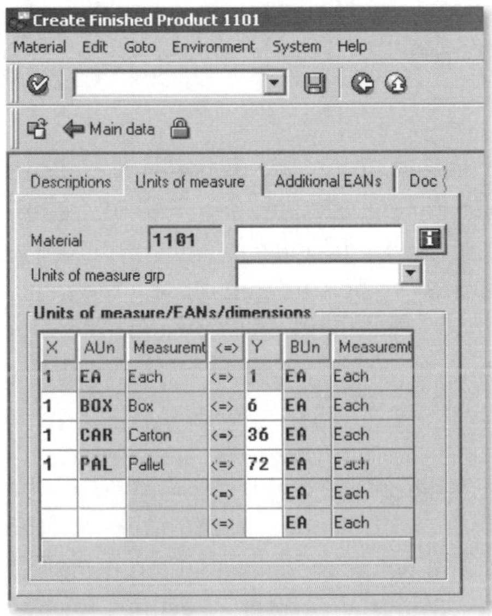

Figure 4.7 Base Unit of Measure and Conversion Factors to Alternative Units of Measure

Material Group

The material group is a method of grouping similar materials. The material group can be defined either by using classification or by configuration. The material group is important not only for searching for materials but also in other areas such as purchasing. For example, a purchase information record can be created without a material number, but must require a material group and a vendor. This is material group/vendor purchase information record is used in production orders where in-process material is sent to vendors for outside processing.

The material group is configured in transaction WG21 or through the navigation path **IMG • Logistics—General • Material Group • Create Material Group**.

It is also possible to create a material group hierarchy. This is difficult and time-consuming, so the best practice is to use an existing hierarchical material structure already defined in the implementing organization.

Changes to the material group hierarchy after the project has been implemented can be very complicated and have far-reaching implications. Therefore, it is important to define material groups and hierarchies early in the project.

Customer Material Number

The customer material number has been called the old material number in past SAP releases. This is useful for customers, as it allows them to enter a number that the material was referred to in legacy systems or systems that they are still interfacing with SAP. This field is 18 characters in length.

Division

Each material can only be assigned to one division, primarily at a sales-and-distribution organizational level. It can be used to distinguish different areas of the distribution channel. The division allows a company to organize its sales structure to work with groups of similar materials. Divisions can be configured using the transaction VOR2 or via the navigation path **IMG • Sale and Distribution • Master Data • Define Common Divisions**.

Laboratory/Design Office

This field is defined to be the laboratory or design office that is responsible for the material. It is used more frequently in Production Planning (PP) to identify the persons responsible for a bill of materials. The field can be configured using the navigation path **IMG • Logistics—General • Material Master • Settings for Key Fields • Define Laboratories/Offices**.

Cross Plant Material Status

There are a number of areas where the material status can be entered. The cross-plant material status field on the basic data screen allows the data entry user to enter a status that will be valid across the client. The material statuses are defined using transaction OMS4 or via the navigation path **IMG • Logistics—General • Material Master • Settings for Key Fields • Define Material Statuses**.

A two-character field defines the material status. The configurator can configure new material statuses. The material status shown in Figure 4.8 is user-defined and shows the process areas where either there is a warning message given, **A**, or an error message, **B**.

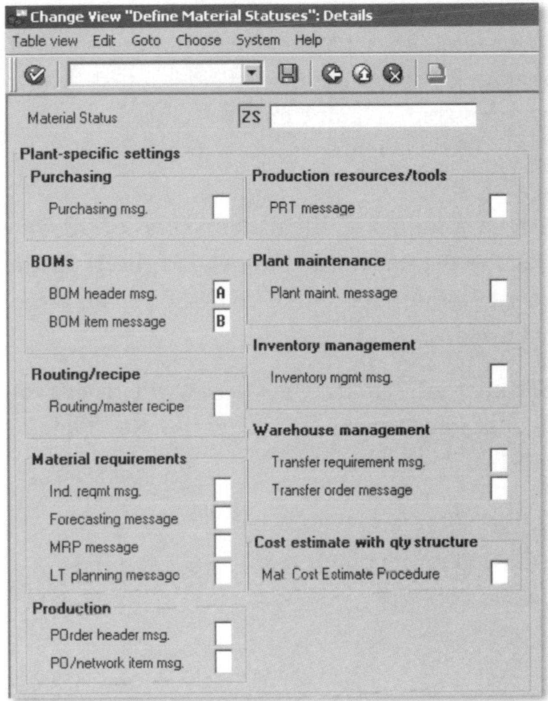

Figure 4.8 Attributes for Process Areas for User-Defined Material Status

Product Hierarchy

The product hierarchy is used in the sales and distribution area for analyses and price determination. The field is an alphanumeric character string that groups together materials by combining different characteristics. In standard SAP, the product hierarchy can have up to 3 levels. Levels one and two have five characters each, level three has eight. The product hierarchy is defined in table T179 using transaction V/76

General Item Category Group

The general-item category group is an entry that allows the system to automatically generate an item type in the sales document being created. This depends on the type of sales document and the general item category group. The item category group can be configured using the navigation path **IMG · Sales and Distribution · Sales · Sales Documents · Sales Document Items · Define Item Category Groups**.

Dimensions

This section of the basic-data screen offers the chance to enter information on gross weight, net weight, and volume. The size/dimensions field is a text field to allow a text description that may be required on a document.

EAN/UPC

The European Article Number (EAN) is assigned by the manufacturer of the particular material. The EAN identifies the manufacturer uniquely. In the U.S., the equivalent to the EAN is the Universal Product Code (UPC). An SAP customer can configure EANs to be used internally.

Some configuration items can be found for EAN/UPC items, using the navigation path **IMG • Logistics—General • Material Master • Settings for Key Fields • International Article Numbers (EANs)**. These are:

- Internal and External Number ranges for EAN (Transaction W4EN)
- Number ranges for Perishables EAN (4 and 5 digit)
- Prefixes for EAN/UPCs
- Attributes for EAN/UPCs

Product/Inspection Memo and Industry Standard Description

These fields are for information only. The product/inspection field allows you to enter a product or inspection memo for the material. The industry standard field allows the entry of the industry standard description of the material. If there is an ISO or ANSI standard name for the material, then this can be added.

Basic Material

The basic material is a selection that can be made in the basic-data screen. It allows a basic material to be chosen that the material being entered can be grouped under. The basic-material field has no specific control function, but is often used in custom reports where end users want to see activity of material at a basic material level. The basic material is found in table TWSPR.

The basic material can be configured using the navigation path **IMG • Logistics—General • Material Master • Settings for Key Fields • Define Basic Materials**.

Dangerous Goods (DG) Indicator Profile

This field is defined in the Environment, Health, and Safety (EHS) module of SAP. A **DG** indicator profile can be selected if the material being added is relevant for dangerous goods and for any documentation that accompanies that type of material.

The **DG** indicator profile can be configured in EHS using the navigation path **IMG • Environmental Health and Safety • Dangerous Goods Management • Dangerous Goods Checks • Common Settings • Specify Indicator Profiles for Material Master**.

Environmentally Relevant

This field is relevant for safety-data shipping. If this field is checked then during the delivery-creation process, an output type of SDB (Safety Data Sheet) is selected via the SD condition table. The output for this delivery will include a MSDS and other documentation that may be defined in EHS Product Safety.

Highly Viscous and In Bulk/Liquid

These two indicators do not have any control features in standard SAP. These can be used to influence the text or documentation of transportation documents, if custom reports are developed.

Design Drawing Fields

The document, document type, document version, page number, document chapter, page format, and number of sheets are all used if there is a design document that is not controlled under SAP Document Management System (DMS). If there is a design document that the users need to be added to the Material Master then these are the fields that need to be entered.

Cross-Plant Configurable Material

This field is used in variant configuration to identify a configurable material that is relevant for the client, not just one plant.

Material Group: Packaging Materials

A packaging material group can be entered for a material that groups similar packaging materials. The packaging material group can be found in table TVEGR. The fields can be configured using the navigation path **IMG • Logistics—General • Handling Unit Management • Basics • Technical Basics • Define Material Groups for Packaging Materials**.

4.4 Classification Data

The classification data is used primarily when searching for materials. The characteristic values entered into the classes for each material can be searched on, and the material with that set of characteristics can be found. This functionality is very powerful when the customer has allocated significant effort into identifying and creating characteristics and classes and entering the characteristic values for materials and other objects, such as vendors or batches.

4.4.1 Class Type

The classification entry screen after the basic data entry allows information to be entered into user defined characteristics and classes that can be assigned to a material.

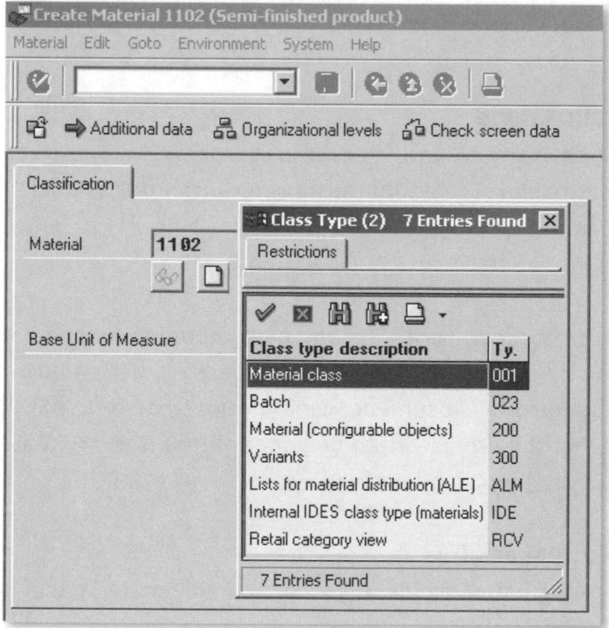

Figure 4.9 Class Types Accessible from Material Master Data Entry Screen

Figure 4.9 shows that for this material, the material user can choose to find a class that has been assigned to one of four class types. The class type is a grouping that is pre-defined in SAP. When a class is created, it is assigned to a class type depending on its function. Figure 4.9 shows class type 001, which is a grouping of classes associated with a material. Class type 022 is for batch records. The class contains the characteristics of where the values are entered. The material user can view the classes of a particular class type, but choosing that class type in the screen, shown in Figure 4.9. The classification system will be defined in detail later in this book.

4.4.2 Classes

Once the class type has been chosen for the material, individual classes can be selected. These classes have been set up in order to group together characteristics that describe the material further than do the fields in the Material Master.

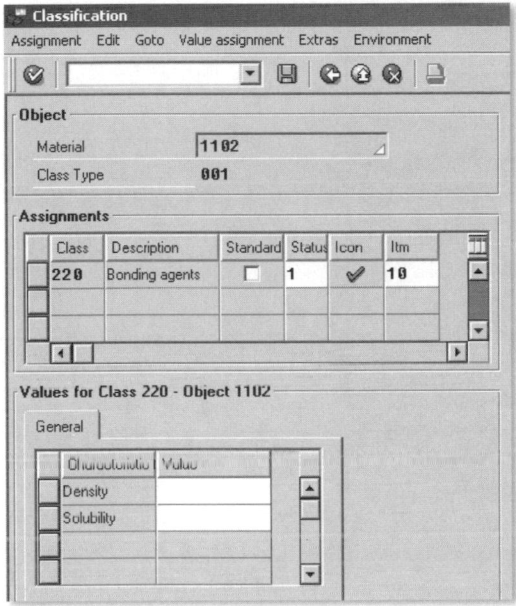

Figure 4.10 Two Classes Selected for Material and Characteristics for One of the Classes

4.4.3 Characteristics

The characteristics are the lowest level of the classification structure. The characteristic is the level at which information or a value is entered. In Figure 4.10, two classes have been selected for this material. The characteristics for the first class are shown and are available for entering values.

The characteristic can be configured to accept certain values or a range of values, and entry can be mandatory or optional.

4.5 Purchasing Data

The purchasing-data screen, shown in Figure 4.11, is displayed when the material being entered is assigned to a material type that allows purchasing. For example, it is normal to have a purchasing data screen for trading goods (HAWA), Raw Materials (ROH), and Production/Resource Tools (FHMI). Some of the fields shown have already been described in other Material Master screens.

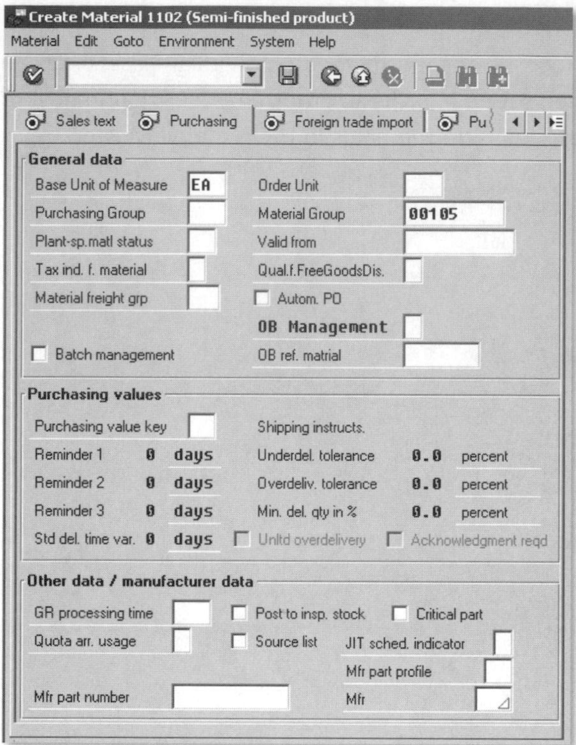

Figure 4.11 Purchasing Data Screen

4.5.1 General Data

Base Unit of Measure

The base unit of measure has been defaulted from the basic data screen and will be defaulted through to the other data screens.

Order Unit

The purchasing order unit of measure is the unit of measure that the material can be purchased in. Therefore, a material that has a base unit of measure of each (**EA**) may be purchased from a vendor in the order unit of carton (**CAR**). If the order unit field is blank, then the base unit of measure is used as the purchasing unit of measure.

Variable Order Unit

Checking this field allows the purchasing unit of measure to be variable. The purchasing unit of measure can be changed for a purchase order or the source list.

Plant-Specific Material Status

The plant-specific material status on the purchasing screen uses the same status fields that are used for the cross plant material status field in the basic data screen as seen earlier in Figure 4.8. The field in this screen defines the material status at the plant level.

Tax Indicator for Material

The tax indicator is used for the automatic determination of the tax code in purchasing. The tax code can be determined automatically by price determination, using purchasing conditions.

Qualify for Free Goods Discount

This indicator specifies whether a material qualifies for a discount in kind. A value should appear if the material does qualify for a discount in kind from vendors.

Material Freight Group

The material freight group is entered to classify materials in order to provide transportation information to the forwarding agents and rail transportation companies.

The configuration for the freight groups and codes is completed in the transportation area of Sales and Distribution. The table containing this information is TMFG. The navigation path for configuring the freight groups is **IMG • Logistics Execution • Transportation • Basic Transportation Functions • Maintain Freight Code Sets and Freight Codes**.

Automatic Purchase Order

The automatic purchase order indicator allows the customer to have purchase orders generated automatically when purchase requisitions are converted to purchase orders. To make the generation automatic, a further indicator must be set in the vendor master record of the vendor associated with the purchase order.

Batch-Management Requirement Indicator

This indicator configures the material to allow batches to be created for the material. This indicator is found in several screens.

4.5.2 Purchasing Value Key

The purchasing value key is configured to allow the entry of the purchasing values of tolerance limits, reminder days, which are the days elapsed before the vendor is contacted regarding the outstanding purchase orders, or similar information, by using one entry. The purchase value key information is found in table T405. Figure 4.12 shows the purchasing value key and the attributes that can be configured.

The configuration of the purchase value key can be selected via the navigation path **IMG • Materials Management • Purchasing • Material Master • Define Purchasing Value Keys**.

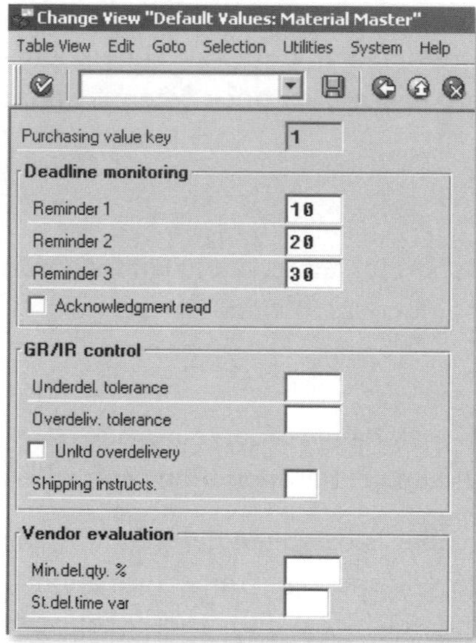

Figure 4.12 Purchasing Value Key and Configurable Attributes

Deadline Monitoring—Reminders

The reminder is entered at the number of days at which reminder or urging letters/messages are to be generated and sent to the vendor. If the figure entered is a positive number, then reminders are sent that many days after the due date given by the purchasing document. If the figure entered is a negative figure that means that the reminder is sent that many days before the due date.

The number of days for the reminders 1, 2, and 3 are used from the purchase information record. If there is no record, then information in the Material Master record is used.

Deadline Monitoring—Acknowledgement Required

If this field is checked, then the vendor is expected to supply an acknowledgement that it has received the purchasing document.

GR/IR Control—Under-Delivery Tolerance

In this field, the customer can enter a percentage figure for the under-delivery tolerance for this material. For instance, if the tolerance is 13%, then on a purchase order to a vendor for 20 units the customer will accept a delivery for 18 units (10%), but not 17 units (15%).

GR/IR Control—Over-Delivery Tolerance

In this field, the customer can enter a percentage figure for the over-delivery tolerance for this material. So if the tolerance is 7%, then on a purchase order to a vendor for 340 units, the customer will accept a delivery for 363 units (6.8%), but not 364 units (7.1%).

GR/IR Control—Unlimited Over-Delivery Allowed

This indicator allows the customer to accept any over-delivery from the vendor. This may not be acceptable for some materials and some vendors, so the purchasing department should understand the ramifications of the unlimited over-delivery.

GR/IR Control—Shipping Instructions

This field allows a shipping instruction indicator to be chosen. The instructions regarding shipping and packaging requirements are sent to the vendor if configured. The shipping instruction indicator is found in table T027A and configured via the navigation path **IMG • Materials Management • Purchasing • Material Master • Define Shipping Instructions**.

Vendor Evaluation—Minimum-Delivery Quantity Percentage

In this field, you can enter the minimum percentage of the purchase order quantity that must be delivered in order for the goods receipt to be included in the vendor evaluation. This field prevents the vendor from receiving a good score for on-time delivery when the delivery quantity was insufficient.

Vendor Evaluation—Standardizing Value For Delivery-Time Variance

The value is entered to determine how many days from the planned delivery date will constitute 100% variance for vendor evaluation. If the entry in this field is 10, then the vendor evaluation system calculates that the vendor will receive a 100% variance if the purchase order is delivered 10 or more days after the expected delivery date.

4.5.3 Other Data

Goods-Receipt Processing Time in Days

This processing time refers to the number of working days required after receiving the material for any quality inspection and movement into storage.

Post to Inspection Stock

This indicator allows the user to indicate whether the material is subject to inspection and the material needs to post to inspection stock.

Critical part

This indicator is only used in inventory sampling. It is for information purposes only. Discuss with the customers how or if they need to use this indicator.

Source List

This indicator is important to the purchasing department. If this indicator is checked, there is a requirement to maintain a source list for procurement for the plant. The source list has to have been created before a purchase order can be entered. Maintenance of source lists is described more fully later in this book.

Quota Arrangement Usage

This field is a key that defines how quota arrangements are used in purchasing. The information for the quota-arrangement usage key is found in table TMQ2 and configured via the navigation path **IMG • Materials Management • Purchasing • Quota Arrangement • Define Quota Arrangement Usage**. Figure 4.13 shows the purchasing functions that can be assigned to a quota arrangement usage key

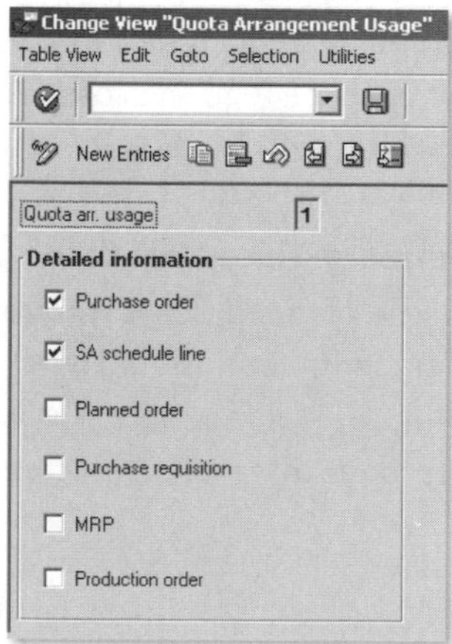

Figure 4.13 Purchasing Functions Assignable to Quota-Arrangement Usage Key

The key controls how the total order quantity is calculated in the quota arrangement and which source of supply is determined for the material. The key can be configured for the following purchasing functions:

- Purchase Order—quantity of the material ordered is included in the quota arrangement
- Purchase Requisition—total quantity requested in purchase requisitions for this material is included
- Scheduling Agreement—quantity scheduled in delivery schedules for this material is included
- Planned Orders—quantity planned in planned orders for this material is included
- MRP—the planned orders and purchase requisitions created by MRP are included in the quota arrangement
- Production Orders—quantity of all production orders for this material is included

Item Relevant to JIT Delivery Schedules

This indicator determines whether the system can generate a just-in-time (JIT) delivery schedule, as well as the forecast schedules, for the material in a scheduling agreement.

4.5.4 Foreign Trade Data

Commodity code / Import code Number for Foreign Trade

This field relates to the harmonized system for the description and coding of merchandise. If selected, the commodity code is used for statistical purposes and must be declared to the authorities for foreign trade transactions. Examples of this are INTRASTAT and EXTRASTAT in the European Union (EU) and the Automated Export System (AES) in the U.S.

The commodity code is defined in table T604 and is configured via the navigation path, **IMG · Sales and Distribution · Foreign Trade/Customs · Basic Data for Foreign Trade · Define Commodity Codes/Import Code Numbers by Country**.

Export/Import Group

This four-character field is a grouping for similar materials based on import and export attributes. The export/import group information can be found in table TVFM and can be configured via the navigation path **IMG · Sales and Distribution · Foreign Trade/Customs · Basic Data for Foreign Trade · Define Material Groups for Import/Export**.

CAS Number for Pharmaceutical Products

This field is only required if the material has a CAS number that is a key to descriptions given by the World Health Organization (WHO) for customs-free materials.

The CAS Number can be defined using transaction code VI36 or via the navigation path **IMG • Sales and Distribution • Foreign Trade/Customs • Specific Data for Customs Processing • Define CAS Numbers**.

PRODCOM Number for Foreign Trade

This field is used to enter a PRODCOM number in EU countries. It allows for harmonized production statistics in the EU. The PRODCOM numbers can be configured by using transaction VE47.

Control Code for Consumption Taxes in Foreign Trade

This field is used for consumption taxes in foreign trade. The values can be updated in table T604F.

4.5.5 Origin of Material

Country of Origin

A country of origin must be specified for export documentation. The material will often require a Certificate of Origin (COO) to be printed and included in the shipping documents. This field uses the country abbreviations in table T005.

Region of Origin

The region of origin, which is a state in the U.S., a county in the United Kingdom, a province in Australia etc., can provide more information for documentation of where the material originated. This field uses the region abbreviations from table T005S.

4.5.6 Preferences

Preference Status

This field specifies whether the preference status is allowed at a plant level. The preference status identifies whether a material is eligible to receive any special or preferential treatment under the terms of a trade agreement between countries.

Vendor Declaration Status

This field specifies whether the vendor declaration status is allowed at plant level. A vendor declaration states where the material was manufactured. The origin of the material is determined with this declaration.

4.5.7 Legal Control

Exemption Certificate/Certificate Number/Issue Date

This field is defined as an indicator for export-certification information. These are given below:

- A—The material does not require a license for import or export.
- B—The material does not require a license for import or export, as a certificate has been obtained.
- C—Application for an exemption certificate has been rejected.
- Blank—the material has no exemption and requires an import or export license.

If the indicator has been set to **B**, then the two fields, "Certificate Number" and "Issue" Date of Certificate, will need to be entered.

Military Goods

This field is for use only in Germany, due to weapons regulations. It can be used as an information only field outside of Germany.

4.5.8 Common Agricultural Policy (CAP)

The Common Agricultural Policy (CAP) is restricted to the countries of the EU and is not used outside of that region.

CAP Product List Number

The CAP product list number is the number of the material as defined in the EU market products group list. The product list numbers are defined in table T618M and can be configured using transaction code VI67.

CAP Product Group

Similar materials can be grouped under a CAP product group. This is for use in the EU only. The product groups are defined in table T618G and can be configured using transaction code VI69.

4.5.9 Manufacturer Parts

Manufacturer Part Number

This field is part of the Manufacturer Part Number (MPN) functionality. The vendor who supplies a material that is used in your production or plant maintenance may be the supplier of the part, but not the manufacturer. For instance, if there are a number of manufacturers that produce oil filters that fit a shop-floor lathe, your company may require that the vendor sell you a specific filter from a specific manufacturer. In turn, that manufacturer may make better quality filters at its plant in Latvia than at its plants in Latin America. Therefore, you as a customer can specify that information, with a specific manufacturer part number to your vendor. The way to store that information is in the MPN field in the Material Master.

Manufacturer

This is the manufacturer corresponding to the MPN number that has been entered in that field.

4.6 Forecasting Data

The forecasting data screen is displayed when the material being entered is assigned to a material type that is applicable to forecasting. A forecast profile can be entered at the organization level screen, if available. The forecasting data that can be entered into the Material Master comprises the initial calculated forecast and consumption values. Some of the fields shown in Figure 4.14 already have been described in other Material Master screens.

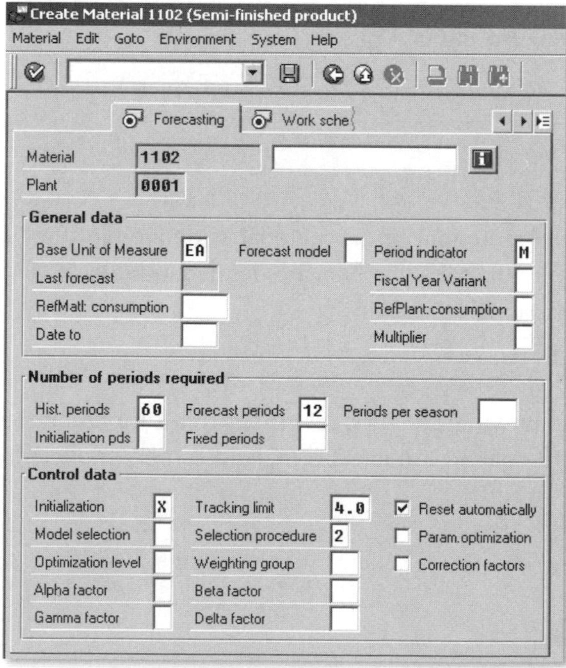

Figure 4.14 Forecast Screen of Material Master Creation Transaction

4.6.1 General Forecast Data

Forecast Model

The forecast model calculates the requirements forecast for the material. The forecast models and analysis of forecasting in general will be discussed later in this book.

Period Indicator

This field specifies the time period for which the consumption values are held for forecasting. The normal time period is one month, and this is the SAP default if this field is left blank.

Fiscal Year Variant

This is an accounting-defined field, which describes the variant for the fiscal year; that is, the number of posting periods. The fiscal year variant can seen in table T009 and configured transaction code OB37 or via the navigation path **IMG • Financial Accounting • Financial Accounting Global Settings • Fiscal Year • Maintain Fiscal Year Variant**

Reference Material for Consumption

If the material you are entering has no historical data from which to create a forecast, you can define a material that may be of similar characteristics to be used as reference material. The consumption figures for the reference material are then used by the system to create a forecast for the new material.

Reference Plant

The reference plant is the plant from which to drive the consumption figures.

Date To

This is the furthest date to which the figures for the reference material should be taken.

Multiplier

The multiplier field is a figure between 0 and 1 where the value relates to the percentage of the consumption of the reference material that should be used for the new material. For example, a figure 1 would mean 100% of the reference material consumption would be used, whereas a figure of 0.6 would indicate that 60% of the reference-material consumption would be used.

4.6.2 Number of Periods Required

Historical Periods

The number of historical periods entered into this field is used to calculate the forecast. If it is blank, then no periods will be used.

Forecast Periods

The number entered in this field is the number of periods over which the forecast will be calculated.

Number of Periods for Initialization

This number is for the historical values that you want to be used for the forecast initialization. If the field is blank, no historical values are used to initialize the forecast.

Fixed Periods

The fixed-period field is used to in order to avoid fluctuations in the forecast calculation or because production can no longer react to changed planning figures. The forecast will be fixed for the number of periods entered.

Number of Periods per Seasonal Cycle

If the customer uses a seasonal forecast model, then this field can be used to define the number of periods that make up a season for this material.

4.6.3 Control Data

Initialization Indicator

If the forecast needs to be initialized, then this indicator can be set to allow the system to initialize the forecast or to allow manual initialization.

Tracking Limit

The tracking limit is the value that specifies the amount by which the forecast value may deviate from the actual value. This figure can be entered to three decimal places.

Reset Forecast Model Automatically

If this indicator is set, the forecast is reset if the tracking limit is exceeded.

Model Selection

This field is only active if the user did not enter a value into the forecast model. This means that the user requires the system to select a model automatically. To assist the system in choosing a forecast model, the model selection field can be set to one of the following three indicators:

- T—Examine for a Trend
- S—Examine for Seasonal Fluctuations
- A—Examine for a Trend and Seasonal Fluctuations

Selection Procedure

The selection-procedure field is used when the system is selecting a forecasting model. There are two selection procedures to choose from:

- Procedure 1 performs a significance test to find the best seasonal or trend pattern.
- Procedure 2 carries out the forecast for all models and then selects the model with the smallest mean absolute deviation.

Indicator for parameter optimization

If this indicator is set, then the system will use the smoothing factors for the given forecast model.

Optimization level

This indicator can be set to fine, middle, or rough. The finer the optimization level, the more accurate the forecast becomes, but at the expense of processing time.

Weighting Group

This key is used with the weighted moving average forecast model. The weighting group can be configured. The navigation path is **IMG • Materials Management • Consumption-Based Planning • Forecast • Weighting Groups for Weighting Moving Average**.

Correction Factor Indicator

This indicator allows the user to decide whether the forecast should include the corrector factors.

Alpha Factor

This is the smoothing factor for the basic value. If it is left blank, the default for the alpha factor is 0.2.

Beta Factor

This is the smoothing factor for the trend value. If it is left blank, the default for the beta factor is 0.1.

Gamma Factor

This is the smoothing factor for the seasonal index. If it is left blank, the default for the gamma factor is 0.3.

Delta Factor

This is the smoothing factor for the mean absolute deviation. If it is left blank, the default for the delta factor is 0.3.

4.7 Work Scheduling Data

The screen seen in Figure 4.15 allows the user entering the work-scheduling information to enter what is relevant to a particular plant. The material may be sold by many plants. Some of the fields in this screen will be defaulted from other entry screens, such as base unit of measure.

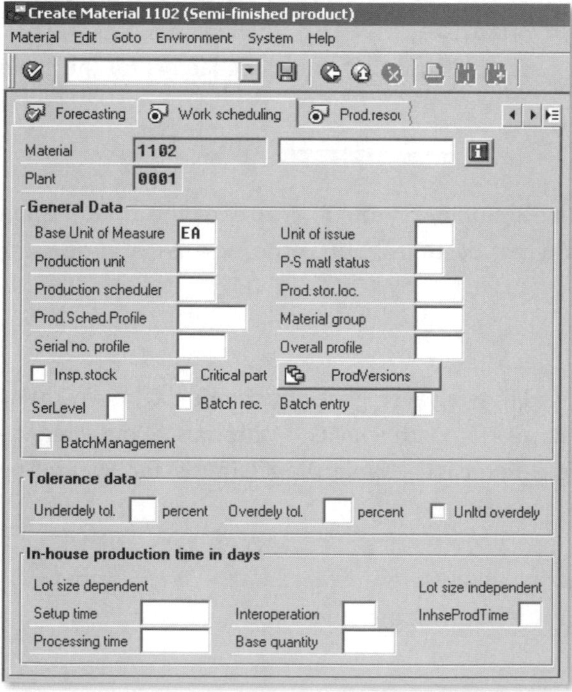

Figure 4.15 Work-Scheduling Screen of Material Master

4.7.1 General Data

Production Unit

The production unit is the unit of measure used for the material in the production process. If no production unit is entered, then the base unit of measure is assumed for the production unit of measure.

Production Scheduler

The production scheduler has an important position in production and has to play many roles. Some of these roles include:

- Generating a collaborative production schedule
- Maximizing plant efficiency through effective use of equipment and personnel
- Determining short-term labor requirements necessary to support plan
- Creating a production plan that meets stated goals for on time delivery
- Monitoring schedule adherence and schedule attainment identify corrective actions to address shortfalls
- Working with management to report current order status and maintain order accuracy
- Coordinating project schedules and incorporate into commercial production schedule
- Identifying and resolving potential capacity constraints

In the Material Master the production scheduler is entered at each plant level. The field is a three-character string and is found in table T024F. The production scheduler can be configured using transaction OPJ9 or using the navigation path **IMG · Production · Shop Floor Control · Master Data · Define Production Scheduler**.

Production Storage Location

This storage location is the key to the production of a material in a plant. This is the storage location used as the issuing storage location for the backflushing process, for a material that is a component for a finished good. If the material is a finished good, then this storage location is where the finished goods will be received after production.

Production Scheduling Profile

The production scheduling profile can be configured using transaction OPKP or via the path **IMG · Production · Shop Floor Control · Master Data · Define Production Scheduling Profile**.

The production scheduling profile can be configured to perform automatic actions on either release or creation of a production or process order. The profile also provides configuration for capacity planning, availability check, goods receipt, batch management, and transport and order type.

4.7.2 Tolerance Data

Under-Delivery Tolerance

This field allows you to define an under-delivery tolerance percentage for the material. This means that if a goods receipt for a production order differs from the expected amount by more than the under-delivery tolerance, then the goods receipt will not be allowed.

Over-Delivery Tolerance

This field allows you to define an over-delivery tolerance percentage for the material. This means that if a good receipt for a production order differs from the expected amount by more than the over-delivery tolerance, then the goods receipt will not be allowed.

Unlimited Over-Delivery

If this indicator is set, then the goods receipt from a production order for this material will accept any amount over the expected goods receipt total.

4.7.3 Lot-Size Dependent In-House Production Time

Setup Time

The setup time is used for determining the dates for planned orders. The setup time is the number of days required to configure the work centers used in the production of the material. For example, if production for material ABC in a machine shop has been completed, the equipment must have the parts used for material ABC removed. Once the machines have been torn down, then the setup for the next production run, material XYZ will start. Once the run for XYZ has finished, the machines will be torn down before the next production run. The setup time for material XYZ is the setup time plus the tear- down time.

This setup time does not take into account the quantity of the material being produced. The setup time may be a standard figure that has been calculated or negotiated. The field can be defined up to two decimal places for partial days.

Processing Time

The processing time is the amount of time the material consumes at the work centers used in the production order. The processing time will take into account the base quantity that is entered

Base Quantity

This processing time is entered for a quantity. The quantity is the base quantity. This quantity can be defined up to three decimal places.

Interoperation Time

The interoperation time is the time that a material is in the state between operations in the production order. There are a number of situations that can go to make up the total interoperation time. These are:

- Move time—the time that is accumulated as the material is moved from one work center to the next
- Wait time—the time the material has to be left after the operation and before the move can take place on the material Examples are curing and temperature reduction.
- Queue time—time that materials are queued for work centers that are bottlenecked or because if production delays in the operations. This queue time can be calculated by production staff.
- Float before production—The production scheduler can enter a float that is the number of days between the start date or the production order and the scheduled start date.
- Float after production—the production scheduler can enter a float that is the number of days from the end of production order to the scheduled end date.

4.7.4 Lot-Size Independent In-House Production Time

In-House Production

This in-house production time is a single value for the material to be produced in-house. The number of days relates to all of the individual elements of in-house production, including floats and interoperation. This figure is used in the material-planning functionality.

4.8 Sales Organizational Data

This screen allows the user entering the sales information to enter data relevant to the particular sales organization. The material may be sold by various sales organizations, and the data for each may differ. Many of the fields in this screen will be defaulted from other entry screens such as base unit of measure. Some of the fields shown in Figure 4.16 already have been described in other Material Master screens.

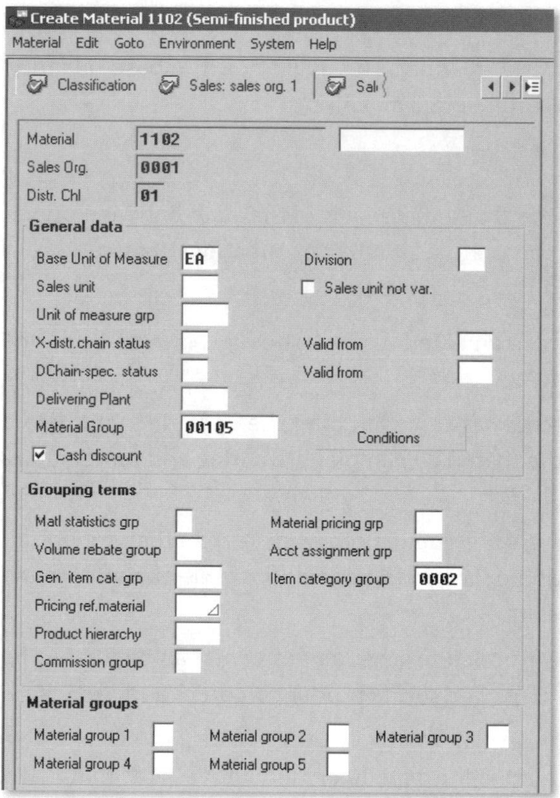

Figure 4.16 Sales Organization Screen for Material Master

4.8.1 General Data

Sales Unit

The unit of measure in which the material is sold is known as the sales unit of measure. For each sales organization, the material can be specified in a sales unit of measure that is used for the sales orders. This unit of measure can be the same as the base unit of measure or a multiple of the base unit of measure. An example would be a material that has bottle as its base unit of measure, but that could be sold in the sales organization for the U.S. as cartons and sold through the sales organization for France as pallets.

Variable Sales Unit Not Allowed Indicator

If this indicator is set, then the sales unit of measure in the Material Master cannot be changed in the sales order. So if the indicator is not set, then the sales representative can change the sale unit of measure in the order from carton to pallet. With the indicator set, the sales representative cannot change the sales unit and it will remain as cartons.

Cross-Distribution Chain Material Status

This field, along with the distribution-chain-specific material status field, is used in SAP retail clients and check whether material can be used in different distribution channels.

Delivering Plant

If the users define this field, it means that this is the default plant where this material is delivered. This field is automatically copied into the sales order as the delivery plant.

4.8.2 Grouping Items

Material Statistics Group

The material statistics group is used as a grouping used in the Logistics Information System (LIS). This field is found in table TVSM. The values can be configured using transaction OVRF or by using the navigation path **IMG · Logistics Information System (LIS) · Logistics Data Warehouse · Updating · Updating Control · Settings: Sales and Distribution · Statistics Groups · Maintain Statistics Groups for Material**.

Volume Rebate Group

This group is just a way of grouping similar materials for rebate-agreement processing. The field can be configured using the following path **IMG · Sales and Distribution · Billing · Rebate Processing · Define Material Rebate Group**.

Commission Group

The commission group field can group together materials that offer similar commissions. The commission group can be used in pricing procedures. This field can be configured via **IMG · Logistics—General · Material Master · Settings for Key Fields · Data Relevant to Sales and Distribution · Define Commission Groups**

Material Pricing Group

The material pricing group is another available field that groups materials for pricing conditions. The field is found in table T178.

Account Assignment Group

The account assignment group can be selected to group together materials that have similar accounting requirements. For example, you can select a group for service revenues, or a group for trading goods revenues. This field is used in sales billing documents. This field can be found in table TVKM. The account assignment groups can be defined in configuration steps. The navigation path is **IMG • Sales and Distribution • Basic Functions • Account Assignment/Costing • Revenue Account Determination • Check Master Data Relevant for Account Assignment • Materials: Account Assignment Groups**.

4.8.3 Tax Data

The tax data can be entered for a number of countries that a material is sold in. The country is entered along with the tax category and the relevant tax classification. There can be a number of tax categories per country.

Tax Category/Tax Classification

The tax category for materials is specific to the sales organization/division/plant level that defines the country-specific taxes during pricing. The configuration of the access sequences in the tax-condition tables for sales and use tax is made in the Financial Accounting Global Settings section of the IMG. That part of the IMG is cross-client and requires careful consideration before any access sequences are added. Consult with the Financial Accounting specialist when considering any changes to the tax-calculation procedures.

The tax category/classification is defined in the IMG, using transaction OVK4 or via the navigation path **IMG • Sales and Distribution • Basic Functions • Taxes • Define Tax Relevancy of Master Records**.

4.8.4 Quantity Stipulations

Minimum Order Quantity

This value is the minimum quantity that a customer can order for this material/sales organization combination.

Minimum Delivery Quantity

This value is the minimum quantity that a customer can have delivered for an order for this material/sales organization combination.

Delivery Unit

The delivery unit is the minimum unit of quantity for a delivery. The second field is for the unit of measure. For example, if the delivery unit is 50 cartons, then the delivery quantity to the customer can only be 50, 100, 150, etc. The delivery quantity should not be 125, as it is not a multiple of 50.

Rounding Profile

The rounding profile defines how a quantity is rounded up to a given value, depending whether a static or dynamic profile is defined. The configuration for a rounding profile allows the user to define the rounding quantities for different thresholds. Table 4.4 shows an example of a static rounding profile.

Threshold Value	Rounding Value
1.000	70.000
211.000	300.000
301.000	450.000
451.000	1000.000

Table 4.4 Configuration for Rounding Profile in Transaction OWD1

Value From	Value To	Rounded Value
1.000	70.000	70.000
71.000	140.000	140.000
141.000	210.000	210.000
211.000	300.000	300.000
301.000	450.000	450.000
451.000	1000.000	1000.000

Table 4.5 Actual Rounding of Quantities

Table 4.5 shows the actual rounding of quantities 1 to 1000 based on the rounding value in Table 4.4 The configuration for rounding profiles can be found in transaction OWD1 or via navigation path **IMG • Material Requirements Planning • Planning • Lot-Size Calculation • Maintain Rounding Profile**.

4.8.5 Material Groups

The material groups that can be entered on this sales organization screen are not used in standard R/3 processing. The five material group fields can be used by the sales department to further define the material based on the sales organization. These fields are available for sales department analysis.

The definition of these five material groups can be configured via the navigation path **IMG · Logistics—General · Material Master · Settings for Key Fields · Data Relevant to Sales and Distribution · Define Material Groups**.

4.8.6 Product Attributes

The product attribute indicators are available to be used by the sales department for analysis. The 10 product attribute fields are found in table MVKE.

4.9 Sales General Data

The sales general data is specific to a material and a particular plant. The screen can be seen in Figure 4.17. Some of the fields shown have already been described in other Material Master screens.

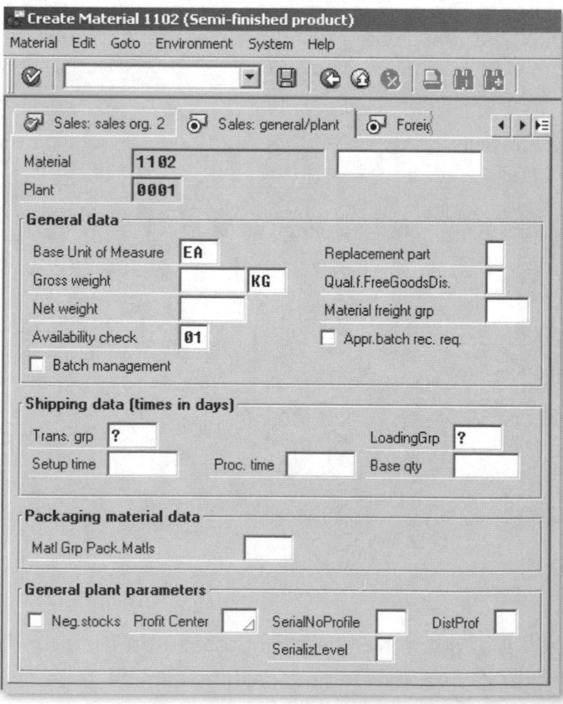

Figure 4.17 Fields on Material Master's Sales General Data Screen

4.9.1 General Data

Replacement Part

This indicator allows the sales department to specify if the material is a replacement part. The options are to indicate that this is not a replacement part, that is must be replacement part, or that there is an optional replacement part.

Availability Check

The availability check field is important to the sales department it defines how an availability check is defined. The configuration can be found using transaction OVZ2 or via the navigation path **IMG • Sales and Distribution • Basic Functions • Availability Check and Transfer of Requirements • Availability Check • Availability Check with ATP Logic or Against Planning • Define Checking Groups**

The availability check can be configured in OVZ2, and new availability checks can be defined based on the sales department's requirements.

Approved Batch Record Required Indicator

This indicator is only valid when the batches are from a process order. It specifies that certain activities can only be performed after a batch record has been entered.

4.9.2 Shipping Data

Transportation Group

This group field is used to group together those materials that have similar transportation requirements, such as truck, tanker, train, etc. This field can be used in the automatic route-scheduling function in sales order and delivery. The transportation group can be configured using the navigation path **IMG • Logistics Execution • Shipping • Basic Shipping Functions • Routes • Route Determination • Define Transportation Groups**.

Loading Group

This field allows the sales departments to group together materials that have similar loading requirements, such as crane, forklift, trolley, etc. This field is required if shipping point determination is to be used. The field contents can be configured via the navigation path **IMG • Logistics Execution • Shipping • Basic Shipping Functions • Shipping Point and Goods Receiving Point Determination • Define Loading Groups**.

Setup Time

The setup time for shipping is similar to the setup times in other Material Master screens such as the Work Scheduling screen. This setup time is strictly the set up time for getting the equipment, such as a forklift or a trolley cart, ready to move the material.

Processing Time/Base Quantity

The processing time for shipping is the actual time it takes to load the material from its location onto the transportation vehicle. This processing time is valid for the amount of material that is entered into the base quantity field.

4.9.3 General Plant Parameters

Negative Stock in Plant

This indicator can be set if there is a requirement to allow stocks of this material to be in a negative stock situation. Negative stock occurs when there is actual physical stock, but that stock has not been receipted into inventory. If a goods issue is made from inventory, then the stock will go negative until the missing goods receipt is made. This allows stock to be shipped without waiting for paperwork to be completed. However, this situation is dependent on the policy of the company.

Logistics Handling Group

The logistics handling group allows materials with similar handling requirements to be assigned the same group. The logistics handling group can be configured via the navigation path **IMG • Logistics Execution • Planning and Monitoring • Rough Workload Estimate • Calculate Workload • Maintain Logistics Load Category**.

Profit Center

A profit center is a function of the Controlling area (CO) of SAP. The profit center is a way of internally managing the company. Profit center accounting is an option that the company has to manage and analyze the financials for. The profit center in this screen can be used if profit centers are to be used.

Stock Determination Group

This field, combined with the stock determination type, provides the stock determination strategy for materials that are used in repetitive manufacturing.

4.10 Production Resources and Tools Data

The PRT screen allows the plant maintenance department to enter the data for the PRT material. The screen can be seen in Figure 4.18. Some of the fields shown have already been described in other Material Master screens.

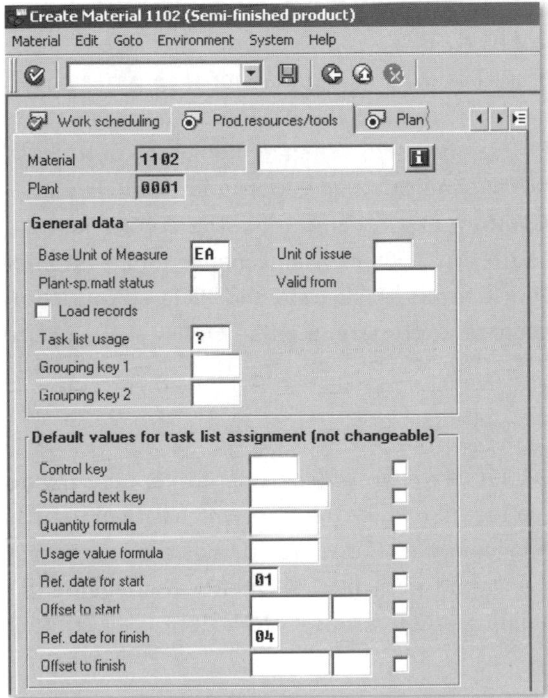

Figure 4.18 Available Fields on Production Resources and Tools Screen of Material Master

4.10.1 General Data

Task List Usage

This field determines on what task lists the PRT is valid for the particular plant. This field can be found in table TC23. The configuration for the task list usage field is found in transaction OP47 or via the navigation path **IMG • Plant Maintenance and Customer Service • Maintenance Plans, Work Centers, Task Lists and PRTs • Production Resources/Tools • General Data • Define Task List Usage Keys**.

Grouping Keys 1 and 2

These fields allow the plant-maintenance department to define groupings for their PRTs. The grouping keys can be defined in configuration and are found in table TCF12. The configuration for the grouping keys is found via the navigation path **IMG • Plant Maintenance and Customer Service • Maintenance Plans, Work Centers, Task Lists and PRTs • Production Resources/Tools • General Data • Define PRT Group Keys**.

4.10.2 Default Values for Task List Assignment

Control Key for the Management of PRTs

The control key specifies how the PRT is used in the maintenance order or the task list. The PRT control key can be found in table TCF10. The control key defines in what parts of the task list the PRT can be used. When defining the control key, the user can check off which of the five indicators are appropriate. The five indicators are **Schedule**, **Calculate**, **Confirm**, Expand and Print. The control key can be configured via the navigation path **IMG • Plant Maintenance and Customer Service • Maintenance Plans, Work Centers, Task Lists and PRTs • Production Resources/Tools • Production Resource/Tool Assignments • Define PRT Control Keys**.

Standard Text Key

The standard text key allows the plant maintenance department to enter a key on the Material Master that defines a standard text for the PRT, which is then used as a default in the task list or maintenance order. The standard texts are maintained in transaction CA10 or via the navigation path **IMG • Quality Management • Quality Planning • Inspection Planning • Operation • Work Center • Maintain Standard Text Keys**.

The standard text has to be maintained in the correct language. Therefore, the standard text key P000010 for PRTs can be defined in a number of different languages.

Quantity Formula

This field is the formula for calculating the total of the PRTs required. This field is copied into the maintenance order or task list. The formula can be defined in configuration transaction OIZM or via the navigation path **IMG • Plant Maintenance and Customer Service • Maintenance Plans, Work Centers, Task Lists and PRTs • Production Resources/Tools • Production Resource/Tool Assignments • Formulas • Configure Formula Definition**.

All formulas are defined in this transaction. For a formula to be selected in the quantity formula field in the PRT screen, the formula must have set the indicator to **PRT Allowed for Requirement**.

Usage Value Formula

This field calculates the total usage value of the PRT. This field is selected from the same formulas as the quantity-formula field.

Reference Date to Start of PRT Usage

This start-date field is used in calculating the start date/time for the PRT usage. It is used with the offset field (next field in the Material Master) and used in the task list or maintenance order. The start date can be selected from entries from table TCA54.

Offset to Start

This field is used in conjunction with the reference date for PRT scheduling. The numeric value can be positive or negative. A negative value indicates a start time before the reference date. A positive value indicates a time after the reference date. The numeric value can have a unit of measure that indicates hours, minutes, days, etc.

Reference Date to Finish/Offset to Finish

These fields are similar to those above, except they are used to determine the finish date rather than the start date.

4.11 General Plant Data

The general plant data screen, shown in Figure 4.19, includes many fields that have been defined in other screens, but also allows the inventory staff to enter information relevant to storage location and to shelf-life characteristics.

4.11.1 General Data

Storage Bin

The storage bin is a field that can be entered by the warehouse staff to identify a location within the storage location where the material is always stored. This is used when Warehouse Management (WM) is not implemented. The storage bin is a 10-character field that is not configurable as it has no functional purpose and is only used as a reference field. The storage bin does not have any functionality within Inventory Management. Please note that there can only be one storage bin defined for each material per storage location.

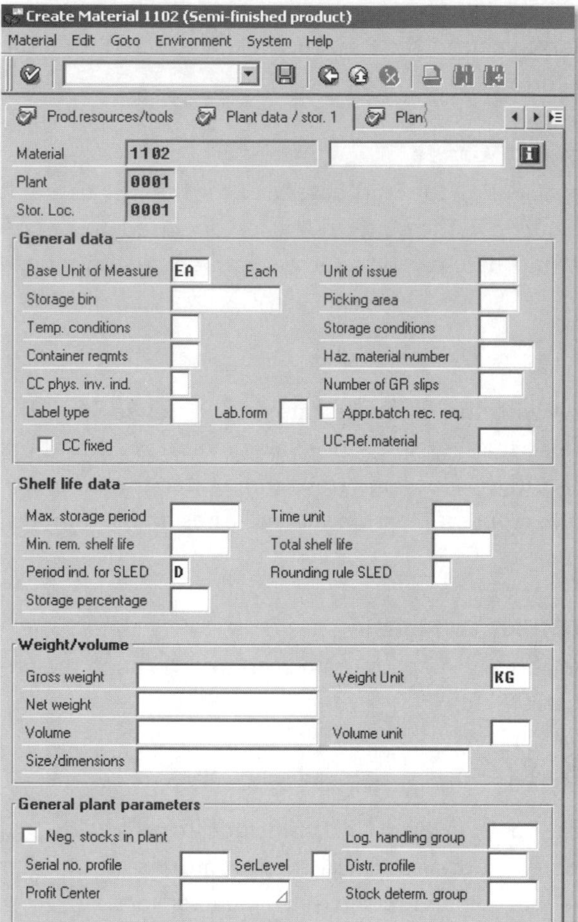

Figure 4.19 General Plant Data Screen.

Picking Area

The picking area is a field that is used in lean WM. It is a group of warehouse management storage bins that are used for picking. The picking area is similar to the definition of storage section. The picking area can be configured using the navigation path **IMG • Logistics Execution • Shipping • Picking • Lean WM • Define Picking Areas**.

Temperature Conditions

This is simply the temperature at which the material should be stored. Certain chemicals and metals need to be stored in low temperatures to avoid chemical reactions. The temperature conditions field is stored at the client level, so is valid for all plants. The temperature conditions field can be configured using the navigation path **IMG • Logistics—General • Material Master • Settings for Key Fields • Define Temperature Conditions**.

Storage Conditions

The storage conditions field is similar to the temperature conditions field in that it is a client-wide field and is valid for all plants. The storage conditions can be defined by the company to be relevant for their requirements. Examples of a storage condition may be refrigeration, outside only, or hotbox. The storage conditions field can be configured using the navigation path **IMG • Logistics—General • Material Master • Settings for Key Fields • Define Storage Conditions**.

Container Requirements

Container requirements is another field that works at the client level and is the same for all plants. It is a field that defines what container a material should be stored and shipped in. The container requirements field can be configured using the navigation path **IMG • Logistics—General • Material Master • Settings for Key Fields • Define Container Requirements**.

Hazardous Material Number

A hazardous material number can be assigned to the material at the client level. This links the material number with the hazardous material information that is defined for that hazardous material number, such as water pollutant, hazardous storage class, or warnings. The hazardous material is not defined in configuration, but in the Logistics Execution functionality. A hazardous material can be created using transaction VM01 or via the navigation path **SAP Menu • Logistics • Logistics Execution • Master Data • Material • Hazardous Material • Create**.

Cycle Counting Physical Inventory Indicator

This indicator is set if the material is to be cycle counted. The indicator can also determine how the count is taken and how often. The cycle count indicator usually is an **A**, **B**, **C** or **D** to coincide with the **ABC** indicators. The cycle counting indicator is defined by four characteristics, which are seen below:

- Number of physical inventories per fiscal year are to be performed
- Maximum interval of days between counts
- Float time allowed for the planned count date after the required date
- The percentage of consumption allocated to each of the indicators (**A**, **B**, **C**, etc.)

The cycle counting indicator can be configured using transaction code OMCO or the navigation path **IMG • Materials Management • Inventory Management and Physical Inventory • Physical Inventory • Cycle Counting**.

Cycle Counting Indicator is Fixed

If this indicator is set then the cycle counting physical inventory indicator, defined above, cannot be changed by the ABC functionality that can be run periodically. If the indicator is not set, the cycle counting physical inventory indicator will be changed if the ABC functionality determines that the material has changed status. If the indicator is set and no changes can be made via the ABC functionality, then the cycle counting physical inventory indicator can still be set by changing it in the Material Master.

Number of Goods Receipt Slips

The field allows the receiving department to enter a figure that determines the number of goods receipt documents that will be printed. If the field is blank, the system assumes that one material document will be printed.

Label Type

Some materials require labels to be printed and affixed to the product or packaging. The label type field defines which labels are printed for which goods movement, how many labels are printed, and which printer they are printed on. The label type can be configured in transaction OMCF or via the navigation path **IMG • Materials Management • Inventory Management and Physical Inventory • Print Control • Set Label Printout • Label Type**.

Label Form

The label form can be used when the label type has been entered for a material. The label form defines the dimensions and characteristics of the label. The label form can be defined in transaction OMCF, as the label type, or via the navigation path **IMG • Materials Management • Inventory Management and Physical Inventory • Print Control • Set Label Printout • Label Form**.

4.11.2 Shelf-Life Data

Maximum Storage Period

This field is for information only and does not have any functionality. The users can define the maximum storage period for a material before it expires. This field can be used for reporting.

Time Unit

This is the unit of measure of the maximum storage period; i.e., days, months, and years.

Minimum Remaining Shelf Life

The minimum remaining shelf-life field determines whether a material can be received via goods receipt based on the remaining shelf life of the material to be receipted. If this field has the value 100 days, and the material to be goods receipted has only 80 days of shelf life left, then the goods receipt will not be accepted. The minimum remaining shelf-life field works at the client level and is the same for the material across all plants.

Total Shelf Life

The total shelf life figure is at the client level and does not vary by plant. The total shelf life is the time for which the materials will be kept, from the production date to the shelf life expiration date. The shelf life is only checked if the expiration date check has been activated. The activation is configured at plant level or movement type level in transaction OMJ5 or via the navigation path **IMG • Logistics—General • Batch Management • Shelf Life Expiration Date (SLED) • Set Expiration Date Check**.

Period Indicator for Shelf-Life Expiration Date

This period field is defined for the shelf life expiration date (SLED) fields used in this Material Master screen. The period can be defined as months, days, etc. The period indicator can be configured in transaction O02K or through the navigation path **IMG • Logistics—General • Batch Management • Shelf Life Expiration Date (SLED) • Maintain Period Indicator**.

Rounding Rule SLED

The rounding rule allows the SLED dates to be rounded up to the nearest unit of the time defined in the period indicator. For example, if the period indicator were months, then the rounding rule either would be the first day of the month, or the last day of the month, or no change if there were no rounding rule. The rounding rule is for calculated dates rather than dates entered into the record.

4.12 Warehouse Management Data

The warehouse management screen of the Material Master allows the user to enter information at the warehouse/storage type level, as shown in Figure 4.20.

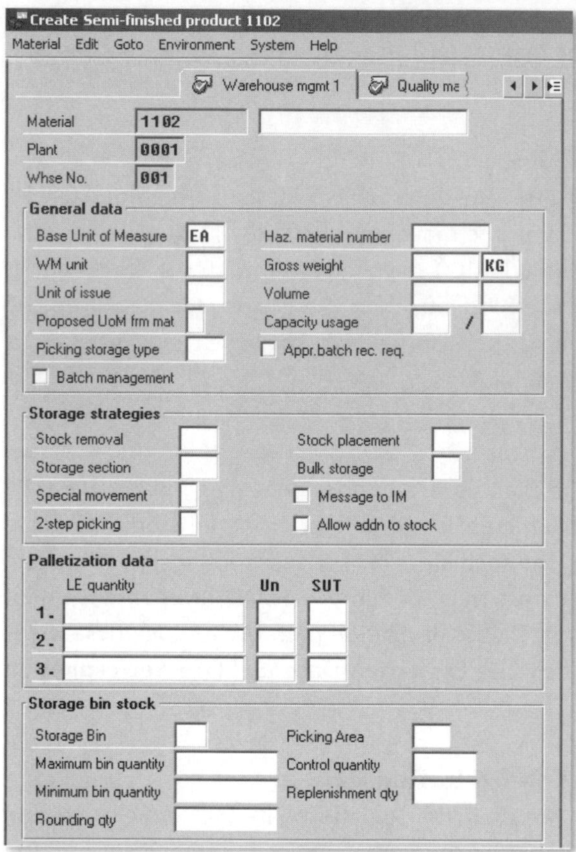

Figure 4.20 Fields of Warehouse Management in Material Master

4.12.1 General Data

Warehouse Management Unit of Measure

Like the other units of measure, this WM unit is the unit of measure defined for the material as it is relates to its movements through the warehouse.

Unit of Measure

This unit of measure field allows the warehouse department to define a different unit of measure for items issued from the warehouse, as an alternative to the base unit of measure.

Picking Storage Type

This storage type is used by planning as the storage type that will contain material that can be used in rough-cut planning.

4.12.2 Palletization Data

Palletization is used in storage unit handling within the WM module. The process uses pallets to store and move material in the warehouse. The palletization data determines how the material should be entered into stock. The material may be able to be placed into storage in different ways depending on what storage unit type is being used.

Loading Equipment Quantity/Unit of Measure

The quantity entered here is the amount of material to be placed on to the storage unit type.

Storage Unit Type

The storage unit type is a description of how the material is stored in the storage bin. For instance, some bins may not be able to allow a full pallet due to height restrictions, but a half-pallet may fit. Therefore, the warehouse can define a storage unit type that defines a half-pallet and the quantity of the material that can fit on that half-pallet.

As an example of this, suppose that for material XYZ, 30 boxes are equivalent to one half-pallet. The storage unit type is configured in the IMG and has to be activated in each warehouse before it can be used. There is a definition of the storage unit type for each plant. The configuration can be made using the navigation path **IMG • Logistics Execution • Warehouse Management • Master Data • Material • Define Storage Unit Types**.

4.12.3 Storage Strategies

Stock Removal

This field allows the warehouse staff to enter the storage type indicator that defines the sequence in which storage types are searched for the material to be picked in the warehouse. The storage type indicator can be defined in transaction OMLY. The navigation path is **IMG • Logistics Execution • Warehouse Management • Strategies • Activate Storage Type Search**.

Stock Placement

The stock placement field acts in a similar manner to the stock removal field, except that the strategy defined in the storage type search is for a placement strategy rather than a removal strategy.

Storage Section

The storage section search is a more specific strategy for stock placement, as it defines one level below the storage type search for stock placement. The storage section indicator must be defined for each warehouse and storage type. The strategy allows up to 10 storage sections to be defined in sequence for the placement strategy. The configuration can be found in transaction OMLZ or via the navigation path **IMG • Logistics Execution • Warehouse Management • Strategies • Activate Storage Section Search**.

Bulk Storage

Within the placement strategies, you can define how bulk materials should be placed in stock. The bulk storage indicator can be used if the bulk storage placement strategy has been activated in WM . The bulk storage indicator can indicate height or width of a particular storage type. The configuration can be found in transaction OMM4 or the path **IMG • Logistics Execution • Warehouse Management • Strategies • Putaway Strategies • Define Strategy for Bulk Storage**.

Special Movement

The special movement indicator allows the material to be identified as requiring a special goods movement. The special movement indicator is configured in warehouse management to allow special processing for a group of materials. The configuration is found using **IMG • Logistics Execution • Warehouse Management • Master Data • Material • Define Special Movement Indicators**.

Once the special movement indicator has been defined, it can be used in the LE-WM interface to inventory management, where the configuration determines the warehouse management movement type. The special movement indicator can allow certain materials assigned with that indicator to behave differently during goods movements. The configuration for the warehouse goods movements can be found using the navigation path **IMG • Logistics Execution • Warehouse Management • Interfaces • Inventory Management • Define Movement Types**.

Message to IM

This field is used if the warehouse management system is decentralized. If the indicator is set, it allows the warehouse management information for this material to be sent to inventory management immediately.

Two-Step Picking

In WM, you can choose between one-step and two-step picking for materials. If the material is large and bulky, then a one-step removal would be optimal. However, if the materials to be picked are small and numerous, then one-step picking may not be an efficient use of warehouse resources. Therefore, two-step picking is used to minimize workload. The two-step process defines an interim storage type (normally 200) where items are picked and transferred to the interim storage type; from there, the final pick takes place. The configuration for two-step picking is found using the navigation path **IMG • Logistics Execution • Warehouse Management • Interfaces • Shipping • Define 2-Step Picking**.

Allow Addition to Existing Stock Indicator

Setting this indicator allows material to be added to the existing stock of the same material in the same storage bin. This is only true if the characteristics of the two quantities of material are the same. If the storage-type table does not allow additions to existing stock for this storage type, the indicator is redundant.

4.12.4 Storage Bin Stock

Storage Bin

The storage bin is the lowest level of storage defined in the warehouse. This field allows the warehouse user to enter a storage bin that this material will be added to for the plant/storage type combination. By selecting F4 the options will show the empty storage bins.

Maximum Bin Quantity

This value can be entered to define the maximum quantity of this material that can be entered into any storage bin defined in the storage type. The quantity is defined in the base unit of measure, not the WM unit of measure.

Control Quantity

The control quantity can be entered to define for this storage type the amount of material that reaches the level where stock removal can take place. Similar to the maximum bin quantity, this control quantity is in the material base unit of measure.

Minimum Bin Quantity

This field allows the warehouse users to define a minimum quantity, which can be stored in the bin locations for this storage type. This makes efficient use of storage bins. So if the material is small, the maximum bin quantity is high, and no minimum quantity is set, then there could be many bins containing small amounts of stock. Entering a minimum bin quantity allows the bin to be used efficiently and minimizes picking. Like the other quantities, the minimum bin quantity is recorded in the base quantity unit.

Replenishment Quantity

The replenishment quantity is defined in order to suggest the quantity that should be placed in the storage bin. Like the other quantities, the replenishment quantity is recorded in the base quantity unit.

Rounding Quantity

This quantity is used if the material is subject to the quantity-dependent picking strategy. The rounding quantity is the figure that the picking quantities are rounded down to for this material/storage type combination. This quantity is also defined in the base unit of measure.

4.13 Quality Management Data

The quality management data screen allows the quality department to define the basic quality requirements for the material at each plant level. Figure 4.21 shows the fields of the Quality Management screen for the Material Master.

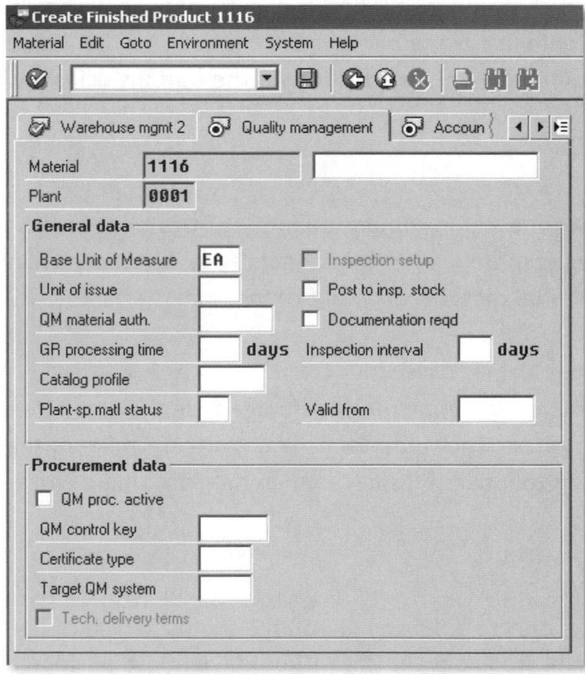

Figure 4.21 Quality Management Screen for Material Master

4.13.1 General Data

Inspection Setup

This indicator is set if a quality management inspection setup already exists for this material/plant combination. If the quality inspection user wants to enter the inspection setup information for this material at this plant, there is a button to the right of the indicator that will bring up the inspection entry screen. The screen will allow a number of inspection types to be entered, such as Goods Receipt Inspection, and Stock Transfer Inspection.

Post to Inspection Indicator

This indicator can be set so as to force material to be posted to inspection stock. This indicator is copied into the purchase order. However, this indicator is ignored if an inspection type that is stock-relevant—in other words, an inspection due to stock movement—has been entered in the inspection setup.

Material Authorization Group for Activities in QM

This field allows the quality department to add a layer of security to the quality information of each material. The authorization group that can be entered in the field will check to see if a quality inspection user has the correct authorization to view the information. The authorization group is defined in configuration via the navigation path **IMG • Quality Management • Environment • Central functions • Authorization Management • Define Authorization Group and Digital Signature**.

Document Required Indicator

Once the indicator is set, it causes the system to record any changes to inspection lots or usage decisions. These status changes are recorded in change documents and can be viewed in the status history for the material. The status can be viewed by using the keys SHIFT + F4.

Inspection Interval

This field allows the quality department to enter the number of days required between inspections of the material at this plant. This figure is copied to the batch record, when a batch is created.

Catalog Profile

This field is a value that is relevant in quality notifications. The catalog profile is defined in configuration. This can be found using the navigation path **IMG • Quality Management • Quality Notifications • Notification Creation • Notification Content • Define Catalog Profile**.

4.13.2 Procurement Data

QM in Procurement Indicator

This indicator switches on the quality-management aspect of procurement. This can be activated at a plant level or a client level. If activated at a client level, then the QM control key should be defined also.

QM Control Key

The control key can be defined during configuration and determines how a material is affected by quality during the procurement cycle. The control key can determine the following:

- If technical delivery terms must exist as a document
- If a quality assurance document must exist between the company and the vendor
- If a valid purchasing information record must exist
- If a quality certificate is required from vendor on each shipment
- If a block can be put in place against the invoice

Certificate Type

The quality certificate can be required by the quality department for each goods receipt item or purchase order item concerning certain materials from the vendor. There can be many different certificate types defined in configuration. The navigation path is **IMG • Quality Management • QM in Logistics • QM in Procurement • Define Keys for Certificate Processing • Define Certificate Types**.

Target QM System

The target QM system field allows the quality department to define the type of QM system they require from their vendors. For instance, the quality department may require that the vendors for the material have a ISO 9001 certification for their sites. The configuration in QM can define the requirements and, in addition, determine what rating vendors can achieve through the quality department's evaluation.

The configuration for the target QM system can be found in transaction OQB7 or via the path **IMG • Quality Management • QM in Logistics • QM in Procurement • Define QM Systems**.

4.14 Material Requirements Planning Data

The MRP data is divided over a number of screens in the Material Master. Figure 4.22 shows the first of these screens. The number of screens may depend on the version of SAP you are working in. This information is important in how material is made, planned, and produced within the plant. Some of the fields from the screens have been discussed in previous sections.

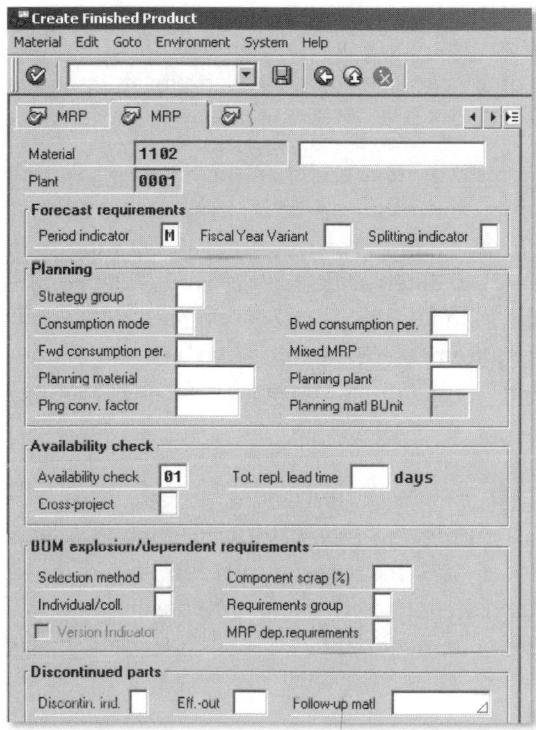

Figure 4.22 First MRP Data entry Screen

4.14.1 Forecast Requirements

Splitting Indicator

The splitting indicator is an important function within forecast based planning. The forecast for a material may determine that production needs to manufacture 1,000 units per month for the next six months. However, the planning function needs to split this into smaller time intervals. It may require the planning run to determine the number of units required to be produced each day for the first month, then weekly for the second month, and then monthly after that. To do this, a splitting indicator can be defined in configuration that determines the number of days, the number of weeks, and the number of forecast periods required.

This configuration can be found using the navigation path **IMG · Production · Basic Data · Material Requirements Planning · Forecast · Define Splitting of Forecast Requirements for MRP**.

4.14.2 Planning

Strategy Group

The strategy group is a field that groups planning strategies. The strategies used in planning are usually predefined in SAP. Examples of strategies include 20—Make to Order Production, 30—Production by Lot Size, and 70—Planning at Assembly Level.

The strategy group is defined with a main strategy and then can have up to seven other strategies as part of that group. For instance, the strategy group 33 may have its main planning strategy defined as 30—Production by Lot Size and then have 40—Planning with Final Assembly defined as part of the group. The configuration for the strategy group can be found using the navigation path **IMG · Production · Basic Data · Material Requirements Planning · Master Data · Independent Requirements Parameters · Planning Strategy · Define Strategy Group**.

Consumption Mode

The consumption mode is simply the direction in which the system consumes requirements. In backwards consumption the consumption of the planned requirements occurs before the requirement date. In a forward-consumption system, consumption occurs after the requirement date.

Backward Consumption Period

This field is a figure that relates to consumption mode. If the consumption mode is defined as backwards consumption, then this field can be defined to the number of workdays that consumption should be carried out. The backward consumption period can last up to 999 workdays from the current date.

Forward Consumption Period

This field also relates to consumption mode. If the consumption mode is defined as forward consumption, then this field can be defined to the number of workdays that consumption should be carried out. The forward consumption period can last up to 999 workdays from the current date.

Mixed MRP

The mixed MRP field can identify the material as being available to one of three options: sub-assembly planning with final assembly, gross requirements planning, or sub-assembly planning without final assembly.

Planning Material

The planning material can be used when the material has a bill of materials that contains variant and non-variant parts. Using another material (the planning material), the planning department can plan the non-variant parts. When planning runs, the planning material is not produced but is only used to plan the non-variant parts. This planning strategy is called planning with a planning material.

Planning Plant

The planning plant is the plant associated with the planning material.

Conversion Factor for Planning Material

If the regular material and the planning material do not have the same unit of measure, a conversion would be needed. The field is a 10-character string and can be defined as appropriate. If the field is blank, the system assumes that the conversation factor is one.

4.14.3 Availability Check

Total Replenishment Lead Time

The total replenishment lead time is the time, in workdays, that it will take before the material is available to be used or sold. This field is not a system calculation but should be the sum of the total in-house production times and the planned delivery times. This field should be entered if the planning department wishes it to be part of the availability check.

Cross-Project Material Indicator

This is used for project stock. This indicator allows the user to take into account all project stock or just the one project segment.

4.14.4 Bill of Materials Explosion

Selection Method

The selection method determines the way in which alternate bill of materials (BOMs) are selected during MRP. There are four selection methods to choose from:

- Selection by Order Quantity—alternative BOM is chosen by lot size
- Selection by Explosion Date—alternative BOM is chosen by date
- Selection by Production Version—alternative BOM is defined in production version
- Selection by Only Production Version—if no production version exists, then no production orders are created

Component Scrap

The component scrap figure is a percentage needed to calculate the correct figure for component stock in MRP. This field is needed if the material is a component in a BOM. If a BOM for a finished material needs 400 units of material X, and material X had a component scrap figure of 10%, then the actual figure needed would be 110%, that is,. 440 units of material X. This figure is not used if it is defined in the BOM.

Individual or Collective Requirements

This indicator allows the planning department to determine whether this material is relevant for individual or collective requirements, or for both. Individual requirements are the quantities of the material that are shown separately. The collective requirements are quantities of the material that are grouped together.

Requirements Group

The requirements group field can be set to allow the system to group together the material requirements for the material, on a daily basis.

MRP Dependent Requirements

This indicator is used for make to stock materials and assemblies. The indicator can be set to indicate that the materials-dependent requirements are relevant for MRP.

4.14.5 Discontinued Parts

Discontinuation Indicator

This indicator is used when a material is being discontinued. For MRP purposes, the system needs to know whether this material has dependent requirements. This indicator can be set to **1** for a single level material and to **3** for dependent requirements.

Effective-out Date

This is the date by which the inventory of the discontinued material will be at zero. At this time, the follow-up material will be used in its place.

Follow-up Material

This is the material number of the material that will take the place of the discontinued material on the effective-out date.

4.14.6 Repetitive Manufacturing/Assembly

Repetitive Manufacturing Indicator

This indicator allows the material to be considered in repetitive manufacturing. If this indicator is set, a repetitive-manufacturing profile also must be entered for the material.

Repetitive Manufacturing Profile

The repetitive manufacturing profile is configured but allows the production user to determine some of these issues:

- Error correction for during backflushing
- Goods issue backflushing at goods receipt
- Planned order reduction
- Which movement types are used

The repetitive manufacturing profile can be configured using the navigation path **IMG · Production · Repetitive Manufacturing · Control Data · Define Repetitive Manufacturing Profiles**.

Action Control

The action control field defines what actions occur and in what sequence they will occur for a planned order. The planning department can define this field in configuration to create actions that can occur during the planned order.

The action keys combined to make up the action control are defined in configuration using the navigation path **IMG · Production · Material Requirements Planning · Procurement Proposals · Planned Orders · Action for Planned Order · Define Action Keys**.

Table 4.6 shows the keys and actions pre-defined in SAP.

Key	Action
BOME	Explode BOM
BEMA	Explode BOM, Check Material Availability
NEMA	Check Material Avail. no BOM explosion
MAAV	Check Material Avail. BOM explosion if nec.
RSMA	Reset Availability Check
SCHE	Schedule Planned Order
CPOD	Change Planned Order
PRNT	Print Component List
ZZxx	User Defined Action

Table 4.6 Action Keys Pre-Defined in SAP

The action control can be defined by selecting these action keys. The configuration can be found using the navigation path **IMG • Production • Material Requirements Planning • Procurement Proposals • Planned Orders • Action for Planned Order • Define Action Control**.

Figure 4.23 shows the second of the MRP data entry screens.

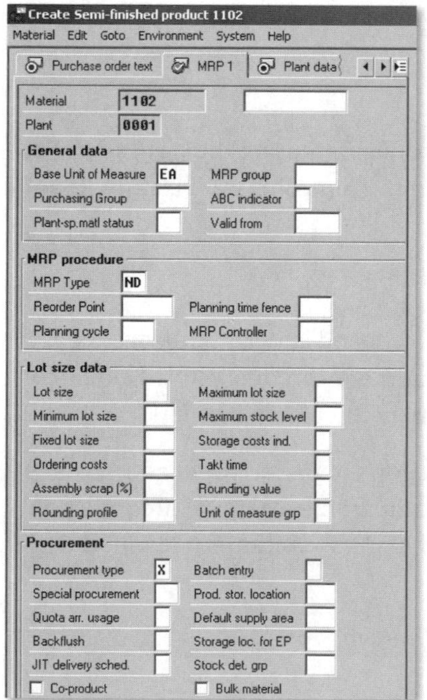

Figure 4.23 Second MRP Data entry Screen

4.14.7 General Data

MRP Group

The MRP group is a combination of special control parameters specific to the total planning run. The MRP group is created at plant level and assigned to materials with similar needs for these parameters.

The MRP group is created in transaction OPPR or via the navigation path **IMG • Production • Material Requirements Planning • MRP Groups • Carry Out Overall Maintenance of Material Groups**.

Figure 4.24 shows the fields available for modification for the MRP group.

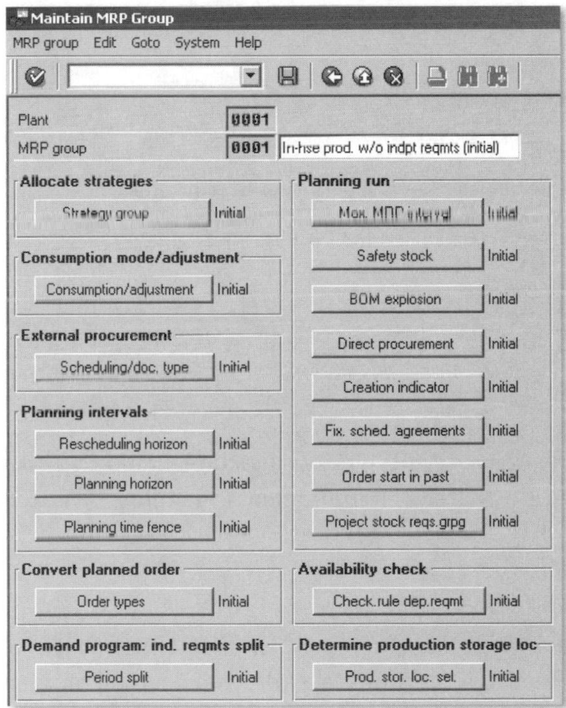

Figure 4.24 MRP Group Parameters

ABC Indicator

The ABC indicator allows a determination to be made based on consumption criteria. The higher the consumption, the more important the material, and the earlier in the alphabet its indicator. The SAP system pre-defines the indicators **A**, **B**, and **C**, but it is possible to define other indicators.

The **ABC** indicator can be configured using the navigation path **IMG • Logistics—General • Material Master • Settings for Key Fields • Define ABC Indicator**.

4.14.8 MRP Procedure

MRP Type

The MRP type is a key to a procedure that is used to plan a material and to control which MRP parameters can be maintained for the material. SAP pre-defines a number of MRP types, but it is possible to create new MRP types in configuration. Table 4.7 shows these standard MRP types and their descriptions.

MRP Type	Description
PD	standard MRP
VB	manual reorder point planning
VM	automatic reorder point planning
V1	automatic reorder point planning (including external requirements)
V2	automatic reorder point planning (without external requirements)
VV	forecast-based planning
ND	no planning

Table 4.7 SAP Standard MRP Types

The planning department can create new MRP types using configuration via the navigation path **IMG • Production • Material Requirements Planning • Master Data • Check MRP Types**.

Reorder Point

This field is used only for reorder point planning. The planning department can enter a reorder quantity for a material. If the stock level drops below the reorder point, then a requirement is created.

Planning Time Fence

The planning department, to create a period of time when there are no automatic changes to the master plan, enters a value for the planning time fence.

Planning Cycle

The planning cycle is a planning calendar that determines when material is ordered and planned. In order for this data to be relevant, the material must be assigned an MRP type that allows time-phased planning. The planning cycle can be configured for the specific planning department. To configure the planning calendar use the navigation path **IMG • Production • Material Requirements Planning • Master Data • Maintain Planning Calendar**.

MRP Controller

The MRP controller is defined as a person or persons who are responsible for the planning of the material. The MRP controller can be configured via the navigation path **IMG • Production • Material Requirements Planning • Master Data • Define MRP Controllers**.

4.14.9 Lot Size Data

Lot Size

The lot-size key field defines the lot-sizing procedure. The procedure calculates the reorder quantity in the planning run. The lot size can be defined for short-term and long-term periods. The production department will determine what lot-size calculation is required for the material. The lot size calculation can be configured in transaction OMI4 or via the navigation path **IMG • Production • Material Requirements Planning • Planning • Lot-Size Calculation • Check Lot-Sizing Procedure**.

Minimum Lot Size

The planning department can enter this field to determine this material's minimum lot size for procurement.

Maximum Lot Size

This is the material's maximum lot size for procurement. This value is used in the lot-size calculation for production orders

Fixed Lot Size

The fixed lot size is the amount of the material that is ordered if there is a shortage of the material. If the fixed-lot size is less than the shortage, then multiples of the fixed lot size will be ordered to cover the shortage.

Maximum Stock Level

This field is only used if the lot-size key "replenish to maximum (HB)" has been entered for this material. This field determines the maximum level of stock for this material at the plant.

Ordering Costs

These costs are only used with the optimum lot-sizing procedure and represent the cost of producing or purchasing the material above the normal purchasing costs. The system assumes the currency is the same as the currency used for the plant.

Storage Costs Indicator

This field is used only with the optimum lot-sizing procedure. It is defined as the cost of storing material based on the quantity and the unit price.

Assembly Scrap

Similar to the component scrap field, this field allows the user to enter the amount of scrap that normally occurs during the assembly of a material. The percentage scrap will allow the lot-size calculation to increase to allow for the scrap. A value should only be entered if this material is an assembly.

Takt Time

»Takt« is the German word for beat or cycle. Production uses takt time as the rate that a material is completed. If the takt time is defined as four hours, that means every four hours a complete material is produced.

4.14.10 Procurement

Procurement Type

The procurement type describes how a material is procured. The material either can be purchased externally from a vendor, produced in-house via a production order, or it can be both produced and purchased.

Batch Entry

The batch entry key is used to identify where the batches have to be entered in the production process. Three options are available for the batch entry field. These are:

- Manual Batch Determination at release of order
- Batch Not Required in Order; confirmation required
- Automatic Batch Determination upon release of order

Special Procurement

The special-procurement key is configured to describe a procurement scenario. The key can determine the procurement type, procurement from another plant and BOM characteristics. The configuration of the special procurement key can be found via the navigation path **IMG • Production • Material Requirements Planning • Master Data • Define Special Procurement Type**.

Production Storage Location

If the material is produced in-house, the storage location entered in this field is used in the planned or production order. It also is used for backflushing purposes.

Default Supply Area

The default supply area is a field used for KANBAN operations. The default supply area is a defined interim storage area, which supplies material to the production operation. The supply area is not part of configuration and can be defined in transaction PK05, or via the navigation path **SAP Menu • Logistics • Production • KANBAN • Supply Area • Maintain**.

Storage Location for External Procurement

This storage location is defined in this field and is used as the storage location defaulted into the planned order for material procured externally.

JIT Delivery Schedule

This indicator can be set to allow a JIT delivery schedule to be generated as well as the forecast schedules for this material.

Co-Product Indicator

A co-product is a material generated by the production process that has the composition or characteristics of a manufactured product or raw material. This field indicates whether this material can be used as co-product.

Bulk Material Indicator

This indicator, if set, defines the material as a bulk material for BOM purposes.

4.14.11 Net Requirements Calculations

Safety Stock

The purpose of safety stock is to ensure that there is no material shortage for production. The safety stock level is designed to offset any unexpected increase in demand.

Service Level

This percentage field is used in the calculation of safety stock. A low service- level percentage will reflect in a low safety-stock level.

Minimum Safety Stock

The minimum safety-stock level is the lower limit of the safety stock range. This should only be used if the planning department in forecasting and calculation of safety stock.

Coverage Profile

The coverage profile defines parameters used in the calculation of dynamic safety stock. The dynamic safety stock is calculated using daily average requirements and the range of coverage. The coverage profile can be found in table T438R. The coverage profile can be configured via the navigation path **IMG • Materials Management • Consumption-Based Planning • Planning • MRP Calculation • Define Range of Coverage Profile**

Safety Time Indicator

The safety time indicator allows the user to define the mechanism for safety time. Two indicators can be used. The first allows the safety time to be active for all requirements; the second is just for independent requirements. The safety time is the time by which the MRP requirements can be brought forward. This inserts a time buffer to allow more time for the delivery of materials, among other things.

Safety Time

This is the actual time that the MRP requirements are brought forward. The figure is the number of actual workdays.

Period Profile for Safety Time

In defining safety time, it can be useful to employ a period profile, given that requirements fluctuate at different times of the year. In configuration it is possible to create a safety time based on the dates the user wishes to enter for each period. It is possible to create a number of safety time-period profiles.

The configuration can be completed in transaction OMOD or via the navigation path **IMG • Materials Management • Consumption-Based Planning • Planning • MRP Calculation • Define Period Profile for Safety Time**.

4.14.12 Deployment Strategy

Fair Share Rules

This field is maintained if the company has, or will, implement distribution requirements planning (DRP). This field allows the planners to determine a rule for materials deployment when demand exceeds supply.

Push Indicator

This field is maintained for DRP. If the material is in surplus, the planners can define whether the material is to be subject to push or pull distribution.

4.15 Accounting Data

The accounting data entry screen in the Material Master (shown in Figure 4.25) allows the accounting department to enter the valuation and price data needed to for inventory transactions.

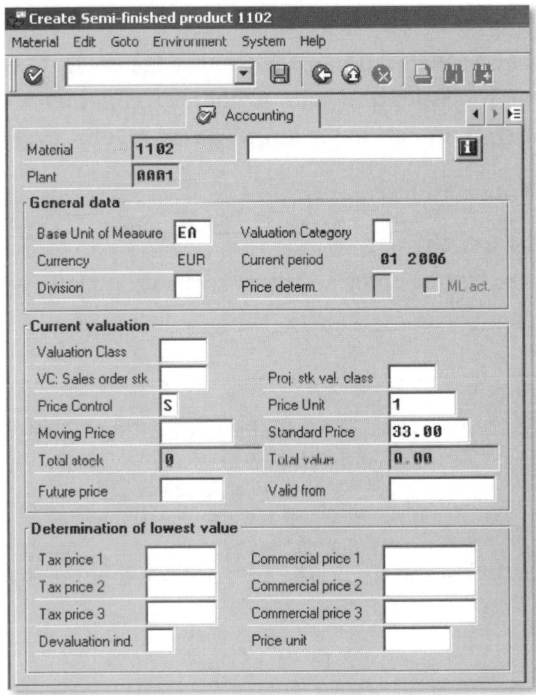

Figure 4.25 Accounting Data Screen in Material Master

4.15.1 General Data

Valuation Category

This field concerns whether the material is subject to split valuation. This means that the material can be valuated in different ways. An example of split valuation is valuation of batches separately. An example of where batches may be valuated differently is in the chemical industry where batches of the same material may have different numbers of days left before the batches expire. A batch with only 10 days before expiry may be valuated differently from a batch that has 100 days left before expiry.

ML Active

This indicator shows if the material ledger has been activated for this material.

4.15.2 Current Valuation

Valuation Class

The valuation class is a mechanism to assign a material to general ledger (G/L) accounts. These G/L accounts are updated when material movements occur that are relevant to accounting. The valuation class is assigned to a material type, via configuration.

The valuation class can be configured in transaction OMSK or via the navigation path **IMG • Materials Management • Valuation and Account Assignment • Account Determination • Account Determination without Wizard • Define Valuation Class**.

Valuation Class for Sales-Order Stock

If the accounting department wishes, it can enter a different valuation class for sales-order stock.

Valuation Class for Project Stock

As with the valuation class for sales-order stock, above, the accounting department can enter a different valuation class for project stock.

Price Control

The price control is used in the valuation of the stock. The two options are moving price (V) and standard price (S).

Price Unit

The figure entered here is the number of units that the moving price or standard price relates to. Therefore, if the standard price for material XYZ is USD 3.24, and the price unit is 1000, then the actual cost per unit is USD 0.00324. The price unit is important when entering materials with very small prices, as it can prevent rounding errors if the number of decimal places in a report are not sufficient.

Moving Price

The moving average price is calculated by dividing the material value by the total stock. This price changes with each goods movement that is relevant for valuation. The accounting department can make an initial price entry if the price control indicator is set to **V** for moving price.

Standard Price

The standard price is a constant that once entered does not fluctuate. It does not take into account invoice prices or any other price-altering movements. The standard price can be entered when the price control indicator is set to S for standard price.

Future Price

The standard price can be changed through an entry in the future price field. The future price is entered in the field and will become valid from the date that is entered in the **valid from** field.

4.15.3 Determination of Lowest Price

Tax Price

This field is not used in the U.S. but is used in some countries. Ask your accounting department if this field is used in your country. This field is available for entering the price of the material for tax purposes.

Commercial Price

This field, also, is not used in the U.S. but is used in some countries. Ask your accounting department if this field is used in your country. This field is available for entering the price of the material for commercial valuation purposes.

Devaluation Indicator

The devaluation indicator can be entered into a Material Master if the company feels that the material is a slow or non-moving item. The accounting department can configure a number of indicators for each material type per company code that has a devaluation percentage attached. The indicator can be changed to increase or decrease the devaluation percentage depending on the movement of the material stock. The indicators can be configured through transaction code OMW6 or via the navigation path **IMG · Materials Management · Valuation and Account Assignment · Balance Sheet Valuation Procedures · Configure Lowest-Value Method · Price Deductions Based on Non-Movement · Maintain Devaluation by Slow/Non-Movement by Company Code**.

4.15.4 LIFO Data

LIFO/FIFO-Relevant

If this indicator is set, it means that the material is subject to LIFO and FIFO valuation.

LIFO (last in, first out) valuation for stock implies that as new stock comes in and then moves out first, the old stock does not change in value and there is no overvaluation of the older stock.

FIFO (first in, first out) valuation calculates the valuation of the stock based on the price of the last receipt. Although this is the most realistic valuation, it can overvaluate older stock.

LIFO Pool

The LIFO pool is ignored if the material is not LIFO relevant. The LIFO pool can be configured to define a group of materials that can be valued together. The LIFO pools can be configured in transaction OMW2 or via the navigation path **IMG • Materials Management • Valuation and Account Assignment • Balance Sheet Valuation Procedures • Configure LIFO/FIFO Methods • LIFO • Configure LIFO Pools**.

4.16 Costing Data

The costing data screen of the Material Master, shown in Figure 4.26, allows the costing department to enter costing information for the material. Some of the fields on this screen have been discussed in previous sections.

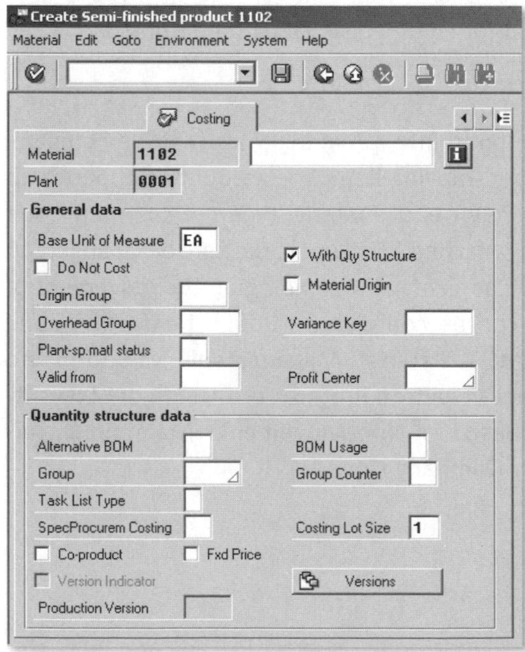

Figure 4.26 Costing Data Entry Screen for Material Master

4.16.1 General Data

Origin Data

The origin group is used to subdivide overhead and material costs. The material can be assigned to an origin group, and overhead costs are assigned to different origin groups at different percentage rates or at a flat cost.

Costing Overhead Group

The costing overhead group applies overhead costs from the costing sheet of a production order to materials in that group.

4.16.2 Quantity Structure Data

Task List Group

A task list group can combine production processes that are similar and are for similar materials. It can be used to group task lists for varying lot sizes.

Group Counter

Combined with the task group list, this identifies a unique task list for the material.

Task-List Type

This field identifies the task list type. The task list type can be maintained using transaction OP8B or via the navigation path **IMG • Production • Basic Data • Routing • Control Data • Maintain Task List Types**.

Costing Lot Size

This field allows the product costing department to enter a lot size for the material that would be used in the product cost estimate.

This chapter discussed the elements that make up the material master file. When you first encounter the SAP material master file, it might seem daunting. Other inventory or integrated systems have item master files that are a fraction of the size of the material master. This is important when bringing on legacy systems. When converting item master files into the SAP material master, it is usual for the legacy master files to only hold few of the necessary fields for the material master. Most companies spend a great deal of time constructing data for the material master. Therefore, if you intend to be involved in the material master and assist in this type of project it is prudent to learn about the material master structure and the implications of entering or not entering information into material master fields.

5 Vendor Master Data

The Vendor Master is as important to accounting staff as it to those in purchasing. The vendor's relationship with any company is twofold; negotiating price and supplying material through purchasing, while invoicing and receiving payment through accounts payable.

The Vendor Master is a collection of data that fully describes the vendor's relationship with the company. The vendor normally will have an initial relationship with the purchasing department. Purchasing may have selected the vendor through its response to a request for quotation or because it is the sole vendor for a required material. However, before a vendor is authorized, the accounting department will ensure that the information it requires is available and satisfactory.

Just as a Material Master record is not complete until all relevant departments have entered their data, the Vendor Master is not complete until both the accounting and purchasing departments have entered their information.

The Vendor Master can be created using three transactions, each of them giving different views of the data to be entered for the vendor. The three transactions are:

- XK01—Create Vendor Centrally
- FK01—Create Vendor via Accounting
- MK01—Create Vendor via Purchasing.

5.1 General Data

The transaction XK01 enables accounting users to enter the account code for the vendor and either the company code or purchasing organization, or both (See Figure 5.1). The vendor number may need to be entered if the account group is defined as allowing only external number assignment.

The Vendor Master can be created by referencing an existing vendor. To do this, use the reference field below the **Account group** field. This can be an efficient method of creating vendors that may have the same or similar data.

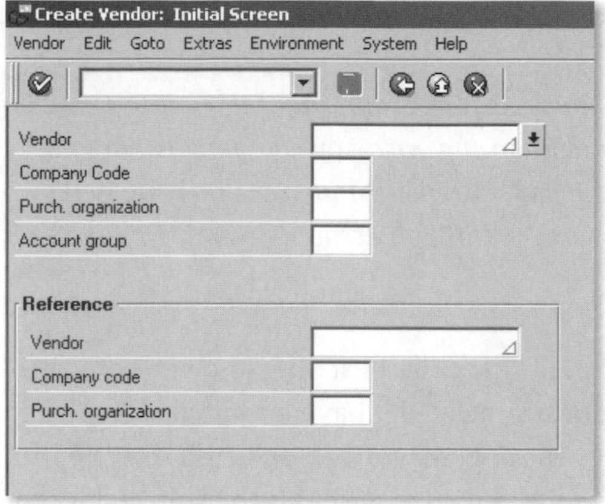

Figure 5.1 Entry Screen for Transaction XK01

5.1.1 Address Screen

The initial screen of the Vendor Master is the address screen is seen in Figure 5.2. The information to be entered relates to address and communication.

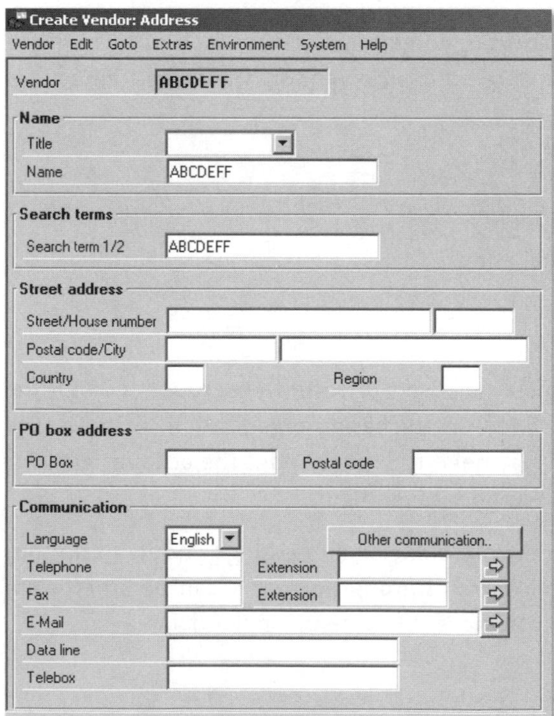

Figure 5.2 Create Address Screen for Vendor Master

Title

This is the title for the vendor. If it is a company, then select the company option; otherwise, select the appropriate salutation. The titles for the business address forms can be configured in the IMG (R/3 Enterprise) via the navigation path **IMG • Flexible Real Estate Management • Address Management • Maintain Texts for Form of Address**.

Name

The name of the vendor should be consistent to avoid duplicate vendor entries. The purchasing department should create a template to follow so that the vendor name always appears the same way as it is entered into the Vendor Master. This will benefit the purchasing users during vendor searches.

Search Terms

The search term is used to find vendors. The entry of data into the search- term field can be structured so that purchasing users can easily remember the criteria for this type of search. For example, the policy may be to enter a search term that is the first five characters of the vendor name plus the two-letter country code for the vendor's country location. For these criteria, the search term for Smith Brothers of London, England would be SMITHGB and for Lakshmi Machines of Coimbatore, India would be LAKSHIN. There is no case sensitivity for this field.

Street Address

The street address is the address of the vendor. The country, region, and postal code will be used to calculate the tax jurisdiction code. If connected to an external tax system, such as Vertex or Taxware, the transaction may validate the address information that you enter to ensure that a valid tax jurisdiction code is obtained.

PO Box Address

Many companies use post-office boxes, and these fields allow that information to be added to the Vendor Master.

Communication

The communication fields should be kept up to date, as fax numbers and email addresses change at the vendor regularly.

5.1.2 Control Screen

The control screen (shown in Figure 5.3) allows the accounting user to enter some general tax information and reference data.

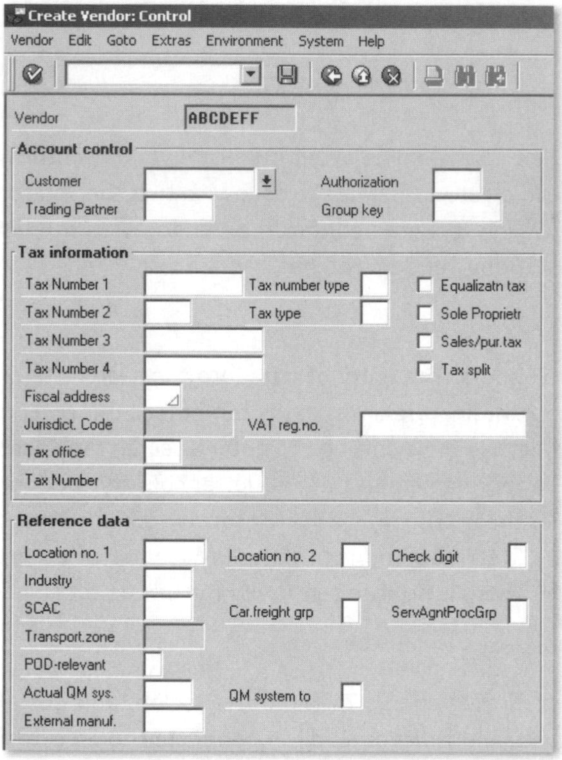

Figure 5.3 Control Screen for Vendor Master

Customer

This customer field allows the purchasing user to enter the customer number for the vendor, if the vendor is both a vendor and a customer of the company. For example, a paper-pulping company may be a vendor for paper products to a particleboard manufacturer, but also may be a customer for scrap particleboard that it can use in pulp creation.

Trading Partner

If the vendor is part of an independent company that has been designated in financial accounting for consolidation purposes, then it is possible to enter that company in this field as a trading partner. The companies are configured as internal trading partners in financial accounting. The navigation path is **IMG • Enterprise Structure • Definition • Financial Accounting • Define Company**.

Group Key

The group key is used to combine vendors to enhance the search capability. The group key is a 10-character string and is not configured. Therefore, a policy for entering a group key would have to be established before any vendor entry commenced.

Tax Numbers 1 and 2

These fields allow the accounting user to enter the tax identification number, or numbers, of the vendor. In the U.S., this would be the Employer Identification Number (EIN), or Social Security number if the vendor were an individual. In France, this field would be the SIRET number, in Spain the NIF number, and so on for various countries.

Tax Type

The tax type can be assigned to the vendor to identify its position as regards sales- and use-tax responsibility.

Jurisdiction Code

The tax jurisdiction code is either determined in SAP by the information entered in the address field or referenced from an external tax package, such as Vertex or Taxware. The tax jurisdiction code is valid only to vendors in the U.S.

Country-Specific Tax Fields

Some of the fields on the Vendor Master control screen are specific to certain countries. These are:

- Tax Number Type—specific to Argentina
- Equalization Tax Indicator—specific to Spain
- Sole Proprietor—specific to 11 countries including Italy, Peru, and Mexico
- Sales/Purchase Tax—specific to countries that levy value-added tax (VAT)
- VAT Registration Number—the VAT number for the vendor, important in EU countries
- Fiscal Address—specific to Italy

Global Location Number (GLN)

In the vendor-control screen, the option is to enter the 13 digits GLN of the vendor. In SAP, the number is divided into three fields, **Location Number 1**, **Location Number 2**, and a **Check digit** field. The GLN is issued to a company and is a number that identifies a legal, functional or physical location within a business or organizational entity. GLN's are governed by strict rules to guarantee that each one is unique worldwide. The identification of locations by GLN is required for an efficient flow of goods and information between trading partners through EDI messages, payment slips, etc. The GLN is often found as a bar code on documents.

Industry Key

The industry key is another grouping that allows similar vendors to be grouped by industry. This field can also be found in customer master records. The industry key can be configured using the navigation path **IMG • Sales and Distribution • Business Partners • Marketing • Define Industry Sector for Customers**.

Standard Carrier Alpha Code (SCAC)

The National Motor Freight Traffic Association (NMFTA) in the U.S. maintains standard Carrier Alpha Code (SCAC). The NMFTA is a nonprofit membership organization with more than 1,000 motor-carrier members, regulated by the U.S. Department of Transportation's Surface Transportation Board and various state and federal agencies.

The SCAC code is a four-letter string used to uniquely identify a shipping carrier. The SCAC code is frequently used in EDI, on the 856 Advance Ship Notice, the 850 Purchase Order, and all motor, rail and water carrier transactions where carrier identification is required. SCAC codes are mandatory when doing business with all U.S. Government agencies.

Certain groups of SCAC codes are reserved for specific purposes. Codes ending with the letter U are reserved for the identification of freight containers. Codes ending with the letter X are reserved for the identification of privately owned railroad cars. Codes ending with the letter Z are reserved for the identification of truck chassis and trailers used in inter-modal service.

Forwarding Agent Freight Group

This group key is assigned to the forwarding agent to group together forwarding agents. For example, the company's transportation department may decide to group its freight forwarders by mode of transport. Therefore, the transportation staff could configure three freight groups; rail, road and shipping. The freight groups are part of the determination of freight costs. The configuration for freight groups can be found via the navigation path **IMG • Logistics Execution • Transportation • Basic transportation Functions • Maintain Freight Code Sets and Freight Codes • Define Forwarding Agent—Freight Groups**.

Service-Agent Procedure Group

The freight costs can be calculated as part of the pricing procedure. To calculate the correct freight costs, the service-agent procedure group has assigned to it a range of forwarding agents. The service-agent procedure group is then assigned to a pricing procedure to calculate freight costs. The group can be configured using the navigation path **IMG • Logistics Execution • Transportation • Shipping Costs • Pricing • Pricing Control • Define and Assign Pricing Procedures • Define Service Agent Procedure Group**.

Vendor's QM System

Many government agencies require that the quality management (QM) systems used by a vendor meet certain levels of verification. These verifications are the level of certification of the system, i.e., ISO 9001, ISO 9002 etc. The verification levels can be configured in transaction OQB7 or via the navigation path **IMG • Quality Management • QM in Logistics • QM in Procurement • Define QM Systems**.

QM System Valid to Date

The date is the expiry date of the certification of the vendor's QM system. For example, a company that has an ISO 9001:2000 certification has to renew it every three years according to ISO certification regulations.

External Manufacturer Code Name or Number

This field can accept a name that may not be the vendor name or number. The field will allow up to 10 characters.

5.1.3 Payment Transactions

The payment transaction screen, shown in Figure 5.4, allows the accounting department to add information on the bank details of the vendor and the payment instructions.

Bank Details—Country

Enter the country where the vendor's bank is located.

Bank Key

The bank key can be selected from the matchcode with the country code entered. The bank key can be entered as the bank-routing number (U.S.) or the bank-sort code (GB), or other country-specific bank identification. The bank key is not entered through configuration, but can be created in financial accounting via transaction code FI01. All details for the bank can be created within that transaction. After entering the bank key in the payment transaction screen, you can see the relevant bank details by clicking on the **Bank data** button beneath the bank details table.

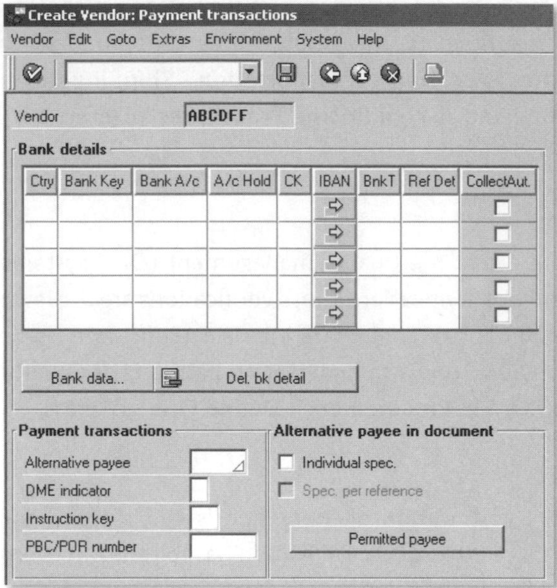

Figure 5.4 Payment Transaction Screen of Vendor Master

Bank Account

This field allows the accounting department to enter the bank account number for the vendor at the bank. The bank-account field can be entered up to 18 characters in length.

Account Holder Name

If the bank account is not in the name of the vendor or the vendor company, then the account holder of the bank account can be entered in this field. This field can accommodate a name of up to 60 characters.

Bank Control Key

The control-key field is specific to each country. In some countries there is no information to enter; in others, such as France, Spain, Japan, and the U.S., the field is used. In the U.S., the field content should be 01 for a checking account and 02 for a savings account. Check with your accounting department to ensure that the correct information is entered into the field for the given country.

International Bank Account Number (IBAN)

The IBAN was designed because of growing pressure to improve the efficiency of cross-border payments in Europe, with respect to cost, speed, and quality. Such improvements required easier validation of foreign bank account numbers. The

IBAN design provided a standard method to enable the cross-border account number formats to be recognized and validated. The IBAN is additional information put on the front of the national account number format of each country.

Check digits and a single simple algorithm perform validation. The algorithm covers the whole IBAN and ensures that individual digits are not transposed.

Recognition is in two parts. The IBAN commences with the ISO 3166 two-letter country code. It is therefore, easy to recognize the country in which the account is held. Within the national account identifier part of the IBAN, it is a requirement of the ISO standard that the bank be unambiguously identified.

The length of the IBAN is not standard across countries. The length can range from 28 characters in Hungary and Cyprus to only 15 characters in Norway.

Partner Bank Type

If the vendor has more than one bank account, then this field allows the accounting user to specify in what sequence the accounts are used by entering a value in this key field. This value can then be used in the line-item payments.

Reference Specifications for Bank Details

This field can be used in countries where additional information or authorization is needed. This information is normally required in Norway and the United Kingdom.

Alternative Payee

The alternative-payee field can be used to enter another vendor number to whom the automatic payments are made. The alternative payee may be needed if the vendor's bank accounts have been frozen.

Report Key for Data Medium Exchange

This key is only used for data medium exchange in Germany.

Instruction Key for Data Medium Exchange

The instruction key controls which statements are given to the banks during the payment order. This is used in Germany, Spain, Norway, Japan, and other countries, as well as for the SWIFT format.

The Society for Worldwide Interbank Financial Telecommunication (SWIFT) is a financial industry-owned co-operative. It supplies secure, standardized messaging services and interface software to more than 7,800 financial institutions in more than 200 countries. Many institutions have been using the MT-100 customer transfer format for one-off credit transfers and repetitive instructions, such as lease payments. Since November 2003, the MT-100 has been replaced by the MT-103 Single Customer Credit Transfer.

PBC/POR Subscriber Number

This field is only relevant for payment orders within Switzerland.

5.2 Accounting Information

The transaction FK01 enables the accounting users to enter the account code for the vendor and the company code. The vendor number may need to be entered if the account group is defined as only allowing external number assignment as seen in Figure 5.5.

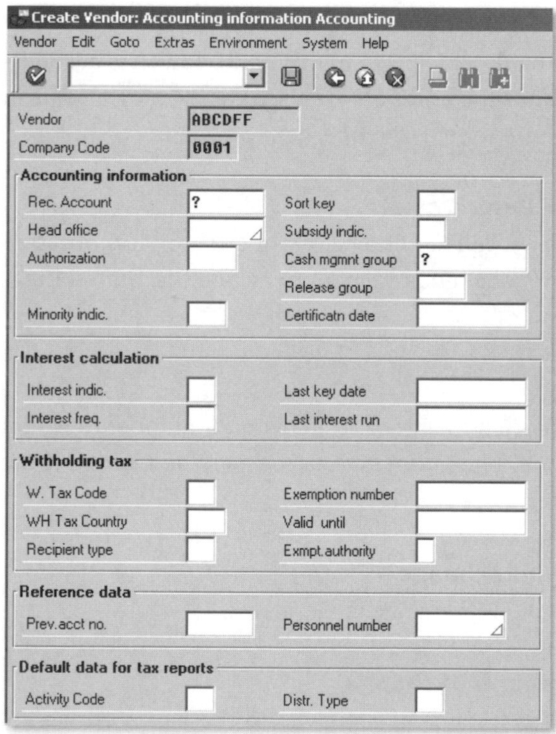

Figure 5.5 Accounting Screen for Transaction FK01

5.2.1 Accounting Information

The accounting screen allows the accounting department to enter relevant data about accounting, interest calculation, and withholding tax as it relates to this vendor within the given company code.

Reconciliation Account

The reconciliation account is an individual general ledger account. A reconciliation account is recorded in line-item detail in the sub-ledger and summarized in the general ledger. The detailed information entered into the reconciliation account is all line-item data from the vendor account. These reconciliation accounts in the sub-ledger are important and must be maintained for vendors, and also for customers and asset accounts.

The reconciliation in the general ledger is at the summary level and is used to reconcile against the vendor account at the total level. However, the sub-ledger can be used to identify line item data if necessary.

A reconciliation account can be created using transaction code FS01. When creating a reconciliation account, remember that the account must be a balance-sheet account, the account group must be selected as a reconciliation account, and the reconciliation account type field must be entered as vendor.

Sort Key

The sort key allows the user to select a sort for the allocation field. The system sorts the document line items based on the key entered in the allocation field. Therefore, if the user selects the sort key 008, then the sort of the line items will be by the allocation 008, which is by Cost Center.

Head Office

This field allows an entry of a vendor number, which represents the head-office or master account for this vendor.

Authorization Group

The authorization group is a way of increasing security on certain objects. By entering an authorization group in this field, it is restricting access to the object to those users who have this authorization group in their SAP profiles.

Cash Management Group

In the cash-management functionality it is possible to allocate vendors to a planning group. This planning group helps the cash-management department to have better information to produce or plan the company's cash forecast.

Release Group

The release-approval group can be defined and configured to allow only those in the group to be able to **release for payment**. The release group can be configured via the navigation path **IMG • Financial Accounting • Accounts Receivable and**

Accounts Payable • Business Transactions • Release for Payment • Define Release Approval Groups for Release for Payment

Minority Indicator

The minority-indicator field is only relevant for implementations in the U.S. Configuration is required to enter the relevant information, as there are no predefined fields in SAP. Many companies are asked by federal and local officials to report on the level of minority vendors supplying material to them.

A definition of a minority vendor, from Virginia Polytechnic Institute's Purchasing Guidelines, 2004, describes it as "a business that is owned and controlled by one or more socially and economically disadvantaged persons. Such disadvantage may arise from cultural, racial, chronic economic circumstances or background, or other similar cause. A minority-owned business is at least 51% owned and controlled by one or more such disadvantaged persons. Additionally, the management and daily business operations must be controlled by one or more such individuals. Minority means any African American, Hispanic American, Native American or Alaskan American, Asian, or a person of Pacific Island descent who is either a citizen of the United States or a permanent resident."

To configure the minority-indicator field, use the navigation path **IMG • Financial Accounting • Accounts Receivable and Accounts Payable • Vendor Accounts • Master Data • Preparations for Creating Vendor Master Data • Define Minority Indicators**.

Certification Date for Minority Vendors

The certification expiration date for the minority-vendor field is only relevant for implementations in the U.S. The certification for a minority vendor has an expiration date. This is required to be entered for the U.S. government.

Interest Calculation Indicator

If this account is suitable for automatic interest, then an interest calculation indicator must be selected. These interest calculations can be configured by the accounting department via the navigation path **IMG • Financial Accounting • Accounts Receivable and Accounts Payable • Business Transactions • Interest Calculation • Interest Calculation Global Setting • Define Interest Calculation Types**.

Interest Calculation Frequency

This field allows the accounting department to select a period that specifies when the interest calculation is run for this vendor. The period can range from monthly to yearly.

Withholding Tax Code

Withholding tax generally refers to an income tax on foreign vendors from country B, and applies to those that are not resident in the country A, but derive incomes form profits, interest, rentals, royalties, and other incomes from sources in country A. The company from country A will be the withholding agent. An income tax of a certain percentage will be withheld on such incomes by the company from country A, which should turn the amount of taxes on each payment over to the local state treasury and submit a withholding income tax return to the local tax authority.

There are a number of exceptions and rules associated with withholding tax and these are best defined by tax experts.

Withholding Tax Country Key

This field can be used in some countries that require this additional country key to calculate or report on withholding tax.

Vendor Recipient Type

In the U.S., Form 1042 is the annual taxable return used by withholding agents to report tax withheld on U.S. source income paid to certain non-resident individuals and corporations. The withholding agent issues a Form 1042S, *Foreign Person's U.S. Source Income Subject to Withholding*. The 1042 requires that a recipient type be entered. That two-digit code can be configured into SAP. Some examples of this code are: 01—individuals, 02—Corporations, 06—Foreign Governments, 11—U.S. Branch treated as a U.S. person, etc.

The recipient type field is also used in Spain for similar reporting. The recipient type can be configured via the path **IMG · Financial Accounting · Accounts Receivable and Accounts Payable · Vendor Accounts · Master Data · Preparations for Creating Vendor Master Data · Check Settings for Withholding Tax · Maintain Types of Recipient**

Exemption Number

If a vendor is exempt from withholding tax and has an exemption certificate, then that number should be entered on the Vendor Master record.

Validity Date for Exemption

The exemption certificate has an expiration date that should be entered in this field. Often, the certificate is extended so the date of expiry should be updated when necessary.

Exemption Authority

On the IRS form 1042S, a code is required for explaining why there is no withholding tax. This code can be configured into SAP and entered on the Vendor Master. Examples of this code are: 01—Income effectively connected with a U.S. trade or business, 03—Income is not from U.S. sources, and 07—Withholding foreign partnership.

Previous Account Number

This field can be used if the Vendor Master has been re-numbered, or you wish to store the legacy vendor number.

Personnel Number

If a vendor is also an employee, then this field will accommodate the employee's personnel number.

5.2.2 Payment Transactions

This screen, shown in Figure 5.6, allows the accounting user to add vendor information on the automatic payment transaction and payment data. Some fields on this screen have been discussed previously.

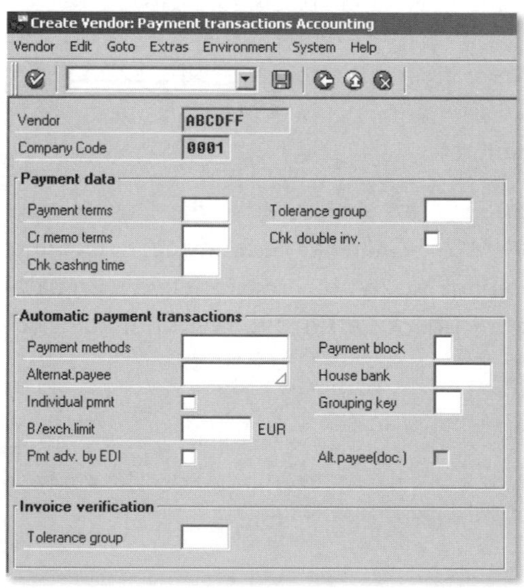

Figure 5.6 Payment Transactions Screen for Transaction FK01

Payment Terms

Payment terms are defined to allow the vendor to offer cash discounts and favorable payment periods to the company. In many accounts-payable departments, before the time of electronic commerce, the rule was to pay the vendor as close as possible to the last day of the agreed payment period in order to maximize the day's payables and to keep the cash within the company. However, over the last 10 years, vendors have been offering incentives to companies for fast payment, and purchasing departments have responded by implementing best practices for paying vendors as soon as the invoice arrives, or sooner.

The payment terms on the Vendor Master record are entered by the accounting department and are configured if the payment terms are not found on the system. The payment terms can be configured via the navigation path **IMG · Financial Accounting · Accounts Receivable and Accounts Payable · Business Transactions · Incoming Invoices/Credit Memos · Maintain Terms of Payment**

Tolerance Group

A tolerance is a percentage or a value that is the limit to which an event can deviate. Therefore, a tolerance of 10% on a line item that is expected to be delivered with 100 units, will allow a delivery of 109, which under the 10% tolerance. A delivery of 111 will not be allowed as it is over the 10% tolerance. A tolerance group is a set of tolerances that are configured and assigned to a vendor if necessary. Each tolerance group is defined for a unique company code. The tolerances that can be defined are seen in Figure 5.7.

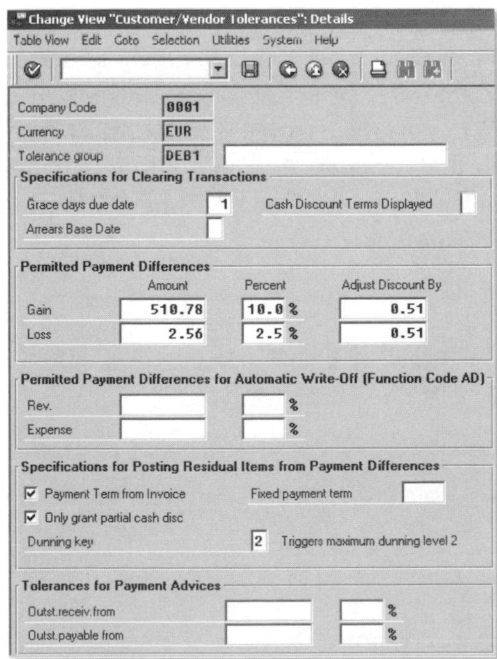

Figure 5.7 Data to be Entered for Tolerance Group

The tolerance group can be configured in transaction OBA3 or via the navigation path **IMG • Financial Accounting • Accounts Receivable and Accounts Payable • Business Transactions • Open Item Clearing • Clearing Differences • Define Tolerances for Customers/Vendors**.

Check Flag for Double Invoices

This indicator should be set if the accounting department wants the system to check for double or duplicate invoices when they are entered.

Check Cashing Time

The value of the check cashing time is used in cash management to calculate the cash outflow. The entry in this field can be calculated by analysis of the issue to cash date and an average used.

Payment Methods

The payment method entered here is used if there is no payment method entered in the line item. The options for this field can be configured via the navigation path **IMG • Financial Accounting • Accounts Receivable and Accounts Payable • Business Transactions • Outgoing Payments • Automatic Outgoing Payments • Payment Method • Set Up Payment Methods per Country for Payment Transactions**.

Payment Block

The accounting department can enter a payment block on the Vendor Master that will prevent any open items for being paid. The payment-block keys are defined in configuration via transaction code OB27 or via the navigation path **IMG • Financial Accounting • Accounts Receivable and Accounts Payable • Business Transactions • Outgoing Payments • Outgoing Payments Global Settings • Payment Block Reasons • Define Payment Block Reasons**.

House Bank

The house bank can be entered if the same bank is always used. This field negates the configuration on the bank-selection screen.

Individual Payment Indicator

If this indicator is set, then every item is paid individually rather than having the items combined and paid.

Bill of Exchange Limit

A bill of exchange is a contract entitling an exporter to receive immediate payment in the local currency for goods that would be shipped elsewhere. Time elapses between payment in one currency and repayment in another, so the interest rate would also be brought into the transaction. The accounting department will determine whether the vendor requires a bill-of-exchange limit.

Payment Advice by EDI

If this indicator is set then all payment advices to this vendor should be sent via EDI.

5.2.3 Correspondence Screen

The correspondence screen, shown in Figure 5.8, allows the entry of data for dunning and correspondence.

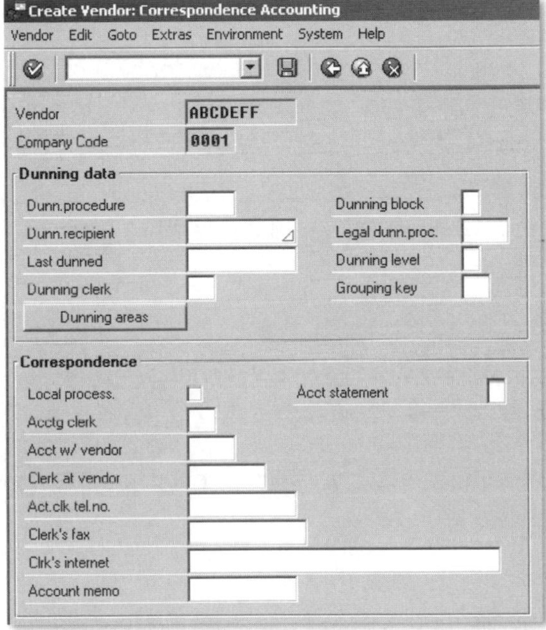

Figure 5.8 Screen for Entering Correspondence and Dunning Information

Dunning Procedure

Normally dunning involves sending reminder letters to customers for payment. However, in this case, dunning relates to reminding vendors to deliver the material from the purchase orders.

The dunning procedure can be selected to reflect how the dunning should be carried out for this vendor. The dunning procedure can be configured in transaction FBMP or via the navigation path **IMG · Financial Accounting · Accounts Receivable and Accounts Payable · Business Transactions · Dunning · Dunning Procedure · Define Dunning Procedures**.

Dunning Block

If a dunning block is selected, then the vendor is not selected for the dunning run. The dunning block can be entered at any time. The dunning block can be defined via the navigation path **IMG • Financial Accounting • Accounts Receivable and Accounts Payable • Business Transactions • Dunning • Basic Settings for Dunning • Define Dunning Block Reasons**.

Dunning Recipient

This field should be completed if the vendor is not the recipient of the dunning notices. If the correspondence should go to a central office or production site, then that vendor number should be entered.

Legal Dunning Procedure

If the dunning procedure that has been undertaken against a vendor has not been successful, then there is the option of legal dunning. Attorneys can carry this out, and documents can be produced through the SAP system. A separate form should be identified for this legal-dunning procedure.

The field on the correspondence screen allows entry of the date when legal dunning procedures began.

Last Dunned

This is simply the date on which the vendor was last sent a dunning document.

Dunning Level

This field indicates how many times the vendor has been dunned. This field is updated when a new dunning notice is sent.

Dunning Clerk

The dunning clerk is the person in the accounting department who is responsible for the dunning of the vendor. A two-character field identifies the dunning clerk. This dunning clerk field is configured via the navigation path **IMG • Financial Accounting • Accounts Receivable and Accounts Payable • Vendor Accounts • Master Data • Preparations for Creating Vendor Master Data • Define Accounting Clerks**.

Account Statement Indicator

This indicator allows the accounting department to define when the vendor will receive its periodic statements. The vendor may receive them weekly, monthly, or yearly.

Accounting Clerk

The accounting clerk field uses the same lookup table as the dunning clerk. The accounting clerk does not necessarily have to be the same as the dunning clerk.

However, if the dunning clerk field is not entered, then the dunning clerk is assumed to be the same as the accounting clerk.

Account with Vendor

If known, the account number that the vendor uses to identify the company should be entered here. It is often found on the vendor invoice.

Vendor Clerk Information

The last fields on this screen relate to information concerning the person at the vendor who has been assigned to manage the day-to-day operations between your company and your vendor.

5.3 Purchasing Data

The purchasing data for the vendor can be entered via transaction MK01. Figure 5.9 shows the purchasing information to be entered in the Vendor Master. Some of the fields on the purchasing data screens have already been discussed in Sections 5.1 and 5.2.

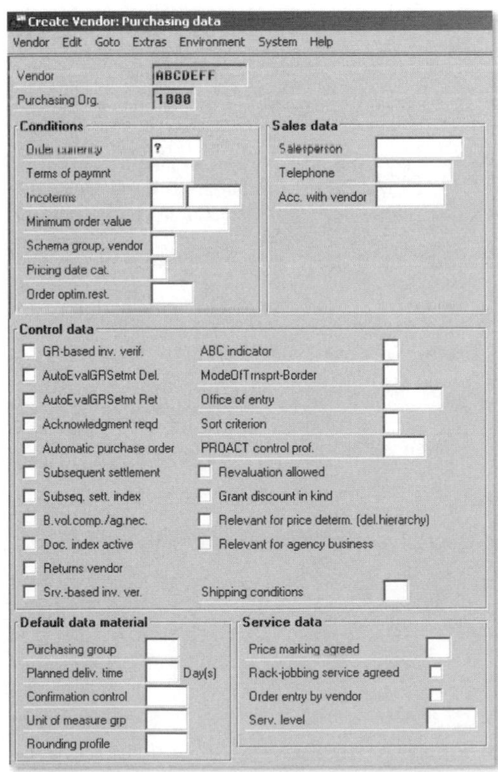

Figure 5.9 Purchasing Information to be Entered in Vendor Master Using Transaction MK01

5.3.1 Purchasing Data Screen

Order Currency

The order currency to be used on purchase order with this vendor can be entered here. The currency is usually that of the vendor's country or that of the purchasing department.

Incoterms

Incoterms make international trade easier and help vendors and customers in different countries understand each other. Incoterms are standard trade definitions used in international contracts. The International Chamber of Commerce (ICC) based in Paris, France devised these. The latest version is Incoterms 2000 and has been translated into 31 languages.

There are 13 Incoterms which are divided into four groups; Arrival, Departure, Carriage paid by seller, Carriage not paid by seller. These are seen in Table 5.1.

Group	Incoterm	Long name	Location
E—Departure	EXW	EX Works	Named Place
D—Arrival	DAF	Delivered at Frontier	Named Place
D—Arrival	DES	Delivered Ex Ship	Port of destination
D—Arrival	DEQ	Delivered Ex Quay	Port of destination
D—Arrival	DDU	Delivered Duty Unpaid	Destination
D—Arrival	DDP	Delivered Duty Paid	Destination
C—Paid	CFR	Cost and Freight	Port of destination
C—Paid	CIF	Cost, Insurance, Freight	Port of destination
C—Paid	CPT	Carriage Paid To	Destination
C—Paid	CIP	Carriage, Insurance Paid	Destination
F—Unpaid	FCA	Free Carrier	Named Place
F—Unpaid	FAS	Free Alongside Ship	Port of Shipment
F—Unpaid	FOB	Free On Board	Port of Shipment

Table 5.1 Table of Incoterms 2000

Vendor Schema Group

The calculation schema is used to determine the pricing procedure for the vendor with relation to purchasing documents. The schema group can be configured via the navigation path **IMG • Materials Management • Purchasing • Conditions • Define Price Determination Process • Define Schema Group**.

Pricing Date Category

The pricing date category is used to determine the date on which the pricing determination will take place. For instance, if the purchasing department decided to select the purchase order date, then the new price is calculated at the creation of the purchase order with the vendor.

Good Receipt-Based Invoice Verification

Setting this indicator allows the system to perform invoice verification based on the goods receipt amounts.

Automatic Evaluated Receipt Settlement

The evaluated receipt-settlement agreement is created between the vendor and the purchasing department. The agreement allows the purchasing department to send payments for the goods received at the time those materials are posted into stock. The vendor will not send an invoice for the material sent. This method of evaluated receipt settlement, sometimes called a two-way match, and is designated a best practice by many purchasing experts.

Automatic Evaluated Receipt Settlement—Returns

If set, this indicator allows returns to be processed under the same evaluated receipt agreement.

Acknowledgement Required

This indicator determines whether the vendor is supposed to send an acknowledgement that they have received the order. This can be electronically sent via EDI.

Automatic Purchase Order

If a purchase requisition has been created and assigned to this vendor, then an automatic purchase order can be created if this indicator is set. This reduces work for the purchasing department.

Subsequent Settlement

The vendor may offer some kind of incentive to the purchasing department to purchase more material. This may take two forms. One may be an instant reduction in price—a promotional price—for a given period. The second incentive may take the form of the subsequent settlement. This is an agreement between the vendor and the purchasing department under which, depending on how much material is purchased, a rebate is offered at the end of an agreed period. So an office supply vendor could agree to give a 10% rebate for the total amount of purchases over a three-month period. This would have a provision that the total amount of purchases would be more than 50% greater than for the same period in the previous year. If the purchases were in excess of the 50%, then the subsequent settlement with the vendor would take place at the end of the period. The vendor would give a 10% rebate on all the purchases over that period.

Business-Volume Comparison/Agreement Necessary

If this indicator is set, data must be compared between the vendor and the purchasing department before any subsequent settlement is posted. In the example of the office-supply vendor, the agreement may depend on the comparison of the files from both parties.

Document Index Active

The document index is a way of automatically adjusting the purchasing documents if the conditions change.

Returns Vendor

This indicator is set if the returns to this vendor are to be issued using shipping processing.

Service-Based Invoice Verification

Some vendors provide services, and the work performed is entered using service-entry sheets. If this indicator is set, the acceptance is carried out at the level of the service-entry sheet.

ABC Indicator

The ABC indicator is used for many objects in SAP. The ABC indicator for vendors relates to the amount of sales the vendor does with the company. The ABC indicator is manually entered.

Mode of Transport for Foreign Trade

This indicator is used if the vendor is involved in foreign trade. The mode of transport is defined for each country; this field determines how the vendor transports material. The field can be configured via the navigation path **IMG • Materials Management • Purchasing • Foreign Trade/Customs • Transportation Data • Define Modes of Transport**.

Office of Entry

The office of entry defines where the material purchased from this vendor will enter the country or leave in the case of a return. The office of entry is the customs office and is configured via the navigation path **IMG • Materials Management • Purchasing • Foreign Trade/Customs • Transportation Data • Define Customs Offices**.

Vendor Sort Criterion

This field allows the purchasing department to sort the delivery items from the vendor in a specific manner. The default is by Vendor Sub-Range (VSR), but the sort can be by material number, material group, or EAN.

Revaluation Allowed

This indicator allows the purchasing department to allow a revaluation of vendor deliveries that have already been settled. Setting this indicator means that all purchase orders from this vendor are included for revaluation.

Grant Discount in Kind

The vendor may offer materials to the purchasing department free of charge as an incentive to purchase. If this indicator is set, then this vendor has been identified as granting discount in kind.

5.3.2 Partner Functions

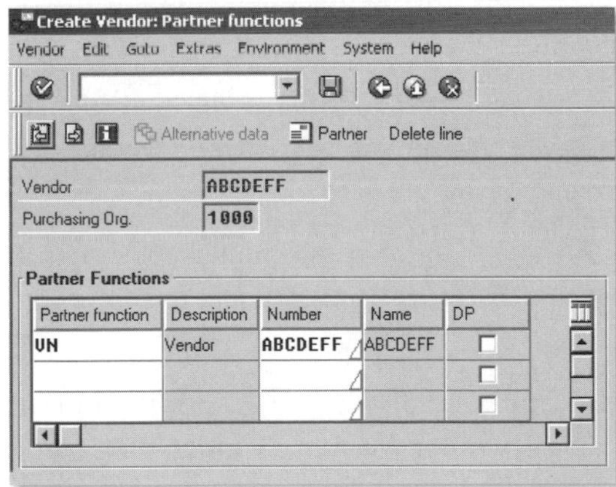

Figure 5.10 Partner Functions for Vendor Master Using Transaction MK01

The partner function screen shown in Figure 5.10 allows the purchasing user to define the relationships between the vendor and the company. A vendor can vary in size from a sole proprietor to the largest multinational company. To best describe the vendor's various operations, partner functionality can be described. The partner functions are used for both customers and vendors. A selection of available vendor partner codes is seen in Table 5.2.

Partner Code	Description
AZ	Alternative Payment Recipient
CA	Contact Address
CP	Contact Person
ER	Employee Responsible
GS	Goods Supplier
OA	Ordering Address
PI	Invoice Presented By
VN	Vendor

Table 5.2 List of Partner Functions

Basically, the partner function allows the purchasing department to determine what function vendors perform within the larger vendor organization. For example, a multinational auto-parts manufacturer may supply material to your company and you have created a vendor number (VN) for them. However, the address to which you send the purchase orders may be a separate address in a separate division of the manufacturer's business. Therefore, you would create a vendor number for the ordering address (OA), and that record is entered into the partner function screen for the VN vendor.

Further, there may be a separate contact address (CA) for a vendor that supplies the invoices (PI), and an alternative payee (AZ). All of these can be created and entered into the partner functions screen of the VN partner.

The partner functions are assigned to the vendor account groups. For example, the vendor account group 0001 may have different partner functions to the vendor account group LIEF.

The partner function can be defined in configuration via the navigation path **IMG • Materials Management • Purchasing • Vendor Master • Vendor Hierarchy • Define Partner Determination**.

In this chapter, the Vendor Master file was fully discussed. There are different ways to enter vendor data and both the purchasing department and the accounting department play a role in this important task. Entering the correct vendor information is important when material needs to be ordered quickly and correctly. Any errors in the vendor master file can be costly if material cannot be sourced in a timely fashion and customer shipments are delayed.

6 Purchasing Information Data

The documented relationship between the vendor and the material is important for the purchasing department. In order to reduce the length of procurement process, the purchase order can be generated from the information in the purchasing information record, thus reducing manual data input.

The information found on the purchasing information record is the information that the vendor and the customer have negotiated in a verbal or written agreement. The information supplied by the vendor or from the contract is entered into the purchasing information record. A normal purchase information record is between a vendor and customer for a specific material. However, the vendor can supply a service that is defined by a material group rather than a specific material and this information can be entered into a purchasing information record.

6.1 Purchasing General Data

There are four distinct purchasing information records:

- standard
- contracting
- pipeline
- consignment

Figure 6.1 shows the initial data entry screen for the creation of a purchasing information record. The screen shows the four types of information records that can be created.

6.1.1 Create a Purchasing Information Record

The transaction code to create a purchasing information record is ME11. The navigation path is **SAP Menu · Logistics · Materials Management · Master Data · Info Record · Create**

At the initial screen (Figure 6.1) of the purchasing information screen, the purchasing user can decide what data to enter in order to create certain types of records.

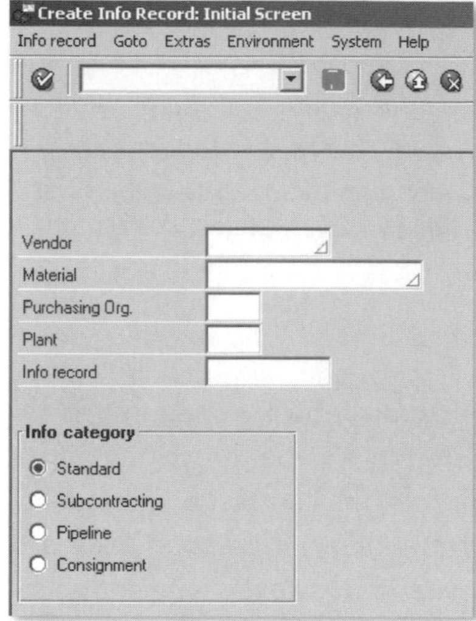

Figure 6.1 Initial Screen for Creating Purchasing Information Record

Standard Purchasing Information Record

This type of purchasing information record contains the information supplied by the vendor for a specific material, service or group of materials or services.

Subcontracting Purchasing Information Record

The subcontracting purchasing information record can be used when the order is a subcontracting order.

Pipeline Purchasing Information Record

Pipeline materials such as electricity, water, oil, etc., are supplied by utility vendors and used by the customer through pipeline withdrawals. The pipeline purchasing information record reflects the information for this vendor/material combination.

Consignment Purchasing Information Record

When a vendor supplies material to be stored at a customer's site for customer withdrawal, the purchasing department can create a consignment purchasing information record for that material.

6.1.2 Create a Purchasing Information Record with Material Number

The purchasing information record can be created for a specific material by entering the supplying vendor. The record can be created with or without a purchasing organization. If no purchasing organization is entered then the purchasing information record will only be created with general data (see Figure 6.2). If a purchasing organization is entered with the material and vendor then the purchasing data screen will be available for the purchasing user to enter specific data that relates to that purchasing organization.

6.1.3 Create a Purchasing Information Record without a Material Number

Only entering a vendor in the initial data screen can create a purchasing information record. This purchasing information record will be valid for the vendor and a material group, which is mandatory entry on the general data screen (see Figure 6.3). It is also mandatory to enter a description for the purchasing information record. This is not required if a material is entered. This description allows the purchasing user to describe the service that the vendor will provide for the materials in the entered material group. This type of record can be created with or without a purchasing organization. If no purchasing organization is entered then the purchasing information record will only be created with general data.

6.1.4 General Data Screen

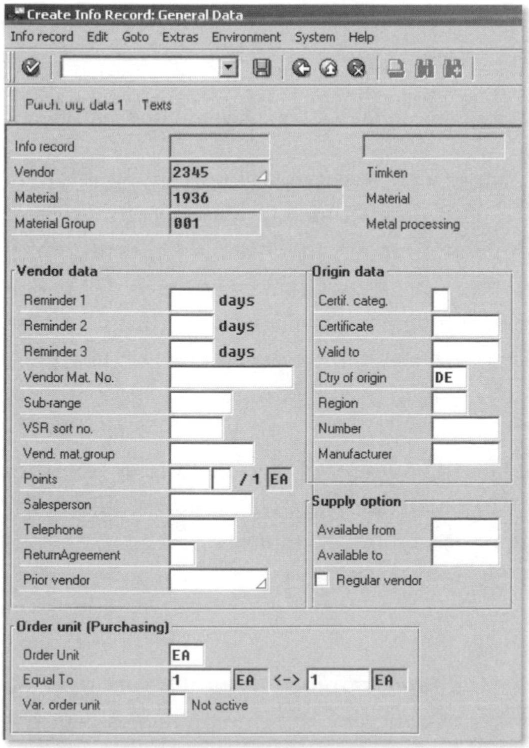

Figure 6.2 General Data screen for Standard Material/Vendor Purchasing Information Record

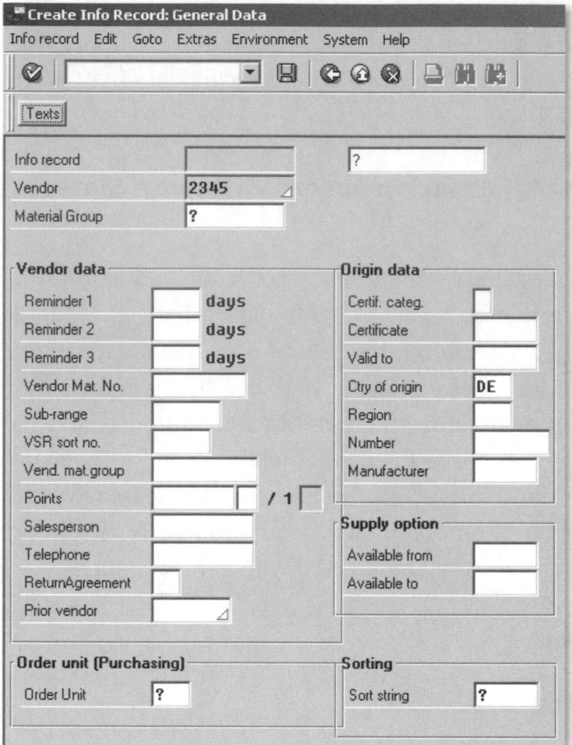

Figure 6.3 General Data Screen for Material Group/Vendor Purchasing Information Record

The general data screen is valid for either a material/vendor purchasing information record or for a material group/vendor purchasing information record. Figure 6.3 shows that for a material group/vendor record, the information record must be given a valid description. Figure 6.3 also shows that only the order unit is shown and not the other unit of measure fields as in Figure 6.2. This is because the materials in the material group may have varying ordering units of measure.

Reminder Fields

The reminder fields (1, 2 and 3) contain the number of days that urging letters or emails can be sent to the vendor for this material. Negative numbers indicate the message is prior to the delivery date, positive numbers indicate messages after the date.

Vendor Sub-Range (VSR)

The vendor can be used to sub-divide the vendor's products into different ranges. So the vendor could be an office products company and the sub ranges could be computer media, paper products, ink products, etc.

Vendor Sub-Range (VSR) Sort Number

The vendor sub-range sort number allows the vendor sub-ranges to have different values, which are used to create a sort sequence. When a purchase order is created it uses the VSR sort number from the purchasing information records to sequence the materials in the purchase order. For example, if computer media has a sort number of 40 and the sort number for ink products is 24, then the ink products are sequenced before the computer media in the purchase order.

Points

The points system can be used where the purchasing department has negotiated with a vendor a subsequent settlement or rebate arrangement. The points field in the purchasing information record allows the purchasing user to enter the number of points that are recorded each time a certain value of the material is ordered. The numbers of points are recorded for the amount ordered rather than the total value ordered.

At the end of the rebate period the number of points accumulated determines the value of the rebate from the vendor.

Return Agreement

The return agreement field determines what arrangement the client has with the vendor for the return of the material. The return agreement field can be configured so that unique return agreements can be defined. The return agreement is usually used for retail implementations and can be configured via the navigation path **IMG · Logistics—General · Material Master · Retail-Specific Settings · Settings for Key Fields · Return Agreement**

In the next section the discussion will proceed to move specific date that is required by the purchasing organization.

6.2 Purchasing Organization Data

Once the general information has been entered the data the next screen is for the purchasing organization data.

The data fields in Figure 6.4 are also found in the vendor master and the material master. However, by entering the information in the purchasing information record will be specific to the vendor/material. This information will be used in purchasing documents.

Depending on the agreement between the vendor and the client, the purchasing department will enter information on the tolerances, delivery time, quantities and the net price.

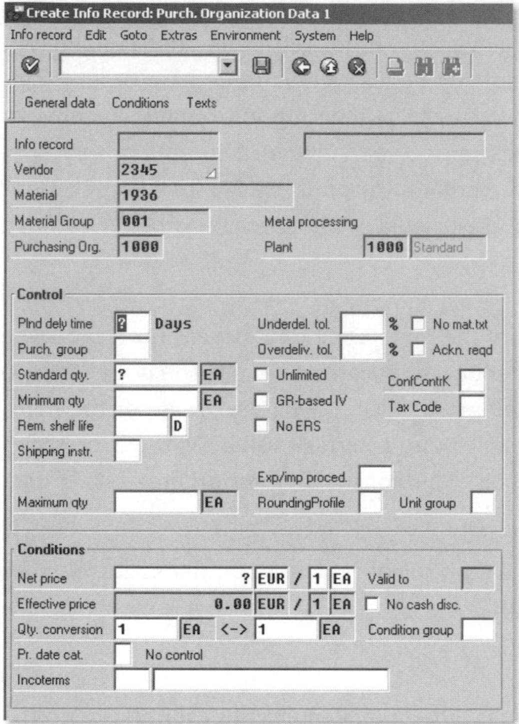

Figure 6.4 Purchasing Organization Screen for Purchase Information Record

6.2.1 Conditions

The purchasing information record contains information that defines the conditions for the material/vendor. The condition screen can be seen in Figure 6.5.

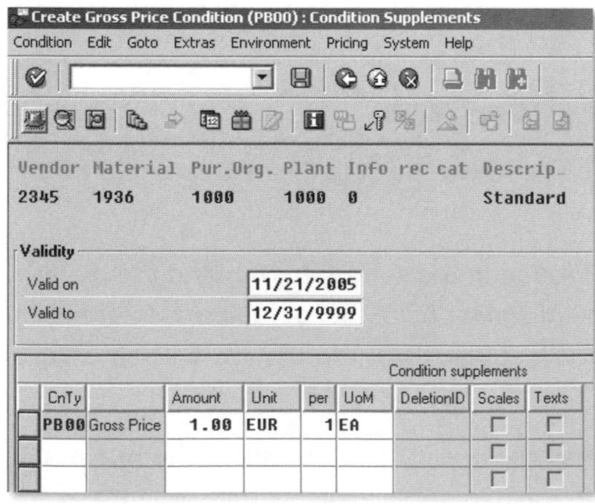

Figure 6.5 Condition Screen for Purchasing Information Record

Validity

The conditions that can be entered for the purchasing information record are valid for a certain time period. For instance, if the agreement with the vendor is valid for three months, then the valid to date should reflect that. If the information is for future agreements, the validity dates can be entered to reflect this.

Price Calculation Schema

In purchasing, the condition types are used in pricing. A condition type can represent a price, a tax, a transportation cost, a discount, etc. The condition types can be grouped together to form a pricing procedure, sometimes called a price calculation schema. The pricing procedure can be defined in the IMG using the navigation path **IMG • Materials Management • Purchasing • Conditions • Define Price Determination Process • Define Calculation Schema**.

The calculation schema is created to produce a step-by-step procedure for a particular event. For instance, in a pricing procedure the first step would be the condition type for a gross price, then a discount condition type, followed by a tax condition type etc.

Condition Type

The condition type is simply a function, which tells the system what type of calculation to perform, e.g., fixed amount, percentage etc.

User defined condition types can be created in the IMG. The navigation path is **IMG • Materials Management • Purchasing • Conditions • Define Price Determination Process • Define Condition Types**.

The screen shown in Figure 6.6 requires that the condition type must be assigned to a condition class. Examples of the condition class include discounts, prices, taxes, expenses etc. It is also mandatory for a calculation type to be assigned to the condition type. The calculation type identifies whether the condition type is a percentage, quantity, formula, points, fixed amount, etc.

The entry screen is where the purchasing user can define how the condition type can be updated, either manually or automatically, and the validity date of the condition type.

The scale fields allow the purchasing user to enter information on the condition type if it is valid for scaling. If a discount from a vendor is not a blanket 4%, but different depending on the amount ordered then this would be scaling. A vendor can give discounts for a specific material that increase the more the client purchases. For example, if the purchase order is for a quantity of up to 30 units the vendor would give the client a 1% discount; from 31–60 the discount is 2% discount; 61–120 the discount is 4% discount and over 121 it is a 6% discount.

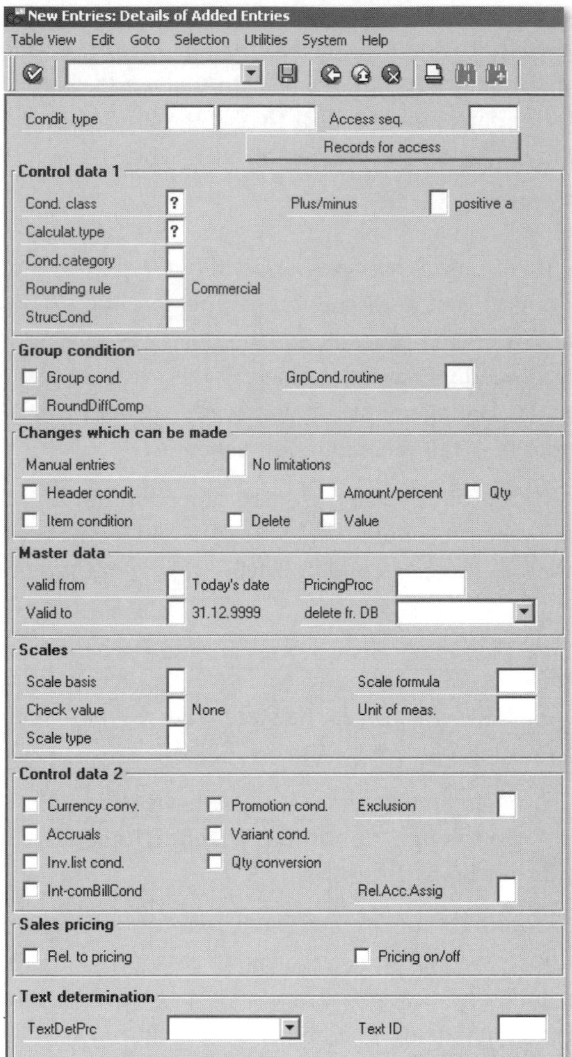

Figure 6.6 Condition Type Creation Screen

Access Sequence

For each condition type there is an access sequence. This allows the condition type to access the condition tables in the correct sequence. The access sequence can be configured using the navigation path **IMG · Materials Management · Purchasing · Conditions · Define Price Determination Process · Define Access Sequence**

Condition Tables

The access sequence defines the sequence in which to read the condition tables. The condition table consists of a number of fields that are selected and records are created to assign values to those fields. A condition table can be created in the IMG using the navigation path **IMG • Materials Management • Purchasing • Conditions • Define Price Determination Process • Define Condition Tables** and is shown in Figure 6.7.

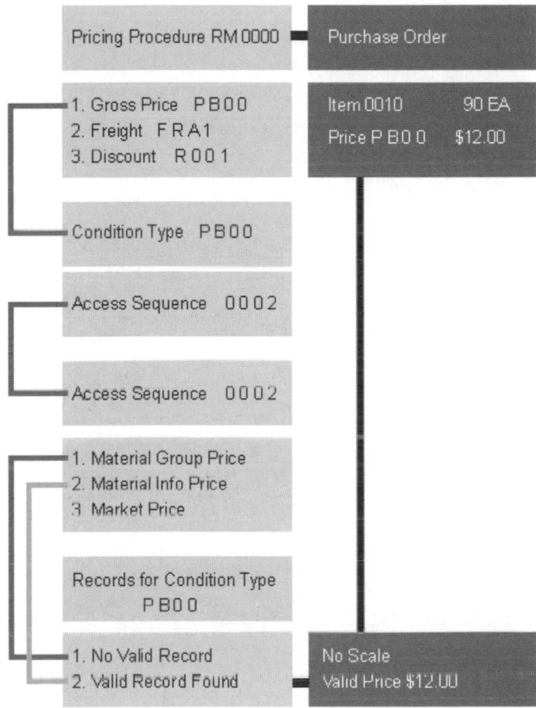

Figure 6.7 Interaction of Calculation Schema, Condition Type, Access Sequence and Condition Table

6.2.2 Text Screen

There are texts fields that can be used to enter specific information regarding the particular purchasing information record. The screen in Figure 6.8 shows the two text fields into which information can be entered; the **info record notes** and the **purchase order text**.

The screen displays five text lines of forty characters etc. However, double- clicking on the **more text** icon will display a free form text input screen similar to a normal word processing program. Here additional text can be added if significant information needs to be included in the purchasing information record.

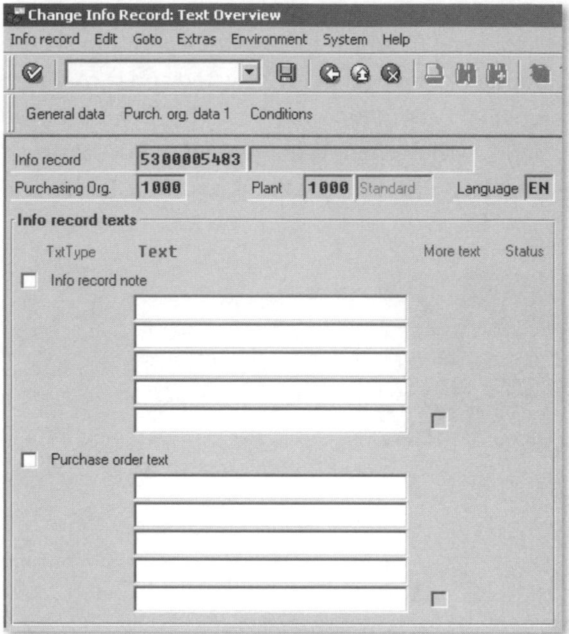

Figure 6.8 Text Input Screen for Purchasing Information Record

To the far right of the test item there is the status field. This shows how the text can be used. The purchasing user can:

- Allow the text to be used as is, with only changes to the original text allowed
- Allow the text to be used and allow any changes to the text to be reflected back in the original text, but adopting the modified text
- Allow the text to be displayed, but not to be printed or changed

The relevance of the text fields can be determined in configuration. For each of the purchasing documents, RFQ, purchase order, contract, etc., the texts defined in master records can be prioritized for each document.

The texts entered on a purchasing information record should be relevant to a purchase order line item. In configuration the configurator can define the priority against other text fields. This transaction can be accessed using the navigation path **IMG • Materials Management • Purchasing • Messages • Text for Messages • Define Texts for Purchase Order**

The configuration for the purchase order texts can be further sub-divided into header, line item, supplement and headings. The purchasing information record text would be most relevant to the document item, which is shown in Figure 6.9.

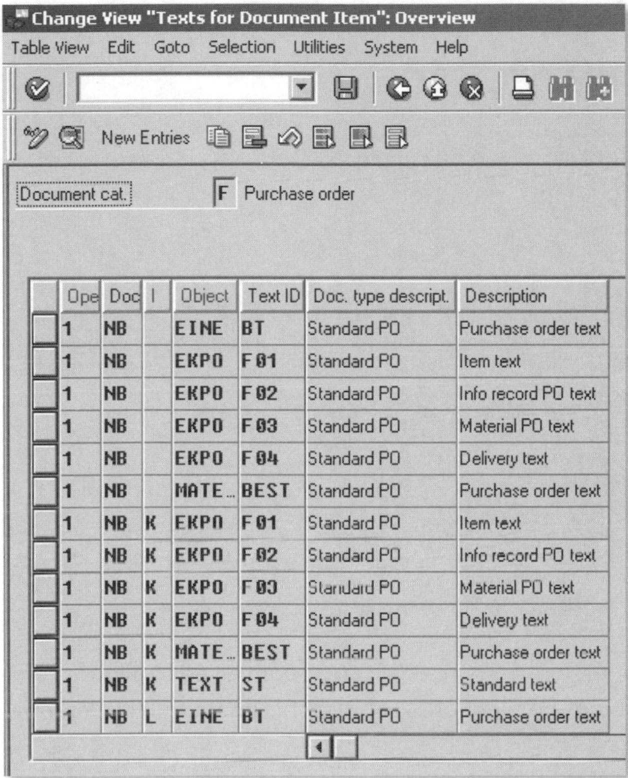

Ope	Doc	I	Object	Text ID	Doc. type descript.	Description
1	NB		EINE	BT	Standard PO	Purchase order text
1	NB		EKPO	F01	Standard PO	Item text
1	NB		EKPO	F02	Standard PO	Info record PO text
1	NB		EKPO	F03	Standard PO	Material PO text
1	NB		EKPO	F04	Standard PO	Delivery text
1	NB		MATE...	BEST	Standard PO	Purchase order text
1	NB	K	EKPO	F01	Standard PO	Item text
1	NB	K	EKPO	F02	Standard PO	Info record PO text
1	NB	K	EKPO	F03	Standard PO	Material PO text
1	NB	K	EKPO	F04	Standard PO	Delivery text
1	NB	K	MATE...	BEST	Standard PO	Purchase order text
1	NB	K	TEXT	ST	Standard PO	Standard text
1	NB	L	EINE	BT	Standard PO	Purchase order text

Figure 6.9 Texts Relevant for Purchase Order Line Item

The configuration screen shows the following:

- Document type, which in this case is **NB** for standard purchase order
- Object type, **EKPO** for purchasing document item texts, etc.
- Text **ID**, which is relevant to the particular object.

New entries can be made to this list to allow new texts or modify the existing text sequence.

6.2.3 Statistical Data

Within the purchasing information record there is statistical information that is recorded and can be reviewed. The statistical screens can be accessed from within the general screen by clicking on **Extras • Statistics**

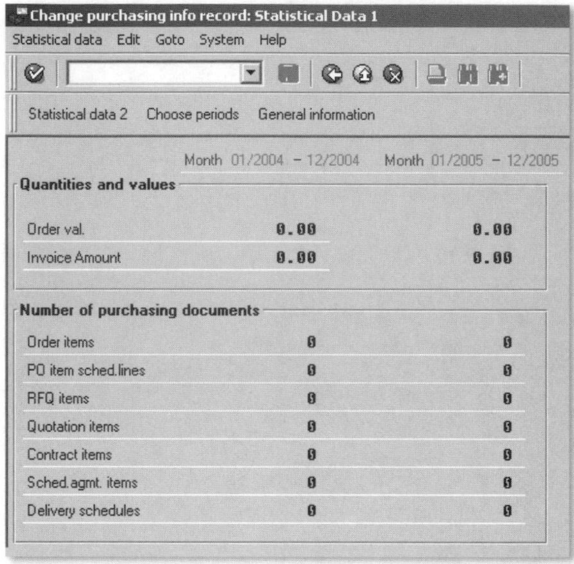

Figure 6.10 Statistical Data for Purchasing Information Record.

The statistical data screens shown in Figure 6.10 can be controlled to allow a comparison between two different time periods. The statistical data reflects information on:

- Order quantity and invoice value
- Number of Purchasing Documents
- Delivery Time Information
- Delivery Reliability Information
- Quantity Reliability Information

This chapter has shown that a significant amount of data is required in the SAP purchasing functionality. This data drives the purchasing of materials and services within a business. Accurate data reduces unnecessary delays of receiving material, which in turn reduces production problems and improves overall customer satisfaction.

7 Batch Management Data

Batch Management is an important part of a company's ability to produce, store, and sell material. The batch defines a quantity of material by characteristics unique to that batch. Those characteristics determine how the material in that batch is used, sold, or moved.

7.1 Batch Management Overview

7.1.1 Batch Definition

The definition of a batch will differ between companies, industries, and countries. For example, in the pharmaceutical industry there are strict guidelines and regulations that determine what a batch is. These regulations on batches and batch control include the ANSI/ISA-88 standard and the Food and Drug Administration (FDA) 21 CFR Part 11 specifications in the U.S.

There is no one correct definition of a batch; however, the following definition from ExxonMobil Aviation Lubricants may help.

"A batch is the specific quantity of a material produced in a single manufacturing process, i.e. under the same conditions, thus featuring identical properties. Each batch of material is given a batch number. Each batch of a material is tested with regard to relevant characteristics to ensure it meets the values or within the range for those characteristics."

A second definition of a batch is from the Marathon Oil Company, which significantly differs from other definitions.

"A batch is a shipment of a single product that is handled through the pipeline without mixing with preceding or following shipments."

This third definition of a batch is from the Hawaiian Coffee Association.

"A batch refers to a quantity of coffee coming to the roaster. Quantities of the same coffee arriving at different times would be viewed as separate batches. Changes from batch to batch—even of the same variety of bean—must be detected by the roaster if he is to produce coffees that are consistently the same."

Whatever the definition, the fact is that the batch has to be identified by a batch record. This can be as simple as identifying bags of coffee beans as they arrive at the plant, or as complex as identifying a batch by numerous qualifying characteristics to ensure quality and safety.

A batch of material can either be purchased from a vendor or produced internally. The need to manage materials by batch has been discussed above; however, in SAP the material must be identified as one that is batch-relevant. The batch-management indicator is found in the material master record on the Purchasing view, Sales/Plant view, Storage/Plant view, Warehouse view and the Work Scheduling view.

The indicator for the material can be changed from "batch managed" to "non-batch managed" only if there has been no stock for the current period and the previous period. This is to allow for any previous period material posting.

7.1.2 Pharmaceutical Industry

The identification of a batch record is especially important for the pharmaceutical industry due the regulations set down by the FDA in the U.S. and other regulatory bodies across the world, such as the Drugs Controller General of India (DCGI), Bundesgesundheitsamt (BGA) in Germany, Health Canada, and the Medicines and Healthcare Products Regulatory Agency (MHRA), in the United Kingdom.

These regulatory bodies are primarily interested in public safety. The regulations such as FDA 21 CFR Part 11, in the U.S., are aimed at improving the efficiency of quality control and the quality assurance process. Each batch produced has to be quality tested, with the results stored electronically against the batch number.

Product Recall

The batch number also can be used as the tracking device for companies in case of subsequent errors or contamination. Manufacturers publish product recalls every day, but for the pharmaceutical industry product recalls could be life-saving.

A pharmaceutical company can voluntarily recall product. If the company finds that a result from a test on a batch was incorrect and that puts the batch out of tolerance, then the product made from that batch could be hazardous. The errors could go all the way back to the vendor, if any of the material was purchased. If a vendor informs the company that a batch of purchased material was out of tolerance, then this batch must be traced through the production process in order to find all finished goods batches that may contain the faulty batch.

In the U.S., the FDA has the power to request that a company initiate a recall when it believes that a drug violates the Food, Drug and Cosmetic Act (FDCA). A recall will be requested when the FDA concludes that:

- A drug that has been distributed presents a risk of illness or injury or gross consumer deception,
- The manufacturer or distributor has not recalled the drug
- FDA action is necessary to protect the public health

In a recall, the manufacturer informs the retailer, wholesaler, or even the consumer how to identify the batch number on the product and what batch numbers are part of the recall.

7.2 Batch Master Record

7.2.1 Creating a Batch

The batch record can be created manually through the SAP menu using transaction code MSC1N. The navigation path is **SAP Menu • Logistics • Materials Management • Material Master • Batch • Create**. Figure 7.1 shows the batch-creation screen.

The batch number can be internally or externally assigned, and the configuration paths are described in Chapter 3.

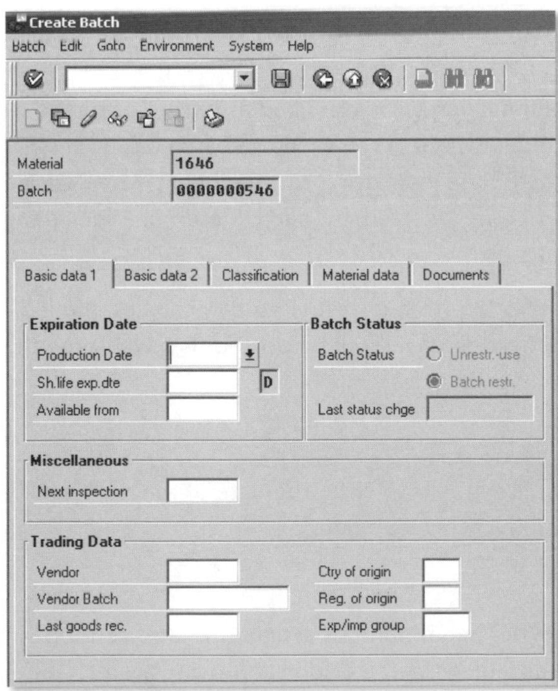

Figure 7.1 Initial Batch-Creation Screen

Production Date

The date when the batch was produced can be entered into this field. In some industries, this field is also used as the date the material was tested or re-tested. If a material is found to be still in tolerance after the shelf-life date has expired, the material can be re-tested, and the date of the re-test is entered into this field, in addition to a new shelf-life expiration date. Check with your clients to see how they need to use this field.

Shelf-Life Expiration Date

This date is the date on which the shelf life of this batch will expire. The shelf life of a product can vary between plants. This date can be used in the sales process, as customers may have set a requirement on the number of days shelf life remaining of a batch is acceptable. Some companies use this field to indicate the date on which a batch needs to be retested.

Available From

This field indicates when the batch will be available. For example, if a material needs to remain in the quality inspection process for a certain amount of days after testing, then the quality department can enter a date to inform other departments of when the batch is expected to be available.

Batch Status

The batch status indicator allows the batch to be classified as having restricted or unrestricted use. If the unrestricted indicator is set, then the batch has no restriction placed on its use. If the restricted use indicator is set, the batch is treated like blocked stock in planning, but can be selected by batch determination if the search includes restricted-use batches.

The batch status can be set to restricted from unrestricted by changing the indicator in the batch record. A material document will be posted that will show the movement of stock between the two statuses.

Next Inspection

This date field allows the quality department to enter the date of the next quality inspection of the batch, if applicable to this material.

Vendor Batch

If the material is purchased, then the batch number assigned by the vendor can be added to the batch record (See Figure 7.2). It is important to any product recall procedure that the vendor batch number is noted. The vendor batch number field allows a 15-character string to be entered.

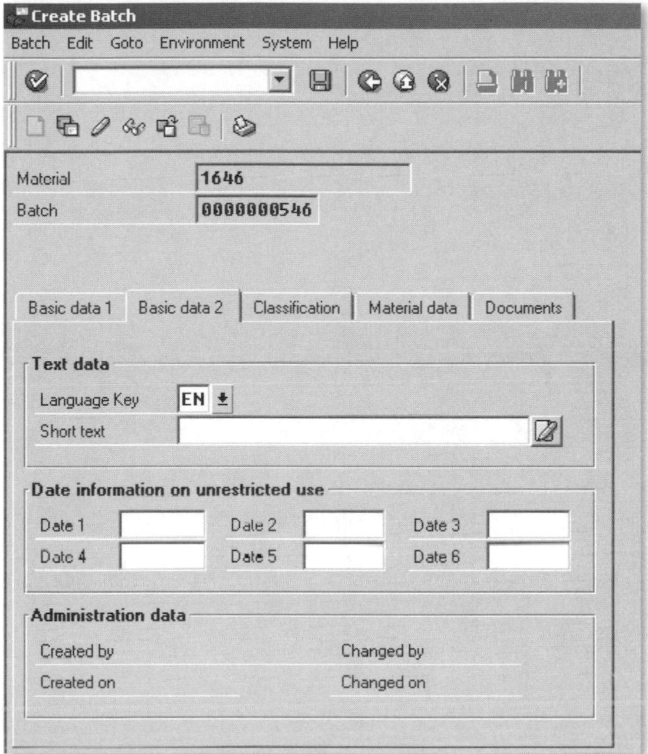

Figure 7.2 Second Batch-Entry Screen

The **short-text** field allows the user to enter a specific text for the batch record. Clicking on the icon next to the short-text field can create a longer text item, if required.

The other fields on the screen are six date fields. These fields do not have any standard functionality. The six date fields can be used for whatever purpose is defined by the client. For example, these fields could contain the dates on which the material was inspected by the quality department.

Class

Figure 7.3 shows the third screen for the batch creation transaction. The classification screen allows the user to classify this batch by using a specific class selected from the class type 23. When the class is created, it must be assigned to a class type. The class type for batch objects is 23.

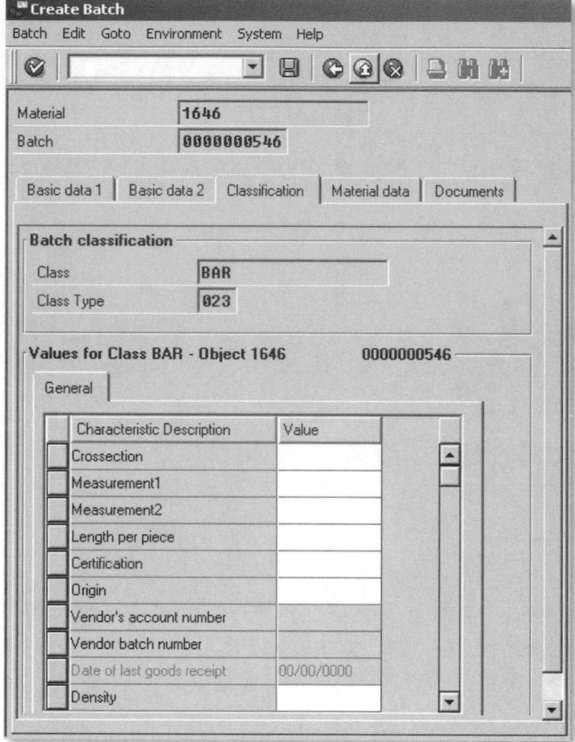

Figure 7.3 Data Entry Into Classification Screen for a Batch

Characteristics

The class has been created using a number of characteristics. The values for this batch are assigned to the characteristics. The values of the characteristics allow users to complete classification searches to find objects, in this case batches, given certain characteristic values. The values also can be used as part of the batch-determination functionality to select batches that have characteristic values within the determination search parameters.

Release Status

Once the values have been entered against the characteristics, the user has the option to change the status of the classification.

The default for the status is released. However, the user has the option to set the status as incomplete or locked. The incomplete status can be used when not all characteristic values are known at the time of data entry. Figure 7.4 shows the status options available to the user.

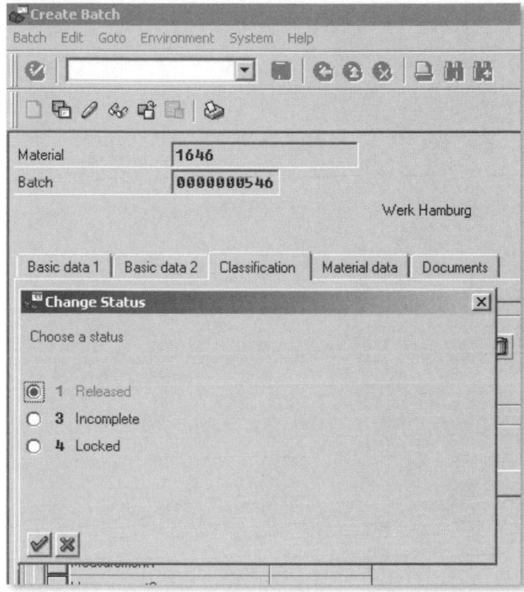

Figure 7.4 Release Status of Batch Record

Linked Documents

The last input screen for the batch record is the documents screen, shown in Figure 7.5. This allows the user to link documents that relate to the batch. These can be as simple as a quality testing document that has to be followed for testing each batch, or an engineering drawing for the specifications.

To allow a document to be linked to a batch a configuration step must be completed.

Use the transaction ODOC or use the navigation path **IMG • Logistics—General • Batch Management • Batch Master • Activate Document Management for Batches**.

The configuration is simply switching on the field to allow document management for batches.

Document Type

Linked documents must be defined in the document management system (DMS). The document type field allows the purchasing user to specify a document. This document for the batch will be that of a certain category. The categories are defined in the DMS. Depending on the industry of the client, the number of document types can vary. Document types can include recipes, specifications, quality inspection worklists, or engineering drawings, among others.

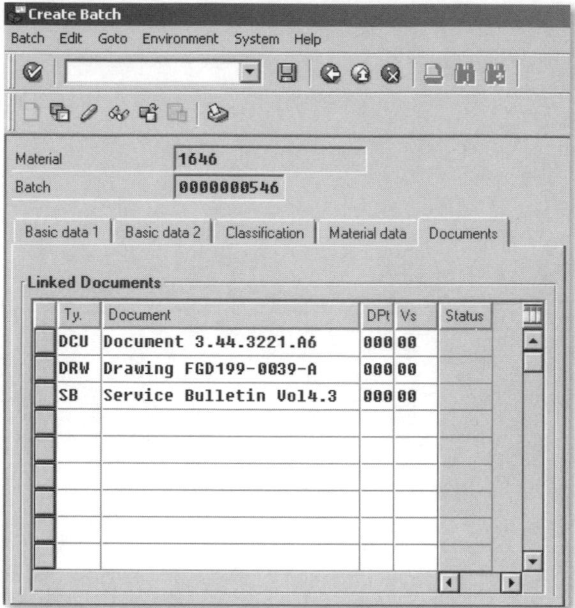

Figure 7.5 Screen for Linking Documents to the Batch Record

Document

Once the document type has been selected, the user can choose the relevant document via the matchcode, using the document type as a key. The document identification is created in the DMS.

Document Part

Two other fields that can be entered by the user include the document part and the version. The document part allows the user to enter a section or part of the document that is relevant to the batch. For instance, if the batch falls under a quality testing protocol that in total is 140 pages long, the relevant text for the batch may be a certain part or section. If this is the case, that information can be entered on this screen.

Version

Documents are continually revised and updated. For a batch record, it is important that the correct version of the document be identified in this section. An incorrect version number may allow incorrect quality testing or inspection.

7.2.2 Changing a Batch

Once the batch has been created, there may be an occasion where the batch record needs to be amended, either to modify a characteristic or to add a new linked document. To change a batch record use the transaction MSC2N or the navigation path **SAP Menu • Logistics • Materials Management • Material Master • Batch • Change**.

The user can make changes to the batch record, but these changes are recorded and are available for review. The batch record screen has an extra tab in the change mode. This tab accesses a screen to view all changes made to the batch record.

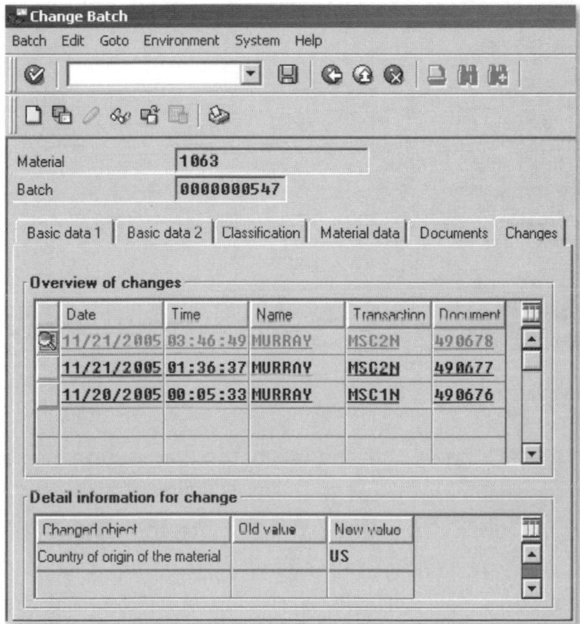

Figure 7.6 Changes to the Batch Record

The changes screen, shown in Figure 7.6, shows the changes made to the batch record. The information recorded includes the user who created and changed the record. It also shows the fields that have been changed, including their values. This information is important to some companies, as a strict audit record is needed to show compliance with federal or local regulations.

7.2.3 Deleting a Batch

There is no specific transaction for deleting a batch. It is possible to delete a batch through the change transaction MSC2N.

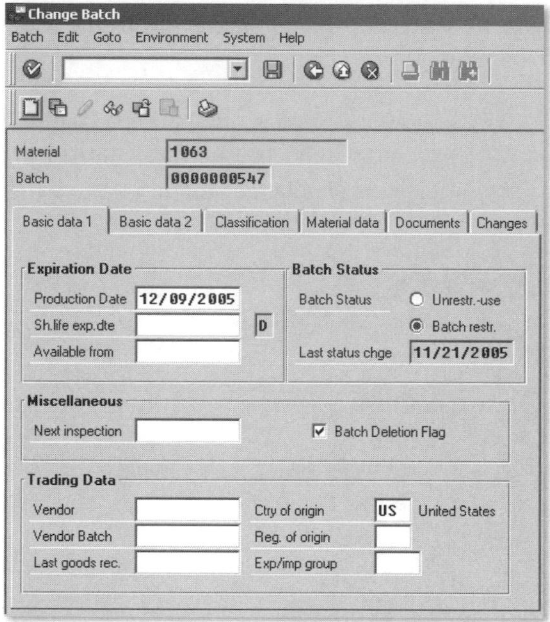

Figure 7.7 Initial Screen for Changing Batch

The initial screen, seen in Figure 7.7 shows the change-batch transaction has a field named **Batch Deletion** Flag that can be set if the batch is to be deleted. However, setting the deletion flag does not immediately delete the batch. The indicator allows the batch to be processed by an archiving program that will determine whether the batch can be deleted. If the batch cannot be deleted, the deletion flag will remain until either the archiving program determines that the batch can be deleted or until the deletion flag is removed.

The archiving process is unique to each company, so the deletion of a batch depends on how frequently information is archived. The BASIS team will be able to explain the archiving process for your particular client.

7.3 Batch Determination

The batch determination process is not unique to Materials Management. The process is important in Sales and Distribution, Production Planning, and Warehouse Management. Batch determination uses strategy types, search strategies, and search procedures in order for a batch to be identified in the relevant area.

The batch determination process uses the same type of selection protocol as described in pricing conditions; that is, the use of condition tables and access sequences

7.3.1 Batch Determination Condition Tables

The batch determination condition table consists of a number of fields that are selected and records that are created to assign values to those fields. A condition table can be created for each of the four areas that use batch determination.

The condition tables can be created in the IMG using the navigation path **IMG • Logistics—General • Batch Management • Batch Determination and Batch Check • Condition Tables**.

There are then five options for condition table creation:

- Inventory Management (Transaction OMA1)
- Process Order (Transaction OPLB)
- Production Order (Transaction OPLB)
- Sales and Distribution (Transaction V/C7)
- Warehouse Management (Transaction OMK4)

7.3.2 Batch Determination Access Sequences

For each batch strategy type, there is a batch determination access sequence. This allows the batch strategy type to access the condition tables in the correct sequence. The access sequences for the five areas, shown in section 7.3.1, can be configured using the navigation path **IMG • Logistics—General • Batch Management • Batch Determination and Batch Check • Access Sequences**.

It is important to note that these access sequences are cross-client. Any changes in one client will affect all clients.

7.3.3 Batch Strategy Types

The batch strategy type is the specification that tells the system what type of criteria to use during the batch determination process. A batch strategy can be defined in the five areas already mentioned. In materials management, a batch strategy type can be defined for different movement types.

The batch strategy type can be configured using the navigation path **IMG • Logistics—General • Batch Management • Batch Determination and Batch Check • Strategy Types • Define Inventory Management Strategy Types**.

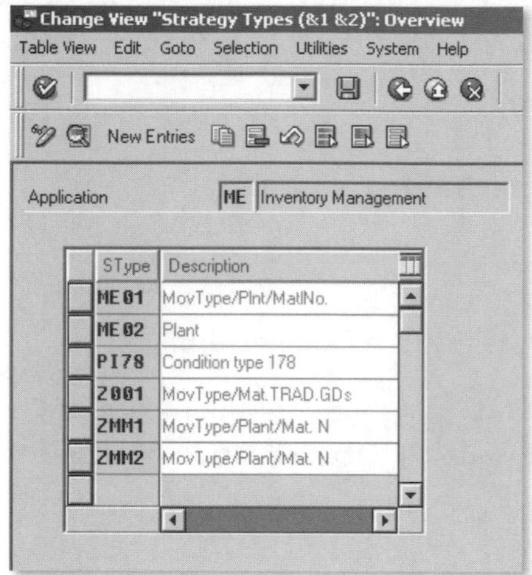

Figure 7.8 Initial Screen When Creating a New Strategy Type for Materials Management

Figure 7.8 shows the available batch strategy types for Materials Management. Strategy types ME01 and ME02 are pre-defined in the system and should not be modified. The other strategy types shown on this screen are user-created.

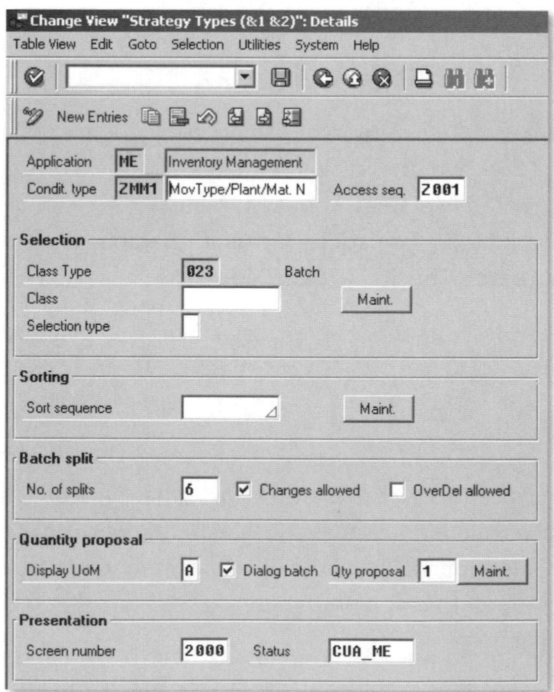

Figure 7.9 Details Needed to Create a Batch Strategy Type

Figure 7.9 shows the fields that have been created for batch strategy type ZMM1. When creating a new strategy type enter the new strategy type into the condition type field. The field is defined as four characters. To indicate a user created strategy type, it should commence with the letter Z.

The batch strategy type has to be assigned to one access sequence. The access sequence must already have been configured.

In the selection fields is an option to define the values of certain characteristics within a class. The values can be maintained by clicking on "maintain."

The selection type field allows the user to determine how the batches are selected at the commencement of the batch selection. If the selection type is left blank, then the system will display the batches that meet the selection criteria.

The sort sequence field allows the user to choose a sort that will define how the batches are sorted if they are selected. The sort sequence can be maintained on this screen if desired.

The batch split field defines the number of batch splits that are allowed during the batch determination.

7.3.4 Batch Search Procedure

The batch search procedure defines how the search is defined. The batch search procedure can be configured using the navigation path **IMG · Logistics—General · Batch Management · Batch Determination and Batch Check · Batch Search Procedure Definition · Define Inventory Management Search Procedure**.

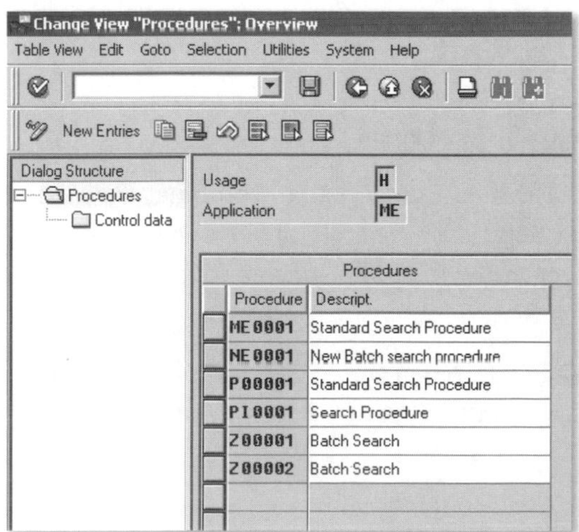

Figure 7.10 Batch-Search Procedures Defined for Inventory Management

The SAP system is supplied with one batch search procedure, ME0001. All user defined search procedures should begin with a **Z**. Once the name of the batch search procedure has been determined, the sequence of strategy types can be configured. To enter the strategy types, click on the **Control data** icon.

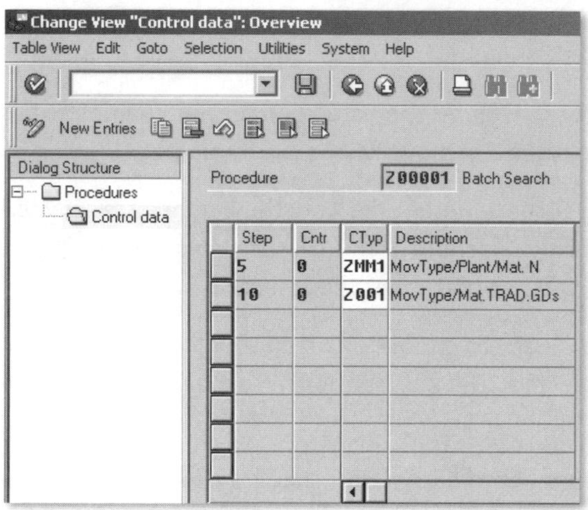

Figure 7.11 Strategy Types for Batch Search Procedure Z0000.

The batch search procedure is created to produce a step-by-step schema for a particular batch determination search. In figure 7.11, the batch search procedure Z00001 is defined to search for batches according to search type ZMM1 and then search type Z001. The batch search procedure can be configured to include other strategy types.

7.4 Batch Information Cockpit

7.4.1 Batch Information Cockpit Overview

The batch information cockpit (BIC) is a transaction that combines views and analyses of batch information in a single location. The BIC allows the user to select batches, display all the information regarding the batch, access follow-up transactions, and use the batch worklists.

The BIC is accessed using transaction BMBC or via the navigation path **SAP Menu • Logistics • Central Functions • Batch Management • Batch Information Cockpit**.

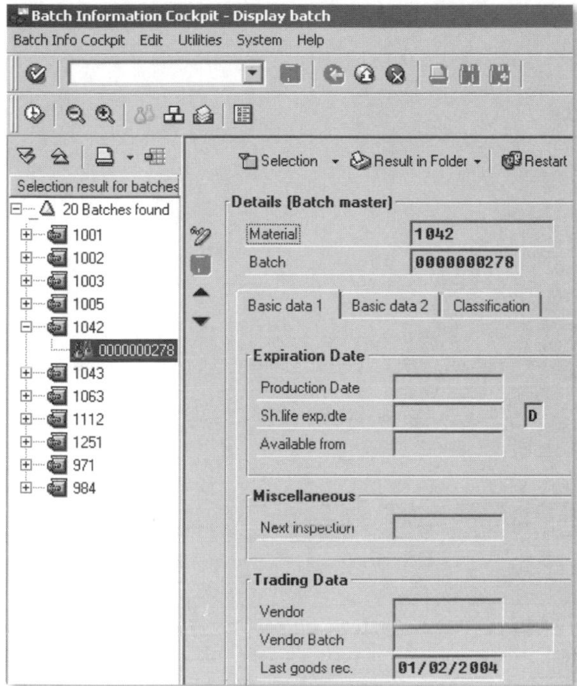

Figure 7.12 Central Area of Batch Information Cockpit (BIC)

In Figure 7.12, the BIC has been run, and 20 batches have been selected. The materials are shown and the matches can be displayed by highlighting the material. The information regarding the batch is then displayed in a main screen. There are a number of different screens with information on this batch, and the tabs indicate those screens.

The user can view the selections of a particular user group, defined in configuration, by selecting **Utilities • User Settings**.

The user can select a user group that has been configured in the IMG. The user group view is a way in which different departments can use the BIC to see batch information relevant to their department.

7.4.2 Batch Information Cockpit Standard Configuration

The SAP system is delivered with a pre-defined configuration for the selection and layout of the BIC. Using transaction OBIC_DIS, the configuration of the BIC layout can be displayed, but not changed. To get to the transaction use the navigation path **IMG • Logistics—General • Batch Management • Batch Information Cockpit • Display SAP Standard Selection**.

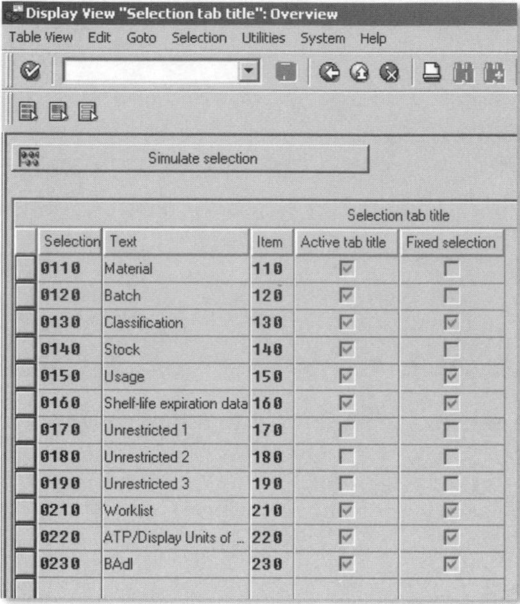

Figure 7.13 SAP Standard Selection for BIC

The SAP standard selection is shown in Figure 7.13. Fields of each of the tabs can be selected and displayed as shown in Figure 7.14

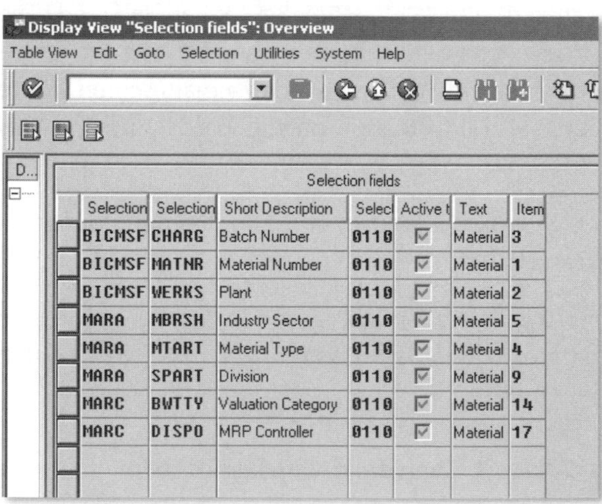

Figure 7.14 Fields Associated with Tabs from the SAP Standard Selection

7.4.3 Batch Information Cockpit User-Defined Configuration

If the standard SAP configuration does not address all the clients' requirements it is possible to modify the BIC. Some clients have found that the standard view of the BIC is not suitable for all departments that need information on batches. Therefore, the user-defined BIC can be modified so that different user groups can have their own view of the BIC.

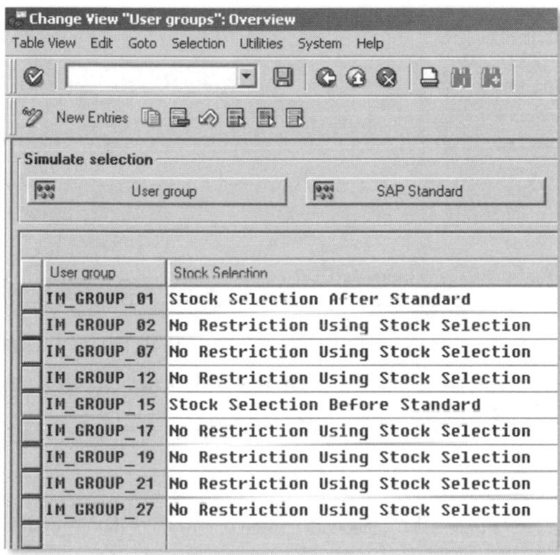

Figure 7.15 User Groups Defined for the BIC

Once the user group has been defined, the attributes to the BIC for that group can be created. In Figure 7.15 the user group can be highlighted and then the selection tab table field screen can be selected. The selection tab title is the structure that defines which fields are viewed in the BIC.

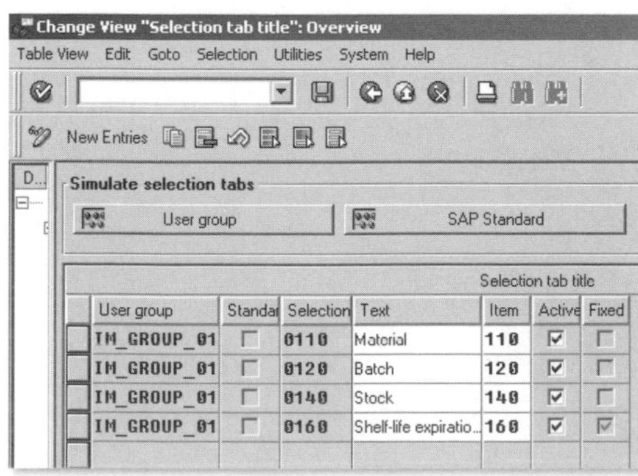

Figure 7.16 Selection Tab Fields Selected for the User Group

The screen shown in Figure 7.16 allows the user to define what tabs will be available to the specific user group and in what order they appear.

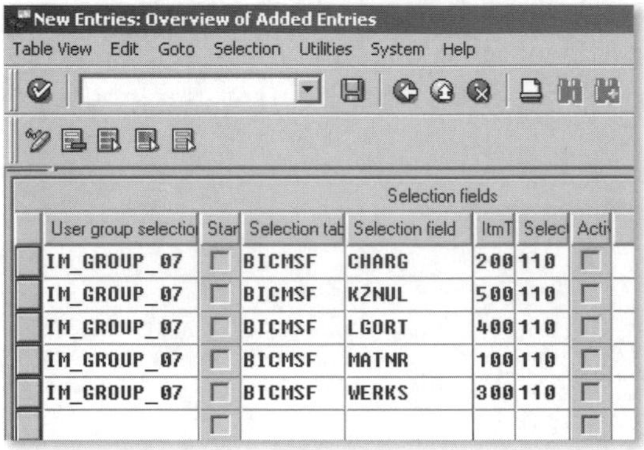

New Entries: Overview of Added Entries

Table View Edit Goto Selection Utilities System Help

			Selection fields			
User group selectio	Star	Selection tab	Selection field	ItmT	Selec	Acti
IM_GROUP_07	☐	BICMSF	CHARG	200	110	☐
IM_GROUP_07	☐	BICMSF	KZNUL	500	110	☐
IM_GROUP_07	☐	BICMSF	LGORT	400	110	☐
IM_GROUP_07	☐	BICMSF	MATNR	100	110	☐
IM_GROUP_07	☐	BICMSF	WERKS	300	110	☐
	☐					☐

Figure 7.17 Fields Selected for One Tab Specific to One User Group

Once the tabs have been selected for the specific user group, the individual fields can be selected, as shown in Figure 7.17. The structure of the tab and the placement of the fields depend on the requirements of the user group.

Batch Management is important to a growing number of industries. It has developed from just an identification of a group of items to a process that allows companies to perform product recalls, select and sell by batch characteristics and identify expiring stock. As the drive for a competitive advantage continues, companies will further investigate how batch information can lower production time and hasten material to the customer.

8 Material Master Record

Creation of a material master record depends on many different departments. Each layer of information is important in its own right, but the material record is not complete until all the relevant data has been entered.

The relevance of the material master data was discussed in Chapter 3. In this chapter, we shall discuss how material master records are loaded, created, modified and deleted.

8.1 Creating a Material Master Record

The standard transaction for creating a material master record is MM01. Other transactions can be used to create a material master. If the material type of the material to be created is known, then the material can be created using a transaction specific to that material type. So, if a material master record for a finished product is to be created, then the material user can use transaction code MMF1 to create a material master record.

8.1.1 Create a Material Master Record through a Schedule

If the material master record for an item has been decided upon, but not ready to be released until a specific date then the material can be created via a schedule. This functionality is part of the Engineering Change Management (LO-ECH).

To create a material based on a schedule, use transaction MM11 or the navigation path **SAP Menu • Logistics • Materials Management • Material Master • Material • Create (General) • Schedule**.

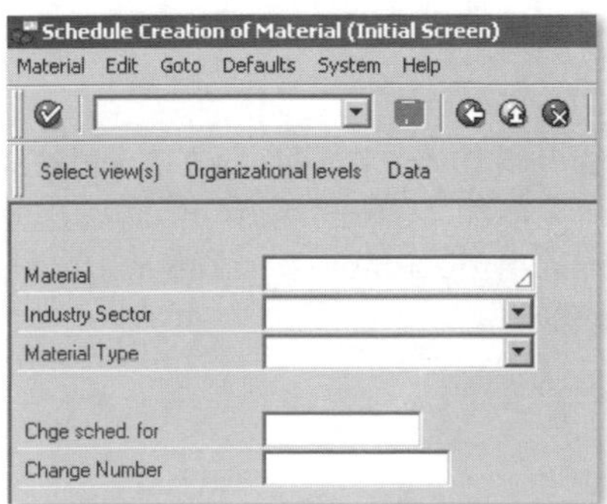

Figure 8.1 Entry Screen for Creating a Material Master Record with a Scheduled Release

The entry of this record, shown in Figure 8.1, is different from a normal material-master creation, as it requires a date to be entered for the creation of the material and, if applicable, an engineering change number. The change number would be created by the engineering department to reflect a change in a specification that requires, in this case, a new material number to be created.

The selection screens for this material creation are limited to the engineering screen and the data for the plant screen, as shown in Figure 8.2 and Figure 8.3.

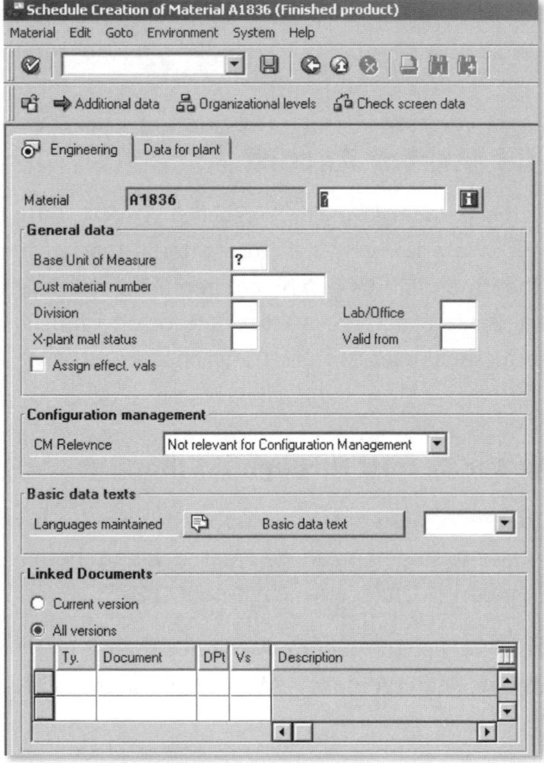

Figure 8.2 Engineering Screen for Transaction MM11

The screen in Figure 8.2, for engineering, requires the material user to enter a material description and a unit of measure for the material. The user can enter other relevant data, and can also link any relevant documents to this material, such as engineering, CAD, or design drawings.

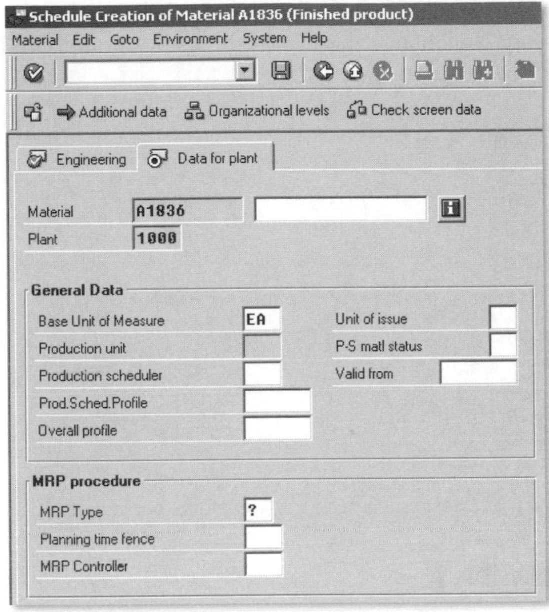

Figure 8.3 Plant Screen Data for Transaction MM11

The second data-entry screen for MM11 requires the material user to enter a MRP type, and if necessary, a MRP controller. There are a number of other fields, which can be entered for the plant level.

After the material master has been created, there will always be an need to update or change material and the next section will explain methods for changing the material master.

8.2 Changing a Material Master Record

8.2.1 Change a Material Master Record—Immediately

This is the most common way a material master is changed. The transaction code is MM02 and can be found via the navigation path **SAP Menu · Logistics · Materials Management · Material Master · Material · Change · Immediately**.

The initial screen for MM02 (see Figure 8.4) allows the material user to enter the material number and, if applicable, an engineering change number. Once a material number has been entered, the user may choose to select the particular area that is of relevance.

Once the material field or fields have been changed, the material is saved. After the material is saved, the system logs the change made and the user who initiated the change (See Figure 8.5 and Figure 8.6).

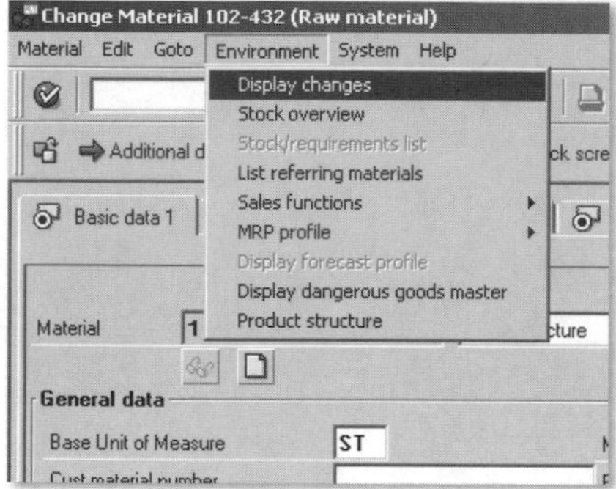

Figure 8.4 Menu Path for Finding the Log of Changes Made to a Material Master Record

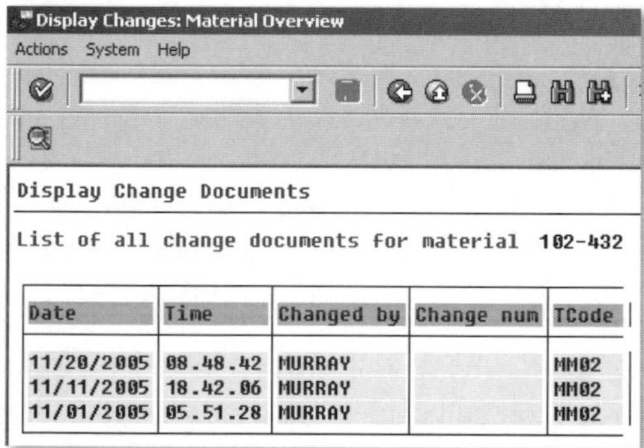

Figure 8.5 Material Change Display Showing Detail Change Information

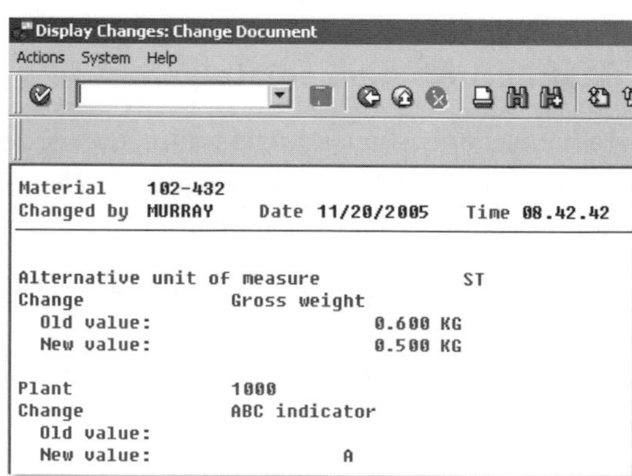

Figure 8.6 Details of a Single change Made to Material

8.2.2 Change a Material Master Record—Schedule

If the material is not scheduled to be changed until a certain date, then the material change can be set ahead of time and a date-activation transaction, MM13, can used to put the change into effect at the right time. The transaction code for this process is MM12 and can be found via the navigation path **SAP Menu · Logistics · Materials Management · Material Master · Material · Change · Schedule**.

The change can also be driven by an engineering change, and there is the opportunity to enter that change number into the scheduling screen, as shown in Figure 8.7.

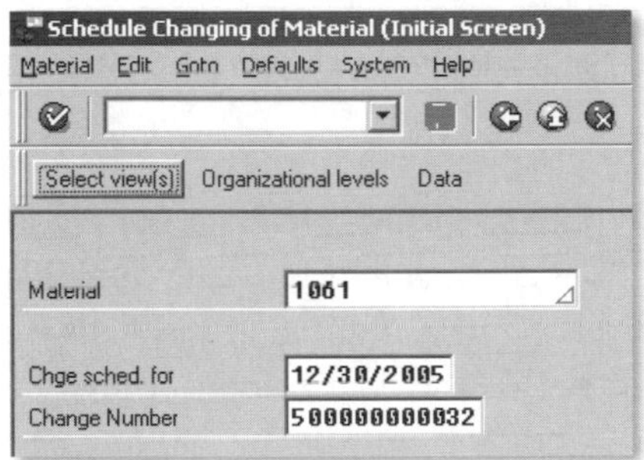

Figure 8.7 Initial Screen Allowing User to Schedule a Material Change

8.2.3 Change a Material Master Record—Activate

This transaction allows the material user to release changes made to a material or a group of materials based on when the changes were made. For instance, if a group of materials was changed because it received a new MRP controller number, then this transaction allows the material user to release the scheduled changes up to a certain date. Users can run this activation in test mode so that the actual changes do not take place.

The transaction code for this process is MM13 and can be found via the navigation path **SAP Menu · Logistics · Materials Management · Material Master · Material · Change · Activate**.

Activate To

This field should contain the key date needed to include all scheduled changes as shown in Figure 8.8. So if the field contains the date 12/21/05 then all changes up to that date will be included. If the date field is blank then the system assumes that today's date should be used.

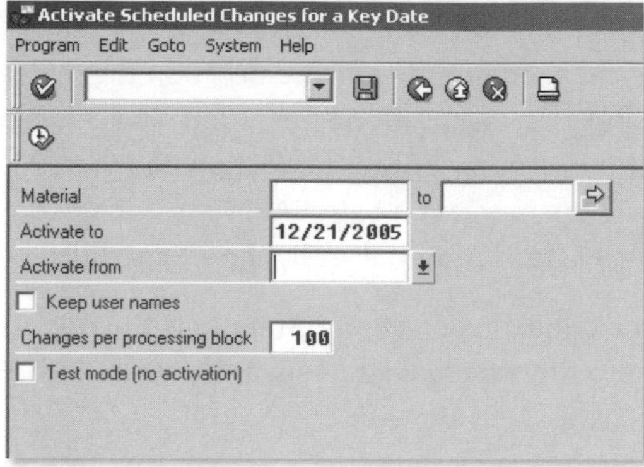

Figure 8.8 Activation Transaction for Scheduled Changes Made Through Transaction MM12.

Activate From

This date is used to define the first date from which to include changes. For example, if this field contains the date 01/01/01, the system will include all scheduled changes made to the material from that date to the date entered in the **Activate to** field. If this field is blank, the system assumes that the field content should be copied from the **Activate to** field, and the activation will only be for that one day.

Keep User Names

This indicator allows the material user to decide what information is copied to the change document. If the indicator is set, then names of the user who made the scheduled changes will be copied across. If the indicator is not set, only the name of the person who ran the activation transaction will be copied across. It would be prudent to confer with your client as to the requirements of any audit trail they may require.

Changes Per Processing Block

This field allows the material user to enter a value of between 100 and 500, which can increase the efficiency of the transaction at runtime. If there is a major change that requires more processing power, then this field can be changed to a higher number. However, if the indicator **Keep user names** is set, then this field must be set to one.

Test Mode

This indicator allows the material user to run the transaction in test mode, which does not activate any of the scheduled changes.

In the next section the deletion of a material master record is discussed. This is something not all companies wish to consider and discussions with your client is important.

8.3 Material Master Deletion

Material master deletion is a process that should be secure and require multiple checks prior to any action.

The path to deleting a material starts with transaction MM06 (or MM16 for scheduling a deletion). This transaction is to flag a material for deletion. Not all companies delete their materials, even if they have stopped using them or producing them. Returns, repairs, and other needs, cause a material to have a life in the system long after its relevance in production has ended.

8.3.1 Flag for Deletion—Immediately

This transaction allows a company to flag a material for deletion if it is decided that the material will never be used in the system again. This transaction does not delete the material, but flags the material master for deletion.

This transaction is called MM06 and can be accessed through the navigation path **SAP Menu · Logistics · Materials Management · Material Master · Material · Flag for Deletion · Immediately**.

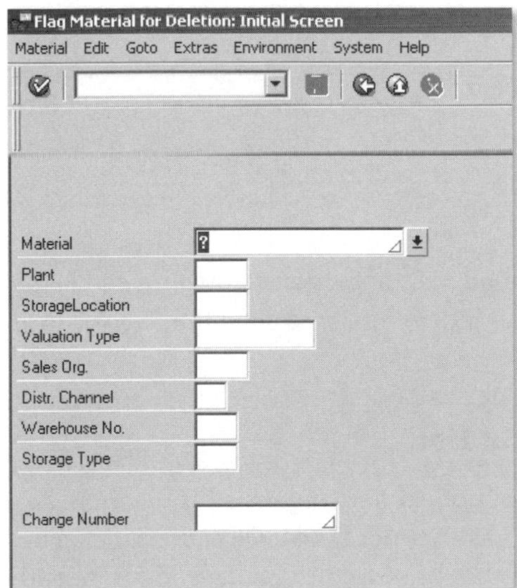

Figure 8.9 Flag-for-Deletion Screen

The screen shown in Figure 8.9 shows the data that can be entered in the transaction. The material user has the option to delete the material at different levels. Entering just the material number will flag the material throughout the system. Entering a plant or a sales organization or a warehouse number will flag the material to be deleted at that same level, i.e., sales organization or warehouse level.

8.3.2 Flag for Deletion—Schedule

This transaction is called *MM16* and can be accessed through the navigation path **SAP Menu • Logistics • Materials Management • Material Master • Material • Flag for Deletion • Schedule**.

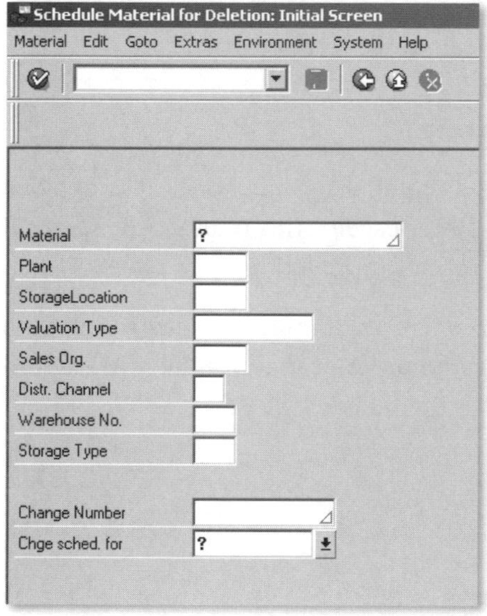

Figure 8.10 Scheduling Flag-for-Deletion Transaction

The difference between this and the immediate transaction, shown here in Figure 8.10 is that the material user has to enter a date for scheduling the flag-for-deletion date, not the actual deletion date.

8.3.3 Flag for Deletion—Proposal List

Within transaction *MM06*, there is an option to flag materials for deletion via a proposal list. Using the screen menu, **Extras • Proposal List** will cause a dialog box to appear with materials that the system has proposed to be flagged for deletion (See Figure 8.11). These materials are without any stock in the system.

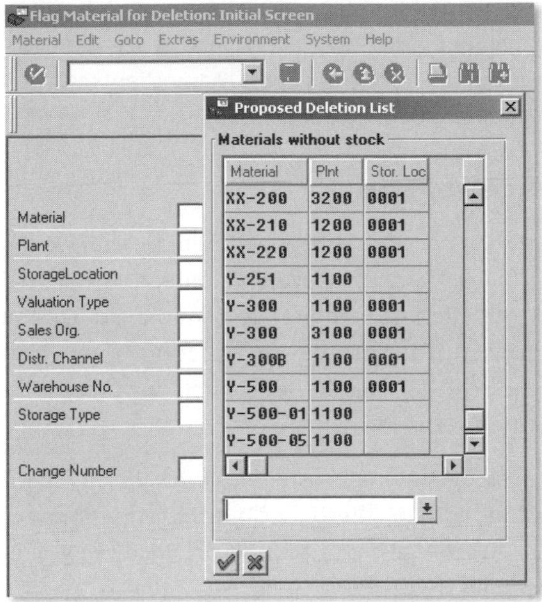

Figure 8.11 Proposal List for Materials That can be Flagged for Deletion

8.3.4 Material Master Archiving

The material master archiving program will delete the materials that have been flagged for deletion and that are suitable for deletion. The transaction for the archiving process is MM71. This transaction can be found using the navigation path **SAP Menu • Logistics • Materials Management • Material Master • Other • Archiving • Archive/Delete**.

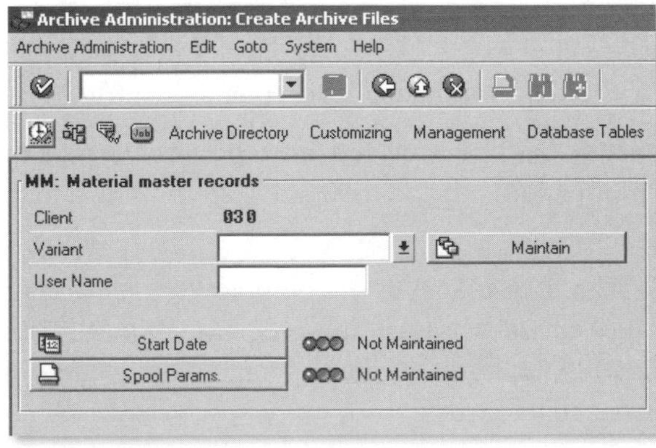

Figure 8.12 Screen for Archiving and Deleting Material Master Records

Companies often delay setting procedures for archiving materials until after the implementation of Materials Management. As an SAP consultant, it is good practice to inform clients about their long-term archiving needs. Many clients will run archiving as part of their monthly or semi-yearly routines.

8.3.5 Remove a Material-Deletion Flag

It is possible to remove the deletion flag once it has been entered, but before the archiving program has been run. Using transaction MM06, enter the material number of the material that has the deletion flag required to be removed. On the initial screen, enter any specific relevant plant or sales organization. The subsequent screen will highlight where the deletion flags are set. By deleting those indicators, the flagged for deletion status is removed.

In the next section, the process of loading material master files is discussed. Loading of materials from a legacy system may be the only time this is performed. However with the number of company mergers and acquisitions increasing, you may the material master loading is more frequent.

8.4 Loading Material Master Records

8.4.1 Loading Material Master Records via Direct Input

When working on a new implementation for a company, you may be asked about the loading of material master records. If the implementation involved re-engineering, the client may have had a project to rationalize and cleanse its material master records from the legacy systems. In order to construct suitable material master records based on legacy records, the client would have needed a process for adding to the SAP material master record necessary details that would not have been available from the legacy item master. This may have included collecting information from other legacy systems, or manual collection and entry.

Once the material master information has been collated in a repository outside of SAP, it is possible to load that information into the new SAP system using a load program.

Initially before any materials are loaded into SAP, it is good practice to clean out any spurious material records. It is advisable to use the program RMMMDE00, run from transaction SE38, to delete all materials from the client. This will ensure a clean environment for the material data load.

Using the material load program RMDATIND, through transaction code SE38, the client can load their items into SAP and into new material master records (See Figure 8.13).

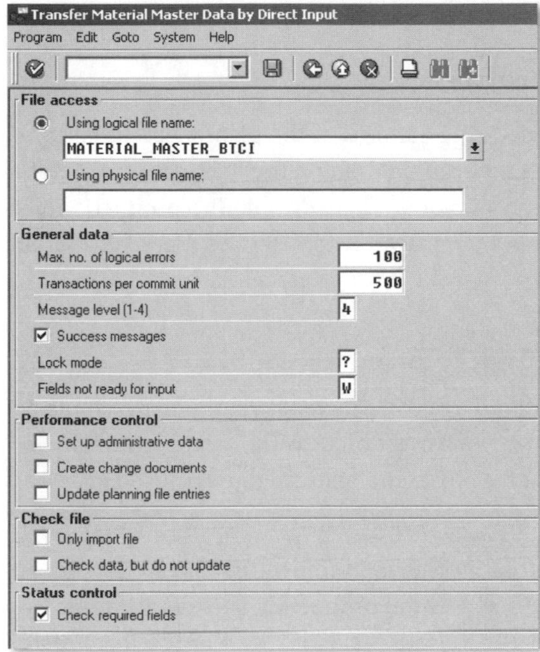

Figure 8.13 RMDATIND Program for Loading Material Master Records

Another program can generate test data for the initial load program. The test-data generation program is RMDATGEN and can be run from transaction SE38.

8.4.2 Distribution of Material Master Records via ALE

Material master records can be moved from one system to another via Application Link Enabling (ALE), a middleware solution in SAP's Business Framework Architecture (BFA). ALE can integrate data and processes between SAP systems and non-SAP systems. Messages between the systems are distributed by IDocs. An IDoc comprises a header, data segments, and a status record.

During a transfer of data, the outbound system creates an IDoc containing the data to be transferred, and this is transferred to the target system. In the target system, the IDoc starts inbound processing. The data is processed and then posted in the application, in this case the material master creation transaction.

An ALE environment that moves material records as described can be found in clients who control the creation of material master records centrally and then push the new materials out to their other SAP systems around the world.

The next section discusses the production version. This is important for the production staff and planning department.

8.5 Production Versions

8.5.1 Production Version Overview

A production version can be assigned to a material at the plant level. It describes the types of production techniques that can be used on the material. The material can have any number of production versions assigned to it. The production version can only be assigned to materials purchased externally and materials that are produced in-house.

8.5.2 Creating a Production Version

The production version can be entered against a material via the material master creation transaction (MM01) or change transaction (MM02). The production version can only be entered at the plant level, so the material must be used in at least one plant.

The production version dialog box can be reached through the MRP, Work Scheduling or Costing screens. Figure 8.14 shows the production version dialog box via the MRP screen. We will explain the various fields in the **Production Version Overview**.

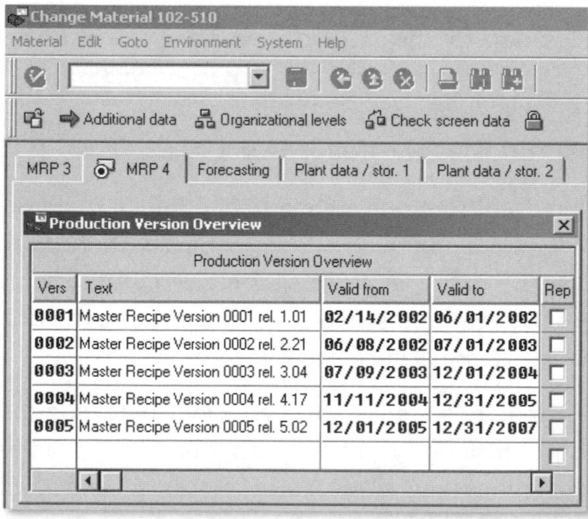

Figure 8.14 Entry Screen for Material Production Versions

Version

This is the production version key field: the key that determines what production techniques are applicable for the material.

Version Text

This field is a description for the production version and is a 40-character field.

Valid To/Valid From

These date fields allow the production user to determine the date range for which the production version is valid.

Repetitive Manufacturing

If this indicator is set, it means that the production version is allowed to be used in repetitive manufacturing.

Once these fields are entered, then the production version details can be added on the next screen, shown in Figure 8.15.

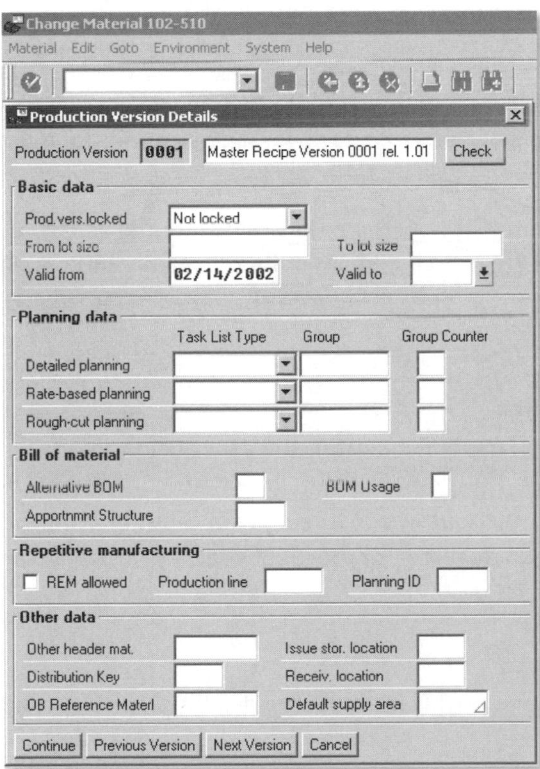

Figure 8.15 Details of Production Value Key for Production Planning

Basic Data

The first field in the basic data section specifies whether the production version is locked or not locked. The next two fields relate to the minimum and maximum lot sizes applicable for this particular production version. The basic data section also includes the validity dates.

Planning Data

There are three planning areas, which can be defined in the production version. These are:

- detailed planning
- rate-based planning
- rough-cut planning

For each of these planning types a task list, a task-list group, and a task counter can be selected. By entering a value for these, a particular task is identified for the production version, and thus a particular task is identified for the material.

Bill of Material Data

The bill of material data that can be entered for the production version includes an alternative bill of materials, a bill of materials usage key, and an apportionment structure.

An apportionment structure determines how the costs are distributed as regards co-products. The system uses the apportionment structure to create a settlement rule that distributes the costs from the order header to the order items, that is, the co-products.

Repetitive Manufacturing Data

In addition to the repetitive-manufacturing indicator, the other fields are for the product line and the planning ID. The product line is one that is identified for repetitive manufacturing. This is important when working with capacity planning. The planning ID is used to group together production versions. This can be selected from the drop-down selection.

Other Production-Version Data

The last group of fields includes the receiving location, the default supply area and the issuing storage location.

8.5.3 Production Versions—Mass Processing

There is a transaction that allows a different approach to entering production versions. A mass processing approach allows the production user to change production versions collectively, thus saving time. Transaction code C223 can be used to enter the information on production version via the Production Planning menu.

The production department uses this transaction when entering large numbers of production versions for a plant.

The navigation path of transaction code C223 is **SAP Menu • Logistics • Production • Master Data • Production Versions**.

8.6 Revision Levels

8.6.1 Revision Level Overview

A revision level identifies a certain change status of a material. It is related to the change status of an engineering change record. The revision level can be assigned to a material within the material master record.

The revision level can be entered into the material master from the MRP screens. There is an icon below the plant field that creates a dialog box, shown in Figure 8.16. The dialog box requires the production user to enter an engineering change number and a revision number.

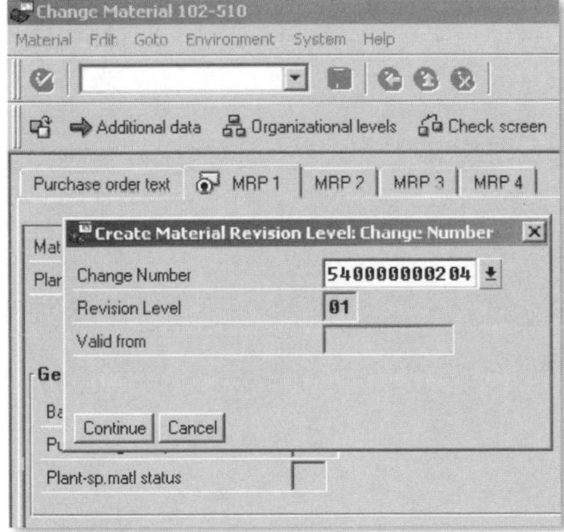

Figure 8.16 Dialog Box for Revision Number Within Material Master Change Record (MM02)

The engineering change document must relate to the particular material being changed; otherwise the revision level cannot be entered.

When the production user enters a revision number, the system will check to ensure that the revision number has not been used before and that it follows the sequence. The revision level functionality is configurable.

8.6.2 Revision Level Configuration

Before any configuration is performed on revision levels, a configuration step needs to be performed in the Engineering Change Management (ECM) area. Transaction code OS54 is the setup transaction for the control data and that needs to be configured to make revision levels active. The navigation path is **IMG • Logistics—General • Engineering Change Management • Set Up Control Data**

The key configuration for the material master is in transaction OS55. This creates the sequence for the revision levels for materials. The navigation path is **IMG • Logistics—General • Engineering Change Management • Revision Levels • Define Revision Levels for Materials**

In this chapter, material creation, modification and deletion were discussed. The material master is a highly complex master file with hundreds of links to transactions in SAP. Errors made in the material master can have serious effects on other modules, such as Sales and Distribution, Production Planning, Quality Management etc. The number of users who have access to the material master file should be limited. Any change should be carefully considered before you make it and should be audited after it is made.

9 Vendor Master Record

The Accounting or Purchasing departments can create the Vendor Master record. The record contains all the relevant data that helps the purchasing choose vendors based on negotiated price and performance, while the financial data aids the accounting department with invoicing and payables.

In previous chapters we discussed the relevant data found in the vendor master. In this chapter we shall discuss the mechanics of vendor master records and the less common elements that are important in vendor management, such as one-time vendors and vendor sub-ranges.

9.1 Creating Vendor Master Record

Earlier, we explained that the vendor master can be created using one of three transaction codes:

- ▶ XK01—Create Vendor Centrally
- ▶ FK01—Create Vendor via Accounting
- ▶ MK01—Create Vendor via Purchasing.

From the vendor menu within Materials Management, the purchasing user has the option to create the vendor master either centrally or through Purchasing. It is not usual for the purchasing department to know all the issues pertaining to the accounting side of the vendor relationship, so the different transaction codes make vendor creation easier for the departmental users.

The purchasing department uses transaction MK01 to create a vendor with just the relevant purchasing information (see Figure 9.1). This transaction can be found using the navigation path **SAP Menu • Logistics • Materials Management • Purchasing • Master Data • Vendor • Purchasing • Create**.

The purchasing user can enter the vendor number if the vendor number field has been defined as allowing external number ranges. This depends on the configuration for the account group. Otherwise, the vendor number is generated by the system, depending on the number range assigned.

The vendor number ranges are defined in the accounting area of configuration. It is possible to define a number range to be between some specific numbers, i.e., 9000 and 99990000, which can be assigned to an account group.

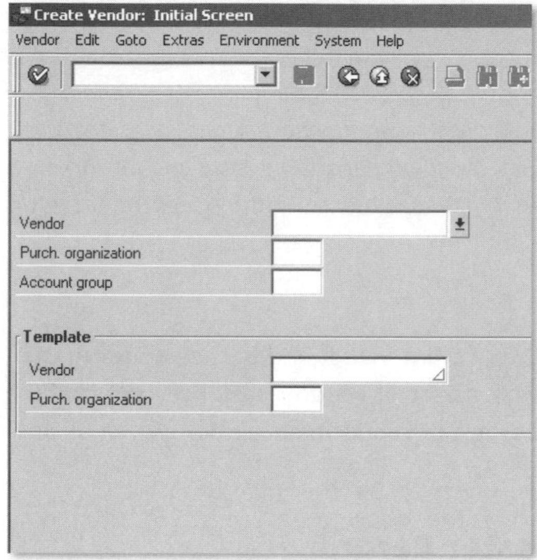

Figure 9.1 Initial Data Entry Screen for Transaction MK01

The vendor number ranges can be defined using the transaction XKN1 or by following the navigation path **IMG • Financial Accounting • Accounts Receivable and Accounts Payable • Vendor Accounts • Master Data • Preparations for Creating Vendor Master Data • Create Number Ranges for Vendor Accounts**.

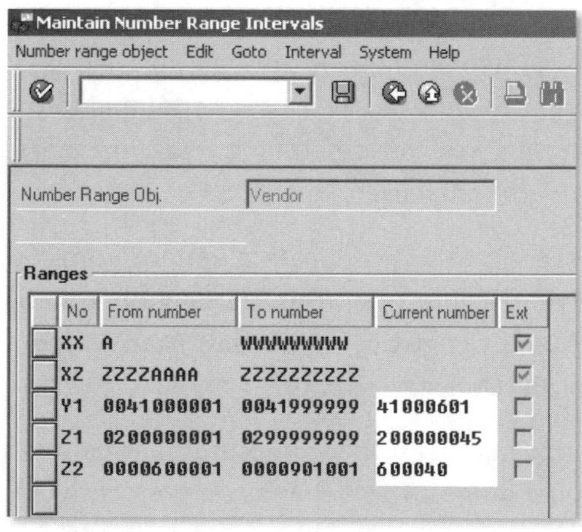

No	From number	To number	Current number	Ext
XX	A	WWWWWWWWW		☑
XZ	ZZZZAAAA	ZZZZZZZZZZ		☑
Y1	0041000001	0041999999	41000601	☐
Z1	0200000001	0299999999	200000045	☐
Z2	0000600001	0000901001	600040	☐

Figure 9.2 Transaction XKN1

In Figure 9.2, you can see that the number range is defined by a two-character code. The purchasing user can enter the code and then define the number range. This cannot overlap with existing number ranges. The user then has the ability to define the number range as external by highlighting the **EXT** field. If the number range is not defined as external, it is defaulted to be internally assigned. The user can define the current number of the vendor master if the internally assigned numbers need to start at a certain point.

Once the number range has been defined, it can be assigned to an account group or many account groups (see Figure 9.3). The account groups are defined for the vendor in the Accounting configuration, using the navigation path **IMG • Financial Accounting • Accounts Receivable and Accounts Payable • Vendor Accounts • Master Data • Preparations for Creating Vendor Master Data • Define Account Groups with Screen Layouts**.

The vendor account group is a way of grouping vendors that have the same number range and have the same attributes entered. The account group is defined to allow certain fields to be seen and entered on the vendor master.

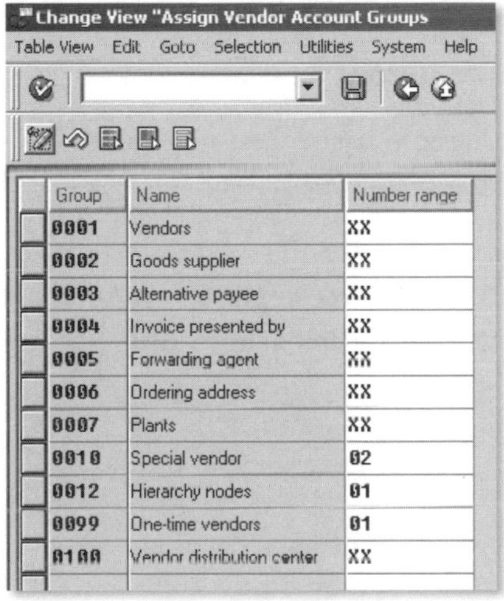

Group	Name	Number range
0001	Vendors	XX
0002	Goods supplier	XX
0003	Alternative payee	XX
0004	Invoice presented by	XX
0005	Forwarding agent	XX
0006	Ordering address	XX
0007	Plants	XX
0010	Special vendor	02
0012	Hierarchy nodes	01
0099	One-time vendors	01
0100	Vendor distribution center	XX

Figure 9.3 Assignment of Number Range to Vendor Account Group

The assignment of vendor number range to the vendor account group can be configured using the navigation path **IMG • Financial Accounting • Accounts Receivable and Accounts Payable • Vendor Accounts • Master Data • Preparations for Creating Vendor Master Data • Assign Number Ranges to Vendor Account Groups**.

The vendor master record is especially relevant to a purchasing organization. When creating the vendor, the purchasing user is determining the data associated with that vendor that is relevant only to the single purchasing organization. A vendor often may deal with many purchasing department of a single company, and the negotiations between the vendor and the company are limited to a specific geographical area, which may relate to a single purchasing organization. For instance, if a global telecommunications company negotiates rates and discounts with a company, the terms may be different for the company's Indian locations than for the Mexican locations or the locations in China. Therefore, when entering the vendor master record for this telecommunications company, the differences between purchasing organizations may be significant.

On the entry screen of transaction MK01, it is possible to use another vendor/purchasing organization as a template for the new vendor. This is useful when entering the same vendor for a number of purchasing organizations, as it saves having to make unnecessary entries. This will also reduce the level of data-entry errors.

9.2 Changing Vendor Master Record

A vendor master record can be changed in two ways, either with a current change, or a planned change.

9.2.1 Change Vendor Master Record—Current

This functionality is the normal way in which a record is changed. The purchasing user will want the change in the record to take effect immediately.

The transaction to change the current vendor master record is MK02 and can be found using the following navigation path: **SAP Menu • Logistics • Materials Management • Purchasing • Master Data • Vendor • Purchasing • Change**. The transaction screen is shown in Figure 9.4.

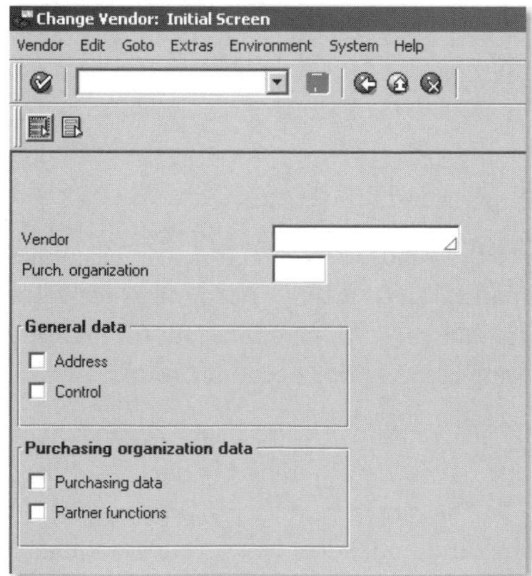

Figure 9.4 Transaction MK02

The purchasing user has the option of selecting the relevant area that needs to be modified from the General or Purchasing screens. The user would not be able to change the accounting data for this vendor via this transaction code. To change the accounting data for the vendor, the user should use transaction code FK02 or the navigation path **SAP Menu • Accounting • Financial Accounting • Accounts Payable • Master Records • Change (Current)**.

9.2.2 Change Vendor Master Record—Planned

This transaction can be used when the purchasing user wishes to have a vendor master record changed at a specific future date.

The transaction to change the current vendor master record is MK12 and can be found using the following navigation path **SAP Menu • Logistics • Materials Management • Purchasing • Master Data • Vendor • Purchasing • Change (Planned)**.

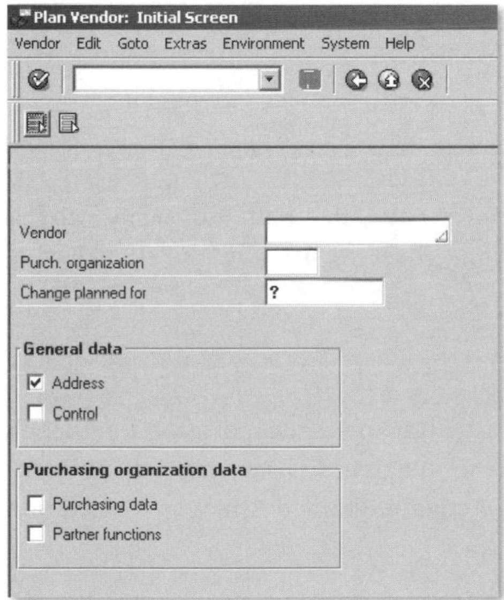

Figure 9.5 Transation MK12

With transaction MK12, the purchasing user can enter a date on which the changes entered for this record will become valid from. Figure 9.5 shows that the **Change planned for** field is a date field. As with transaction MK02, the user only has the option of selecting the relevant area that needs to be modified from the General or Purchasing screens.

9.2.3 Display Planned Changes to Vendor Master Records

After the planned changes have been specified for the vendor master records, it is possible to view all the planned changes. Transaction MK14, shown in Figure 9.6, allows the purchasing user to enter a range of variables in order to view the planned changes made to vendors. The resulting report shows the vendors that have planned changes pending and what changes have been made.

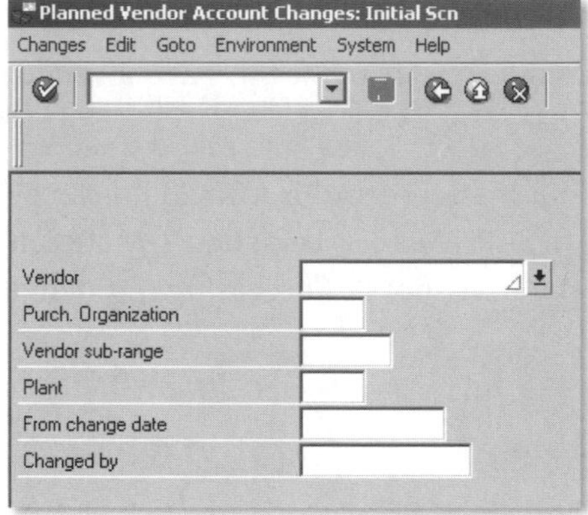

Figure 9.6 Transaction MK14 and Selection Fields for Viewing Vendor Master Changes

The transaction MK14 can be found using the navigation path **SAP Menu • Logistics • Materials Management • Purchasing • Master Data • Vendor • Purchasing • Planned Changes**.

9.2.4 Activate Planned Changes

The planned changes to the vendor master can be activated using transaction MKH3 or via the navigation path **SAP Menu • Logistics • Materials Management • Purchasing • Master Data • Vendor • Activate Planned Changes • Activation Online**.

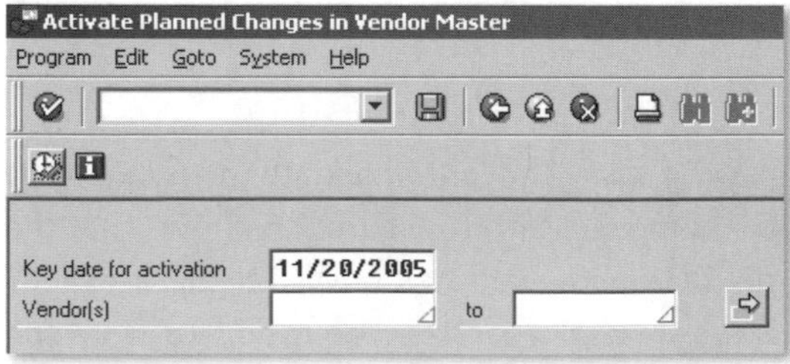

Figure 9.7 Screen for Activating Planned Changes for Vendor Master

As Figure 9.7 shows, the purchasing user can enter a single vendor or a range of vendors. The key date for activation is the final date on which changes can be activated. The field defaults to the current date.

A further transaction, MKH4, allows the purchasing user to create a session to perform the activation of the vendor master changes. This should be used for large mass changes of vendor information, where system performance may be an issue and online activation is not practical.

9.2.5 Change Vendor Account Group

There is a transaction that can change the account group a vendor is assigned to. This is a difficult transaction to use and should only be offered to the client with a strong warning.

Transaction XK07 (see Figure 9.8) allows the purchasing user to change the account group, but the vendor master number must be compatible with the number range of the new account group.

Figure 9.8 Changing of Account Group for Vendor Master Record.

The change of vendor account group can be found via the navigation path **SAP Menu • Logistics • Materials Management • Purchasing • Master Data • Vendor • Central • Account Group Change**.

9.3 Deleting Vendor Master Record

The decision to delete a vendor master record needs to be made carefully, and by more than one user. All concerned parties, including accounting and purchasing, need to be involved.

9.3.1 Flag a Vendor Master Record for Deletion

A vendor master record can be flagged for deletion using the purchasing transaction MK06. This can be reached through the navigation path **SAP Menu • Logistics • Materials Management • Purchasing • Master Data • Vendor • Purchasing • Flag for Deletion**.

On the initial data entry screen, the purchasing user can enter the vendor number and the purchasing organization. Figure 9.8 shows the next screen where the user can determine how the deletion should proceed.

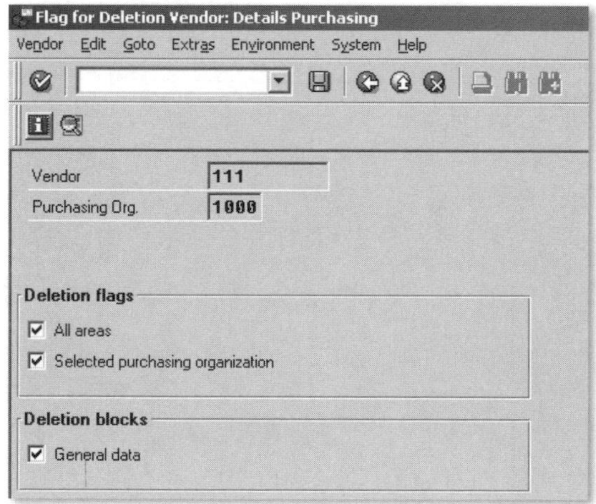

Figure 9.9 Flag-For-Deletion Fields of Transaction MK06

The two indicators in Figure 9.9 allow the purchasing user to determine what can be deleted and what should not.

Deletion Flags—All Areas

If this indicator is set, then all the information in the vendor master will be deleted.

Deletion Blocks—General Data

Setting this indicator prevents the information in the general data area from being deleted.

9.3.2 Deleting Vendor Records via Archiving

Once a vendor master record has been flagged for deletion, then the actual deletion can take place by running the archiving program in the financial accounting functionality.

The transaction F58A allows the financial users to run an archiving program for vendor master data. The transaction (See Figure 9.10) can be found using the navigation path **SAP Menu • Accounting • Financial Accounting • Accounts Payable • Periodic Processing • Archiving • Vendors**.

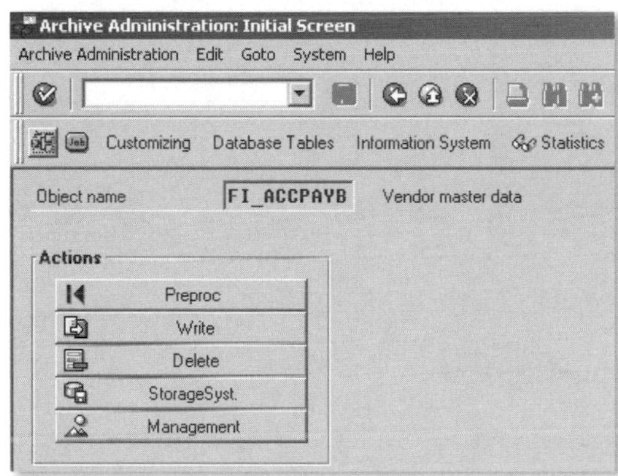

Figure 9.10 Archiving Transaction F58A

9.4 Display Vendor Master Record

Vendor master records can be displayed in a number of ways.

9.4.1 Display Vendor Master Record—Current

The vendor record is normally displayed via the transaction MK03 or via the navigation path **SAP Menu • Logistics • Materials Management • Purchasing • Master Data • Vendor • Purchasing • Display (Current)**.

9.4.2 Display Vendor Master Record—Per Key Date

The vendor master record can also be displayed by how it will be defined at a future date (See Figure 9.11). If many changes are to be made to a vendor master record, users may want to view the vendor master record at a certain date in the future. This can be performed with transaction MK19 or via the navigation path **SAP Menu • Logistics • Materials Management • Purchasing • Master Data • Vendor • Purchasing • Display (Per Key Date)**.

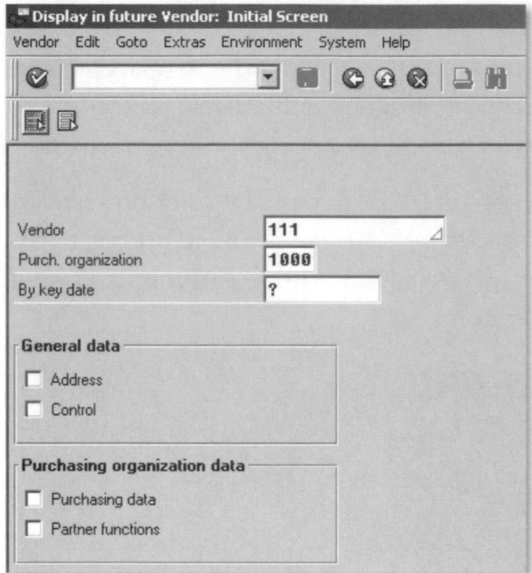

Figure 9.11 Selection Screen for Displaying Vendor Master at a Future Date

9.4.3 Display Vendors—Purchasing List

Transaction MKVZ allows the purchasing user to display the vendors for a given selection criteria. As Figure 9.12 shows, the selection can be made by vendor, purchasing organization, search term, and account group.

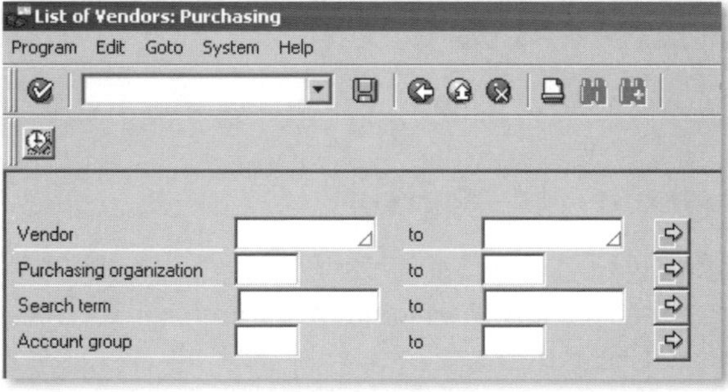

Figure 9.12 Selection Screen in Transaction MKVZ

The transaction MKVZ can also be located by using the navigation path **SAP Menu • Logistics • Materials Management • Purchasing • Master Data • Vendor • List Display • Purchasing List**.

9.5 Blocking Vendors

Vendors can be blocked for a variety of reasons that the client may determine. Often a vendor is blocked due to poor adherence to delivery dates, unsatisfactory material quality, or outside market events. The client has to the option to block a vendor master account, which can stop any future purchase orders being placed with the vendor until the vendor master record has been unblocked.

9.5.1 Block a Vendor—Purchasing

The vendor master record can be set to blocked status by using the transaction code MK05. This can be found using the navigation path **SAP Menu • Logistics • Materials Management • Purchasing • Master Data • Vendor • Purchasing • Block**.

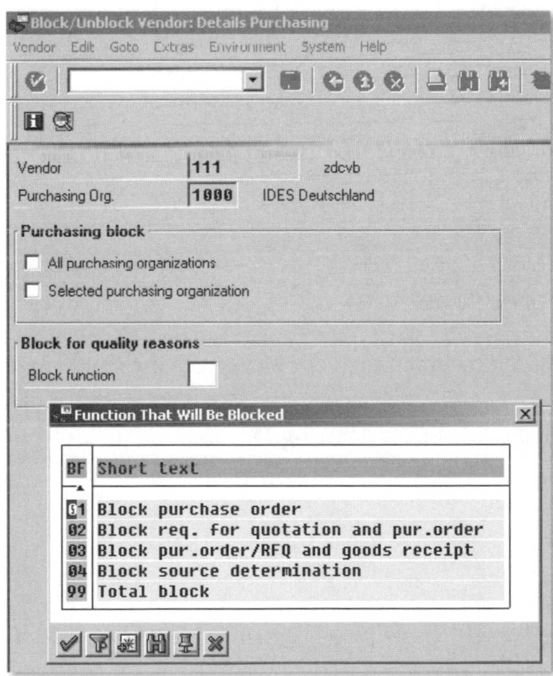

Figure 9.13 Fields Applicable for Blocking of a Vendor

Transaction MK05 is used for blocking vendors via Purchasing. The initial screen of the transaction allows the purchasing user to enter the vendor number and the purchasing organization.

The second screen, shown in Figure 9.13, shows the fields that are relevant to block the vendor. The first indicator is for the user to determine whether the block should be for the vendor in all purchase organizations or just the single purchasing organization entered.

The other field on this screen allows the purchasing user to enter a block function code that describes the how the vendor block is to be used. The block-function code is defined in configuration.

The delivery-block function is defined in the IMG using the following navigation path **IMG • Quality Management • QM in Logistics • QM in Procurement • Define Delivery Block**.

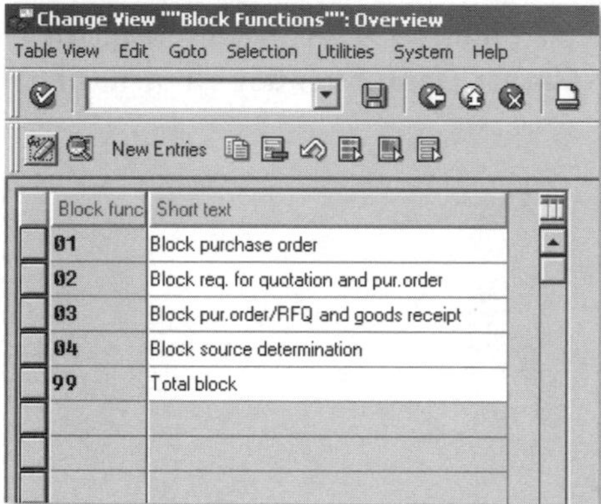

Figure 9.14 Configured Delivery Blocks and Associated Text

Each delivery block can be configured to block the vendor from being valid some part of purchasing functionality. As Figure 9.14 shows, the purchasing block can be for any single option or combination of the following options:

- Request for quotation
- Source determination
- Purchase order
- Goods receipt

9.6 One Time Vendor

A one-time-vendor record (see Figure 9.15) can be used for vendors that are used once or very rarely. An example of this is where a material is needed in an emergency and the normal vendor for that material cannot supply the item in the requested time. In this instance, a local vendor or an unapproved vendor may be used for this one off purchase. Such a record can be used for a number of vendors, as this reduces the amount of data entry and data maintenance.

Clients also use one-time vendor records for travel, expense reimbursement, and vendors who cannot accept the client's purchase orders.

A one-time vendor record can be created in the same way as any normal vendor. The difference is that a one-time vendor uses a special account group for one-time vendors. One-time vendor records do not usually contain any significant data or any bank and financial information.

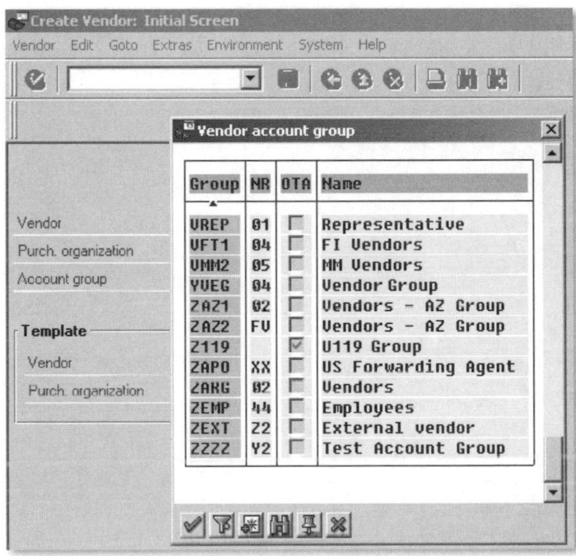

Figure 9.15 Account Groups, Including One-Time Vendor Account Group, in Transaction MK01

Many clients have policies in place that ensure that vendor master records are not created for one-time or limited-use vendors. Some of these policies include establishing a limit on the number of transactions per year and restricting the yearly spending on these vendors. So if a vendor has more than four transactions a year or the total annual spending with a vendor is more than $4,000, then it cannot be called a one-time vendor. A vendor master record must be maintained for that vendor.

9.7 Vendor Sub-Range Functionality

The vendor sub-range can be used to subdivide the vendor's products into different ranges. The vendor could be an office-products company, and the sub-ranges could be computer media, paper products, and ink products.

The vendor sub-range can be entered into the purchasing information record of a particular vendor/material combination. The allocation of a material to a certain vendor sub-range allows the vendor to see the items sorted on its purchase order in sub-range order.

Configuration is required to allow vendor sub-ranges to be used. The transaction OMSG allows the configurator to edit the vendor account groups. The indicator can be highlighted to allow vendor sub-ranges to be relevant for that vendor account group.

The transaction (shown in Figure 9.16) can be reached via the navigation path **IMG • Logistics—General • Business Partner • Vendor • Control • Define Account Groups and Field Selection**.

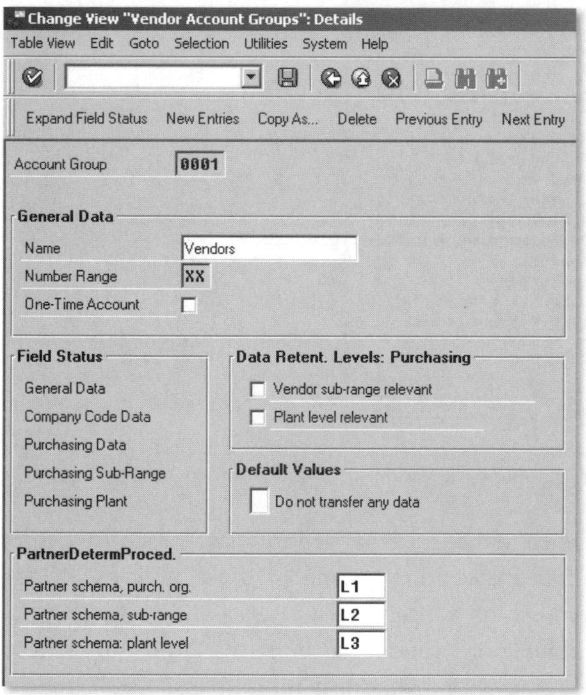

Figure 9.16 Detailed Data for the Vendor Account Group

This chapter looked at the vendor master file. It is important for the purchasing department and the accounting department. The vendor master file is key to allow the purchasing users to the ability to provide material to production at the lowest cost, at the right quantity and quality and at the correct time. The accounting department use the vendor master file to pay the vendors in the correct fashion at the agreed upon time. The vendor master file is important in materials management and requires adequate securtity to minimize the number of user who can create and modify vendor records.

10 Purchasing Overview

Every company that operates a business has to purchase materials: raw materials, office supplies, services, or other items. The science of purchasing has become part of today's efficient business operation. The purchasing department can research and negotiate significant savings for a company through policies and technology.

Purchasing departments have come a long way from a few people doing business with paper requisitions and card files of vendors, and working to get the best deal with long-term local vendors. Technology has brought the purchasing department into the front line of cost-efficiency. Purchasing departments now have tools and procedures that allow them to negotiate larger savings, better quality, and more secure supply.

Today's purchasing department has a plethora of information from associations, purchasing think tanks, and specialist purchasing consultants. Companies can introduce best practices along with specialized technology to ensure that the information is available to the purchasing professional for negotiating and managing contracts.

10.1 Purchase Requisition

The purchase requisition is the procedure by which general users or departments can request the purchases of goods or services that require processing by the purchasing department. Companies can allow certain authorized users to enter purchase requisitions directly into the SAP system, but in situations involving a particular dollar value or type of goods and services the company may request another method of informing the purchasing department of the purchasing requisition, such as fax or email. An example of a purchase requisition is shown in Figure 10.1.

Many companies have implemented an Internet front-end to purchase requisitioning, and authorized users can go to a URL and enter the material or services they need instead of having direct access to SAP.

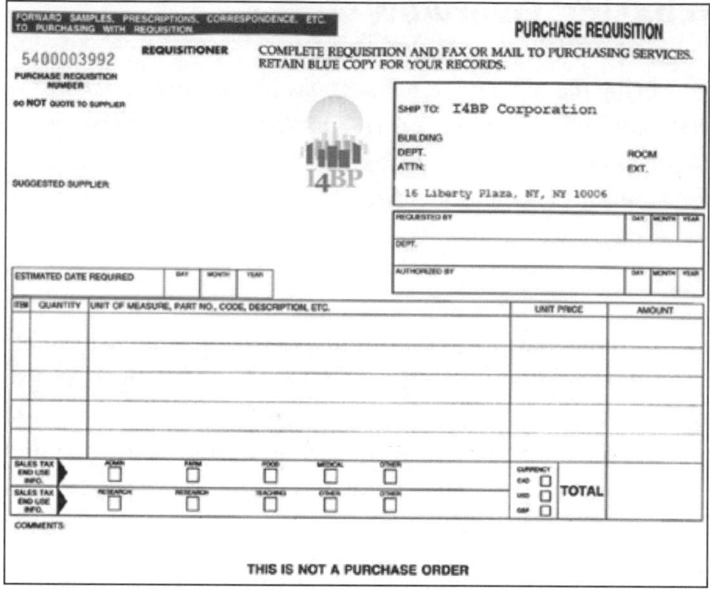

FORWARD SAMPLES, PRESCRIPTIONS, CORRESPONDENCE, ETC. TO PURCHASING WITH REQUISITION

PURCHASE REQUISITION

5400003992

PURCHASE REQUISITION NUMBER

DO NOT QUOTE TO SUPPLIER

REQUISITIONER

COMPLETE REQUISITION AND FAX OR MAIL TO PURCHASING SERVICES. RETAIN BLUE COPY FOR YOUR RECORDS.

I4BP

SHIP TO: I4BP Corporation

BUILDING

DEPT. ROOM

ATTN: EXT.

16 Liberty Plaza, NY, NY 10006

SUGGESTED SUPPLIER

REQUESTED BY | DAY | MONTH | YEAR

DEPT.

AUTHORIZED BY | DAY | MONTH | YEAR

ESTIMATED DATE REQUIRED | DAY | MONTH | YEAR

ITEM	QUANTITY	UNIT OF MEASURE, PART NO., CODE, DESCRIPTION, ETC.	UNIT PRICE	AMOUNT

SALES TAX END USE INFO. ▶ ADMIN ☐ FARM ☐ FOOD ☐ MEDICAL ☐ OTHER ☐

SALES TAX END USE INFO. ▶ RESEARCH ☐ RESEARCH ☐ TEACHING ☐ OTHER ☐ OTHER ☐

CURRENCY CAD ☐ USD ☐ GBP ☐ TOTAL

COMMENTS:

THIS IS NOT A PURCHASE ORDER

Figure 10.1 Typical Paper Purchase Requisition

10.2 Request for Quotation

Once the purchasing department has received the purchase requisitions and have processed them, there may be an item that requires the purchasing department to offer a request for quotation (RFQ), see Figure 10.2. There are a number of reasons why this would occur, and these could involve:

- Material not previously used at the company
- Material previously that now has no identified vendor
- New vendor required due to termination of contract, i.e. quality issues
- New vendor required due to bankruptcy of vendor
- New vendor required due to government regulations
- New vendor required due to logistical issues

When selecting the vendors who will be invited to submit quotations, the purchasing department will use a number of inputs. They can use:

- Vendor suggestions from the requisitioner—especially for a new material
- Research on vendors, using professional associations and buying groups
- Trusted vendors with whom the company has contracts

In traditional purchasing, before advancements in information technology, many companies would carry out RFQs by selecting prospective vendors, physically sending out RFQ documents, and packages of information, and receiving data and prices back. It could then review these documents and select a vendor after some period of time. However, this process meant that much of the vendor evaluation was performed after the RFQ was produced, sent, and received back.

Request for Quotation (RFQ)

RFQ Number 610000782
Contact : John Smith
Telephone : 212.555.9292
Fax : 212.555.9303

Date : 29 Nov 2005

Your Vendor Number : 88930021
Financial Computers LLC
6199 Hawley Street
Boston, MA 02110

Remit Quotation to
I4BP Corporation
16 Liberty Plaza, 2300
New York, NY 10006

Important RFQ Dates

RFQ Closing Date : 22 Jan 06
RFQ Closing Time : 5 PM EST

Deliver Goods/Services to
I4BP Research Labs
Attn: Dr. Robert Jones
3403 Hickman Road
Des Moines, IA 50310

For information on other RFQ's refer to www.i4bp.com/purchasing/rfq.htm

Goods/Services required by 14 Feb 2006

USER CONTACT: Bidders requiring clarification of technical aspects of these specifications should contact :
Dr. Robert Jones by fax only 515.555.9540

Item	Qty	Description
001	30	Apple iMac G5, MA064LL/A, 2.1GHz PowerPC G5 2.5GB SDRAM, 500GB Serial ATA 7200rpm HD, 8X DVD-R Media Kit, Keyboard M9270LL/A, Video Adapter M9109G/A, Wireless Mouse M9269Z/A

NOTES
A. No substitutions will be permitted as all parts must be configurable with equipment currently in use at the Research Labs.
B. To ensure efficient communications during the performance of this project we require that you provide the names and contacts information of any subcontractors used.

NEED HELP? Suggestions and hints to help you complete a successful quotation are available from our website at www.i4bp.com
If you do not have access to the internet, please request a copy from the Purchasing Dept., 16 Liberty Plaza, 2300, NY, NY 10006
A copy will be sent to you by mail or by fax.

**** I N S T R U C T I O N S O N T H I S R F Q ****

By submitting a response to this RFQ, you acknowledge that you have read and complied with the applicable purchasing documents.

Figure 10.2 Typical RFQ Sent to Vendors

Today, the RFQ can be sent to vendors via mail, fax, or electronically via email or EDI. The EDI transaction set for sending the RFQ to a vendor is 840.

With today's level of company spending, the purchasing department has to evaluate the vendors' volume capabilities, on-time performance, quality performance and their understanding of the company's business, long before the RFQ is sent.

For their part, vendors are becoming more aware of companies needs to reduce purchasing cost and are preparing for RFQ's in a more strategic way. Many vendors are using technology to calculate the threshold of what a purchasing department is willing to pay, based on their quality and logistical factors. Vendors know that being the lowest bidder is not necessarily going to win the bid, but they also know that being a low bidder for a RFQ is important.

10.3 Quotation

The quotation is sent by the vendor to the purchasing department that offered the RFQ. The response from the vendor should follow the stipulations set down in the RFQ. Should the vendor fail to follow the instructions in the RFQ, the customer can disqualify the quotation from the vendor. Many vendors fail to read and understand RFQs before submitting quotes. An example of a quotation sent by a vendor is shown in figure 10.3.

The quotation can be sent by the vendor by EDI, using transaction set 843.

Quotation

RFQ Number:	610000782	**Our Customer #:**	8888292339
Attn of	John Smith	**Terms of Payment:**	14 Days
Address	16 Liberty Plaza	**Delivery Promise:**	14 Days
	NY, NY 10006	**Valid Until:**	28 Jan 2006
		Taxes:	NYC 8.375%
Vendor #:	88930021	**Shipping:**	FEDEX Ground
Date	17 Dec 05	**Warranty:**	90 Day

Item	Part #	Description	Qty	Price	Disc.	Total $
01	xxx	Apple iMac G5	30	672.22	43%	20,166.60
xx	xxx	xxxxxxxxxxxxxx	xx	xxxxxx	xxx	xxxxxxxxx

Acknowledgement:
Financial Computers LLC acknowledges that it has abided my all relevant documents supplied by the customer with the RFQ.
This quotation is valid until the date specified on this document. Any extension to this quotation must be sort in writing and no later than 7 days before the expiry date.
All discounts are calculated based on MRSP.
Tax rates are subject to change.

Financial Computers LLC, 6199 Hawley Street, Boston, MA 02110
Tel : (617) 555-9939 Fax : (617) 555-9934

Financial Computers

Figure 10.3 Typical Quotation in Response to a RFQ

10.4 Purchase Order

A purchase order, as shown in Figure 10.4, is a commercial document issued by a purchasing department (the buyer) to a vendor (the seller), indicating the materials, quantities and negotiated prices for materials or services that the seller will provide to the buyer.

The purchase order will usually contain the following:

- purchase order number
- date of the purchase order
- billing address of the buyer
- ship-to address of the buyer
- special terms or instructions
- list of items with quantities
- negotiated price of each item

International Purchase Order

P.0 #: 450000043 — **17 Jan 2006**

Billing Info:

I4BP Corporation
16 Liberty Plaza
New York, NY 10006
U.S.A.
Email: john.smith@i4bp.com
Phone: 212.555.9292
Fax : 212.555.9303

Vendor:

Ganesvoort De Mevre
Parkstraat 83 (9th floor)
2519 JG, The Hague
Nederland
Email: t_ree@ganesvoort.nl
Phone: +31 70 303 92 35
Fax : +31 70 303 92 93

Prod ID	Name	Qty	Price	Amt
7990220	Steenland Packaging Cartons	6	$120.45	$722.70
8893393	Steenland Packaging Inserts (Doz.)	8	$101.16	$809.28
			Total	$1531.98

Please confirm receipt to john.smith@i4bp.com

John Smith
Director of Purchasing
I4BP Corporation

Figure 10.4 Typical Purchase Order

Companies use purchase orders for many reasons. Purchase orders allow purchasing departments to clearly communicate their intentions to vendors, and they protect vendor in the event there is any dispute over the items, quantities, or price. The purchase order is also a component of the three-way match; that is, matching a purchase order, to a goods-receipt document and a vendor's invoice.

Purchase orders can be printed and sent to a vendor. They can also be faxed to a vendor. With EDI technology, the purchase order can be sent electronically and be directly uploaded into the vendor's sales system. The transaction set for this EDI purchase order is 850. If a change is made to the purchcase order, the document can be sent to the vendor using EDI transaction set 860.

10.5 Source List and Source Determination

In order for a purchasing decision to be made, a buyer will look at something called the source list. A contracted or certified vendor will be on the source list for a particular material.

10.5.1 Single Source

Many companies are trying to implement single-sourcing for their materials. This can cut cost substantially if companies also give vendors the chance to to single-source a range of products, but it can leave the buyer in a problematic situation if there is a disruption in that source.

Many purchasing departments are asked by requisitioners to single-source a particular item. The purchasing department will ask the requisitioner to justify this in a document called a Sole Source Justification. This is often used by government and state authorities.

Compatibility

The requisitioner may have a valid reason to purchase a particular material, which was purchased earlier, if no other vendor can supply the requisitioner with a compatible material. For example, a request for information (RFI) project may have found that there are no other vendors able to supply the material in question. If the requisitioner needs to produce a Sole Source Justification, then it is important to describe what equipment is involved and explain why there is no solution except to purchase from the vendor who originally supplied the product. In many research situations, the identical materials are needed to replicate experiments and materials from an alternative vendor may not be acceptable for verifying results.

The purchasing department will usually require some verification that an extensive search has been made and the parts cannot be located at a lower price from a wholesaler or an alternative source. The larger the unit price of the material, the more investigation will be required. If the cost is large enough, then the RFQ process may be suggested by the purchasing department to ensure the correct procedures have been followed.

Economic Justification

Requisitioners can use economic justification to suggest a single source for a material. Opting for the lowest price is not always the most economical way of purchasing a material. There are other factors, such as performance and the cost of incidentals, that should be taken into account.

A common example of this is the PC-printer market. The prices of printers have been falling substantially in the last few years, but in order to create the cheaper printer, the manufacturers have produced printers that can cost less than the ink-jet or toner refill. When looking at the cheapest printer in economic terms, the requisitioner needs to look at the number of prints per refill, the cost of the machines, and the cost of the refill. Therefore, the requisitioner can submit the sole supplier based on the economic justification.

10.5.2 Multi-Source

It is common for purchasing departments to use more than one vendor as a supplier of a material. Although best practices lean towards single sourcing with a trusted vendor, many companies do not wish to risk a failure in the supply of material and thus will have more than one vendor qualified to supply it.

In SAP, each vendor can be entered into the source list for a certain material for a particular plant and/or purchasing organization. The maintenance of the source list in SAP can be accessed using transaction code ME01 or via the navigation path **SAP Menu · Logistics · Materials Management · Purchasing · Master Data · Source List · Maintain**.

Figure 10.5 shows the initial screen of ME01. The purchasing user has to enter the material and the plant where the source list is being maintained. Different plants may have different vendors for the same material, due to logistical issues or the cost of transportation. Other reasons may include the fact that the vendor has different regional outlets with different vendor numbers. The screen in Figure 10.5 shows the fields that are relevant to maintaining the source list.

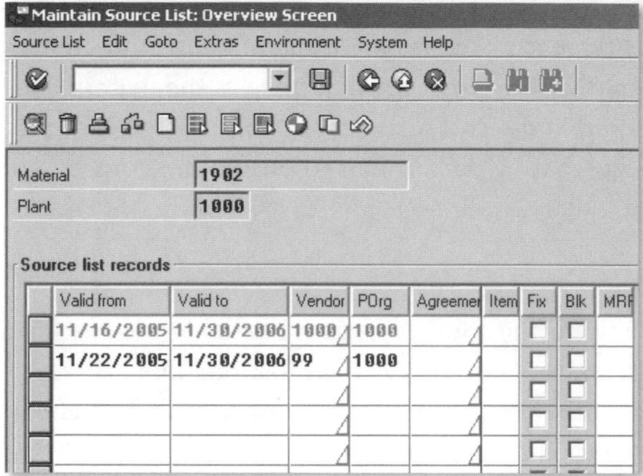

Figure 10.5 Maintenance Screen for the Source List of a Material

Valid To/Valid From

These fields allow the purchasing user to give a validity range showing when the vendor will be allowed to be a source for the specified material at the specified plant.

Agreement/Item

These fields can be completed if there is an outline agreement between the vendor and the company. This outline agreement can be either a contract or a scheduling agreement. The item-number field relates to the item number on the outline agreement.

Fixed Source

This indicator should be set if this vendor is the preferred source of supply for the material at this plant. The system uses this indicator to select the fixed source in the source-determination process.

Blocked Source

This indicator can be set if the vendor is blocked from supplying the material for a specified time, based on the validity period. The blocked-source indicator does not allow any purchase order to be created with this material/vendor/plant combination. Note that the blocked and fixed indicators cannot both be set. Only one of the indicators can be set, or neither.

MRP Field

The source list can be used in the materials resource planning (MRP) process to determine the vendor for requisitions and instigating schedule lines from scheduling agreements. The indicator in this screen allows the planning department to determine how this source vendor influences MRP.

If no indicator is set for this field, the vendor is not taken into account in source determination within MRP. If the indicator is set to **1**, this vendor is taken into account as the source for purchase requisitions generated in MRP. If the indicator is **2**, then this vendor is identified as the source for the scheduling agreement, and delivery schedule lines can be created if there is a scheduling agreement in place.

10.5.3 Generate a Source List

There is a transaction in SAP that allows the purchasing user to generate a source list for a single material or for a range of materials, rather than manually creating the lists. The transaction code is ME05 and can be found via the navigation path **SAP Menu • Logistics • Materials Management • Purchasing • Master Data • Source List • Follow-on Functions • Generate**.

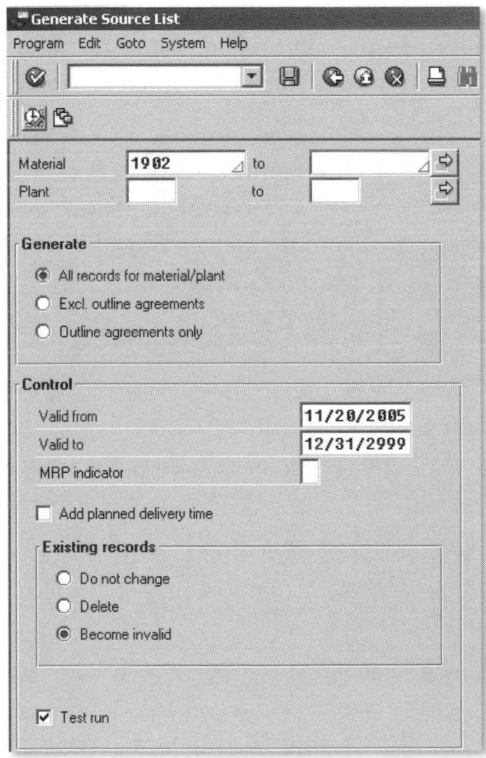

Figure 10.6 Selection Screen for Generating a Source List for a Material or Range of Materials

The selection screen in Figure 10.6, shows that the generation can be for a range of materials at a range of plants. This is useful if no source lists have been created, and a mass-maintenance program is a fast way to generate the lists.

There is a selection to include, exclude, or only allow outline agreements. Most clients will include all material or vendor scenarios in an initial source- list creation.

The other selection fields are similar to those that can be created in transaction ME01, including validity dates and MRP relevance. There is also an option to delete all existing source list records or allow them to remain. Finally, there is a test-run indicator to allow the purchasing user to run the program without actually creating the source lists. We advise running this program with the indicator set to a test run, as changes in the selection parameters are often required.

10.5.4 Source Determination

Source determination allows the buyer to find the most suitable source of supply for a purchasing need, based on various sourcing information. This information does not necessarily have to come directly from the source list. There are other areas where sourcing information is found.

Outline agreements can offer the buyer information about current contracts in place with regard to the vendor/material combination. An agreement such as a quota arrangement can influence sourcing, as it informs buyers of the level of commitment the vendors have contracted to for a given time period.

Other source-determination information can be found from the purchasing information record and plant information.

Within the system there is a source-determination procedure for determining the best source of supply for the buyer-s need. The order of relevance for source determination is as follows:

- Quota Arrangement: If the system finds a quota arrangement for the material that is valid for the date needed, then the system will determine that vendor as the source of supply.
- Source List: If there are no valid quota arrangements, then the system will review the entries on the source list for the required material/plant combination. If there is a single source or a source that is flagged as the preferred vendor, then the system will offer this vendor as the determined source. However, if there are a number of vendors on the source list that are valid by date selection, then the system will stop and offer the selection to the purchaser. A vendor can then be selected from the list.

- Outline Agreement and Info Records: If there is no valid source list or no valid source-list line items, the system will review the contracts, outline agreements and info records for the required material. The system will check all information records for the material for all purchasing organizations, but will only offer a source if the supply region specified by the vendor is applicable to the relevant plant. Once the system has reviewed all documents and info records, a selection will be available to the buyer, providing that any vendors have been determined by the system to be valid.

10.6 Conditions in Purchasing

10.6.1 Condition Processing

The condition procedure in purchasing is used to calculate the purchase price by processing all relevant pricing factors. By using the defined conditions, the purchasing process arrives at a determined price for purchasing transactions, such as purchase orders.

As discussed in previous chapters, condition processing is made up of four distinct areas: calculation schemas, condition types, access sequences, and condition tables.

Condition Types

Condition types represent pricing dynamics in the system. The system allows condition types for absolute and percentage discounts, freight costs, duty, and taxes. With the condition type, the buyer can see how the price is calculated in the purchasing document.

Examples of Condition Types

- PB00 Gross Price
- RB00 Absolute Discount
- ZB00 Absolute Surcharge
- FRB1 Absolute Freight Cost
- ZOA1 Percentage Duty
- SKTO Cash Discount
- NAVS Non Deductible Input Tax

10.6.2 Pricing Conditions

Pricing conditions allows the purchasing department user to enter the details of the pricing agreements negotiated with the vendor into the system. These contractual agreements can include discounts, surcharges, agreed freight costs, and other pricing arrangements. The buyer can enter any of these conditions in purchasing documents such as quotations, outline agreements, and purchasing information records. These conditions are then used in purchase orders to determine prices.

Time-Dependent Conditions

This type of condition is mostly used for scheduling agreements and quotations. Time-dependent conditions allow the purchasing department user to introduce limits and scales into the condition record. A pricing scale is a scale based on quantity. It can determine that, the more the buyer orders of a particular product, the lower the price. It is also possible to create condition records with graduated scales.

A pricing scale can be created using the following criteria: quantity, value, gross or net weight, and volume. The purchasing department user can create a rate for each level of the scale. For instance, if a buyer orders up to 100 units, the price may be $10 per unit, and if the buyer orders between 101 units and 150 units, the price may fall to $9.45. Above 151 units, the price may fall again, to $9.12 per unit. The price will apply to all units purchased.

There is a different pricing scale called a graduated price scale. Here, the price of unit changes at a certain level as described above, but the price of the unit is not applicable to all the units sold. For instance, using the regular pricing scale, a purchase of 155 units would mean the total cost would be 155 multiplied by the unit cost of $9.12, which is equal to $1,413.60. Using a graduated price scale, the calculation for 155 units would be 100 units at $10, 50 units at $9.45. and five units at $9.12, for a total of $1,518.10.

Time-dependent conditions are always used in purchasing information records and contracts.

Time-Independent Conditions

Time-independent conditions do not include any pricing scales or validity periods. Purchase orders contain only time-independent conditions. Quotations and scheduling agreements can include both types of conditions.

10.6.3 Taxes

Tax information can be calculated during the price-determination process using tax conditions. The tax rate is coded into the tax field in the purchase- order item. The tax calculations are determined by the tax conditions described in the purchase order.

10.6.4 Delivery Costs

Delivery costs can be determined via conditions in the purchase order. The planned delivery costs are entered in the purchase order for each order item. These costs have been negotiated with the vendor or the freight company. The planned delivery costs usually include the actual freight charges, any relevant duty payments, a quality-dependent cost, and a volume cost.

10.7 Vendor Evaluation

Vendor evaluation is an important part of the function of the purchasing department. Selecting vendors to supply material or services can now be a formalized procedure requiring significant information gathering and analysis. Purchasing departments generally have written policies that determine a set of criteria for selecting vendors initially and then selecting from a list of suitable vendors for a purchase document, see Figure 10.7 on page 234. The process of evaluating vendors will vary from company to company and will depend largely on the specific industry of the company and company policy.

Vendor evaluation in SAP is a configurable scoring system that allows the purchasing department to design the evaluation to align with the company's policies and procedures.

10.7.1 Vendor Evaluation Overview

The vendor-evaluation function can be configured to replicate some or all aspects of a company's written procedures on vendor selection. The functionality is based on criteria that can be objective or subjective. The objective criteria are calculated with the data from the purchasing transactions. The subjective criteria are not calculated values, but rather are entered by the purchasing department. In order to determine what level of importance is attributed to each criteria, a weighting key is used. The weighting key can be defined as equal weighting or unequal weighting.

Northern Connecticut State University
College Building, Post Office Rd, Enfield, CT 06082
Tel: (860) 555-3293

Vendor Selection Policy Document
Control Document - 3200-930-Section 2.1

Criteria for Selecting a Vendor

Certain basic evaluations should be included in the selection process of an approved vendor, including:

1.The vendor provides the best mix of quality, service and price for the specified need.
2.The vendor has the financial stability, size and service infrastructure to be capable of meeting the need.
3.The product quality and performance reputation of the vendor is acceptable in the context of University use.
4.The vendor warranty, service reliability and format, shipping or delivery procedures, and terms and conditions of sale protect University interests.
5.The vendor is given preference, to the extent practical and economically feasible, for products and services that conserve natural resources, are energy efficient and protect the environment.

Strategic Partnership Vendors

The procurement services department is establishing relationship with a select group of vendors based on a thorough evaluation of users' needs for specific goods and services (including their active participation in this evaluation) and a thorough evaluation of the potential vendors in that area. The evaluation also includes a commitment to work together on improving the price and service provided for those specific goods and services throughout the life of the relationship.

Small and Disadvantaged/Minority Vendors

The University is committed to the support of small, disadvantaged, minority and/or women-owned vendors. It is recommended that those units engaged in the purchasing function should encourage the use of small, disadvantaged, minority and enterprises owned by women as vendors whenever they are willing and able to compete for University business under the same terms and conditions as defined for all vendors.

1.Authorized individuals are encouraged to use the following organizational guidelines and/or manuals regularly when selecting vendors:
2.The Connecticut Minority Purchasing Council
3.The New England Group of the National Association of Educational Buyers
4.The Connecticut Department of Economic Development - Minority and Women Business Directory
5.Try Us, the publication of the National Minority Council
6.Other directory of enterprise that meets the federal definitions of small and/or disadvantaged businesses.
7.Authorized individuals may also participate in trade fairs and other public programs that serve to introduce small/disadvantaged enterprises to the business community of the state and region. The procurement services department maintains a membership in the Connecticut Minority Purchasing Council and attends various functions it sponsors.

Figure 10.7 Vendor Selection Document from a University Purchasing Department

10.7.2 Vendor Evaluation Criteria

Main Criteria

In the standard SAP system there several criteria. Four of the main criteria relate to the procurement of material, while the fifth is used for vendors supplying services. The criteria are given below:

- Price
- Quality
- Delivery
- Service and Support
- External Service

Although the system has the five main criteria defined, the evaluator does not need to include all of the criteria. The purchasing user can include new criteria and up to 99 main criteria are permitted by the vendor evaluation functionality.

The main criteria can be defined in configuration, see Figure 10.8. The navigation path is **IMG · Materials Management · Purchasing · Vendor Evaluation · Define Criteria**.

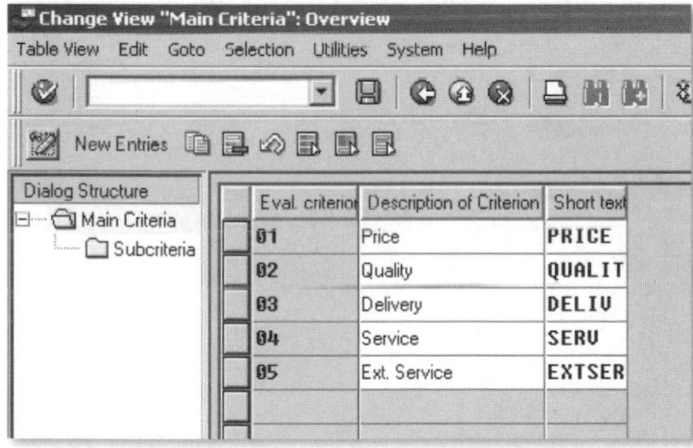

Figure 10.8 Main Criteria Defined in Vendor Evaluation

Subcriteria

Within the main criteria there are smaller elements called subcriteria. There can be up to 20 subcriteria to each of the defined main criteria. The combined scores for subcriteria produce the overall score for each main criteria.

The standard SAP system includes the following:

- Subcriteria for Price includes Price Level, Price History
- Subcriteria for Quality includes Goods Receipt, Quality Audit, Complaints

▶ Subcriteria for Delivery includes Confirmation date, Compliance, On-time delivery, Quantity

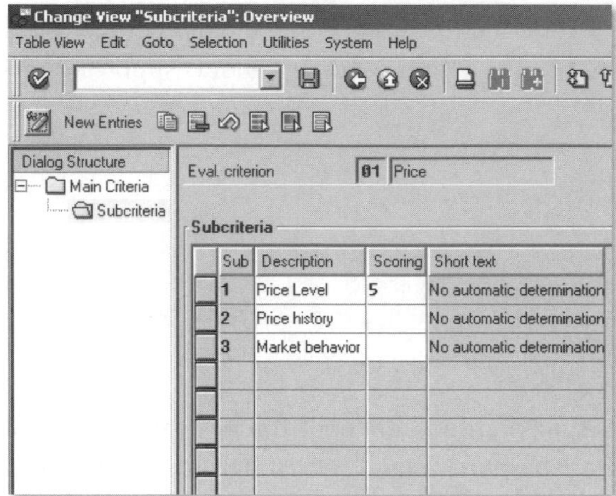

Figure 10.9 Subcriteria for the Price Main Criteria

The subcriteria, shown in Figure 10.9, can be configured for each of the main criteria. To add new subcriteria enter the description and the scoring method. The scoring method can be automatic, semi-automatic, or manual. The defined scoring methods are shown in Figure 10.10.

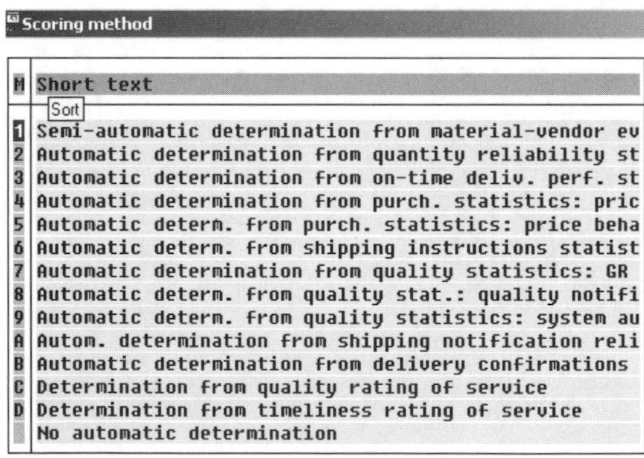

Figure 10.10 Scoring Methods Available for Subcriteria

10.7.3 Vendor Evaluation Weighting

In the vendor-evaluation configuration steps, the weighting of the criteria can be defined for each valid purchasing organization. The configuration can be found using the navigation path **IMG · Materials Management · Purchasing · Vendor Evaluation · Define Purchasing Organization Data for Vendor Evaluation**.

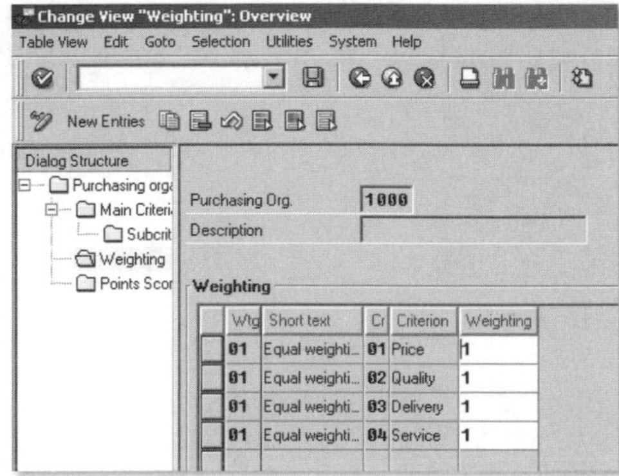

Figure 10.11 Weighting for the Purchasing Organization

Figure 10.11 shows that the weighting for purchasing organization 1000 is equal for all the main criteria. In this case, the purchasing department has determined that no special weighting is required for one of the main criteria. If the there was a change in policy to recognize price as being more important than the other criteria then the weighting would be different, i.e., unequal weighting.

10.7.4 Points Scoring for Criteria

In the configuration for the purchasing organization, the configurator can also configure the points given for levels of evaluation. The system can calculate any variances that the vendor may have— in price, e.g., —and the purchasing user can determine how many points to award for certain variance ranges from 100 percent to plus or minus a certain total variance. This is shown in Figure 10.12.

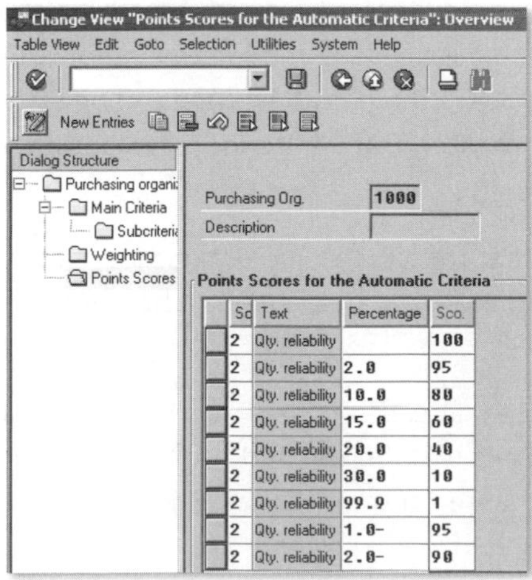

Figure 10.12 Points Score Defined for Variance on Quantity Reliability, Automatic Criteria

The points awarded are reduced, as the variance gets further away from a perfect score, that is, a zero variance. A graphical representation is shown in Figure 10.13 for points awarded to a vendor on delivery quantities.

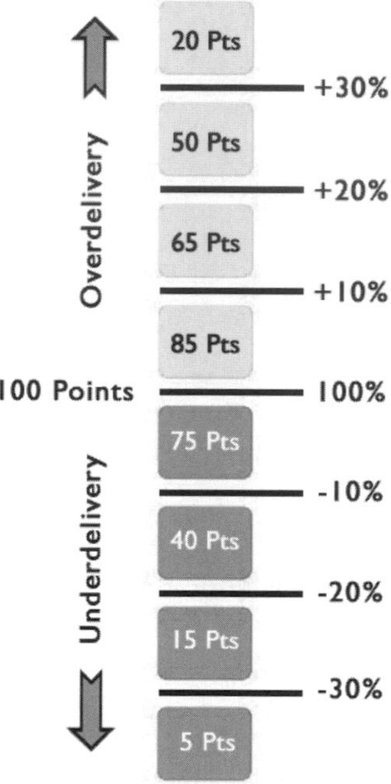

Figure 10.13 How the Point Score Varies Based on Configuration

10.7.5 Maintain Vendor Evaluation

Once the configuration is complete, the maintenance of a vendor's evaluation record can be performed. The maintenance of individual vendor evaluation can be performed using transaction code ME61 or via the path **SAP Menu • Logistics • Materials Management • Purchasing • Master Data • Vendor Evaluation • Maintain**.

The maintenance of a vendor's evaluation is at the purchasing organization level. This means that a vendor can be evaluated differently between purchasing organizations.

The evaluation data shows the weighting key and the overall score. There is a deletion indicator that can be set if the record is to be deleted. In Figure 10.14, the overall score for this vendor is zero, because no transactions have been processed.

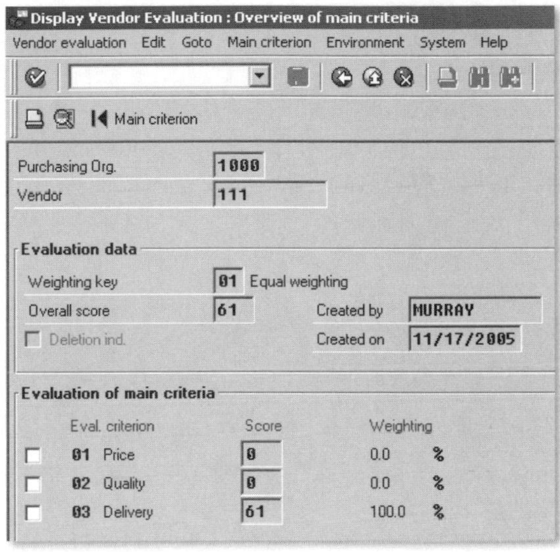

Figure 10.14 Maintaining a Vendor Evaluation: Transaction ME61

The bottom part of the screen shows the evaluation of the main criteria. There are only three main criteria for this evaluation. The **Price** and **Delivery** are calculated scores, while the **Quality** score is a subjective value and must be entered. The subjective score can have a significant effect on the overall score for a vendor, and companies will generally implement a manual scoring system for the subjective or non automatic scoring criteria. This can be as simple as a list of a questions or as complex as a detailed spreadsheet. Whatever method is used, the continuity of method used to calculate the subjective score is important. Otherwise, vendors will be scored differently, and the comparison between vendors will be unsound.

10.7.6 Scoring for Automatic and Semi-Automatic Criteria

The automatic and semi-automatic criteria can be calculated via a transaction to provide the latest scores. The transaction code ME63 allows the purchasing department user to enter a vendor and the relevant purchasing organization. The transaction can be found using the navigation path **SAP Menu • Logistics • Materials Management • Purchasing • Master Data • Vendor Evaluation • Automatic New Evaluation**.

The system will calculate the scores for the subcriteria defined and give an overall score for each of the objective scores, i.e. the automatic and semi-automatic criteria, as shown in Figure 10.15.

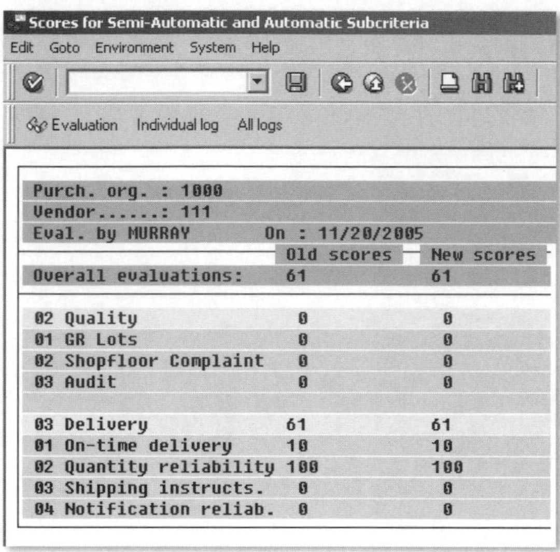

Figure 10.15 New Calculated Scores for Vendor After Running Transaction ME63

10.7.7 Evaluation for a Material

It is possible to perform a check on a material or a material group that will evaluate the supplying vendors and show the results. The transaction code ME6B will allow the purchasing user to enter a purchasing organization and the material or the material group. This is shown in Figure 10.16.

Purchasing Organization 1000

Rank	Vendor Name	PRICE	DELIV	QUALIT	SERV	Av.Var
1	1050 Global Market Ltd	46	80	86	60	12.20
2	1010 Global Pvt Ltd	44	93	92	60	7.32
3	1000 C.B.B.	40	59	97	78	2.44-
4	1005 L.E.N.	40	75	97	80	2.44-
5	1234 APC	40	79	85		2.44-
6	1006 TFFC Ltd	35				14.63-
7	111 Global Pages		61			100.00-
8	2345 Tark			20		100.00-
Average Values		41	75	80	70	

Figure 10.16 Evaluation Results for a Material Group

The navigation path for transaction ME6B is **SAP Menu • Logistics • Materials Management • Purchasing • Master Data • Vendor Evaluation • List Displays • Evaluations per Material**.

In this chapter we discussed the purchasing functionality in SAP. The purchasing of materials and services is a large part of a company's business function. Selecting vendors and obtaining the best price and service for a material is key to producing products at a competitive price for the customer while maximizing company profits

11 Purchase Requisition

The purchase requisition is the procedural method by which users or departments can request the purchase of goods or services. The purchase requisition can be entered manually by a user or generated automatically as a result of a demand from requirements planning.

Purchasing requisitions are the first step in the demand for material either entered by the requisitioner or generated out of a requirements system such as materials resource planning (MRP). The requisition will contain the material or services to be procured, a required date of delivery, and a quantity. The purchase requisition will not contain a vendor. As it is a document that is internal to the company, it is generally not printed.

11.1 Indirectly Created Requisition

An indirectly created purchase requisition is one created via other SAP functionality. The purchase requisition is created if some functionality needs to have materials or services assigned to it.

11.1.1 Purchase Requisition Created by Production Order

In a production order, there are two elements that determine how the production order functions. The routing is a sequence of the operations that take place, and the bill of materials (BOM) is the recipe used to produce the final material.

A purchase requisition can be generated automatically when the routing in the production order involves an operation whereby the material needs to be sent out for external processing, e.g., subcontracting work.

Another way a purchase requisition can be produced is when the bill of materials calls for a material that is not a non-stock item. This may occur when a special item is required for the production order, or if the material is no longer purchased by the company.

11.1.2 Purchase Requisition Created by Plant Maintenance Order

This type of order produces purchase requisitions similar to the production order. The maintenance order is created for plant maintenance operations on a technical object (in other words, equipment) at the plant. Similar to a production order, a maintenance order has a list of operations that have to be performed. The operations give the maintenance user a step-by-step list of what needs to be performed and the materials and equipment needed for each step.

In the operation, there may be a need for a certain non-stock material, and this may cause a purchase requisition to be created. The maintenance order may also have an operation that requires performance of an external operation by a subcontractor. This will also cause an indirect purchase requisition to be created.

11.1.3 Purchase Requisition Created by Project Systems

Within the Project System (PS) module, there are objects called networks. A network consists of a set of instructions that tell the projects user what tasks need to be performed, in what order, and by what date.

The network has two options for creating material requirements. The network can create purchase requisitions for non-stock materials and external services, similar to the production and maintenance orders. The network can also be configured to allow creation of purchase requisitions as soon as the network has been released.

11.1.4 Purchase Requisition Created by Materials Planning

The consumption-based planning module can create purchase requisitions based on its calculations. The planning module creates purchase orders with quantities and delivery dates that are calculated. The planning run can also produce planned orders for in-house production, but these can be converted to purchase requisitions.

The purchasing requisitions are internal purchasing suggestions that can be modified before being converted to purchase orders. Once the MRP controller has determined the accuracy of the external purchasing requirements, he or she can convert some planned orders to purchase requisitions and perhaps convert some purchase requisitions to purchase orders. The level of interaction between the planning department and the purchasing department will determine what procedures are in place that allow a MRP controller to create purchase requisitions and purchase orders.

11.2 Directly Created Requisition

A directly created purchase requisition is one that is created by a requisitioner and not by other SAP functionality. The majority of non-production purchase requisitions are created this way.

In this section the transactions described will include the *EnjoySAP* purchasing transactions that were delivered with SAP with Release 4.6 and in later releases. The purchasing transactions prior to Release 4.6 are also included here, as many SAP users still use systems below Release 4.6.

11.2.1 Create a Purchase Requisition with a Material Master Record

The most common way a requisition is created is by using an item or service that has a material master record.

The purchase requisition can be created using transaction ME51N. This transaction has a different look and feel than the previous purchase requisition transaction, ME51. The transaction can be accessed via the SAP menu using the navigation path **SAP Menu · Logistics · Materials Management · Purchasing · Purchase Requisition · Create**.

This transaction allows the requisitioner to define what fields are viewed on the screen when entering the requisition data. Many fields that can be viewed and entered, but the screen capture in Figure 11.1 only shows a few of them.

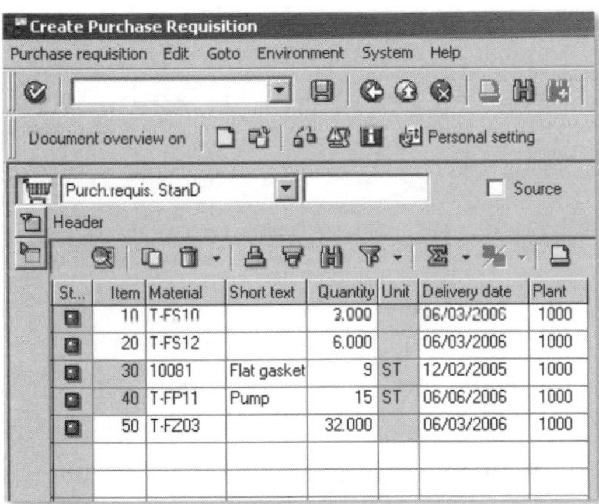

Figure 11.1 Purchase Requisition Screen for Transaction ME51N

The requisition for the materials that have a material master record requires the requisitioner to enter the following information:

- Material Number of item or service
- Quantity to be procured
- Date of delivery of the material
- Plant location of delivery

The requisition process will default the information into the purchase requisition screen. Examples of this include, the material group and purchasing group.

Transaction ME51 can also create the purchase requisition, but has been superceded by the new EnjoySAP transaction ME51N. The purchase requisition, using ME51, has to be a two-screen process, whereas in ME51N the purchase requisition can be created in a single screen. The initial data-entry screen for ME51 can be seen in Figure 11.2.

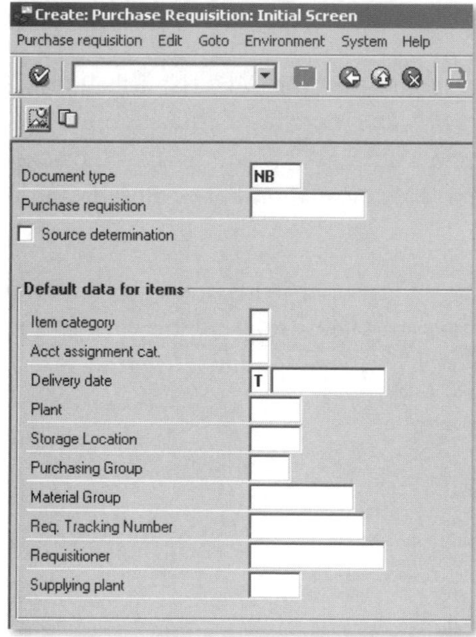

Figure 11.2 Initial Data Entry Screen for Transaction ME51

The initial screen of ME51, as shown in Figure 11.2, allows the requisitioner to enter the purchasing group, delivery date, and plant for the material item. However, as this is a two-screen process, no other information needs to be entered until the detail screen.

Document Type

The document type for a purchase requisition is important, as it defines the internal and external number ranges that are used for requisitions, it can defines the item categories that can be valid and the follow-on functions. A configuration specialist can also configure the item number interval and the screen layout.

The standard SAP system is delivered with the document types **NB** for a standard purchase requisition and **TB** for a transport order. The number ranges are already in place for these document types. More document types can be created for other types of purchase requisitions that are appropriate for your client.

The transaction to configure the document type for the purchasing requisition can be found using the navigation path **IMG • Materials Management • Purchasing • Purchase Requisition • Define Document Types**.

Purchase Requisition Number

The purchase requisition number can be defined as internal or external. This is an attribute of the document type that has been configured.

Source Determination

This field can be selected if the system needs to carry out an automatic source selection.

Item Category

The item category is another control field that allows the purchase requisition to follow the correct path for that category of purchase requisition. The SAP system is delivered with a set of item categories. These are:

- Blank—Standard
- K—Consignment
- L—Subcontracting
- S—Third-party
- D—Service
- U—Stock Transfer

The item category will allow the display of certain fields and not others. For example, if a purchase requisition item has an item category K for consignment, then invoice receipts will not be allowed.

Account Assignment Category

The account-assignment category determines what type of accounting assignment data is required for purchase requisition. Examples of account assignments are cost centers, cost objects, general ledger accounts, and assets.

The account-assignment categories can be configured in the IMG. The configurator can create a new account assignment category by following the navigation path **IMG • Materials Management • Purchasing • Purchase Requisition • Account Assignment • Maintain Account Assignment Categories**.

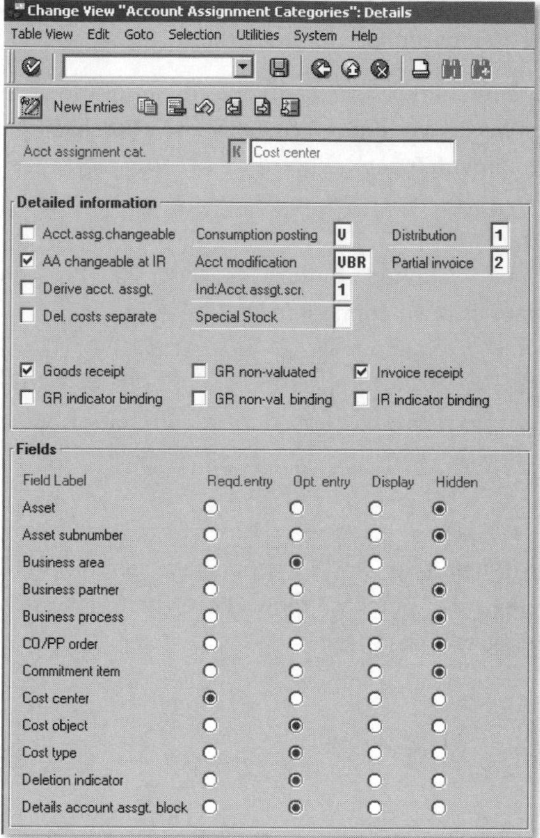

Figure 11.3 Configuration Data for Account Assignment Category

The configurator can create a new account assignment category and configure the fields shown in Figure 11.3. The accounting department would primarily be involved in creating new account assignment categories.

Required account-assignment data is needed for specific account assignments, which can be seen below:

- Asset (A)—Asset number and sub-number
- Production Order (F)—Production order number
- Cost Center (K)—Cost Center and G/L Account number
- Sales Order (C)—Sales Order and G/L Account number
- Project (P)—Project Number and G/L Account number
- Unknown (U)—None

Plant/Storage Location

The plant- and storage-location fields can be entered if the location where the materials are to be shipped to is known. If there is one receiving dock for the whole plant, then this can be defaulted.

Purchasing Group

The purchasing group number is the number for the buyer or buyers for a material. If a purchasing group is entered at the order level, then this will be defaulted for each of the purchase requisition line item.

Requirement Tracking Number

This is not the number of the requisition or the number for the requisitioner, but a free-form field in which a tracking number can be entered. This can be useful to purchasing users in order to search for requisition without knowing the requisition number.

Requisitioner

This field is another free-form field that allows the purchasing user to add the requisitioners name in order to search and order the purchase requisitions.

Supplying Plant

The supplying plant is only entered in a stock-transport order between plants. The supplying plant can be entered in this field.

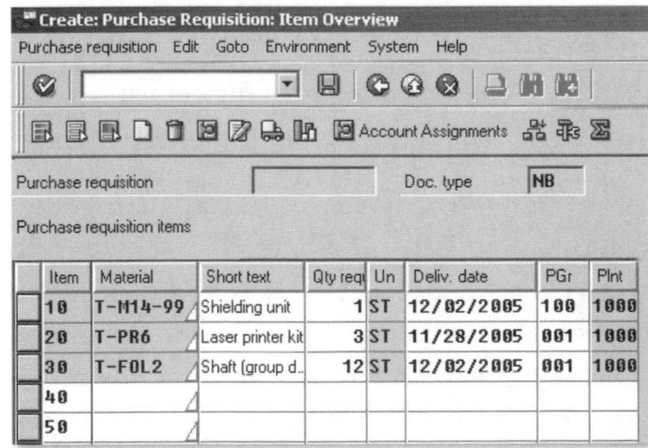

Figure 11.4 Primary Version of Detail Screen for Transaction ME51

The detail screen has a set display unlike ME51N and only allows the requisitioner to select another version of the entry screen, by selecting from the header menu, **Edit • Change Display**. This screen is shown in Figure 11.5 with the same information as displayed in Figure 11.4.

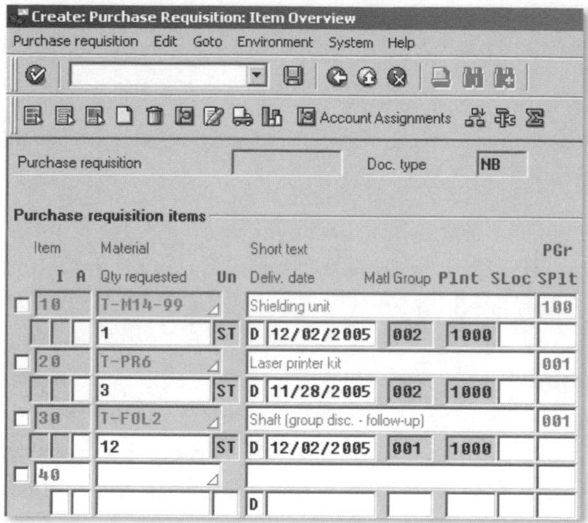

Figure 11.5 Alternative Version of Detail Screen for Transaction ME51

11.2.2 Create a Purchase Requisition without a Material Master Record

When a purchase requisition is to be created without a material master record for the item, then the purchase requisition has to use account assignment to direct the cost to a specific account.

The account-assignment categories described in the last section allow the requisitioner to allocate the costs of the purchase to the correct accounts.

To enter a purchase requisition for an item without a material master record, the transaction is still the same as before ME51. The requisitioner can enter information on the initial screen or enter nothing and go directly to the line-item screen.

In the detail line-item screen, the information has to be entered, as there is no material master record to refer to. The requisitioner must enter a short description of the material, an account assignment category, the quantity to be supplied, the unit of measure, the delivery date, the plant, the purchasing group, and the material group. Once that information is added on the line item, the system will display a dialog box. The information that is required to be entered into the dialog box will correspond to what account-assignment category was entered in the line item. Figure 11.6 shows the dialog box and the account information that can be required. The dialog box will not appear if the account assignment category **U** is entered.

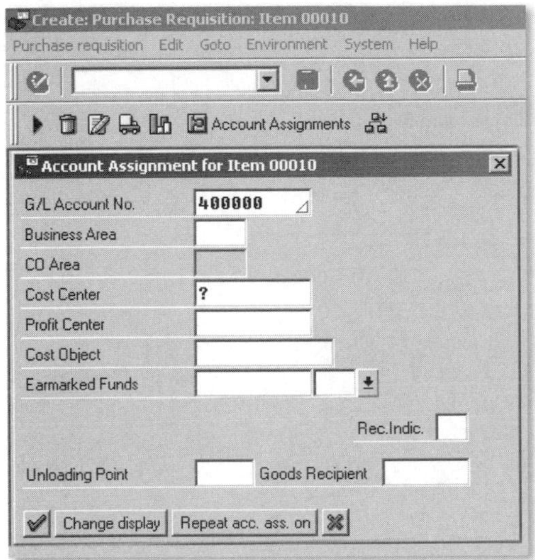

Figure 11.6 Account-Assignment Information Required for Purchase-Requisition Line Item with no Material Master Record

11.3 Processing a Purchase Requisition

11.3.1 Change a Purchase Requisition

The purchase requisition can be changed as part of the material planning process, that is, by the MRP controller, or by the requisitioner prior to being processed by the purchasing department. Using either transaction ME52 or ME52N can change the purchase requisition.

11.3.2 Display a Purchase Requisition

Purchase Requisition—Display

The purchase requisition can be displayed using the transaction code ME54N or ME54 or via the navigation path **SAP Menu • Logistics • Materials Management • Purchasing • Purchase Requisition • Display**.

Purchase Requisition—List Display

There is a display-purchase-requisitions transaction, ME5A, which can be run by the requisitioner to show a list of purchase requisitions. This transaction can be found using the navigation path **SAP Menu • Logistics • Materials Management • Purchasing • Purchase Requisition • List Displays • General**.

The ME5A transaction allows the requisitioner to enter a wide range of selection criteria in order to display the valid requisitions.

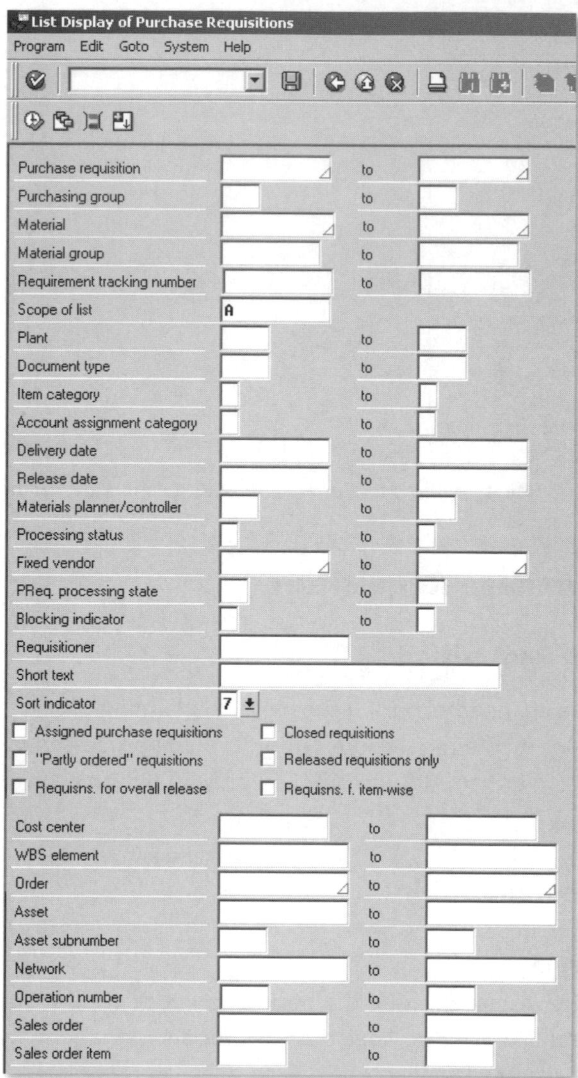

Figure 11.7 Criteria for Selecting a List of Purchase Requisitions

Purchase Requisitions by Tracking Number

Transaction MELB can be used to select purchase requisitions by the requirement tracking number. This number is not the requisitioner but a tracking number entered by the requisitioner to identify their particular purchase requisitions. This transaction can be found using the navigation path **SAP Menu • Logistics • Mate-**

rials Management • Purchasing • Purchase Requisition • List Displays • By Account Assignment • Transactions per Tracking Number.

11.3.3 Close a Purchase Requisition

A purchase requisition can be closed if an indicator is set within the item detail screen. Normally, the purchase requisition is closed when the amount requested to be ordered on the line item of the purchase requisition is equal to the amount that has purchased via a purchase order.

To close a line item on a purchase requisition, the requisitioner needs to access the change-purchase-requisition transaction, ME52 or ME52N. The line item that needs to be flagged for deletion must be selected, and the requisitioner should select **Edit • Delete**. The delete indicator on the line item then will be checked. This is shown in the Figure 11.8.

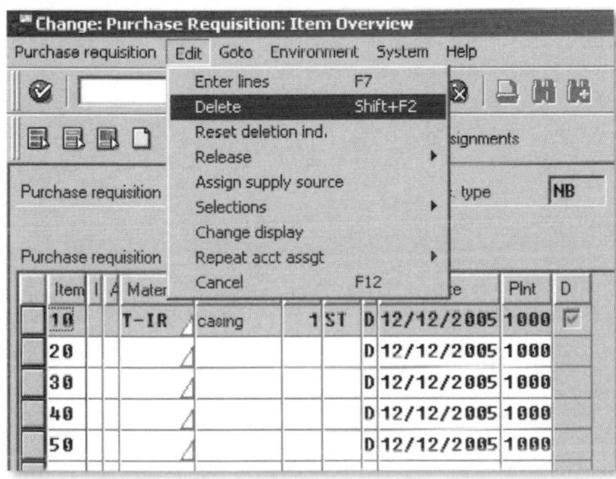

Figure 11.8 Delete Indicator Set for a Purchase Requisition Line Item

11.3.4 Follow-on Functions

As the purchase requisition has been processed, it is possible to carry out some follow-on functions before the purchase requisition is converted to a purchase order.

Assign Source

The transaction ME56 allows the purchasing user to select a range of purchase requisitions to have a source assigned. The purchase requisitions can be selected via a large range of selection criteria, including material group, item category, delivery date, cost center, etc.

The transaction can be found via the navigation path **SAP Menu • Logistics • Materials Management • Purchasing • Purchase Requisition • Follow-on Functions • Assign**.

This chapter examined the purchase requisition process. Most companies use a requisition process. It allows the company to identify where material is needed and allows the purchasing department to review and create the optimum purchase order for each vendor taking into account volume discounts and favorable terms offered by the vendor. Without the purchase requisition purchasing, decisions would be made by the end user and not by the purchasing department.

12 Request for Quotation

Once the purchasing department has received a purchase requisition and processed it, there may be a line item that requires the purchasing department to send out a request for quotation (RFQ) to certified vendors for that material at a particular plant.

In some cases, purchase requisition items cannot be processed by the purchasing department by simply selecting a vendor or issuing a purchase order to a single-source vendor. In cases where the material has never been used by the company or when a new vendor is required due to vendor bankruptcy or de-certification, an RFQ will be issued by the purchasing department.

12.1 Creating a Request for Quotation

A request for quotation can be created using transaction ME41, shown in Figure 12.1, or via the navigation path **SAP Menu • Logistics • Materials Management • Purchasing • RFQ/Quotation • Request for Quotation • Create**.

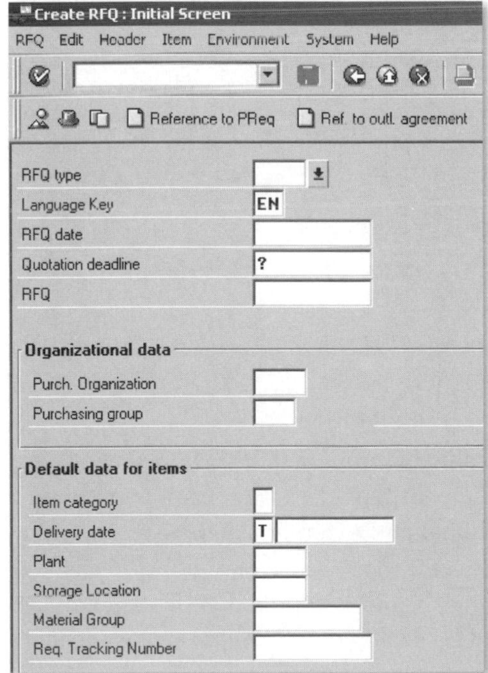

Figure 12.1 Initial Entry Screen for Transaction ME41

12.1.1 RFQ Type

The RFQ type can be defined in the configuration and allows the company to distinguish between the types of RFQs that they may send out. The pre-defined RFQ type is AN, which does not need any configuration changes if the company has simple RFQ needs. If the company wishes to distinguish between RFQs and needs to create more RFQ types, this can be carried out in the IMG.

The configuration transaction can be found using the navigation path **IMG • Materials Management • Purchasing • RFQ/Quotation • Define Document Types**.

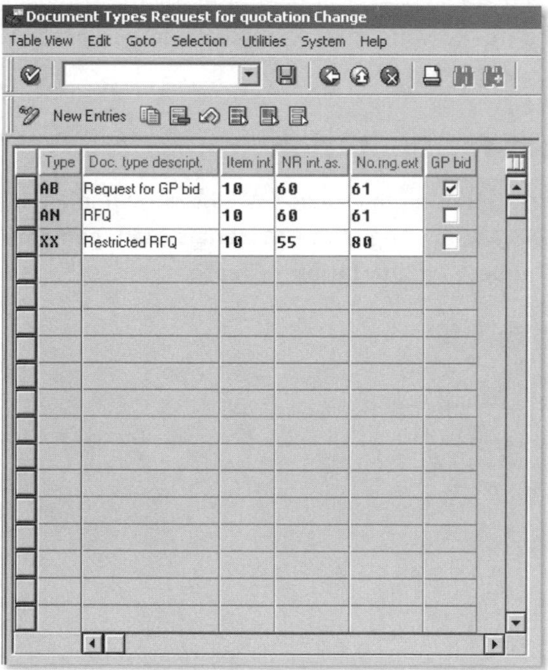

Type	Doc. type descript.	Item int.	NR int.as.	No.rng.ext	GP bid
AB	Request for GP bid	10	60	61	☑
AN	RFQ	10	60	61	☐
XX	Restricted RFQ	10	55	80	☐

Figure 12.2 Configuration for RFQ Document Types

In Figure 12.2, the screen shows the configuration for the RFQ document type. The two-character field defines the document type, and it is necessary to enter a description and number ranges for internal and external assignment. The other field to note is the GP Bid field. This is set if the RFQ is for a global percentage (GP) bid. The standard **RFQ type** for the **GP bid** is supplied with standard SAP, which is document type AB. The **GP bid** is used by purchasing to send suppliers a price that purchasing is willing to pay for a service, rather than having the supplier send in a bid. In this case, the supplier will send back a percentage, either positive or negative, to indicate the level below or above the bid amount sent by the purchasing department it can accept. Although uncommon, this is method is less complicated than the normal RFQ procedure.

12.1.2 RFQ Date

In Figure 12.1 there is a field described as the **RFQ date**. The field is defaulted with the date of entry, but can be overwritten with the appropriate date.

12.1.3 Quotation Deadline

The date entered in this field is the date by which the suppliers need to reply to the RFQ with their quotation. This field is mandatory and should be clearly identified to suppliers on the RFQ print or fax document.

12.1.4 RFQ Document Number

The document number for the RFQ is determined to be either externally or internally assigned, shown by the **RFQ** field in Figure 12.1. This is defined in the configuration shown in Figure 12.2. The field should be entered if the number assignment is external.

12.1.5 Organizational Data

The purchasing organization and purchasing group should be entered for the RFQ.

12.1.6 Default Data for Items

The purchasing user can enter information that is pertinent to items that are to be included in the RFQ.

Item category

The item category can be entered as **L** for subcontracting, **S** for third party and **D** for a service. The field can be left blank for a standard item category.

Delivery Date

This is the delivery date for the item to be delivered or service to be performed to the client by the supplier.

Plant/Storage Location

This would be the client location where the item should be delivered to or the service to be performed.

Material Group

The material group can be used in lieu of a material number or service (if these are not known)

Requirement Tracking Number (RTN)

This tracking number can be traced back to the original requisition if the RTN was entered at that level.

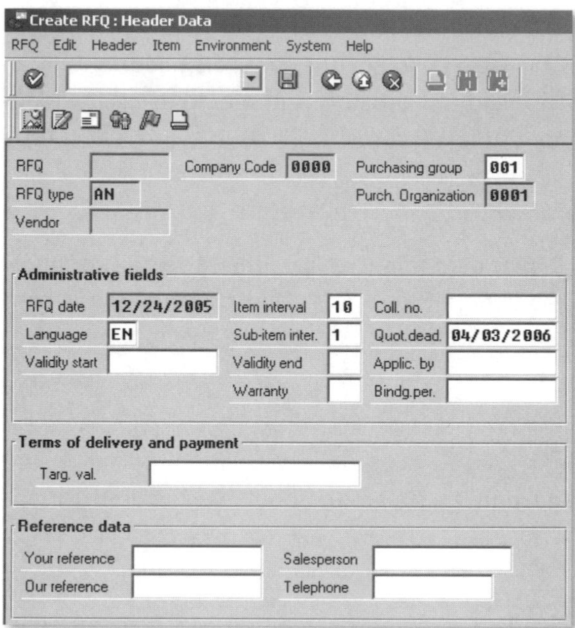

Figure 12.3 RFQ Header Details Screen.

The header details for the RFQ can be seen in Figure 12.3. The data entered in the initial screen are defaulted through and further information can be added in the administrative fields.

12.1.7 Collective Number

The collective number can be used by clients who send out RFQs for a collective bid. For example, if a client is creating a new product, there may be dozens of new materials that it needs to use, as well as new services. In order to collectively identify the many RFQs, the client may use a collective number to ensure that the individual RFQs are tied to the single project. The collective number can be used for search purposes.

12.1.8 Validity Start/Validity End

The validity date range is defined as the dates between which the material or services should be delivered or performed.

12.1.9 Application By

The application date is different from the quotation deadline date. The application date is the date by which the suppliers need to inform the client that they will submit quotations. This date does not necessarily need to be entered, but if it is, then this date would need to be clearly identified to the prospective suppliers.

12.1.10 Binding Period

The binding period is the period of time after the quotation deadline during which the quotation should be valid. For example, if the quotation deadline is April 1, then the client may insist upon a binding period until May 31. This allows the client to process the quotations sent by the suppliers.

12.1.11 Reference Data

The reference data can be added to the RFQ header that relates to the client reference and its contact information. This data can be printed on the RFQ document sent to the supplier.

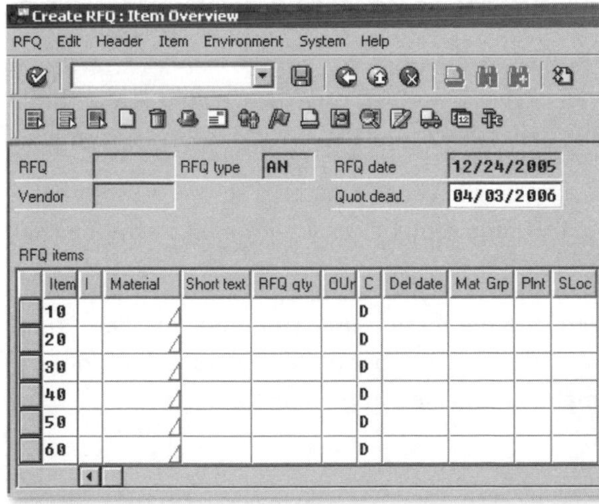

Figure 12.4 RFQ Item Detail Screen

The item detail screen, seen in Figure 12.4, allows purchasing users to add the materials or services that require the creation of the RFQ.

12.1.12 RFQ Item Detail

The line-item details include the item category, material number, and description, quantity for the RFQ, delivery date, and material group.

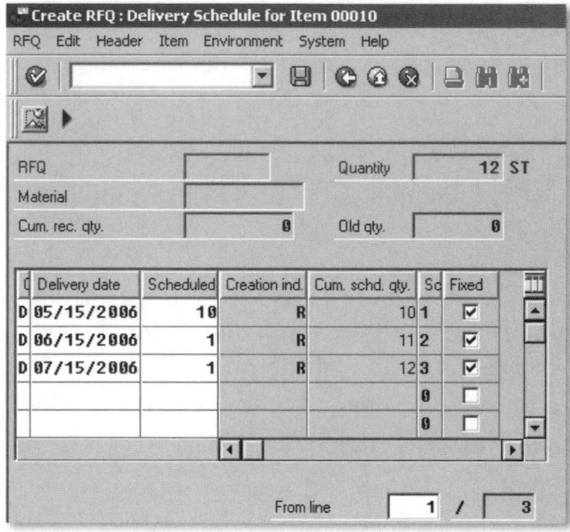

Figure 12.5 Delivery Schedule Screen for the RFQ Item.

12.1.13 RFQ Delivery Schedule

After the item detail information has been added, additional information can be entered if relevant.

To access the delivery scheduling screen, the purchasing user would select **Item • Delivery Schedule** or by pressing SHIFT + F5.

So if the RFQ requires that the supplier deliver the material to the plant in a certain sequence on certain dates, this requirement can be entered in the delivery scheduling screen, shown in Figure 12.5.

In the delivery scheduling screen, the purchasing user can enter the date, time, and the amount required on that date. Any number of delivery schedule lines can be entered for the amount of material specified in the line item.

12.1.14 Additional Data

To enter any further data for the line item, the purchasing user can access the additional data screen as seen in Figure 12.6. This can be found by selecting **Item • More Functions • Additional Data** or by pressing CNTL + F1.

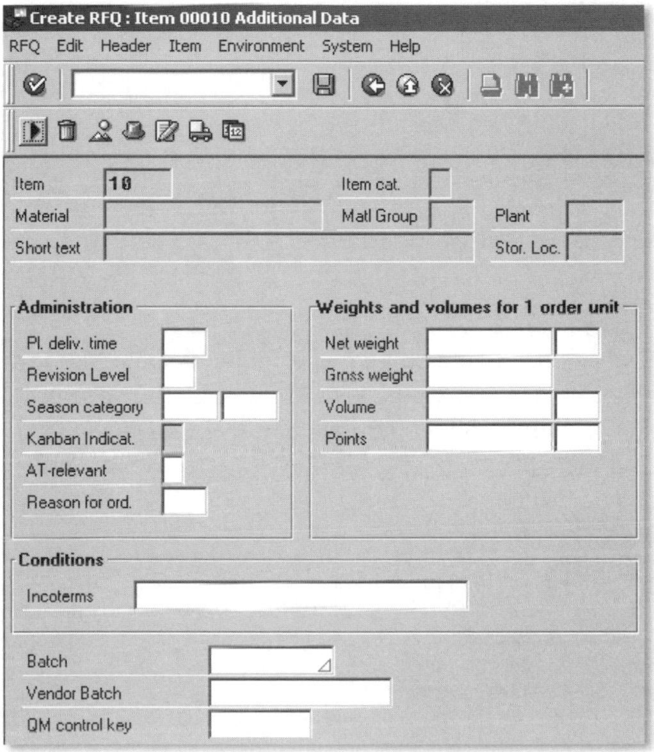

Figure 12.6 Additional Data Screen for RFQ Line Item

The data that can be added here includes the planned delivery time and the reason for the order. The **reason-for-order** field is configurable and can be used by the purchasing department for statistical data collection.

The **reason-for-order** field can be defined in configuration using the navigation path **IMG • Materials Management • Purchasing • Purchase Order • Define Reasons for Ordering**.

The reason code is a three-character field and a short description can be added that is appropriate for the client. This screen is shown in Figure 12.7.

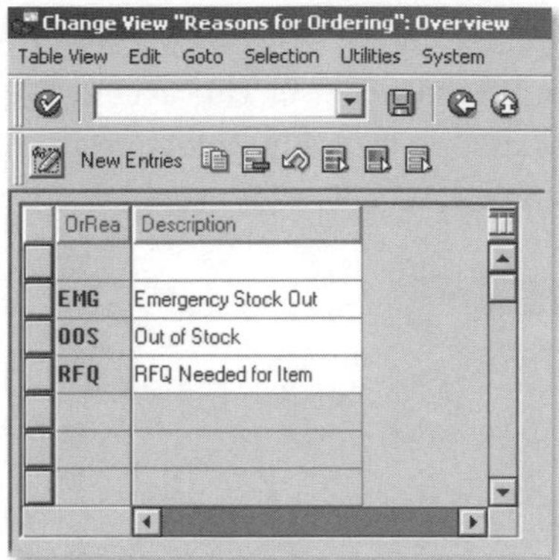

Figure 12.7 Configuration for Reason-for-Ordering Field

12.1.15 Vendor Selection

Once the material details have been entered with any additional data, the RFQ requires that a vendor be selected to receive the RFQ. The vendor can be selected by using the menu selection **Header • Vendor Address** or by pressing the function key F7.

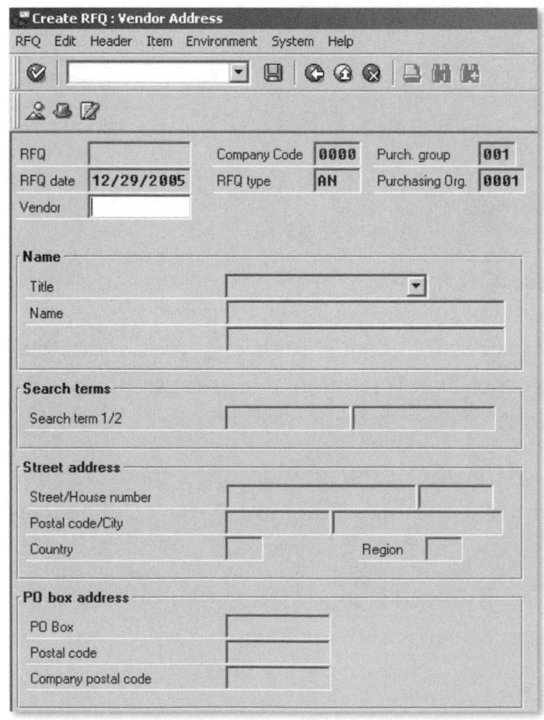

Figure 12.8 Vendor Address Screen Where Vendors are Assigned to RFQ

The vendor address screen, shown in Figure 12.8, allows the purchasing user to select a vendor for the RFQ and once the vendor has been entered the RFQ can be saved. The screen will be refreshed, and the RFQ number will appear on the status line at the bottom of the screen.

The screen shown in Figure 12.8, will allow another vendor to be entered, and if the RFQ is to be sent out to more than one vendor further vendor numbers can be entered, saving after each to create a number of RFQ documents for the same item details.

12.2 Changing a Request for Quotation

A request for quotation can be changed using transaction ME42 or via the navigation path **SAP Menu · Logistics · Materials Management · Purchasing · RFQ/Quotation · Request for Quotation · Change**.

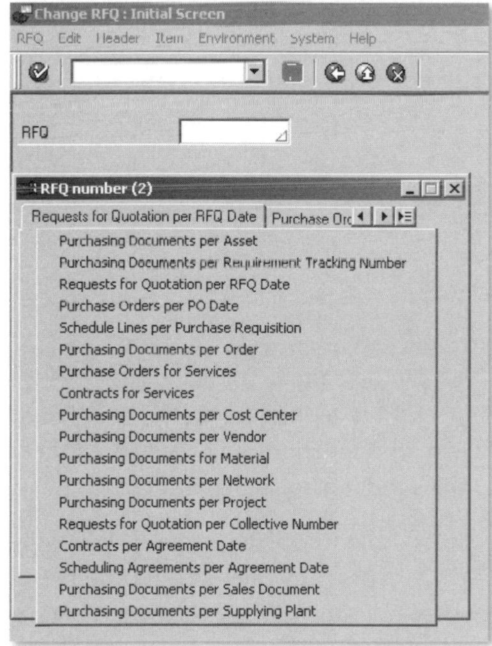

Figure 12.9 Initial RFQ Change Screen with Valid Matchcodes Available to Find RFQ

If the purchasing user does not know the RFQ number that needs to be changed, then a matchcode can be selected. Figure 12.9 shows the valid matchcodes that can be used to find the RFQ.

Note that in Figure 12.9 two matchcodes can be used if the relevant data was added to the RFQ. Those would be:

- Purchasing Documents per Requirement Tracking Number
- Requests for Quotation per Collective Number

Once the correct RFQ number has been entered or selected via a matchcode, the RFQ line item detail is then displayed and certain fields are available for editing.

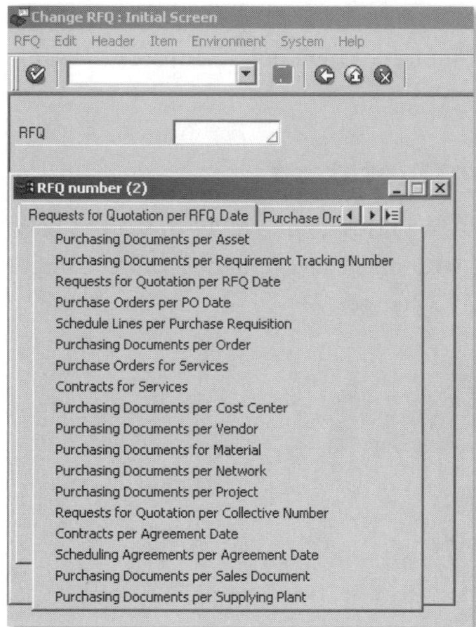

Figure 12.10 Line Item Detail for the RFQ

Figure 12.10 shows a number of fields that can be edited. These include the RFQ material quantity, the quotation deadline, and the required delivery date. Please note that if the RFQ has already been sent to the vendor any changes to these dates will need to be communicated to the vendor associated with the RFQ.

If a line item has been entered incorrectly or if the RFQ is no longer needed, the line item can be deleted in transaction ME42. In order to delete the line item, first select the line item and then set the delete indicator using the menu selection, **Edit • Delete** or by pressing the function keys SHIFT + F2. The deletion indicator can be removed by using the menu selection **Edit • Reset Deletion Ind**.

If the line item does not need to be deleted but the status of the RFQ is in doubt the line item can be blocked using the same transaction, ME42. This screen is shown in Figure 12.11. In order to block the line item, it should first be selected and the blocking indicator then can be set by using the menu selection **Edit • Block** or by pressing the function keys CONTROL + SHIFT + F2. The blocking indicator can be removed by using the menu selection **Edit • Reset Deletion Ind**.

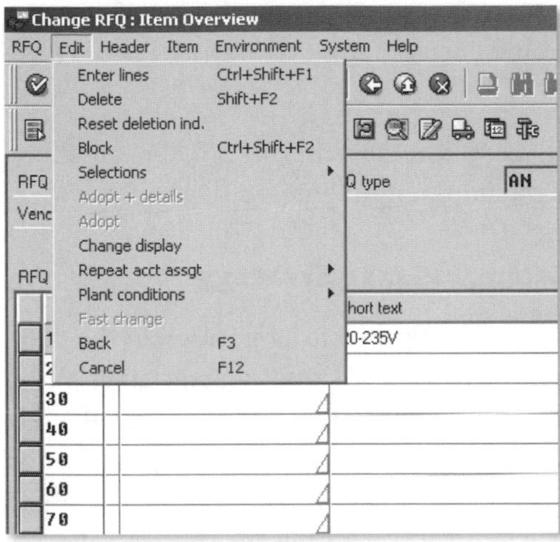

Figure 12.11 Options for Line Item

12.3 Releasing an RFQ

Once the request for quotation has been completed, the document can be subject to release as seen in Figure 12.12. The release procedure is more often associated with purchase requisitions or purchase orders, but can be relevant on RFQs, depending on your clients needs.

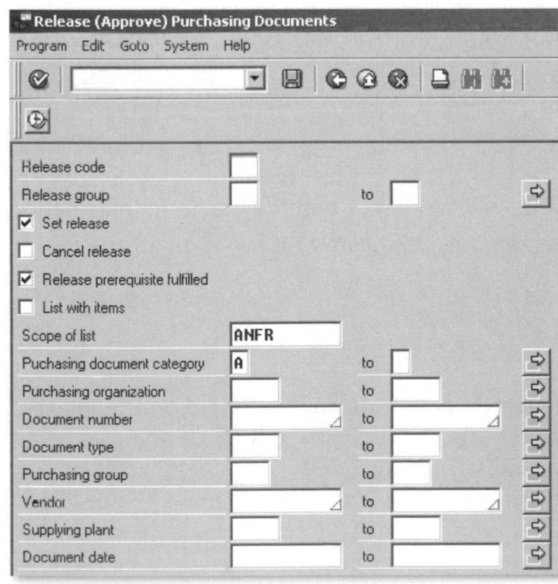

Figure 12.12 Release Screen for Request for Quotations in Transaction ME45

The release procedure for request for quotations only allows the RFQ to be released at the header level and not at the line item level. Therefore the RFQ as a whole is released or not released.

The screen in ME45 allows the purchasing user to enter information that will allow them to release RFQs based on the information entered.

12.3.1 Release Code/Release Group/Release Strategy

The release code is the code that has been configured for a position in the company, such as manager, supervisor, etc. The release code is associated with a release group. The release group contains a number of release strategies that are defined in configuration. The release strategy is configured using classification characteristics. The characteristic can be defined to allow ranges of values for the RFQ. Below a certain value, the RFQ is not subject to release strategy, above a certain amount it would be and the release can be made using ME45.

12.3.2 Set Release/Cancel Release

These indicators can be set to allow the purchasing user to release the relevant RFQs or to cancel their release.

12.3.3 Release Prerequisite Fulfilled

This indicator, when set, allows the purchasing user to view only those RFQs that are ready to be released. If the indicator is not set, all RFQs are released, even if they have not fulfilled all the pre-requisites.

12.3.4 List With items

If this indicator is set then the RFQs will be shown with all line item information shown. If the indicator is not set, then only the header information for the RFQ is shown.

12.3.5 Scope of List

The scope of list is variable that shows different information based on the selected value. The default value for ME45 is the value ANFR, which in this case is for RFQs with collective number. Pressing F4 will cause a selection of scope of list to appear, and a different choice can be made.

12.3.6 Purchasing Document Category

The purchasing document category for request for quotations is the single character **A**. Other documents are **F** for Purchase Orders, **K** for Contracts, and **L** for Scheduling Agreements.

12.3.7 Other Selection Criteria

There are a number of other selection criteria fields that can further narrow down the search for RFQs to be released in ME45. These criteria include purchasing organization, purchasing group, vendor, document number, and document date.

12.4 Issuing a Request for Quotation to a Vendor

Once the RFQ has been entered into the system, the purchasing department has to decide either fax or send a copy to the particular vendor as seen in Figure 12.13. The RFQ document can be printed using transaction ME9A or via the navigation path **SAP Menu · Logistics · Materials Management · Purchasing · RFQ/Quotation · Request for Quotation · Messages · Print/Transmit**.

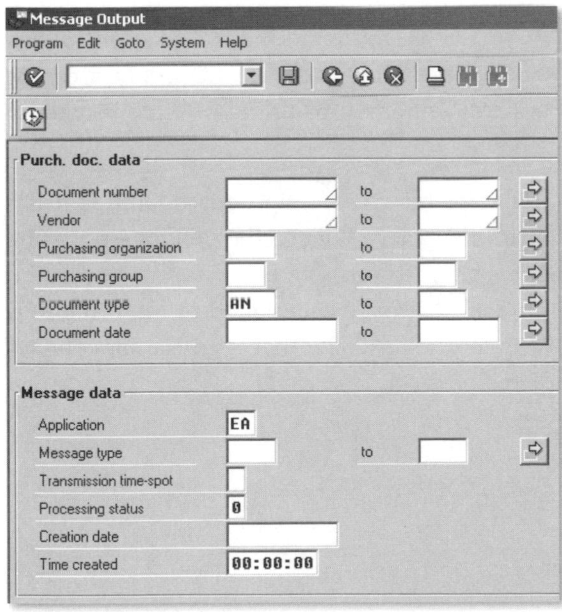

Figure 12.13 Screen for Printing or Transmitting RFQ

The RFQ can be selected by a number of criteria. If the document number is not known, the document can be found by entering the vendor, purchasing organization, purchasing group, or date the RFQ was created.

Once the selection criterion has been entered, the transaction is executed, and the results for the selection criteria will be shown, if any RFQs are found.

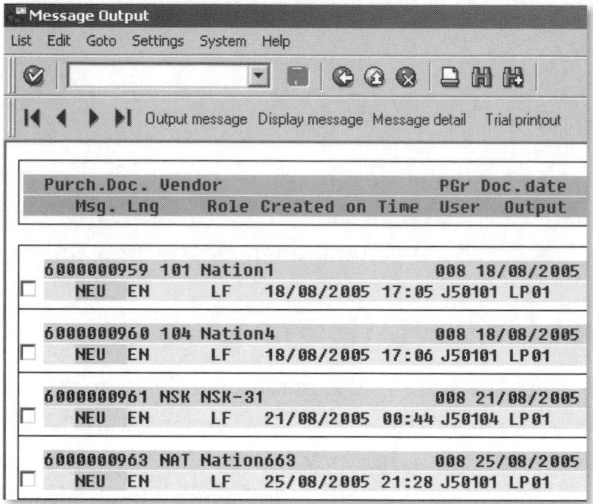

Figure 12.14 Result for Selection Criteria Entered into Transaction ME9A

From the results seen in Figure 12.14, the appropriate RFQ can be selected, and then the RFQ can be printed or transmitted. The resulting RFQ printout can be modified to reflect your client's requirement either by using ABAP, SAPScript, or a tool such as Adobe Form Designer.

A request for quotation is important for the purchasing department, as it is a powerful tool with which the department can influence the vendor's price and terms and conditions in a competitive bid situation. The process examined in this chapter looked at the tools available in SAP that are designed to make the RFQ process simple to use while allowing for the flexibility that is crucial for complex situations found in purchases for large projects.

13 Quotation

Once the purchasing department has received responses from the selected vendors that were sent RFQs, the quotations are entered into the system and comparisons made so the most appropriate vendor bid is accepted.

In Chapter 12 we saw that there is significant purchasing department effort involved in creating the RFQs and selecting appropriate vendors for bid submission.

Once the vendors have replied to the RFQs within the bid submission deadline, the purchasing department then has to enter the bids and process them in order to make an informed decision on the best bid for the RFQ.

13.1 Entering a Quotation

The quotation that has been returned by the vendor should be entered into the SAP system in a timely manner due to the deadline determined within each RFQ. The quotation can be entered into the system by using transaction ME47 or via the navigation path **SAP Menu • Logistics • Materials Management • Purchasing • RFQ/Quotation • Quotation • Maintain.**

The initial screen of ME47 will require the purchasing user to enter a single RFQ number. The RFQ also can be found using the matchcodes discussed in Chapter 12.

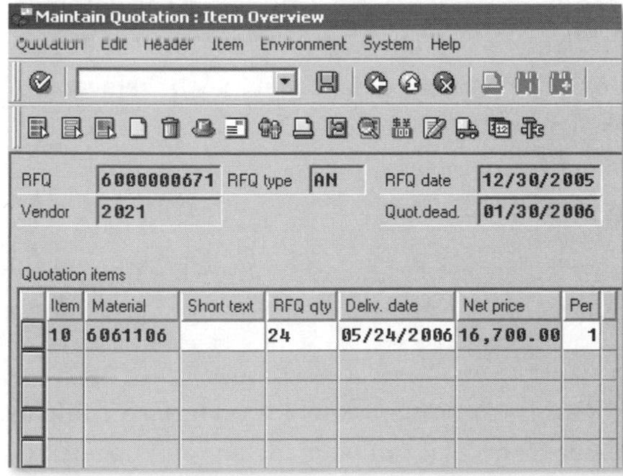

Figure 13.1 Line-Detail Screen for Quotation Maintenance Transaction ME47

The vendor's bid details for the line items needs to be entered into the screen. In Figure 13.1, the vendor has entered a bid for Rupees 16,700 per item on the RFQ. For each vendor quotation submitted, the appropriate RFQ is updated with the quotation.

The price quotation can be entered as a single figure in the net-price field. If there are discounts, taxes, or other conditions, these can be added into the system using the conditions screen.

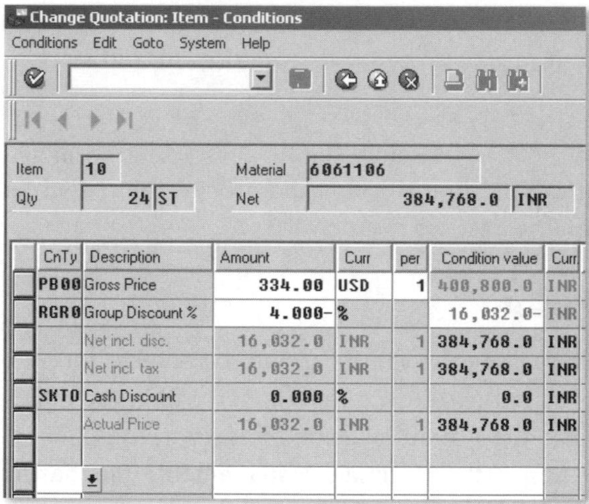

Figure 13.2 Quotation Price Entered into Condition Screen with a Discount

Figure 13.2 shows the purchasing user has entered the quotation of USD 334 per item, which is calculated to Rupees 16,700 (Figure 13.1). The user has entered a condition for Group Discount (RGRO) of 4%. This gives a discount price of Rupees 16,032 per item. On the conditions screen any tax details that may be relevant for the purchase and estimated freight costs can be added

13.2 Comparing Quotations

Once the quotations have been entered for the RFQs and sent to vendors, then it is up to the purchasing department to review them and decide upon selecting a vendor for the material or service put out to bid.

One element of the quotation process is to compare the bids on a price comparison basis. This is the most basic comparison that can be made and not necessarily the deciding factor. Each purchasing department will have a procedure for selecting vendors based on RFQ/Quotation replies.

13.2.1 Price Comparison Factor in Quotations

The price comparison can be found using transaction code ME49 or via the navigation path **SAP Menu • Logistics • Materials Management • Purchasing • RFQ/Quotation • Quotation • Price Comparison**.

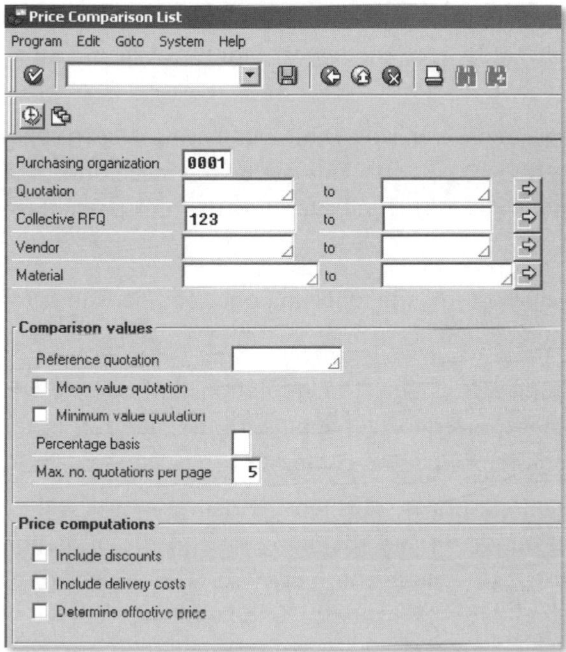

Figure 13.3 Price Comparison Selection Screen for Transaction ME49

The price comparison can be performed between several quotations, as seen in Figure 13.3, and these can be selected by a number of selection criteria, such as purchasing organization, vendor, material, or collective RFQ number. The collective number is the most useful field when sending a number of RFQs to different vendors. The collective number can be used to easily obtain a comparison.

The other criteria in the ME49 transaction include the following comparison value criteria:

- Reference Quotation—This is the quotation that all others would be compared against. If no reference quotation is entered then the quotation will be compared against each other.
- Mean Value Quotation—If this indicator is set, then the comparisons will be made against the average price of the quotations. The quotations will be averaged, and the average quote will be ranked at 100%. The quotes will then

reflect a percentage that shows if it is above or below the average. For example, a lower-than-average quote will show a percentage below 100%; a higher than average quote will show a percentage of greater than 100%.

- Minimum Value Quotation—If this indicator is set, then the comparisons will be made against the lowest price quotation. This means that the first rank (or the best price quote) will be a 100% rank. All other more expensive quotes will show a percentage that is calculated from the lowest bid, i.e., 124%, 136%, etc.
- Percentage Basis—The percentage basis will allow the purchasing user to specify which value will be used as the 100% basis. This can be the mean price, the maximum price, or the minimum price. This will alter how the rank percentage is shown in the quotations.

In addition to the comparison value criteria, the following price comparison criteria indicators can also be set:

- Include Discounts—If this indicator is set, the quotation comparison will include any price discounts that the vendor has applied. If the indicator is not set, then the discounts will not be used in the comparison.
- Include Delivery Costs—If the indicator is set, then the delivery costs will be included in the price on the quotation and therefore used in the quotation comparison. The delivery costs can include the freight costs, duty levied, or other procurement costs such as packing, insurance, and handling.
- Determine Effective Price—This indicator is set if the cash discounts and delivery costs are to be used in the price comparison.

Once the selection criteria have been decided upon and entered, the price comparison can be obtained.

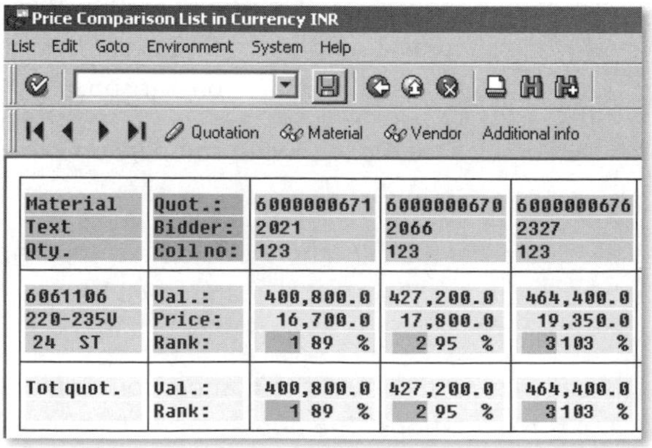

Price Comparison List in Currency INR

List Edit Goto Environment System Help

Quotation Material Vendor Additional info

Material Text Qty.	Quot.: Bidder: Coll no:	6000000671 2021 123	6000000670 2066 123	6000000676 2327 123
6061106 220-235V 24 ST	Val.: Price: Rank:	400,800.0 16,700.0 1 89 %	427,200.0 17,800.0 2 95 %	464,400.0 19,350.0 3 103 %
Tot quot.	Val.: Rank:	400,800.0 1 89 %	427,200.0 2 95 %	464,400.0 3 103 %

Figure 13.4 Price Comparison Between Three Quotations for a Collective RFQ Number

Figure 13.4 shows the price comparison for collective RFQ number 123. It shows three quotations from three vendors for a quantity of material. The price comparison has been used with the Mean Value Quotation indicator set. In other words, the average price has been set as 100%, and bids will be a lower percentage or a higher percentage.

13.2.2 Other Qualitative Factors in Quotations

The price comparison report clearly indicates to the purchasing department, which bidder is giving the client the best price for the material. However, this may only be one of the factors that the purchasing department takes into account. Many purchasing organizations believe that bidding based only on the low-bid dollar amount often results in purchasing a lower quality of goods. Successful bids are more often awarded on comparative evaluation of price, quality, performance capability, and other qualitative factors that will prove the most advantageous to the client.

Other qualitative factors that may be identified by a purchasing department could be:

- Previous Relationship with the Client—if the bidder has a successful relationship with the client, this may be taken into account in any final decision on the winner of bid.
- Compliance with the Equal Opportunity Act (U.S.)—many clients insist that any vendor must be in compliance of equal employment opportunity laws.
- Strategic Alliances—the client may have a number of strategic alliances with vendors or trading partners, which may weight the decision of awarding a bid. For example, a client may have put an RFQ out to vendors for a new Unix Server, and the lowest bidder by price was HP. However, if the client had a strategic relationship with IBM, the bid may be placed with IBM despite the lower bid from HP.
- Minority-Owned and Women-Owned Businesses (U.S.)—some clients may have a preference to give minority-owned or women-owned businesses certain contracts or purchase orders. If the RFQ falls into an area where the client has indicated a preference for this type of vendor, then this may have more weight in the award decision that the price.
- Warranty and Return Process—the warranty period of an item or the return policy offered by the bidder may be very important to the purchaser. For example, if the RFQ was for personal computers, the purchaser may be more inclined to accept a bidder with a higher price per unit if the warranty was two years, than to select a bidder offering a six-month warranty. The same is true

for return policy. The easier the return procedure, the more attractive a bid from a supplier becomes.

- Creative Pricing—often a bidder may not offer the best price in response to an RFQ, but may offer a creative pricing schedule. Purchasing departments are often looking for ways of reducing cost outlay and welcome vendors who can offer the company ways of purchasing material with delayed payments or payments on performance.

13.3 Rejecting Quotations

Once the purchasing department has evaluated the quotations from the bidders, they will determine, based on their criteria, which has been selected as the successful vendor for the material in the RFQ.

13.3.1 Flagging the Quotation as Rejected

The unsuccessful quotations can be flagged as rejected in the system using transaction ME47 or via the navigation path **SAP Menu • Logistics • Materials Management • Purchasing • RFQ/Quotation • Quotation • Maintain**.

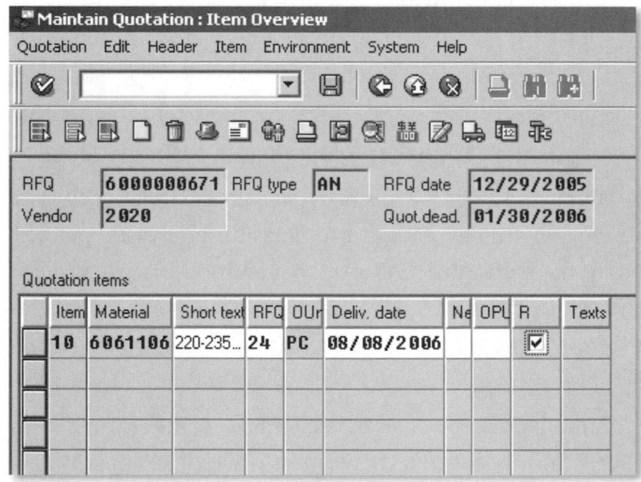

Figure 13.5 Quotation Flagged as Rejected

The purchasing user enters the RFQ number for the quotation to be rejected, as shown in Figure 13.5. The line item can be selected. The line item is then flagged in the rejected column (noted with the letter **R**) to reflect that the quotation has been rejected.

13.3.2 Printing the Quotation Rejection

If appropriate, all unsuccessful vendors in the RFQ process will be notified by the client representative, usually the purchasing department, in writing. Notification will be made as quickly as possible following the award of the contract, or when it has been determined that the vendor will not be asked to continue in the RFQ process.

The rejection letter can be printed from the system using transaction ME9A or via the navigation path **SAP Menu • Logistics • Materials Management • Purchasing • RFQ/Quotation • Request for Quotation • Messages • Print/Transmit**.

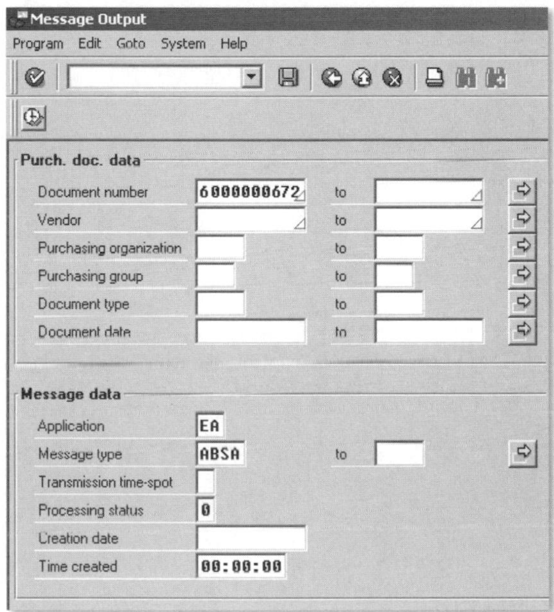

Figure 13.6 Transaction ME9A

For each rejected quotation, a rejection notice can be printed based on the RFQ number, as shown in Figure 13.6. The purchasing user would need to enter the correct message type rejection quotation, which is ABSA. The client can modify the standard rejection notice with SapScript or a tool such as Adobe Form Designer or JetForm.

13.3.3 Advising Unsuccessful Bidders

Sometimes the rejection notice is not an appropriate manner of rejecting a vendor's quotation submission. If the RFQ is for a particular project or of a large monetary value, the client may decide that all the unsuccessful vendors should be given (or may request) a debriefing session with respect to their submissions. These sessions with the client should concentrate on the strengths and weaknesses of the individual vendor's response.

This chapter described the receiving and processing of the quotation. The quotation allows the purchasing department to review the price and terms offered by each vendor and to make the best decision for the company based on the replies given by vendors. The acceptance of a quotation should mean that the vendor has the right to supply the material to the customer for a period of time. Purchasing departments will periodically seek quotations from other vendors to ensure that the material cannot be procured at a better price elsewhere.

14 Purchase Order

The purchase order is the document that shows the intent of the buyer to buy a certain quantity of product at a certain price from a specific vendor. In accepting a purchase order, the vendor agrees to supply the quantity of product to the buyer on or before the required delivery date.

A purchase order is an external document issued by a purchasing department to send to a vendor. The purchase order will contain details that will include the required products, the quantity of the products needed, and the price agreed to by the client and the vendor. As well as the products, quantity, and price, the purchase order usually contains the purchase order number, the order date, delivery address, and terms.

Purchase orders are used to communicate the request to the vendor and to give the vendor a written confirmation of the request. Depending on the legal jurisdiction involved, the purchase order can be considered a legal and binding document.

In some cases, the purchase order does not specify the specific item number, but rather gives a detailed description of the item. This occurs where the material number does not exist or when the customer does not know the material number.

14.1 Create a Purchase Order

The purchase order can be created without any other specific purchase-related documents being created. For instance, a purchase order can be created from a purchase requisition. Depending on the complexity of the client's purchasing activities, the client may not wish to implement purchase requisitions and may allow purchase orders to be created directly.

14.1.1 Create a Purchase Order with Vendor Known.

To create a purchase order without any reference to a purchase requisition, but with the vendor known, the purchasing user can use the new *EnjoySAP* transaction, ME21N, or the traditional purchase order create program ME21. This is illustrated in Figure 14.1. The navigation path used to find the transaction is **SAP Menu • Logistics • Materials Management • Purchasing • Purchase Order • Create • Vendor Known**.

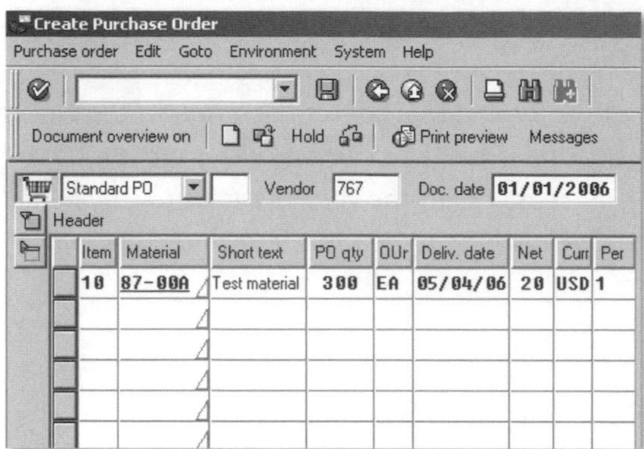

Figure 14.1 Detail Screen from EnjoySAP Transaction ME21N

The new *EnjoySAP* transaction allows the purchasing user to enter most of the information in one location. The left column of the screen can be used to select purchase orders and quickly see the purchasing information. The line detail and header detail can be seen on the one screen, and these can be minimized to make the screen clearer. In Figure 14.1, the purchasing user has chosen to display the purchase line-item detail, but the header detail is filtered out.

This sample purchase order is a standard purchase order, type **NB**, but the purchasing user can choose to select another order type from the drop down menu. Figure 14.2 shows the same purchase order created with the traditional SAP transaction ME21.

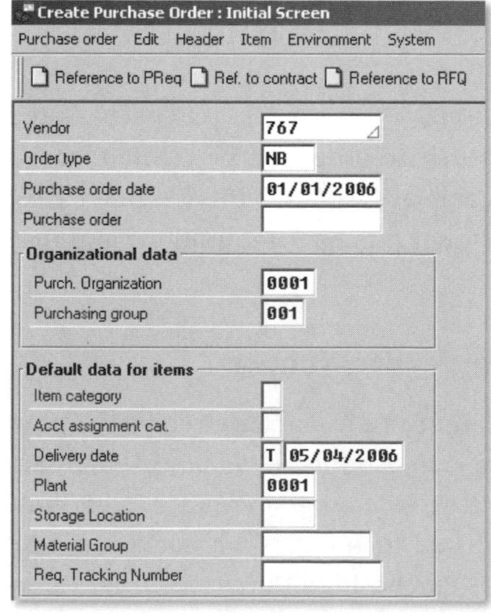

Figure 14.2 Initial Purchase Order Screen for Transaction ME21

14.1.2 Create a Purchase Order Where Vendor is Unknown

Where the purchasing user has to create a purchase order and if the vendor is not known, transaction ME25 should be used, as shown in Figure 14.3. The purchasing user will be able to enter information on the initial screen including date required, purchase group, plant, and item category, if required. This transaction can be found using the navigation path **SAP Menu • Logistics • Materials Management • Purchasing • Purchase Order • Create • Vendor Unknown**.

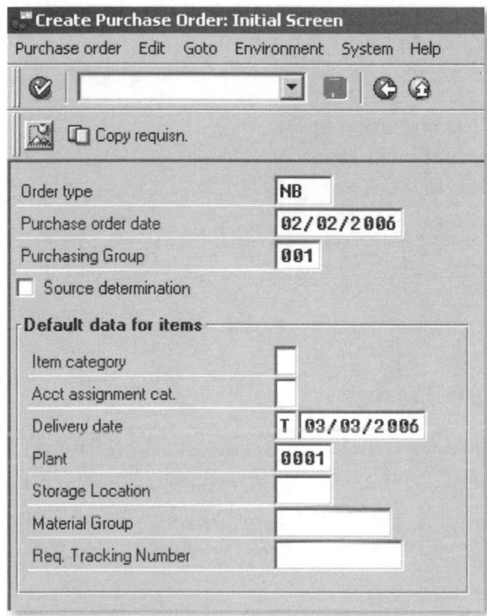

Figure 14.3 Initial Screen for Transaction ME25

Once the initial data is entered, materials on the line-item detail screen can be added. The user can add materials and quantities for the purchase order, as shown in Figure 14.4.

Once the material has been added, the purchasing user can assign a source of supply, i.e., a vendor. If a source list is created for the material, the purchase order program will review all relevant source lists and offer a list of vendors or select the vendor if there is only one source list.

Once the vendor has been assigned, the purchasing user has the option of saving the document as a purchase order. Once posted, the purchase order number will be displayed.

The completed purchase order should be forwarded to the vendor by the method agreed to between the purchasing department and the vendor. If EDI is being used to transmit the purchase order, then EDI code 850 will be used.

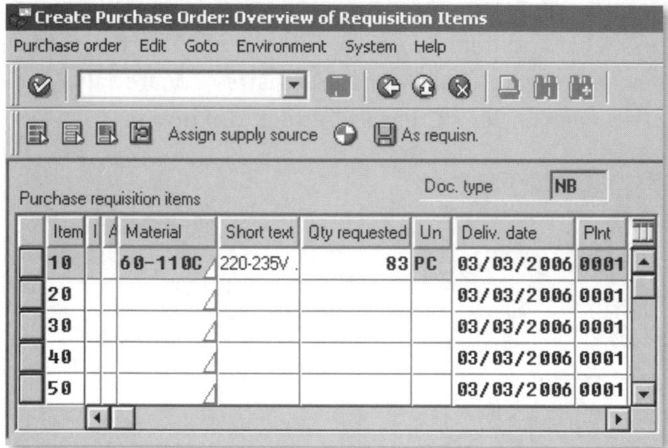

Figure 14.4 Material Added to Transaction ME25 When Vendor is Not Known

14.2 Maintaining a Purchase Order

Once a purchase order has been created there may be an occasion where the purchasing department needs to modify the purchase order. This may be due to a change of vendor, a change in the material quantity required or removal of a line item altogether.

To change the purchase order, the transaction to be used is ME22N. This can be found using the navigation path **SAP Menu • Logistics • Materials Management • Purchasing • Purchase Order • Change**.

Apart from changes to a line item, the purchasing department can add a purchase order line for another material or delete a line item.

Once the purchase order is changed, then it will have to be re-sent to the vendor. The purchase order should be forwarded to the vendor by whatever method is appropriate: fax, email, EDI, etc. However, if the vendor has already delivered an amount against the purchase order, the purchasing department will not be able to reduce the ordered quantity below that which the vendor has already delivered.

If the vendor's invoice has been received, then any changes to the purchase order will not be valid.

14.3 Blocking and Canceling a Purchase Order

14.3.1 Block a Purchase Order Line Item

The purchasing department may wish to block a purchase order after it has been created. This will stop any goods receipt for the relevant line item. The reason for a block on the line item may due to many different reasons, including quality issues with the material that has already been received at the plant.

Using the purchase order change transaction, ME22N, a purchase order line item can be blocked, as shown in Figure 14.5.

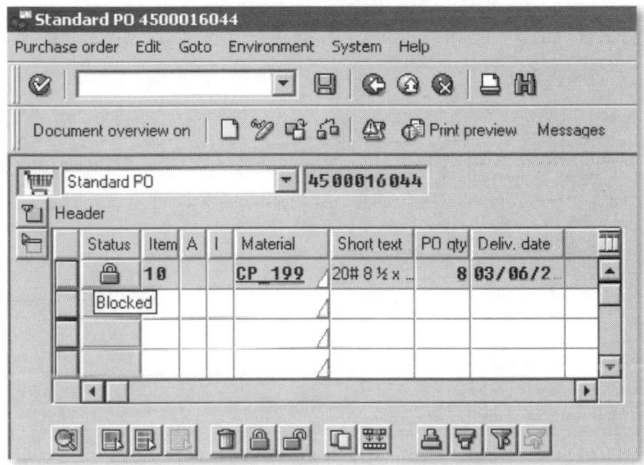

Figure 14.5 Line Item in Purchase Order Blocked by Using Transaction ME22N

14.3.2 Canceling a Purchase Order Line Item

The purchasing department may decide to totally cancel a line item, rather than just block it. There may be issues with the vendor, or the material is no longer required. The material can be canceled by using the purchase order change transaction ME22N. The delete icon can be chosen for the selected line item.

If the purchase order line item has already been subject to a partial goods receipt, the line item cannot be fully deleted because of the delivery. If the line item does not show any delivery, then the purchase order can be set to zero to cancel out the line item.

Once the line item has been canceled, the purchasing department needs to contact the vendor to inform them of the change of purchase order. This can be performed by whatever method has been agreed upon between the purchasing department and the vendor. If EDI were employed, the EDI 860 code would be used, as shown in Figure 14.6.

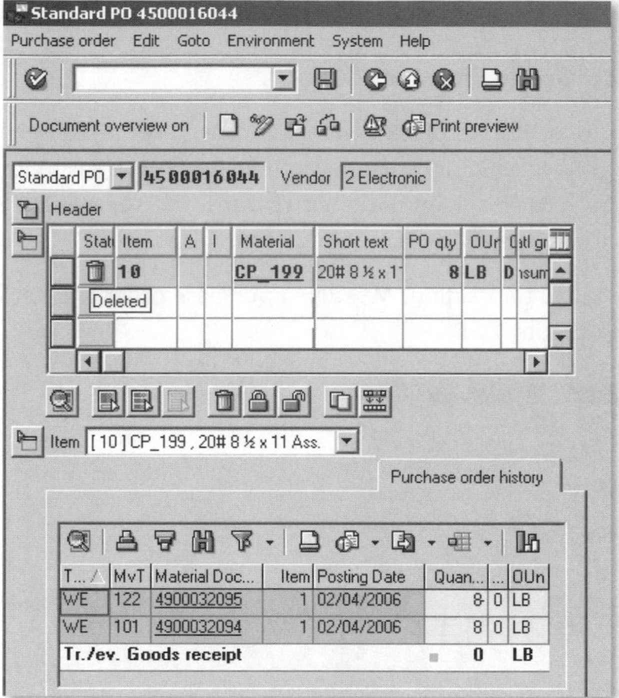

Figure 14.6 Cancellation of Line Item in Transaction ME22N.

14.4 Account Assignment in a Purchase Order

14.4.1 Account Assignment Overview

It is possible to assign a single account code or a number of account codes to a purchase order. Assigning account information describes how the purchased material is being used, such as fulfilling a sales order, or consumption by a cost center. The account assignment also determines what accounts are to be charged when the goods receipt has been posted or the invoice received.

14.4.2 Account Assignment Categories

A number of account assignment categories can be used in the purchase order. On the initial screen of ME21, purchase order creation, the purchasing user can enter an account assignment, as shown in Figure 14.7. The account assignment category determines what account assignment details are required for the item. So if account assignment category **K** is selected, then the transaction would, depending on the specific configuration, require a G/L account and cost center to be entered.

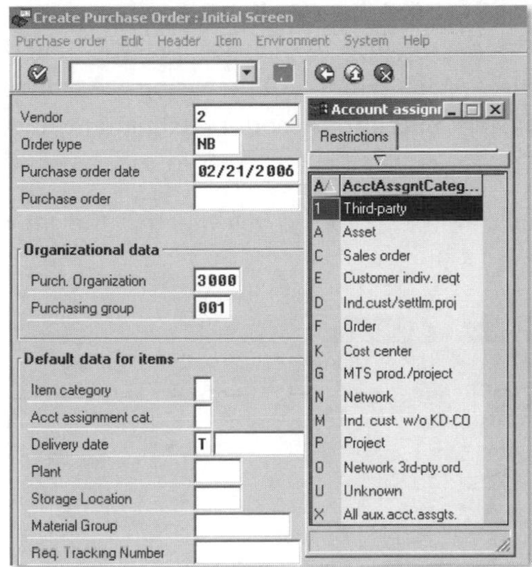

Figure 14.7 Account Assignment Categories to Choose from in Transaction ME21

The different account assignments can be configured in the IMG. The configuration allows a new account assignment to be added and the fields modified to be required, optional, or hidden. The transaction, shown in Figure 14.8, can be found using the navigation path **IMG • Materials Management • Purchasing • Account Assignment • Maintain Account Assignment Categories**.

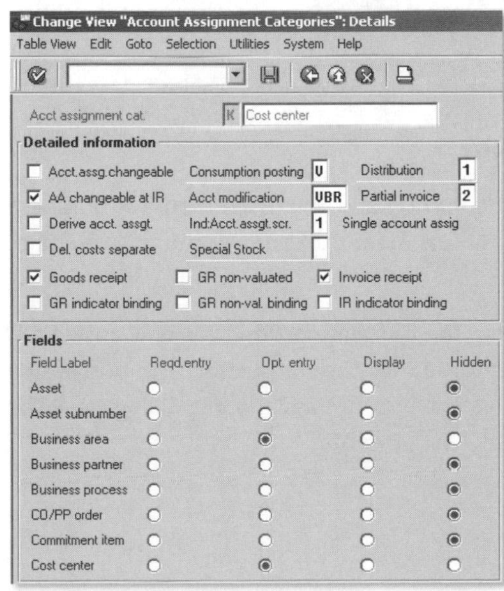

Figure 14.8 Detail Information Screen for Account Category Configuration Transaction

Once a new account assignment has been created, it has to be assigned to an item category in configuration. The transaction to complete this assignment is found via the navigation path **IMG • Materials Management • Purchasing • Account Assignment • Define Combination of Item Category/Account Assignment Categories**.

The purchasing user can decide which item category is relevant for the new account assignment, as shown in Figure 14.9.

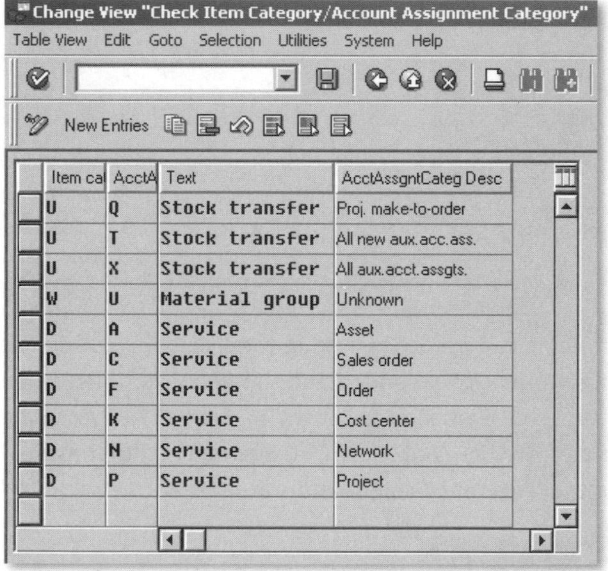

Item ca	AcctA	Text	AcctAssgntCateg Desc
U	Q	Stock transfer	Proj. make-to-order
U	T	Stock transfer	All new aux.acc.ass.
U	X	Stock transfer	All aux.acct.assgts.
W	U	Material group	Unknown
D	A	Service	Asset
D	C	Service	Sales order
D	F	Service	Order
D	K	Service	Cost center
D	N	Service	Network
D	P	Service	Project

Figure 14.9 Configuration for Item Category and Account Assignment Combination

14.4.3 Single Account Assignment

Single account assignment is the most common account assignment for purchase orders. The single account assignment simply means that one account is assigned, as can be seen in Figure 14.10.

The account assignment can be made in the purchase order creation transaction, ME21. Once the line item has been entered into the transaction, the purchasing user can use the header menu to access the account assignment dialog box. The user should navigate to **Item • Account Assignments**.

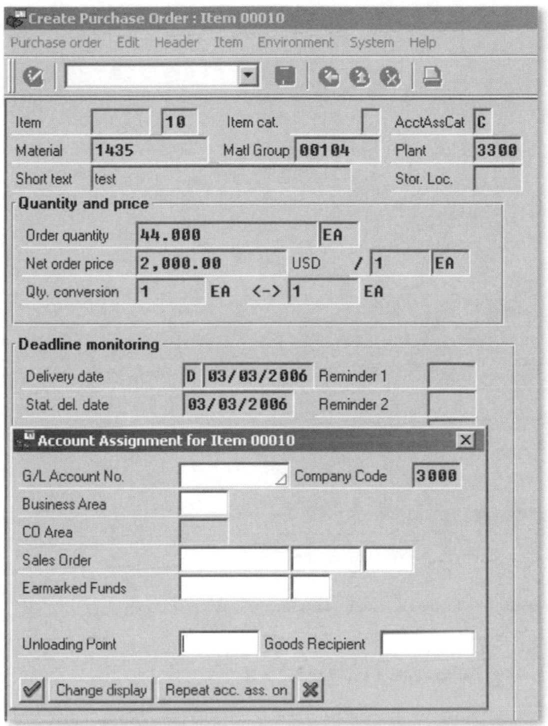

Figure 14.10 Account Assignment Dialog Box for Transaction ME21

14.4.4 Multiple Account Assignment

The multiple account assignment allows a number of accounts to be assigned to one purchase order line. This scenario could occur if a line item is for a material or service that is used by three laboratories and the cost is split between the three. There is the option to divide the amount of the material into that used by each lab, or the user can decide to split the charge by a percentage.

To assign multiple accounts access the multiple account screen from the account assignment dialog box as shown in Figure 14.10. The purchasing user accesses the dialog box as if they were entering one account, and they can then access the multiple account screen by clicking on the icon **Change Display**.

Once the multiple account screen is displayed, see Figure 14.11, the purchasing user can opt to change the Distribution field to **1** for quantity assignment or **2** for percentage assignment.

Any number of accounts can be added for the line item, as long as the total percentage does not exceed 100%, or the total quantity exceeds more than the quantity entered in the line item.

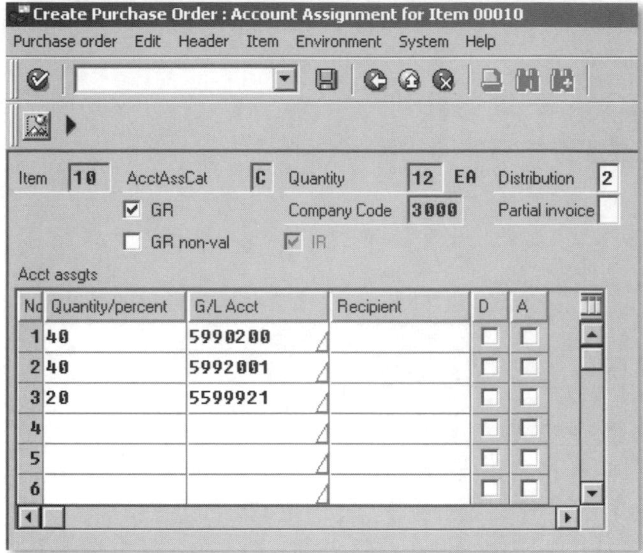

Figure 14.11 Multiple Assignment Screen in Purchase Order Transaction ME21

14.5 Outline Purchase Agreement pause

14.5.1 Outline Purchase Agreement Overview

The outline purchase agreement is often referred to as a blanket or umbrella purchase order. It is basically a long-term agreement between the purchasing department and a vendor for materials or services for a defined period of time. The purchase department negotiates with the vendor a set of terms and conditions that are fixed for the period of the agreement.

14.5.2 Outline Purchase Agreement Types

There are two types of outline purchase agreements: contracts and scheduling agreements. These are:

- A contract is an outline purchase agreement against which release orders can be issued for materials or services when the customer requires them.
- A scheduling agreement is an outline purchase agreement whereby the purchasing department has arranged to procure materials based on a schedule agreed upon between the purchasing department and the vendor. This type of outline purchase agreement is useful to customers who operate repetitive manufacturing, where production consumes the same materials each month and can plan accordingly.

14.6 Scheduling Agreement

14.6.1 Scheduling Agreement Overview

A scheduling agreement can be created manually or it can copied with reference to purchase requisitions, quotations, and centrally agreed contracts. Before creating a scheduling agreement, the purchasing user must define account assignment, purchasing organization, and purchasing group. A scheduling agreement can be created for subcontracting, consignment, and stock transfer.

14.6.2 Create a Scheduling Agreement Manually

Creating a scheduling agreement manually requires the purchasing user to enter the details rather than referencing a quotation, purchase requisition, or contract. Transaction ME31L is used to create the scheduling agreement. This can be found in the navigation path **SAP Menu • Logistics • Materials Management • Purchasing • Outline Agreement • Scheduling Agreement • Create • Vendor Known**.

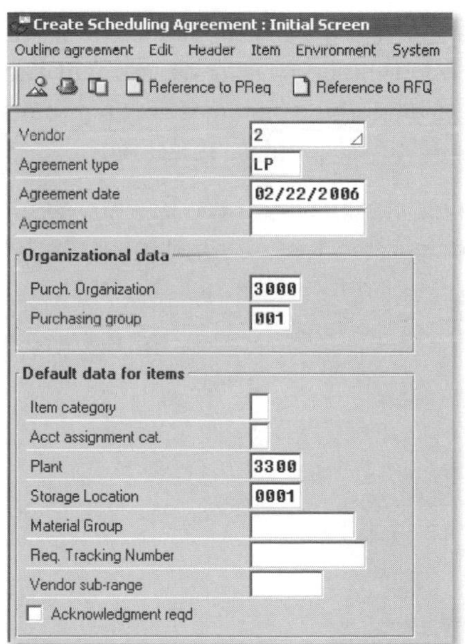

Figure 14.12 Initial Screen for Creating a Manual Scheduling Agreement

In Figure 14.12, there is an option to enter an agreement type, which can be either **LP** for a scheduling agreement or **LU** for stock transport scheduling agreement. There is also the opportunity to enter a scheduling agreement number if an external number has been assigned.

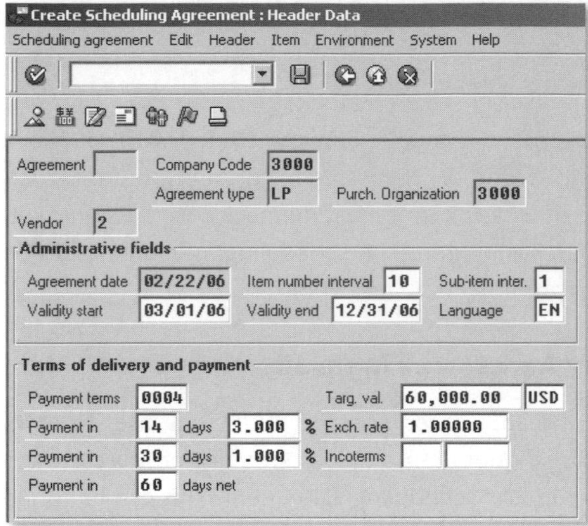

Figure 14.13 Header Data for Manual Scheduling Agreement

Figure 14.13 shows the validity dates of the scheduling agreement and the terms of delivery that have been agreed upon between the purchasing department and the vendor. The purchasing department could have agreed a target dollar amount for the contract. This value can be entered into the scheduling agreement.

Once the header information has been entered the line items can be entered for the scheduling agreement. Each line item requires that a target quantity be entered, as seen in Figure 14.14. The target quantity is the quantity that was agreed upon by the purchasing department and the vendor.

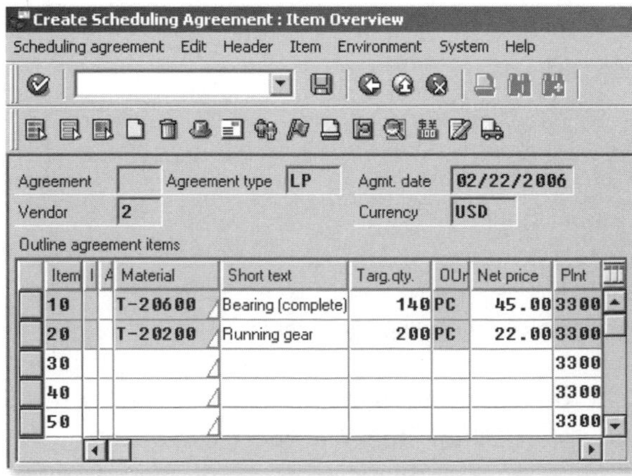

Figure 14.14 Detail Line Items for Scheduling Agreement Using Transaction ME31L

14.6.3 Create a Scheduling Agreement with Reference

If there is a purchase requisition or quotation that should reference the scheduling agreement, the document can be identified when transaction ME31L is run.

When the transaction is run the user has the option of referencing other documents. In Figure 14.15, you can see that a scheduling agreement can be created based on the details from a purchase requisition.

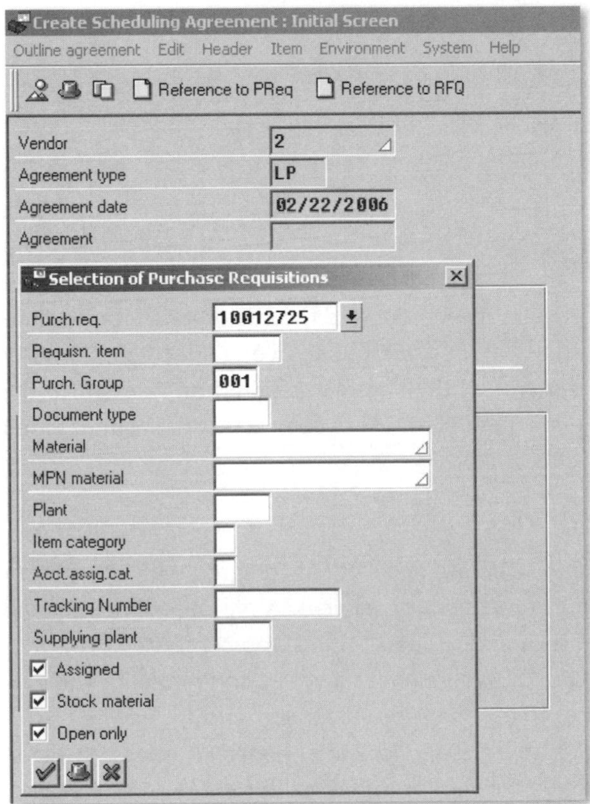

Figure 14.15 Scheduling Agreement Created With Reference to a Purchase Requisition

Once a purchase requisition is chosen, the details from the requisition are available to be adopted and entered into the scheduling agreement. The purchase requisition line items can be seen in Figure 14.16. The purchasing user can then use the **Adopt + Details** icon to copy the details into the scheduling agreement.

Once the purchase requisition lines are copied to the scheduling agreement, the agreed price can be entered, and the scheduling agreement can be posted.

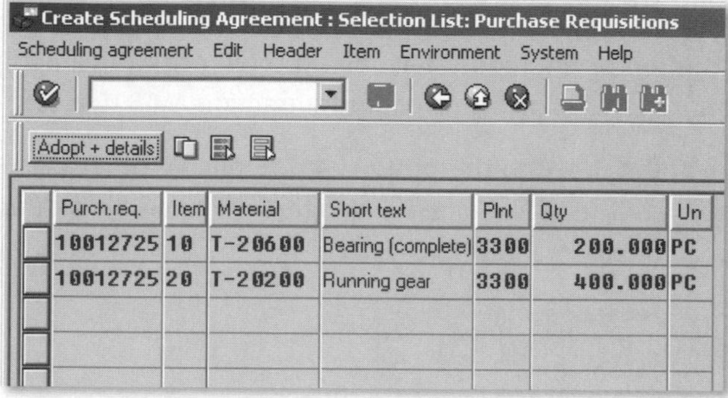

Figure 14.16 Referenced Purchase Requisition for Scheduling Agreement

14.7 Contracts

14.7.1 Contract Overview

A contract is an agreement between the vendor and the customer for the vendor to supply material to the customer at an agreed price over a specified period of time. Unlike the scheduling agreement, the contract is based on releases to the contract, or blanket order, as it is often called. These contracts can be either based on a total quantity or a total value.

Quantity Contract

A quantity contract allows the purchasing department to agree with the vendor on a contract for a set quantity of material, or services. A typical example would involve a vendor that supplies technical support for desktop computers. The vendor may have agreed to provide 480 hours under a yearly contract with the customer. This allows the customer to use the support service without having to create a new purchase order each time the services are needed. A release is made against the contract, which allows the vendor to be paid for the service provided. When all of the hours have been used, the contract has been fulfilled and a new contract can be negotiated.

Value Contract

A value contract allows a purchasing department to cap the spending with one particular vendor. The value contract is not concerned with the quantity of material supplied by the vendor but by the total spending with the vendor for that material. The process of supply is the same as with the quantity contract, as release orders are used to receive material.

However, the release orders are only valid until the total spending for the value contract reaches the total agreed to. In this way, the purchasing department can limit spend at vendors to allow other vendors to supply material.

14.7.2 Centrally Agreed Contract

The centrally agreed contract allows a central purchasing organization to create a contract with a vendor that is not specific just to one plant. In this way the purchasing organization can negotiate with a vendor by leveraging the whole company's spending for certain materials.

Many companies allow plants to negotiate deals with vendors independently of each other and it often turns out that the plants have chosen the same vendor for materials, but have negotiated an array of prices and terms that place some plants at a disadvantage. By creating a central contract, a central purchasing organization can combine the spending of all plants and work on a obtaining the best price for the whole company. The materials and services involved can be as complex as specialized chemicals or as simple as telephone service or express-mail services. Many companies have hundreds of contracts for express-mail service that have been negotiated by local staff over a long period of time, and a central contract could achieve a tremendous cash saving if one was in place.

14.7.3 Creating a Contract

The contract is created in a very similar way to the scheduling agreement. The purchasing user will use transaction ME31K to create a contract. This is found in the navigation path **SAP Menu • Logistics • Materials Management • Purchasing • Outline Agreement • Contract • Create**.

The initial screen, as shown in Figure 14.17, is similar to the initial screen for creating a scheduling agreement.

The agreement-type field, shown in Figure 14.17, should be entered to determine what type of contract is being created. The options are:

- **WK**—Value Contract
- **MK**—Quantity Contract
- **DC**—Distributed or Centrally Agreed Contract

After the initial information has been entered, the transaction will display the header information that needs to be completed, as shown in Figure 14.18. The value contract requires a target value to be entered for the contract.

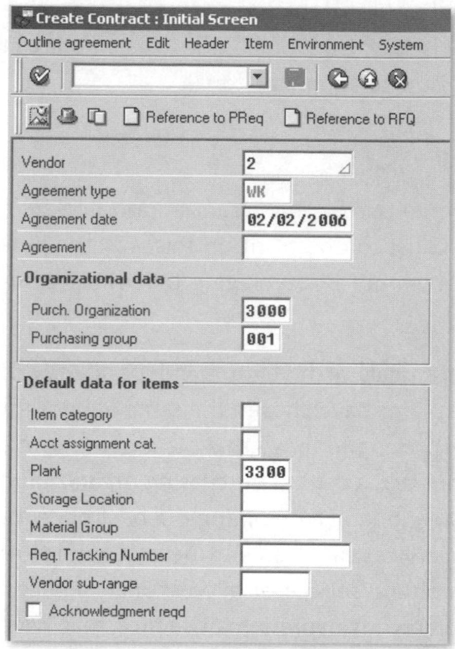

Figure 14.17 Initial Screen of Transaction ME31K

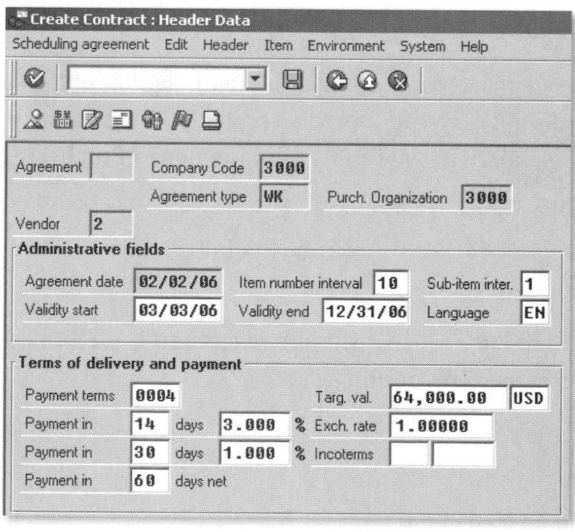

Figure 14.18 Header Information for Value Contract Using Transaction ME31K.

The line items that need to be added to the detail screen are shown in Figure 14.19. The purchasing user will need to add a target for the line item.

Create Contract : Item Overview

Contract Edit Header Item Environment System Help

Agreement		Agreement type	WK	Agmt. date	02/02/2006
Vendor	2			Currency	USD

Outline agreement items

Item	I	A	Material	Short text	Targ.qty	OUn	Net price	Plnt
10			SM-COMP1	ID board for server	100	PC	32.00000	3300
20			SM-COMP2	Memory	100	PC	23.00000	3300
33			T-20600	Bearing (complete)	100	PC	299.00000	3300
40								3300
50								3300

Figure 14.19 Detail Line-Item Information for Value Contract

14.7.4 Release Order Against a Contract

Once the contract is in place, material can be requested from the vendor by using a release order against the contract. This release order can be created via the purchase order screen in transaction ME21. On the initial screen, as seen in Figure 14.20, the purchasing user can access the contract by selecting the **Ref to Contract** icon.

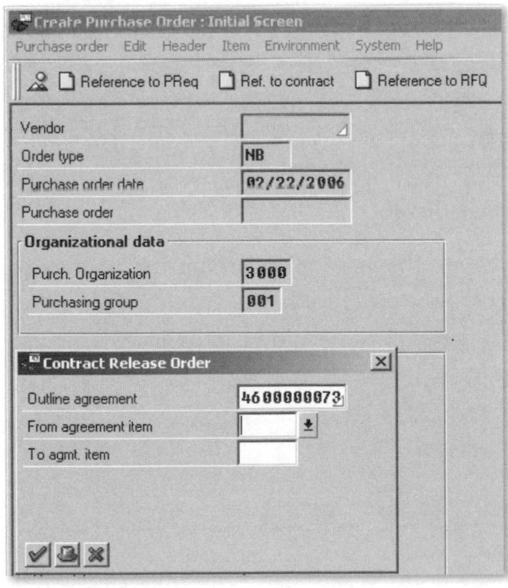

Figure 14.20 Initial Screen for Creating Release Order for Contract

A dialog box will appear where the contract number to create a release for can be entered, as shown in Figure 14.20. Once the contract number is entered the detail lines will be displayed and a quantity entered for each line item on the release order against the contract. The line item will also show the quantity available on the contract, as shown in Figure 14.21.

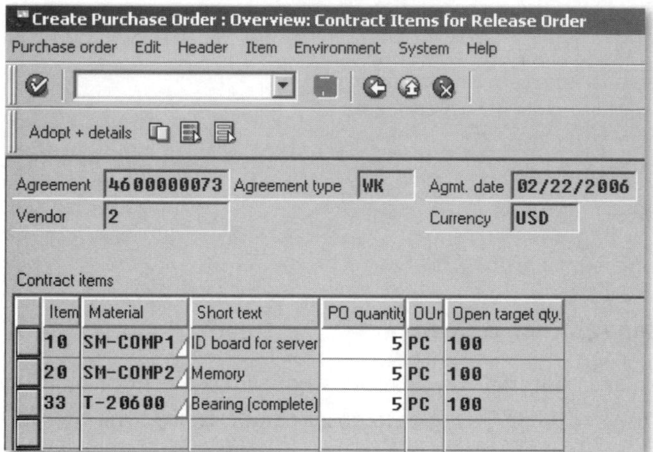

Figure 14.21 Contract Line Items Assigned to Release Order in Transaction ME21

Once the quantities are entered for the release order, the **Adopt + Details** icon can be used to copy the details into the release order. The release order can then be saved.

14.8 Vendor Confirmation

14.8.1 Vendor Confirmation Overview

Vendor confirmations are defined as when the vendor communicates to the customer regarding a purchase order or inbound delivery. The communication can be in the form of a fax, email, or EDI. The communication can be for:

- Order Acknowledgement
- Transport Confirmation
- Advance Ship Notification (ASN)
- Inbound Delivery

The vendor confirmations are manually entered into SAP. The only case where confirmations are loaded automatically is when the confirmation is sent from the vendor using EDI.

Vendor confirmations are important to a client because they provide updated information on delivery of goods. This means that the client does not have to rely solely on the delivery dates agreed to by the vendor at the time of purchase order creation, or even before. This allows the planning department to adjust the production schedule based on the vendor's information.

14.8.2 Confirmation Configuration

The confirmation categories can be configured in the IMG for external or internal confirmations. External categories are defined for manual entries of vendor confirmations, while the internal categories are for the vendor confirmations through EDI. The EDI transaction sets for vendor acknowledgement include 855 for Purchase Order Acknowledgement and 856 for Advance Ship Notification (ASN).

External Confirmations

The external confirmation categories can be configured using a transaction found on the navigation path **IMG • Materials Management • Purchasing • Confirmations • Define External Confirmation Categories**.

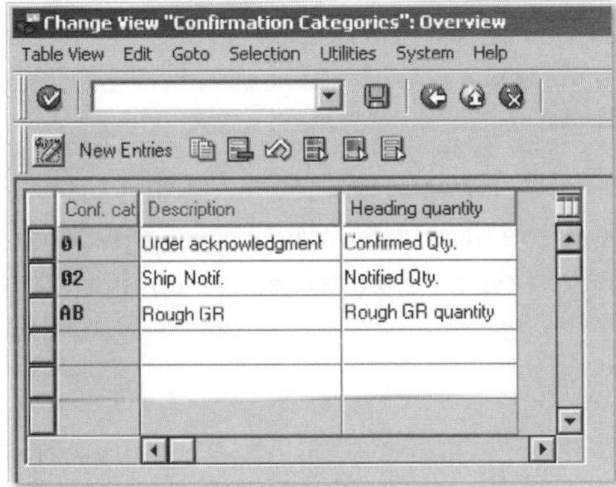

Figure 14.22 Configuration Traction for External Confirmation Categories

It is possible to add new categories, as shown in Figure 14.22, for confirmations, depending on the requirement for confirmations.

Internal Confirmations

Three internal confirmation categories for EDI are supplied in the standard system. These are:

- Category 1—used for order acknowledgments
- Category 2—advance shipping notification (ASN) or inbound delivery is used
- Category 3—rough goods receipt is used

An external confirmation category can be assigned to each internal confirmation category, as shown in Figure 14.23. This enables purchasing documents to be automatically updated with data from the relevant confirmations. The external confirmation categories can be configured using a transaction found on the navigation path **IMG · Materials Management · Purchasing · Confirmations · Define Internal Confirmation Categories**.

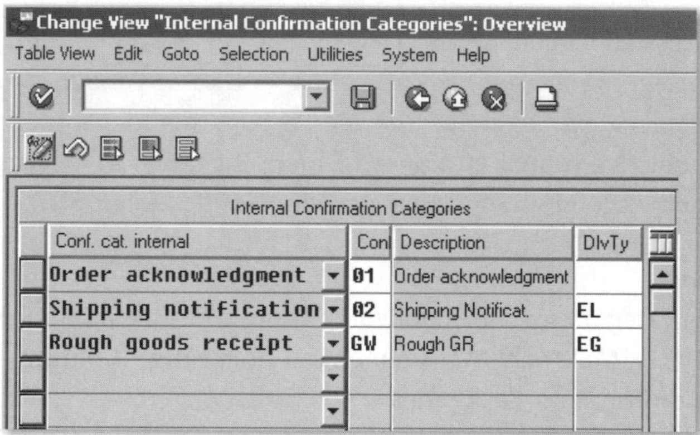

Figure 14.23 Internal Categories and Their Assignment to External Categories

14.8.3 Enter a Manual Confirmation

When a vendor has sent or faxed a confirmation, the acknowledgement can be entered manually into the purchase order line item. However, before the confirmation can be entered, the line item should be checked to see if a confirmation is relevant for confirmation control.

The way to check a line item for confirmation control is to display the line item detail screen within the purchase order-change transaction, ME22, as shown in Figure 14.24.

From the detail line-item screen, the purchasing user can enter the confirmation from the header menu **Item · Confirmations · List**.

The screen then displayed, shown in Figure 14.25, will allow confirmations to be manually added. The confirmation can be added by selecting the type of confirmation; in this case the confirmation control is **AB**, which represents order acknowledgement. The purchasing user then adds the information related to delivery date, time of delivery, and quantity. If the ASN is available, then that also can be entered using confirmation control, LA.

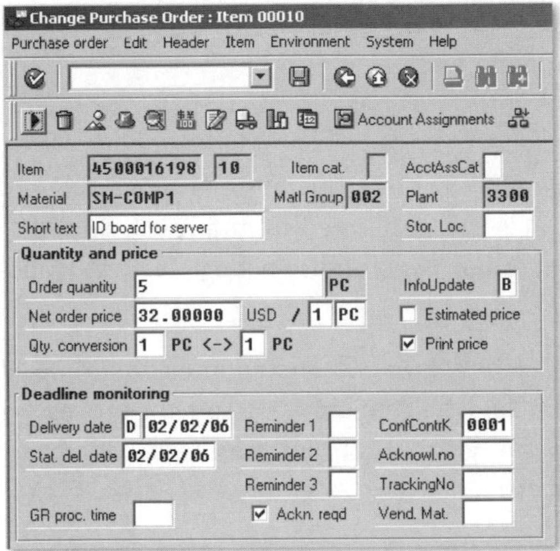

Figure 14.24 Detail Line Item for Purchase Order

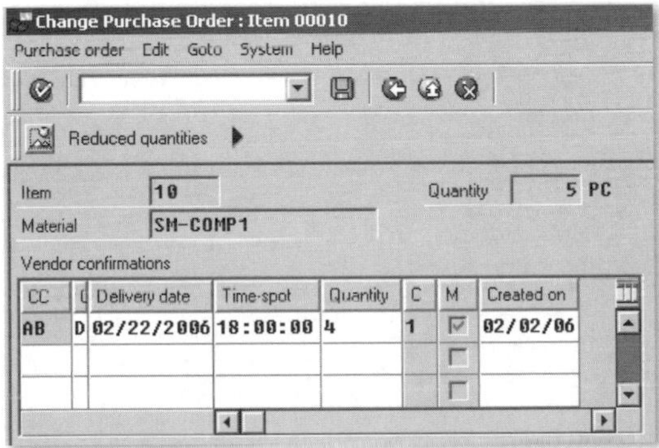

Figure 14.25 Manual Entry of Vendor Confirmation for Purchase Order Line Item

14.9 Messages and Outputs

14.9.1 Message Overview

Once the purchasing user has created a purchase order or changed a purchase order, they will require that the document be in a format where it can be sent to the vendor either by fax, mail, or EDI. The system will generate a message for each document posted.

The output message is created by the same conditions technique that is used for price determination. Once a message is produced for a purchase order, contract. etc., the message is placed in the message queue that contains all messages that are still to be processed. Messages in the queue are available to be processed immediately or at a later time.

14.9.2 Message Creation

The message is created when a document is posted. The message-processing can be seen within the purchase order. This can be viewed from a purchase order, transaction ME22, by accessing the header menu and selecting **Header • Messages**.

The message that has been created can be viewed, as shown in Figure 14.26. If the message can be processed the status will be green. By selecting the processing log icon, the purchasing user can view any error or warning messages that may be causing the document not to be processed.

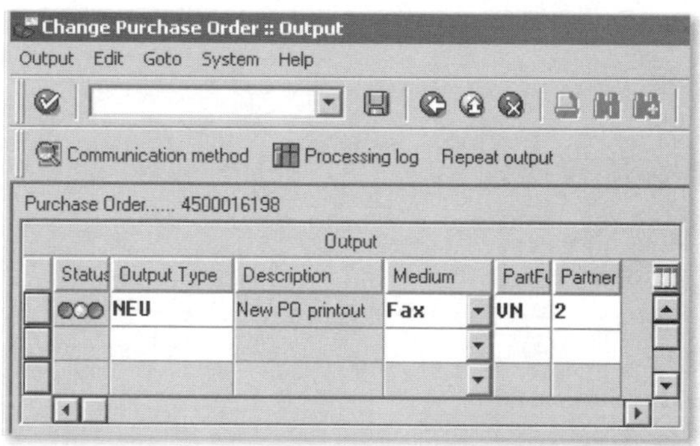

Figure 14.26 Fax Output for Purchase Order: Transaction ME22

14.9.3 Message Output Definition

The output format of the message can be configured in the IMG if the standard format is not suitable. The format can be changed for the purchasing outputs, RFQ, contract, purchase order, and scheduling agreement.

To change the texts for a purchase order, the transaction can be found using the navigation path **IMG • Materials Management • Purchasing • Messages • Text for Messages • Define Texts for Purchase Order**.

The text for document header can be changed and also the document items for any of the different print operations, such as change, rejection of RFQ, or new purchase order. In Figure 14.27, the first line that can be changed is for print operation **1**, which is for a new output of document type **NB**, which is a purchase order. The text is **F01**, which is the header text.

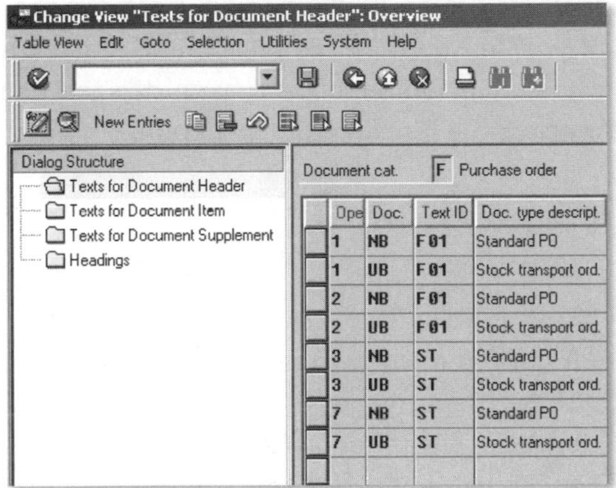

Figure 14.27 Structure of Document That can be Modified

14.9.4 Output Messages

Messages can be processed either by a scheduled batch job or manually. The batch job that can be run to process the output is RSNAST00, and this should be run when it is appropriate.

Messages produced by purchasing documents can be processed by transaction ME9F. This transaction can be found via the navigation path **SAP Menu • Logistics • Materials Management • Purchasing • Purchase Order • Messages • Print/Transmit**.

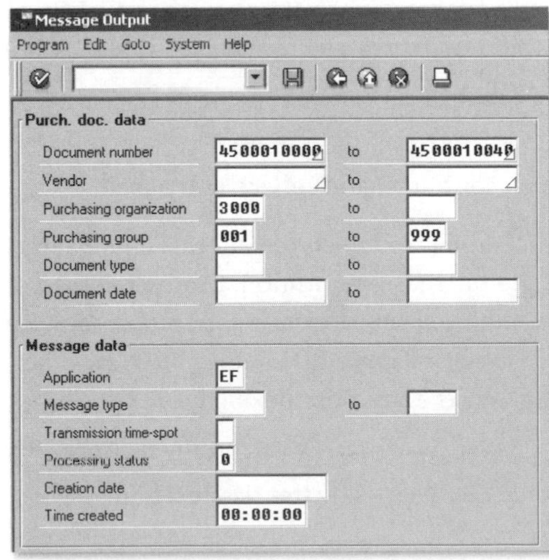

Figure 14.28 Selection Criteria for Printing Purchase Orders in Transaction ME9F

This transaction allows a range of purchase orders, purchasing organizations, vendors, etc, to be entered. This can be seen in Figure 14.28. Once the selection criteria are entered, the transaction will return a number of purchase orders that can be printed. The purchasing user can select the purchase orders to print.

14.10 Reporting

14.10.1 Reporting Overview

The purchasing functionality in SAP does contain a large number of standard reports that can be run on an ad hoc basis. Reports such as the archived purchasing documents (ME82), subcontractor stick per vendor (ME20), and the monitoring confirmations program (ME2A) all can be run from the standard SAP menu.

A number of companies use a large number of standard reports, SAP queries, and customized reports to provide them with an overall view of the purchasing function.

Before customizing reports for a client, it is always worth reviewing the standard reports with the client to ensure that they would not fit their purposes.

14.11 Release Procedures

14.11.1 Introduction to Release Procedures

The release procedure in SAP is the process that allows documents to be held because of specific conditions and only released when they are approved or go through a series of approvals. These approvals are electronic signatures, as the process is conducted within the SAP system.

The release procedure is valid for purchase requisitions, purchase orders, scheduling agreements, request for quotations, contracts, and service entry sheets.

The main difference in the release procedure is between the internal and external documents. The internal document, the purchase requisition, can be released at the item level or the header level. In addition, the purchase requisition can also be released with classification or without classification. However, it is important to realize that release with classification gives a lot more flexibility.

The external documents, such as the purchase order and the RFQ, can only be released at the header level and can only be released by the classification method.

14.11.2 Release with Classification for a Purchase Requisition

For the release with classification, the characteristics and appropriate classes need to be defined in the classification system. It is important to remember that a class should be created for each purchasing document.

The configuration for release of a purchase requisition without classification is already pre-defined in SAP. The release with classification within the IMG, must be configured.

The configuration for the release of purchase requisitions is found in the IMG using the path **IMG • Materials Management • Purchasing • Purchase Requisition • Release Procedure • Procedure with Classification**.

Edit Characteristics

Each characteristic represents a release condition. Characteristics can be set up that describe the conditions that need to be satisfied for a release strategy to be assigned.

Characteristics can be created easily as they would be in classification. The chapter for further discussion on classification will appear later in this book.

Edit Class

The class is created, and as part of that creation the characteristics defined for the purchase requisition are assigned to the class. The class for release strategy does need to be linked to class type 032, which is the class type for release strategy.

Release Groups

The release groups are defined in standard SAP. Release group 01 is defined for purchase requisitions; release group 02 is defined for purchase orders.

Release Codes

The release code is a two-character field that usually represents the person responsible for the approval.

Release Indicator

The release indicator represents the document that was released of the purchasing document.

Release Strategy

The strategy defines the release codes with which a purchase document must be released and the sequence in which release must be used.

The purchase order is probably the most familiar process in materials management. The purchase order is important in that it provides material to the production process or requestor in a timely fashion, at the best available price and with the best terms. For the materials management user, especially for a purchasing user, all aspects of creating and maintaining purchase order should be studied. Links with finance should be understood, e.g., account assignment. Two areas that were discussed here often create many issues for purchasing users. These are message output and release strategy. If purchase orders cannot be printed it can cause delays in receiving material and understanding the process of printing purchasing output is very important. Release strategy can be complex to implement, but this depends on the client. Understanding how the release strategy is configured and how it works within the purchasing documents will help a client adopt a successful and straightforward release policy.

15 External Service Management (ESM)

Companies purchase as many services as they do materials. Services can be managed and analyzed in the same way as any material. However, services have some unique aspects and require the SAP user to understand the differences to benefit from the ESM functionality.

External Service Management (ESM) incorporates functionality that is relevant to the procurement and execution of services at a company. The service master record is the document that contains the information on a service. The service specifications are listed services that can make up a particular task or project that a company needs to procure.

Services can be planned—using a service master record—or unplanned, therefore not referencing a service master but rather referencing a monetary limit for the services performed. The service can be entered using a service entry sheet, whereby the documented hours can be approved, and authorization given for payment.

15.1 Service Master Record

The service master record is the document that contains the basic information of the service, similar to a material master record.

The service master record can be entered using the transaction AC03, or via **SAP Menu • Logistics • Materials Management • Service Master • Service • Service Master**. Figure 15.1 (page 306) shows the initial screen.

15.1.1 Service Number

The service number is similar to the material number, and this field can be defined for external or internal numbering. The number ranges can be defined in configuration using transaction ACNR or via the navigation path **IMG • Materials Management • External Service Management • Service Master • Define Number Ranges**.

15.1.2 Service Category

The service category differentiates between different types of services, similar to the same way that a material type does for materials. The service category, as shown in Figure 15.2, can be configured in the SAP IMG using the navigation path **IMG • Materials Management • External Service Management • Service Master • Define Service Category**.

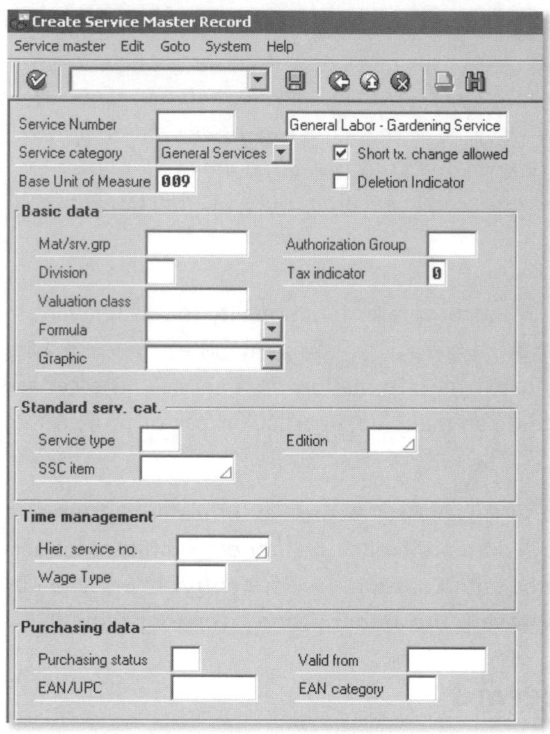

Figure 15.1 Entry Screen for Creating Service Master Record

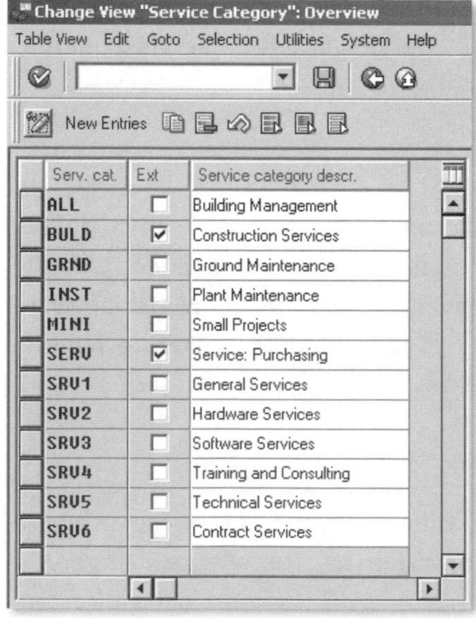

Figure 15.2 Configuration for Service Category

15.1.3 Material/Service Group

The material/service group field allows the material group to be selected for grouping purposes. The selection is the same for the service master as it is for the material master.

15.1.4 Tax Indicator

The tax indicator for the service master allows the purchasing user to enter a "not taxed" code if the service is not taxed or a tax code for taxable service.

15.1.5 Valuation Class

The valuation class for the service master is the same field that is used in the material master. Using the valuation class, the system can find the general ledger accounts that are associated with the service financial postings.

15.1.6 Formula

The formula field allows a defined formula to be chosen for a service that has been pre-defined in configuration. Depending on the service to be performed, the effort involved in performing a task may be definable by a number of variables. For instance, there may be a formula for lawn maintenance that is variable depending on the size of the area to be maintained.

Formula can be defined in configuration using the navigation path **IMG • Materials Management • External Service Management • Formula for Quantity Determination • Define Formulas**.

The formula is defined by entering a formula key and then the formula with variable names. The formula can use variables that are defined elsewhere in configuration. The formula must also have a base unit of measure.

The variables in the formula calculation must be defined in configuration also, as shown in Figures 15.3 and 15.4. The variables are defined using the navigation path **IMG • Materials Management • External Service Management • Formula for Quantity Determination • Specify Names of Formula Variables**.

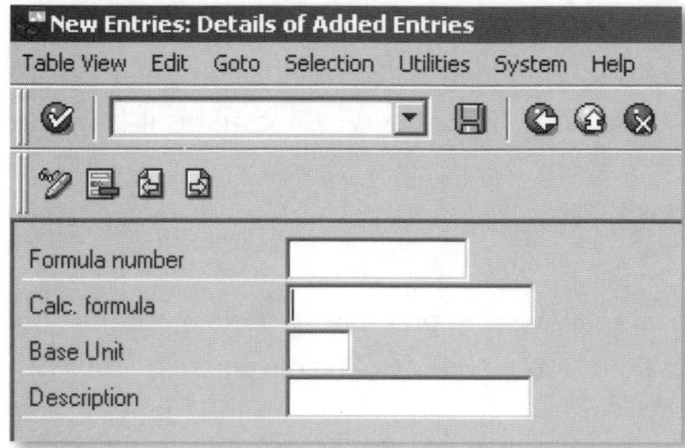

Figure 15.3 Configuration Screen to Create Formula for Quantity Determination in Service Master

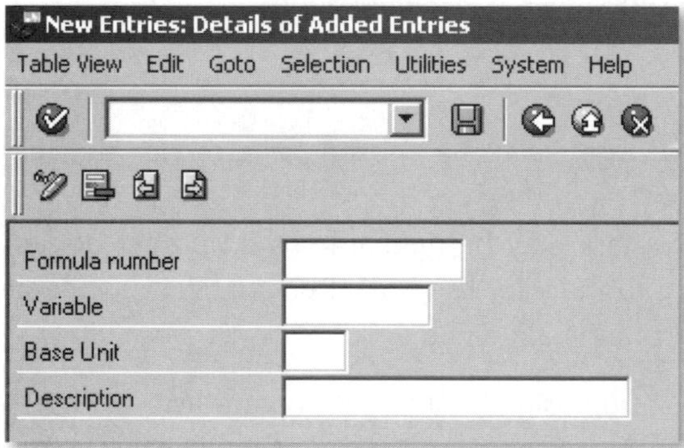

Figure 15.4 Configuration of Formula Variables for Service Master Calculation

15.1.7 Graphic

The service master includes a graphic field where the purchasing user can select a picture or graphic that can aid the supplier of the service. For example, the service may be to polish a finished good, and the company may have a specific way of completing the task. The graphic could be included with the purchase order or RFQ to ensure the service was performed correctly.

In the next section, the standard service catalog is discussed. This is a list of the service description that reduces the number of entries the purchasing user has to make.

15.2 Standard Service Catalog (SSC)

15.2.1 Overview

The standard service catalog is a record containing service descriptions that are used when the service master has not been created. The SSC is used to keep a standard list of the description that eliminates the need for descriptions to be created each time a non-service master record is entered. This prevents a great deal of data duplication.

15.2.2 Creating a SSC Entry

The SSC entry can be created by using transaction ML01 or by following the navigation path **SAP Menu · Logistics · Materials Management · Service Master · Standard Service Catalog · Create**.

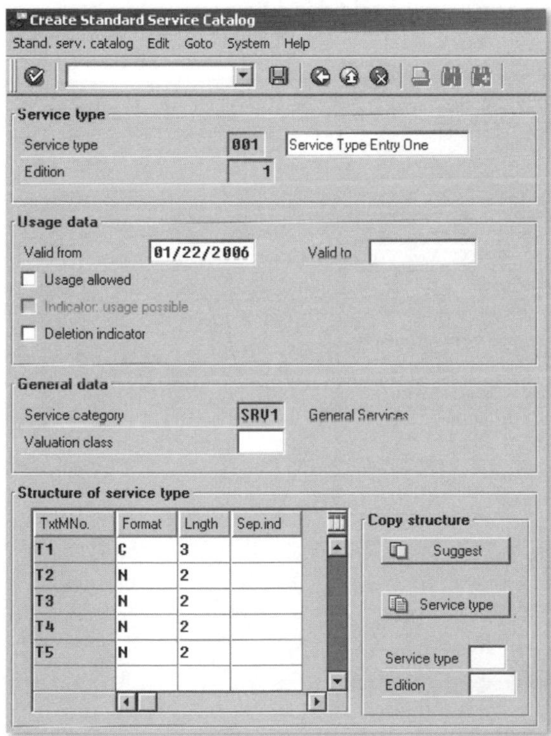

Figure 15.5 Detail Screen for Creating Standard Service Catalog Entry

On the initial screen for entering a SSC, the user can enter a service type number and an edition (or version number) can be entered. The detailed information for the service type includes a validity period and the service category, as seen in Figure 15.5.

The structure of the service type is defined where the structure can be divided into a number of meaningful sections. The maximum number of characters in the structure is 18.

For instance, in Figure 15.5 in the **Structure of a Service Type** section, the SSC entry for service type 001 will have an 11-character structure made up of a three-character string followed by four separate numeric strings of two characters each.

Figure 15.6 shows how the different elements of the structure are made up. The first four characters are the highest in the hierarchy in column T2, then the next three in column T3, and so on. The structure can be thought of as a service tree where the lowest elements where the actual time is reported, i.e. in column **T5**. In Figure 15.6, note that the unit of measure should only be added to the lowest level of the structure, **T5**, otherwise an **invalid text module** error will occur.

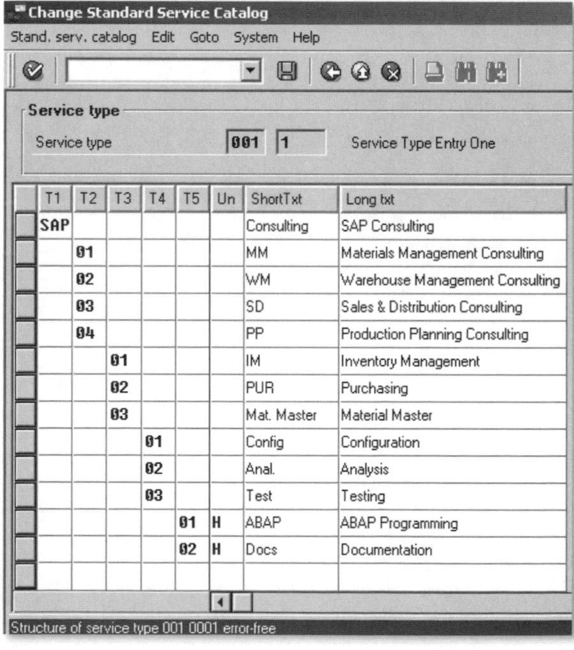
Change Standard Service Catalog

Stand. serv. catalog Edit Goto System Help

Service type

Service type 001 1 Service Type Entry One

T1	T2	T3	T4	T5	Un	ShortTxt	Long txt
SAP						Consulting	SAP Consulting
	01					MM	Materials Management Consulting
	02					WM	Warehouse Management Consulting
	03					SD	Sales & Distribution Consulting
	04					PP	Production Planning Consulting
		01				IM	Inventory Management
		02				PUR	Purchasing
		03				Mat. Master	Material Master
			01			Config	Configuration
			02			Anal.	Analysis
			03			Test	Testing
				01	H	ABAP	ABAP Programming
				02	H	Docs	Documentation

Structure of service type 001 0001 error-free

Figure 15.6 Elements of Service Type Hierarchical Structure

15.3 Conditions in ESM

Conditions are found in service management similar to those found in normal purchasing. Conditions apply to services such as discounts, surcharges, and taxes.

15.3.1 Total Price Condition

One method of entering a condition for a service is to enter a total price condition. This can be achieved by using the transaction ML45 or via the navigation path **SAP Menu • Logistics • Materials Management • Service Master • Service • Service Conditions • For Service • Add**.

This transaction allows the purchasing user to enter a condition that gives an overall estimate of the service to be performed over a certain time period.

Create Total Price Condition (PRS) : Fast Entry

Condition Edit Goto Extras Environment Pricing System Help

Service Conditions

Service	Description	Amount	Curr	per	UoM	Valid on	Valid to
3000111	Consulting	50,000.00	USD	2,000	H	01/03/06	12/31/06

Figure 15.7 Total Price Condition for Service for Given Validity Period

In this case, as can be seen in Figure 15.7, the service has been given a total price condition of $50,000 for 2,000 hours of work until December 31, 2006. The total price condition can also be defined as a scale, by selecting the F2 function key or using the menu path **Goto • Scales**.

The condition can be entered with a different value being valid for a different level of the scale as defined by the purchasing user, see Figure 15.8.

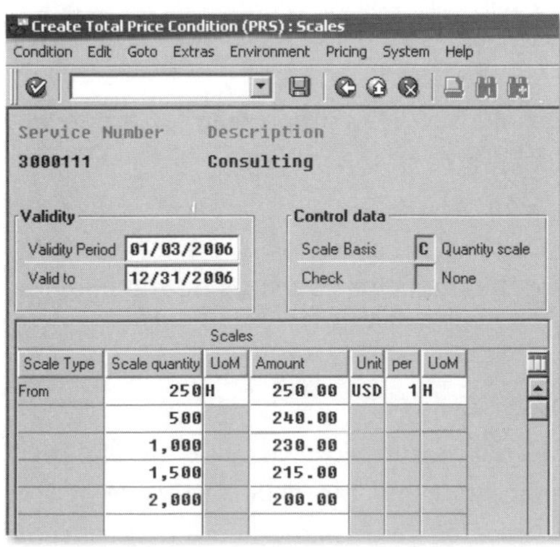

Scale Type	Scale quantity	UoM	Amount	Unit	per	UoM
From	250	H	250.00	USD	1	H
	500		240.00			
	1,000		230.00			
	1,500		215.00			
	2,000		200.00			

Figure 15.8 Condition Defined Using Scales for Given Time Period

15.4 Procurement of Services

15.4.1 Using a Purchase Order

Services can be purchased using the normal purchase order creation transaction, ME21. The item category needs to be entered and set to **D** for services.

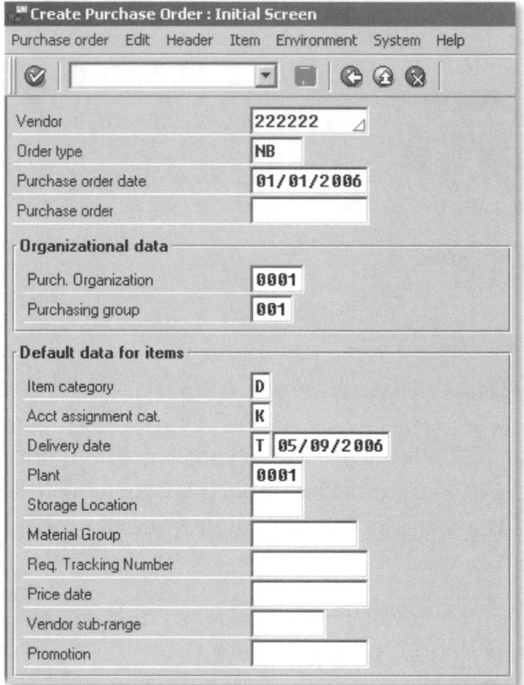

Figure 15.9 Purchase-Order Entry Screen for Services

The screen shown in Figure 15.10 will show the data entry screen for the service specification. A number of items can be entered in this screen.

Overall Limit

An overall limit can be entered for all of the unplanned services on the purchase order. This limit may not be exceeded.

Expected Value

An expected value of unplanned services can be entered. This value does not necessarily need to be equal to the overall limit, and the expected value can be exceeded unlike the overall limit. The expected value is the figure that is used if there is an appropriate release strategy in place.

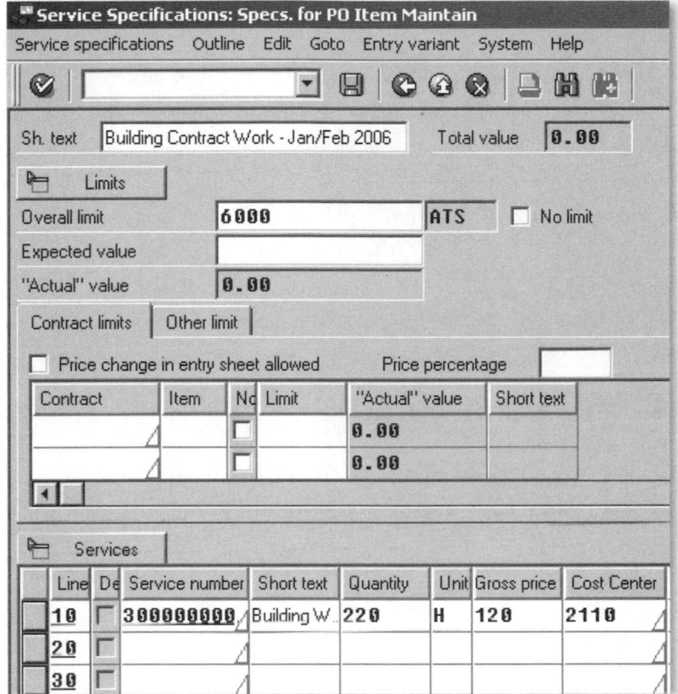

Figure 15.10 Detail Screen for Purchase Order for Services

Actual Value

This field is calculated by the system and is updated continually from service sheet entry or from goods receipt transactions.

Contract

The service purchase order can allow the purchasing user to add one or a number of purchase contracts. A limit to the services purchased against the contract can be added.

Services

A purchasing user can add a number of services that are required for the purchase order. The service number is entered with a quantity and price per unit of measure. Once the information is entered for the individual services, the purchase order can be completed once the header information shown in Figure 15.11, has been verified.

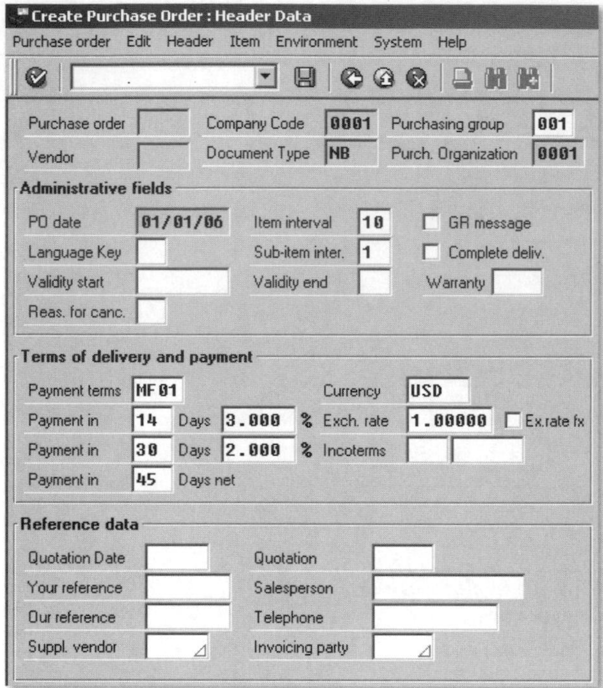

Figure 15.11 Header Information Screen for Service Purchase Order

15.5 Entry of Services

When a supplier has completed a service or the service has been partially performed, the information can be entered into the SAP system. The entry of this data is recorded on the service entry sheet. The information on the service entry sheet would be for planned and unplanned service.

15.5.1 Service Entry Sheet

The service entry sheet is the transaction where data is entered with respect to the service that has been ordered via a Purchase Order. The service entry sheet is found using transaction ML81N or via the path **SAP Menu • Logistics • Materials Management • Service Entry Sheet • Maintain**.

The service entry sheet, shown in Figure 15.12, is based on the service in a purchase order, so the entry point for the transaction is the selection of a purchase order number. Once the purchase order number is entered, the service number that was entered as a line item in the purchase order will be displayed. The purchasing user can enter the quantity of the service, either partial or complete.

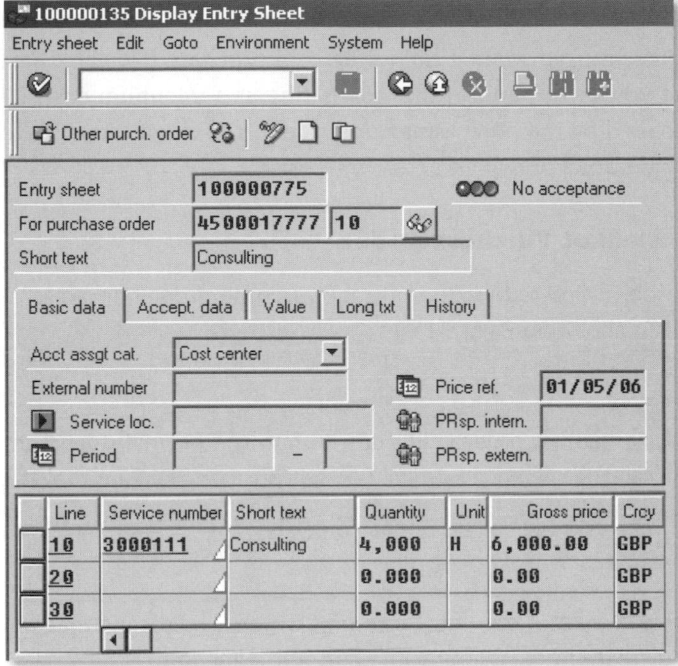

Figure 15.12 Service-Entry Sheet for Given Purchase Order

Once the data has been entered then the data sheet can be accepted. Once accepted, the service entry sheet will appear as accepted or ready for being accepted on the ML81N initial screen, shown in Figure 15.13.

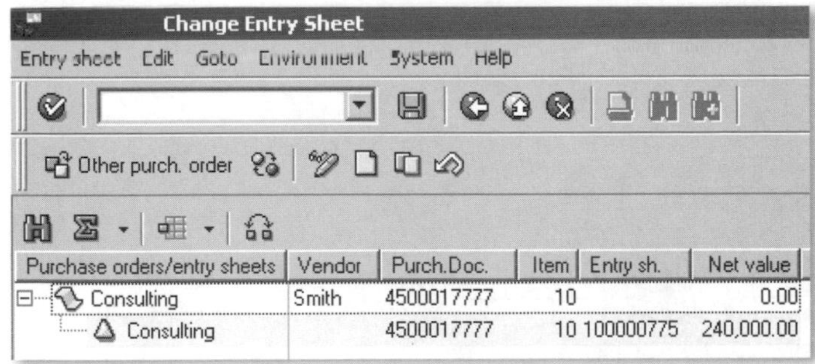

Figure 15.13 Purchase Order and One Service Entry Sheet Ready to be Accepted

Once there are no more service entry sheets to be entered against the purchase order the final entry indicator can be set by selecting from the service entry sheet menu **Entry Sheet · Set Status · Final Entry**.

15.6 Blanket Purchase Order

A blanket purchase order is used when a client needs to purchase low value services or materials and wishes to perform this purchasing at a minimum cost. By reducing the effort needed by the purchasing department, the client can achieve some monitoring of the transaction at an economic cost.

15.6.1 Creating a Blanket Purchase Order

A blanket purchase order is created via the normal purchase order transactions, ME21 or ME21N. This is shown in Figure 15.14.

Document Type

The document type for a blanket order is **FO** rather than the normal document type for a purchase order, **NB**. When creating a blanket order, make sure that the correct document type is used.

Item Category

The item category for a blanket order is B for a limit order. This means that the purchase order will be created with a limit value and not a line item.

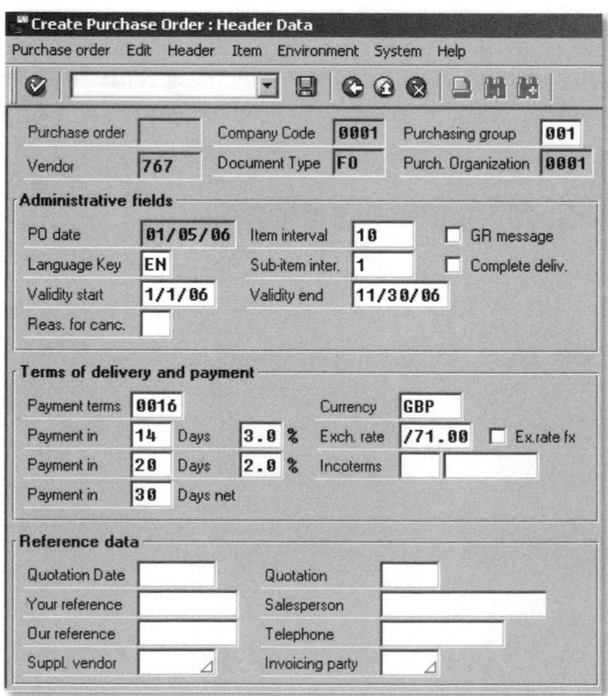

Figure 15.14 Detail Information for Blanket Purchase Order

Validity Period

Using the blanket purchase order requires that the value limit be contained within a period of time. Therefore, the vendor has a limited period in which to submit invoices up to the value limit entered within the blanket order.

Vendor Invoicing

The vendor will send invoices to the purchasing department with reference to the purchase order. The accounts payable department will process the invoices, if the invoices fall within the validity period of the blanket purchase order. The invoices will also only be processed if the total amount of the combined invoices from the vendor does not exceed the value limit in the blanket purchase order, as shown in Figure 15.15.

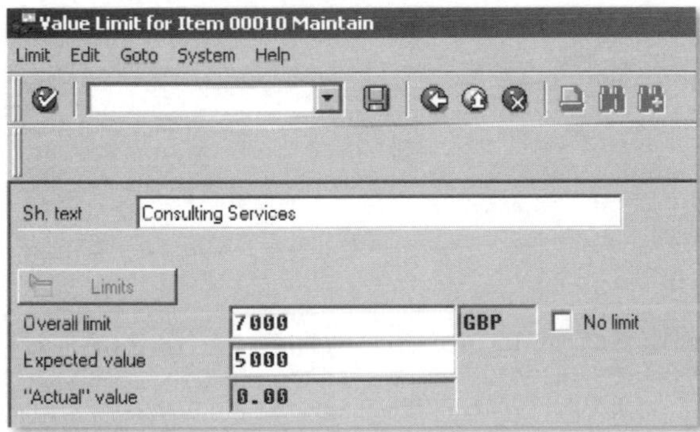

Figure 15.15 Value Limit Entry for Blanket Purchase Order

In this chapter we discussed the ESM functionality. Companies purchase services, as well as, materials and the functionality in ESM allows the purchasing department to influence how services are purchased and to monitor their consumption of those services. As more companies use SAP to purchase and record service usage, purchasing personnel will be required to be fully familiar with this functionality.

16 Consumption-Based Planning

In any company, material is consumed either in the production of items, by performing a service, or by daily operations. In order to replenish the stock of material, the company can use consumption-based planning (CBP) to determine when future purchases need to be made.

Consumption-based planning (CBP) is a planning method based on past consumption of a material and using the entered forecast to determine future material requirements. CBP is not calculated via independent or dependant requirements, such as found in master production scheduling. The level of material hitting a defined reorder point initiates CBP or by the forecast requirements calculated using consumption values found in the material master record. The CBP used in SAP is known as MRP or Materials Requirements Planning.

16.1 Master Data in CBP

16.1.1 Material Master Record

Consumption figures for a material are stored in the material master record and are calculated for unplanned and total consumption. Either figure can be viewed and/or updated in the material master record.

The consumption figures for a material are held within the material master record and are updated by transaction data from inventory management. The data can be viewed in the format shown by the period indicator; in the case of Figure 16.1, it is **M** for monthly consumption.

The transaction to view/change the consumption values is MM02 and this can be found using the navigation path **SAP Menu • Logistics • Materials Management • Material Master • Change • Immediately**.

The material number should be entered, then the organizational level icon should be pressed, and a view requested, such as MRP or Forecasting. On the detail screen there is an icon for **Additional Data**. This will show a number of tabs, and there is one called **Consumption**.

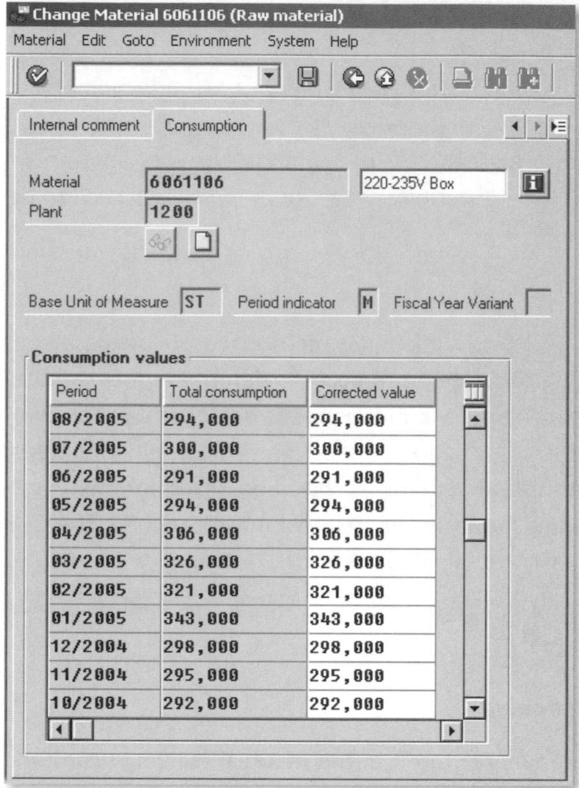

Figure 16.1 Total Consumption Figures per Month for a Material Using Transaction MM02

The consumption screen for the material is shown in Figure 16.1. All the consumption figures for the material will be displayed in chronological order. The unplanned consumption and the total consumption per time period can be viewed. If the material has been entered and there is missing consumption data, this can be added in this screen for the relevant time periods.

16.1.2 Planning Calendar

The planning calendar is used to define the period lengths for CBP at the plant level, shown in Figure 16.2. The planning calendar is defined by using transaction MD25 or using the path **SAP Menu • Logistics • Materials Management • MRP • MRP • Master Data • Planning Calendar • Create Periods**.

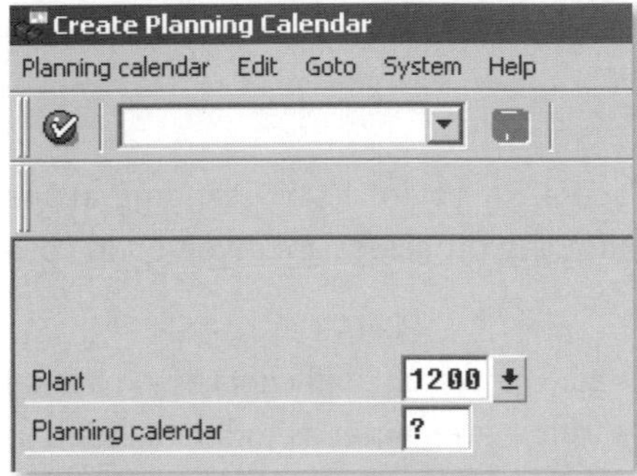

Figure 16.2 Initial Screen for Transaction MD25

The planning calendar is created for each plant. When creating a new planning calendar, a three-character code for the new calendar can be entered.

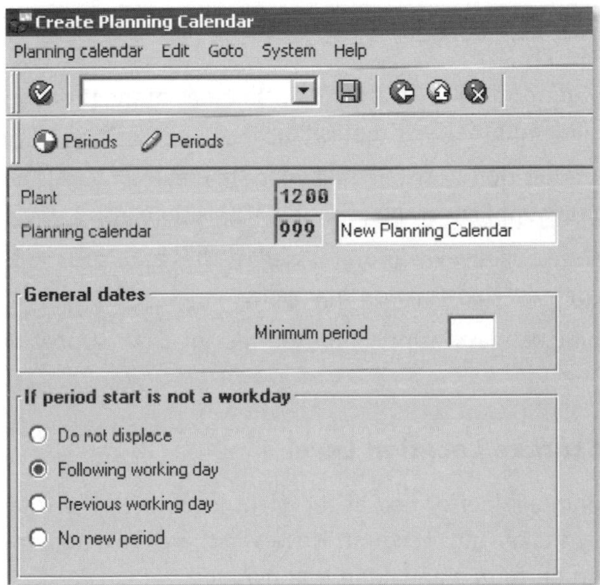

Figure 16.3 Variables for New Planning Calendar

When creating the planning calendar it is possible to define certain variables, such as in Figure 16.3, where the calendar has been flagged to start a period as a weekday. Other options allow the first day of the period to be a workday or not a workday, previous to a non-working day, or after a non-working day. The planning calendar will ascertain whether a day is a working day or a non-working day by referencing the relevant factory calendar configured in the IMG.

16.2 Planning Process

16.2.1 Planning at the Plant Level

The planning process will normally take place at the plant level. Planning at the storage location level can be defined. The following processes are involved in consumption-based planning:

- Initially, SAP checks the planning file entries. The system will check if a material has been changed, relevant to MRP, and if this material needs to be included in the planning run.
- SAP will then complete a net-requirements calculation for every material. SAP checks the available warehouse stock and receipts from purchasing and production to ensure that the requirement quantity is covered. If the net requirement quantity is not covered, a procurement proposal is then created.
- Lot-sizing calculation is then performed. Rounding up or down of values are carried out, if this is necessary.
- Scheduling is performed to determine the start and finish dates of the procurement proposals, such as planned orders, or requisitions.
- Planned orders, purchase requisitions, or schedule lines are created by SAP for the procurement proposal. A supplier can be assigned at this time also.
- Critical situations are identified using exception messages. These are situations where the planner has to process the situation manually.
- Finally, SAP calculates the actual days' supply and the receipt days' supply of the material.

16.2.2 Planning at the Storage Location Level

The planning of material is normally performed at the plant level, with the total amounts of all storage locations taken into account. However, there are occasions when a client may not wish to perform planning in that manner.

A common reason for storage-location planning is a logistical one. Clients with storage locations remote from the associated plant may want to perform planning at lower level. In addition, storage locations that are unique—e.g., locations that only contain a certain type of material relevant to plant maintenance or repairs—may want to plan these separately.

Two options are available to the client who wishes to identify some storage locations as unique for planning purposes: plan at the storage location level, or exclude the storage location from planning.

Storage Location Planning

In this scenario, the planning department needs to ensure that the reorder level for the material and the replenishment quantities are defined at the storage-location level.

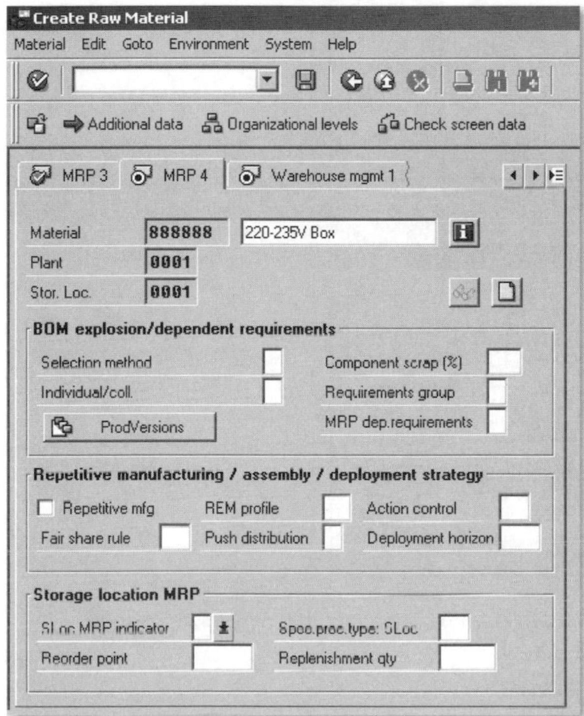

Figure 16.4 Storage Location MRP Fields in Material Master Relevant for Storage-Location Planning

For the planning to be completed at the storage-location level, the storage location MRP fields in the material master need to be completed. Depending on the version of SAP your client uses, these fields may appear on a different MRP screen from that in Figure 16.4.

The procurement proposals for the storage location that is planned separately will not be part of the plant stock levels.

Excluding Storage Location from Planning

A storage location can be excluded from planning and the stock not be included in the available stock totals. The storage location can be excluded from the planning process by selecting the appropriate value for the MRP Indicator for the storage location, as shown in Figure 16.5.

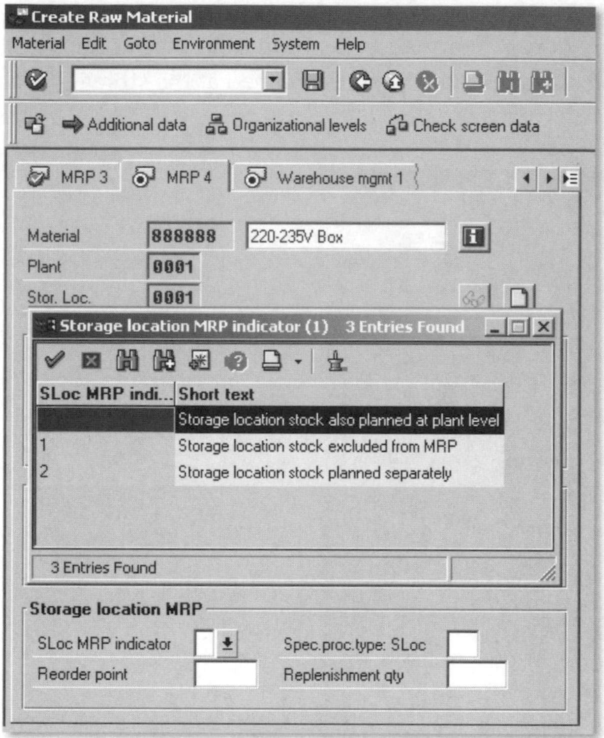

Figure 16.5 Options Available for Storage Location MRP Indicator in Material Master

16.3 Planning Evaluation

Two methods are available to evaluate the planning results in CBP: the MRP list and the stock/requirements list.

16.3.1 MRP List

During the planning run, the nature of MRP lists depends on how the creation indicators are configured. The basic MRP list contains the planning result information for the material. The MRP list is the initial working document for the MRP controller to work from. The MRP list is a static list and changes are not reflected on the list until the next planning run.

The MRP list for an individual material can be displayed using the transaction MD05 or via the navigation path **SAP Menu • Logistics • Materials Management • MRP • MRP • Evaluations • MRP List—Material**.

In Figure 16.6, the MRP list shows that a purchase requisition has been created. This is due to the fact that the stock has fallen below the safety stock level. The error messages in the dialog box relate to the column **EX** on the MRP list.

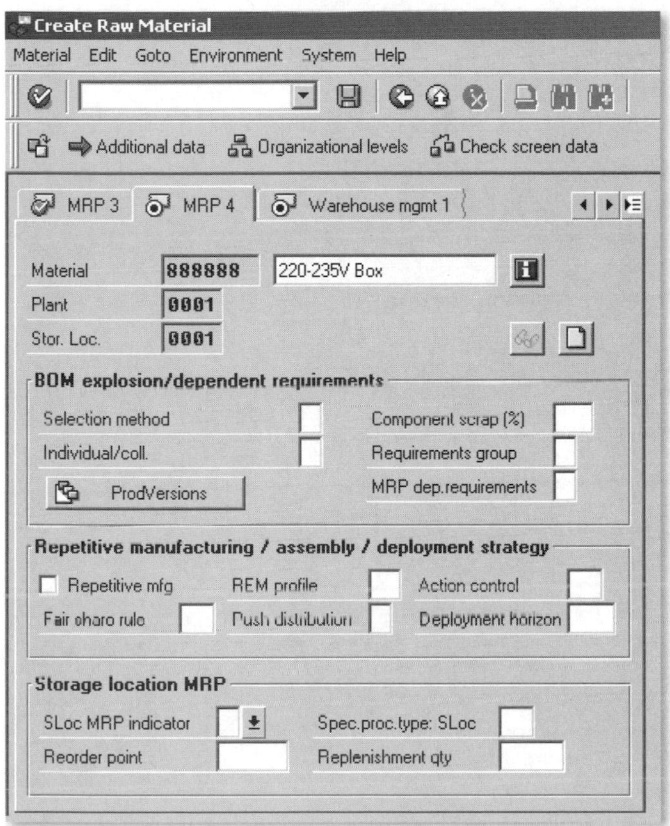

Figure 16.6 MRP List for Material Fallen Below Its Safety Stock Level

16.3.2 Stock/Requirements List

The stock/requirements list shows the current stock and requirements situation. The stock/requirements list is dynamic, as it is updated each time it is displayed (unlike the MRP list). The Stock/Requirements list shown in Figure 16.7 displays two purchase requisitions that would not appear on the MRP list for the same material. The requisitions were created after the MRP list was created and will not appear until another MRP list is created via planning.

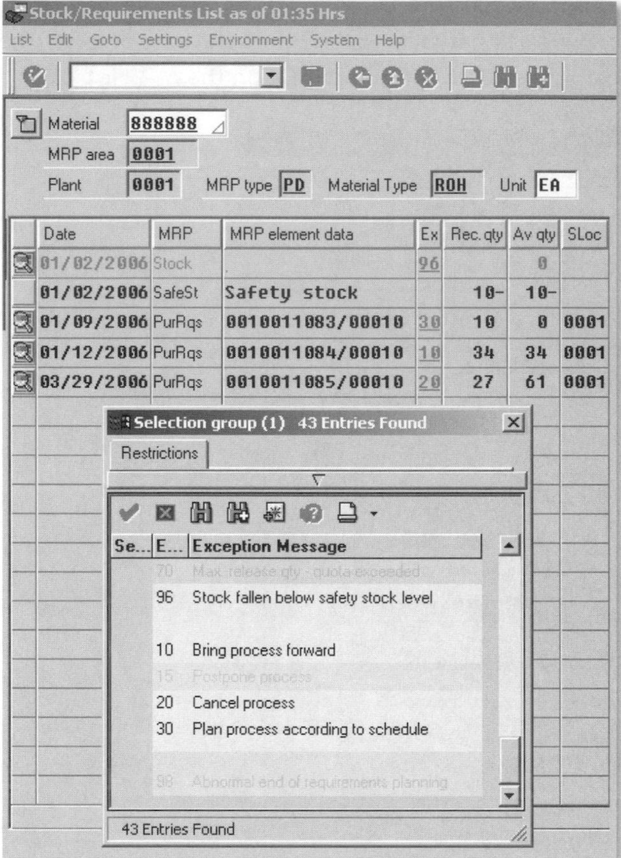

Figure 16.7 Stock/Requirements List for Same Material

16.4 Procurement Proposal

During the planning process, the system will determine the requirements for the material and create procurement proposals based on settings defined by the purchasing department. The procurement proposals created by the system specify when stock movements should be made and the quantity of stock required.

Three types of procurement proposals are used in the planning process: purchase requisitions, schedule lines, and planned orders.

16.4.1 Purchase Requisitions

The planning process will determine that a purchase requisition is required for material that is procured externally. The purchase requisition can be seen on the MRP list as a line item. The planning process also determines the quantity for that purchase order. The MRP controller will review the MRP list and determine whether the purchase requisition is appropriate before passing it on to the purchasing department. The purchase requisition is an internal planning element and can be changed or deleted if necessary.

16.4.2 Schedule Lines

A schedule line is the result of the planning process when the material is procured externally and the material has a source and a scheduling agreement in place. The schedule line is unlike the purchase requisition, which involves a fixed agreement and, therefore, cannot be changed. This makes it much more flexible than the purchase requisition.

16.4.3 Planned Orders

The planned order is a result of the planning process for materials that are produced internally. Like the purchase requisition, the planned order is an internal planning element that can be changed or deleted if deemed necessary. The planned order can be converted to a production or a process order, depending on the production methods of the client. If the material is procured externally as well as produced in-house, the planned order can be converted to a purchase requisition. The MRP controller can use transaction MD14 to convert an individual planned order, or by using the path **SAP Menu • Logistics • Materials Management • MRP • MRP • Planned Order • Convert to Purchase Requisition • Individual Conversion**.

This chapter described the basics of consumption-based planning. This type of planning is found in the vast majority of manufacturers today. This functionality shows the integration between the Production Planning module and the purchasing functionality. It is important to understand how purchasing is involved in planning and the responsibilities the purchasing department has to provide timely action to ensure that material is available for production.

17 Material Requirements Planning

Material Requirements planning (MRP) has to meet three objectives simultaneously: first, to ensure to material is available for production and delivery to customers, second, to maintain the lowest possible level of inventory, and third, to plan manufacturing activities, delivery schedules, and purchasing.

Manufacturing companies face the problem that their customers want finished goods available in less time than it takes to produce them. In order to achieve this, manufacturing companies need to adopt a planning strategy, and this is found in MRP.

Companies need to control the quantities of materials they purchase, plan which materials are to be produced and in what quantities, and ensure that they are able to meet current and future customer demand, at the lowest possible cost.

MRP was first developed in the early 1960s and has been modified and improved to the level found today in SAP and in the methodology adopted by organizations such as the American Production and Inventory Control Society, commonly called APICS.

There are three procedures within MRP:

- Reorder-point planning
- Forecast-based planning
- Time-phased planning

17.1 Reorder Point Planning

The basic premise behind reorder-point planning is that procurement is triggered when the sum of the stock in the plant, plus the firmed receipts, falls below the reorder point.

17.1.1 Manual Reorder Point Planning

In manual reorder-point planning, the planner manually enters the reorder point and the safety stock in the individual material master record. This is shown in figure 17.1.

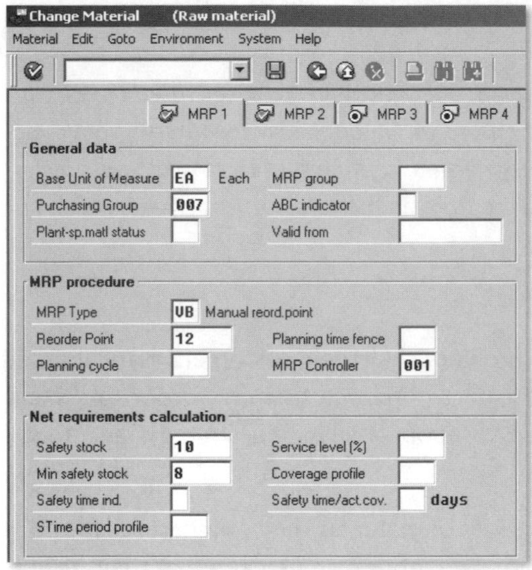

Figure 17.1 Material with MRP Type VB for Manual Reorder-Point Planning

17.1.2 Automatic Reorder Point Planning

In automatic reorder-point planning, the system calculates the reorder level and the safety stock level. To do this, the system uses past consumption data of the material to forecast future requirements of the material.

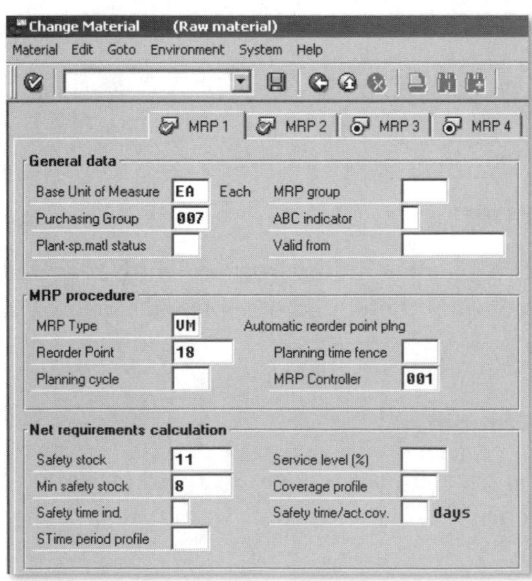

Figure 17.2 Material with MRP Type VM for Automatic Reorder-Point Planning Based on Consumption

The system then uses these forecast values to calculate the reorder level and the safety stock level. Figure 17.2 shows a material with the MRP type that facilitates automatic reorder point planning.

17.2 Forecast-Based Planning

Like the reorder-point planning, forecast-based planning relies on the historical material consumption. Similar to reorder-point planning, forecast-based planning uses the historical values, while the forecast values and future requirements are determined by the forecasting program. The forecast values are used in MRP as the forecast requirements.

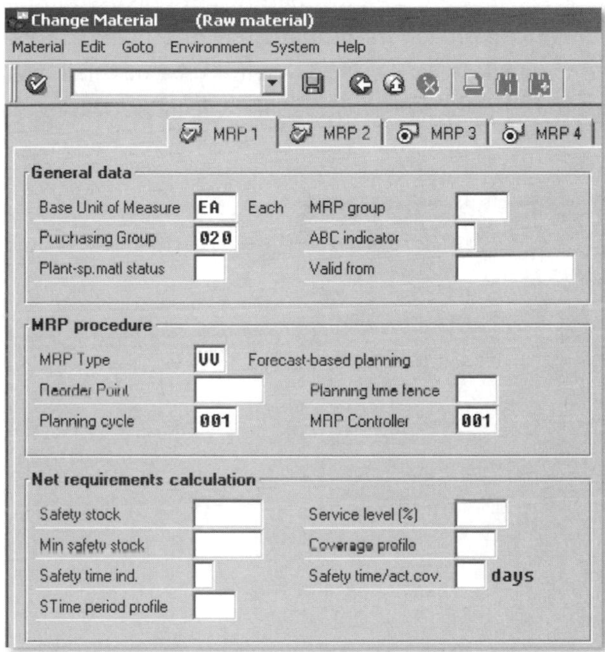

Figure 17.3 Material with MRP Type VV for Forecast-Based Planning

The forecast-based planning procedure, MRP Type **VV** shown in Figure 17.3, can be described in three phases. These are given below:

1. The system takes the forecast it has produced and makes sure that every future period forecast is covered by the available stock, planned purchases, or planned production. If the forecast is greater than the total of the available stock, planned purchases, or planned production, then the system will generate a procurement proposal (purchase requisition or planned order).

2. The procurement proposals are checked against the lot-size procedures in the material master, and forecasts are combined or not, depending on the lot size required for purchasing/production.
3. On each of the procurement proposals, the system defines the date on which the proposal must be converted into a production/process order or a purchase order.

17.3 Time-Phased Planning

The premise of time-phased planning is that the date of the planned requirement should coincide with a known date, such as the date when the supplier delivers. If delivery from a vendor is always on the same day, then this can be used in the planning of a material. This planning procedure requires that the material forecasting be completed for the material. This can be done within the material master record. Figure 17.4 shows the forecast amounts that are calculated within the material master.

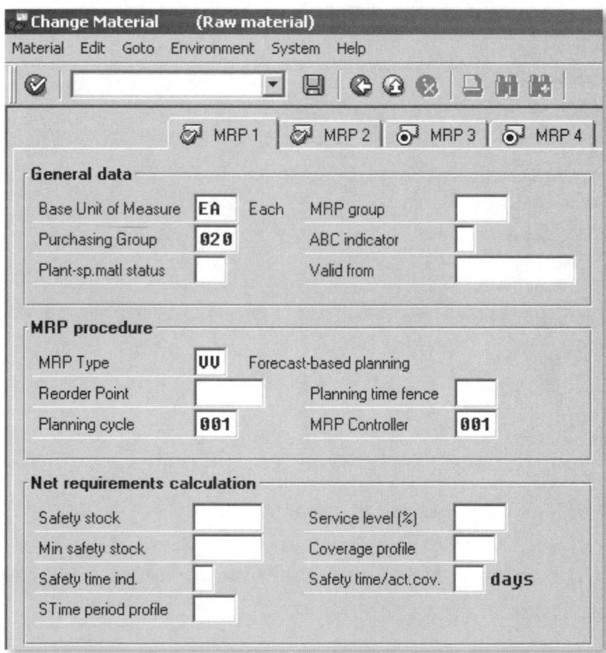

Figure 17.4 Material Forecast Calculated Within Material Master Transaction MM02

To run the time-phased planning procedure, the MRP type needs to be entered as **R1**, as shown in Figure 17.5. The planning cycle is to be entered, and the lot size set as lot-for-lot order quantity.

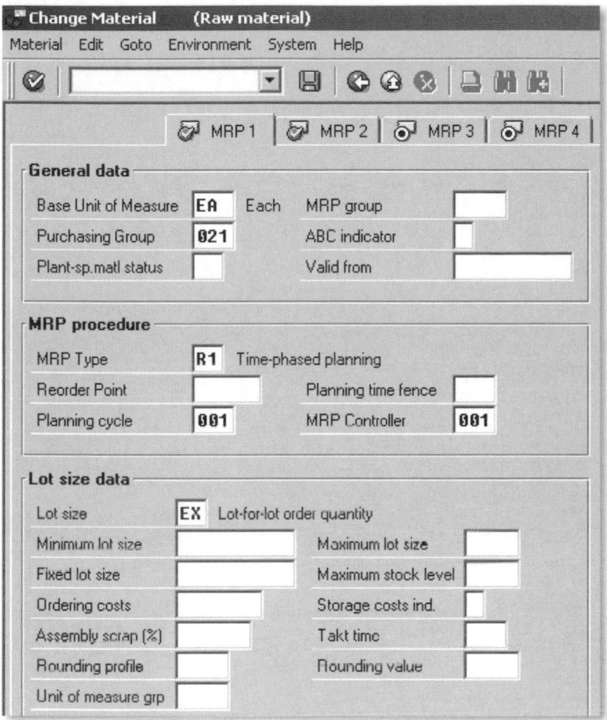

Figure 17.5 Prerequisites for Time-Phased Planning in Material Master Record

During the planning run, the system takes into account the scheduled delivery dates. The system calculates against the forecast requirements and determines whether the forecast can be covered by total of the available stock, planned purchases, or planned production. Again, if there is a shortfall based on the scheduled deliveries, a procurement proposal will be generated. As lot-for-lot sizing is used, the procurement proposal will cover the shortage.

This chapter described the three main objectives for Materials Requirements Planning (MRP). Materials management users should understand the basics of production planning, as there are many touch points between MM and PP. Terms like reorder points, MRP types, lot sizes and forecast models should be familiar to those who work alongside production personnel.

18 Forecasting

Business decisions are based on forecasts. Decisions of material requirements are based on forecasts of future conditions. Forecasts are continually needed, and over time as the impact of the forecast on actual results are measured, the initial forecasts are updated, and decisions are modified

Forecasting is a prediction of what will occur in the future, and therefore, is an uncertain process. Due to this uncertainty, the accuracy of a forecast is as important as is the outcome predicted by the forecast.

18.1 Forecast Models

Forecast modeling has been devised to aid in forecasting particular events. The forecast model can be designed around factors that the client believes are important in influencing the future use of a material. The client also uses past performance of a material to determine future use. Both of these methods will produce a forecast that may be accurate.

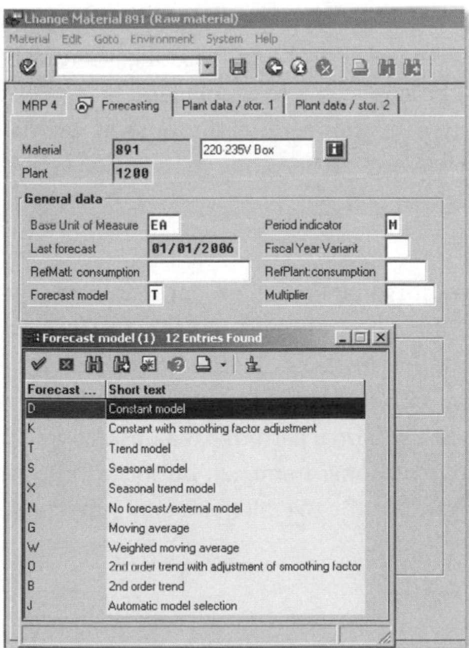

Figure 18.1 Forecast Model

A number of forecast models are available in the forecasting functionality within SAP, as shown in Figure 18.1.

18.1.1 Constant Model

The constant forecast model assumes that the use of material is constant. This is not to say that the use of material is the same each month, but that the variation in material usage fluctuates little and a constant mean value is calculated. This forecast model would apply to electricity consumption in an office. The consumption would not vary a great deal from the mean value.

18.1.2 Trend Model

The trend model is found where there is an identifiable increase or decrease of material over a period of time. The trend may include areas of movement away from the trend, but that the overall movement follows the trend. For example, a downward trend over time may represent the model for use of printer cartridges for certain model printers that become obsolete over time.

18.1.3 Seasonal Model

The seasonal model is one that affects many businesses due to the weather, holidays, or vacations. The seasonal model is defined as a pattern that repeats for each period. So an annual seasonal pattern has a cycle 12 periods long, if the periods are months. A seasonal model may be applicable to a company that makes patio furniture and that experiences a greater demand in the months of May through September, and this pattern is repeated each year.

18.1.4 Seasonal Trend Model

The seasonal trend model is similar to the seasonal model, except that instead of the same pattern occurring each period, the pattern is moving further away from the mean value, either positive or negative. For instance, California sparkling wine manufacturers can see a positive seasonal trend. They have a seasonal pattern in demand for their products, and for them the seasonal pattern has a positive trend, as sales have continued to rise. A negative seasonal trend can be shown in beer manufacturers who have a seasonal market, but the overall trend continues to be negative as sales slow each year.

18.2 Forecast Parameters

The parameters on the forecast screen in the material master record can be predefined using a forecast profile. The forecast profile allows the user to create a default that copies the parameter values directly into the material master record.

18.2.1 Create Forecast Profile

The forecast profile for the forecast parameters can be created using transaction MP80 or via the navigation path **SAP Menu • Logistics • Materials Management • Material Master • Profile • Forecast Profile • Create**.

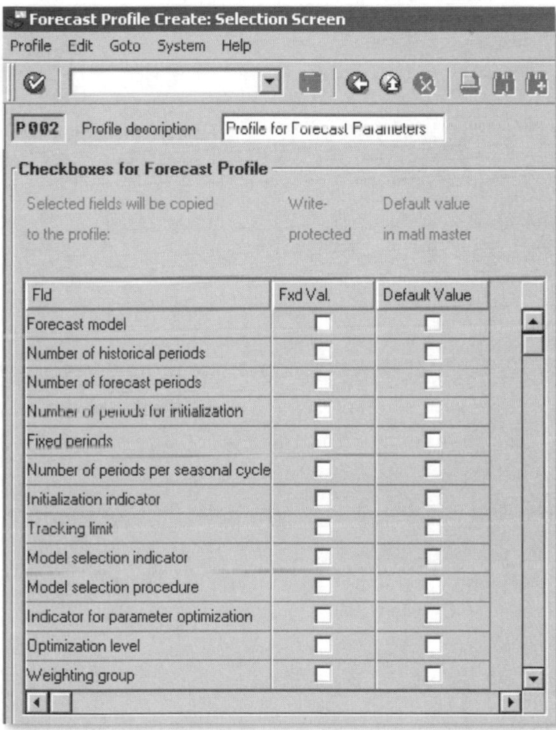

Figure 18.2 Selection Screen for Transaction MP80

In the initial screen of transaction MP80, shown in Figure 18.2, the user can select the parameters for which they wish to enter values. In addition, the user can determine if the value is defaulted into the material master or whether the parameter is write-protected and cannot be changed in the material master.

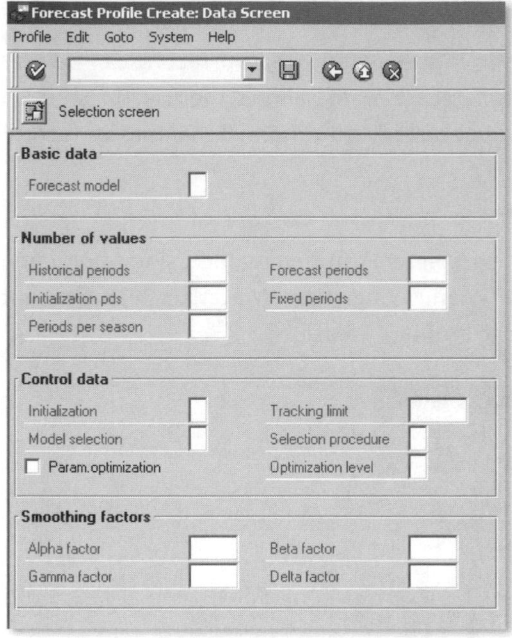

Figure 18.3 Detail Screen for Transaction MP80

The fields shown in Figure 18.3 for the Forecast Data creation screen are described in the section below.

Forecast Model

The forecast model has been discussed in Section 18.1. The selection for the forecast model can be made from the following choices:

- No Forecast Model or External Model (N)
- Automatic Model Selection (J)
- Constant Model (D)
- Constant with Smoothing Factor Adjustment (K)
- Trend Model (T)
- Seasonal Model (S)
- Seasonal Trend Model (X)
- Moving Average Model (G)
- Weighted Moving Average Model (W)
- Second Order Trend Model (B)
- Second Order Trend with Smoothing Factor Adjustment (O)

Historical Periods

The number of historical periods entered into this field is used to calculate the forecast. If this field is left blank, no periods will be used in the profile.

Forecast Periods

The number entered in this field is the number of periods over which the forecast will be calculated.

Number of Periods for Initialization

This number is for the historical values that the user wishes to be used for the forecast initialization. If the field is blank, no historical values are used to initialize the forecast.

Fixed Periods

The fixed-period field is used to in order to avoid fluctuations in the forecast calculation or because production can no longer react to changed planning figures. The forecast will be fixed for the number of periods entered in this field.

Number of Periods per Seasonal Cycle

If your client uses a seasonal forecast model, then this field can be used to define the number of periods that make up a season for this material.

Initialization Indicator

If the forecast needs to be initialized, this indicator can be set to allow the system to initialize the forecast. It also allows manual initialization.

Tracking Limit

The tracking limit is the value that specifies the amount by which the forecast value may deviate from the actual value. This figure can be entered to three decimal places.

Model Selection

This field is only active if there is no value entered for the forecast model. This allows the system to select a model automatically. To aid the system in choosing a forecast model, the model selection field can be set to one of the following three indicators:

- T—Examine for a Trend
- S—Examine for Seasonal Fluctuations
- A—Examine for a Trend and Seasonal Fluctuations

Selection Procedure

The selection procedure field is used when the system is selecting a forecast model. There are two selection procedures to choose from:

- Procedure 1 performs a significance test to find the best seasonal or trend pattern.
- Procedure 2 carries out the forecast for all models and then selects the model with the smallest mean absolute deviation.

Indicator for parameter optimization

If this indicator is set, then the system will use the smoothing factors for the given forecast model.

Optimization Level

This indicator can be set to fine, middle or rough. The finer the optimization level, the more accurate the forecast, but this comes at the expense of processing time.

Smoothing Factors

Some form of random variation is found in a collection of data taken over time, that is, in consumption of material over a given period. There are methods for reducing or canceling the effect due to random variation. A common technique used in forecasting is smoothing. This technique clarifies the underlying trend, seasonal, and cyclic elements.

Four smoothing factors can be used in the forecast profile:

- Alpha Factor—the smoothing factor for the basic value.
- Beta Factor—the smoothing factor for the trend value
- Gamma Factor- the smoothing factor for the seasonal index
- Delta Factor—the smoothing factor for the mean absolute deviation

18.3 Forecast Options

The user can make the forecast model selection manually, or the system can automatically select the forecast model, using option **J** in the **Forecast Model** field in the material master record.

18.3.1 Manual Forecast Model Selection

The forecast model selection is often determined manually as companies have often been developing forecast models for many years. Large companies have departments of analysts working on historical data to fine tune forecasts. Given this wealth of analysis, your client may wish to manually determine the forecast model.

18.3.2 Automatic Forecast Model Selection

If your clients have not developed forecast models in the past, they may wish to allow the SAP system to analyze the historical data and determine an appropriate forecast model to use. Once this has been selected, the client can use this as a starting point and make modifications in the future.

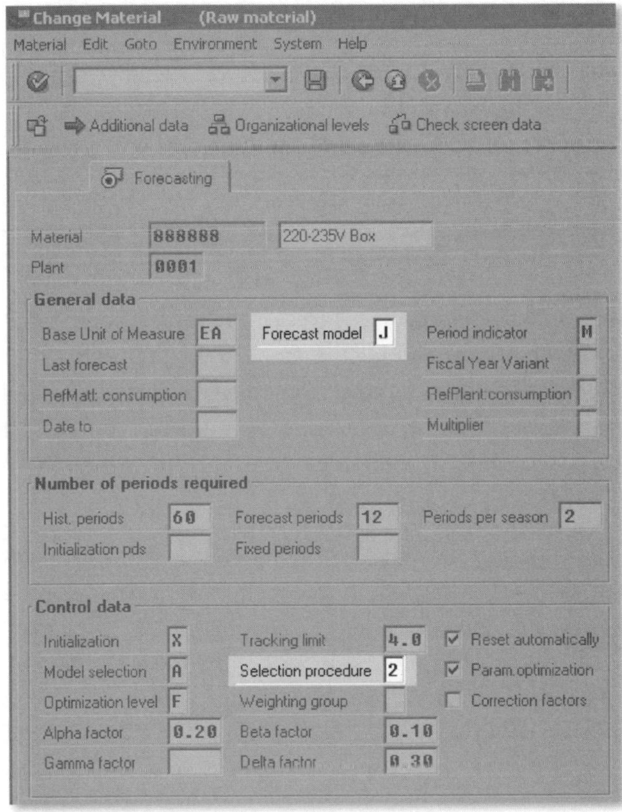

Figure 18.4 Settings for Automatic Forecast-Model Selection in Material Master

To set the system to automatically determine a forecast model for the material, the user must complete two fields in the forecast screen of the material master, as seen in Figure 18.4

Forecast Model

Earlier in this chapter, we have established that to prompt the system to automatically select the model, the option **J** has to be selected in the forecast model field.

The system has two selection procedures that can aid the system in the selection of a forecast model. These are examined below.

Selection Procedure 1

Selection procedure 1 carries out checks to see if a trend or seasonal pattern exists in the historical data. The system checks for a trend pattern by completing a regression analysis on the data and then checks for a trend. To check for a seasonal pattern, the system dismisses any trend pattern and then carries out an autocorrelation test.

Selection Procedure 2

The second procedure is a more detailed analysis of the data at different levels of the smoothing factors to determine the most appropriate model based on the lowest mean absolute deviation.

If neither of these procedures finds an appropriate forecast model to use, the system will propose a constant forecast model, which may not be suitable for your clients, and this should be drawn to their attention. The constant forecast model would continue to forecast amounts that are the same over time. This forecast model is used for materials where consumption does not vary from period to period.

This chapter discussed the forecasting methods available in SAP. Forecasting is important to companies as it can help determine how much material needs to be produced, how much material is needed and when the product needs to be marketed. However, for a forecast to be close to being accurate, the forecast must be run with complete and verified data.

19 Inventory Management Overview

The processes supported by the SAP Inventory Management functionality allows a company to meet customer needs for the availability of material, while maximizing the company's profits and minimizing its costs.

Management is under constant pressure to reduce the time between customer order and customer delivery. A customer will use order-to-delivery time as a factor in deciding on a vendor. Therefore companies must use effective inventory management processes to reduce this time to a minimum. Companies are re-engineering the order to delivery process. Improvements can be made by doing the following:

- Improving the EDI process with customers and vendors
- Increasing the single sourcing of materials
- Increasing the level of just–in-time (JIT) inventory
- Reduce dependence on long-term forecasts for stocking levels
- Using real-time reports and inventory figures

Inventory management within SAP gives the client an effective set of processes for all types of goods movement within the plant. The streamlining plant processes can help companies compress order-to-delivery time, decrease costs, reduce inventory and improve customer service.

The inventory in the plant is managed by quantity or value. The inventory movements are entered in real time, and a snapshot can be taken at any given moment to inform the inventory user of any material status.

This snapshot, see Figure 19.1, is called the Stock Overview transaction (MMBE) and can be found using the navigation path **SAP Menu • Logistics • Materials Management • Inventory Management • Environment • Stock • Stock Overview**.

The stock overview will give the material stock balance across the company, plant, storage location, and batch.

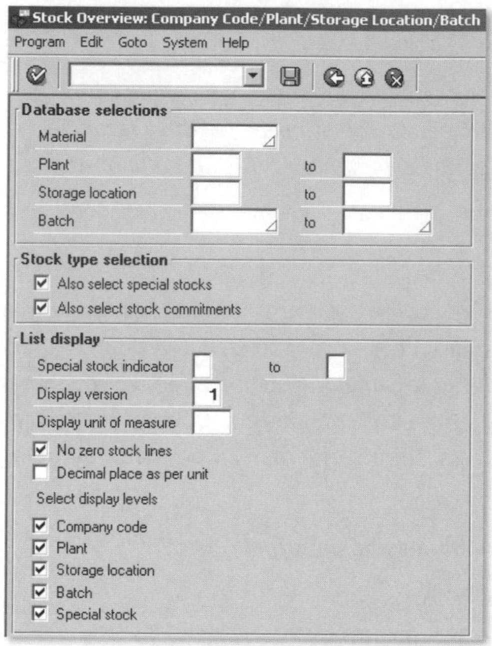

Figure 19.1 Selection Screen for Stock Overview Transaction MMBE.

19.1 Goods Movements

The inventory-management processes within SAP are, in essence, movements inside the plant that can create a change in stock levels within the storage locations designated to that plant. The movement of stock is either inbound from a vendor, outbound to a customer, a stock transfer between plants, or an internal transfer within a plant.

For every goods movement, the SAP system can create two types of documents: a material document and an accounting document. The SAP system follows the accounting principle that for every material movement there is a corresponding document that provides details of that movement. In addition, an accounting document is produced that describes the financial aspects of the goods movement. However, the accounting document is only relevant if the material is valuated.

19.1.1 Material Document

The material document is produced for each movement and is an audit of the details of the material movement. The material document contains the date of the material movement, the material number, and the quantity of the material moved, the location of the movement, the batch number if applicable, and the movement type.

The material document number is displayed after any material movement is made, (see Figure 19.2); it is the user's audit that the movement was made. The inventory user then can view the material document to check the details of the movement.

View the material document by using the transaction MB03 or using the navigation path **SAP Menu • Logistics • Materials Management • Inventory Management • Material Document • Display**.

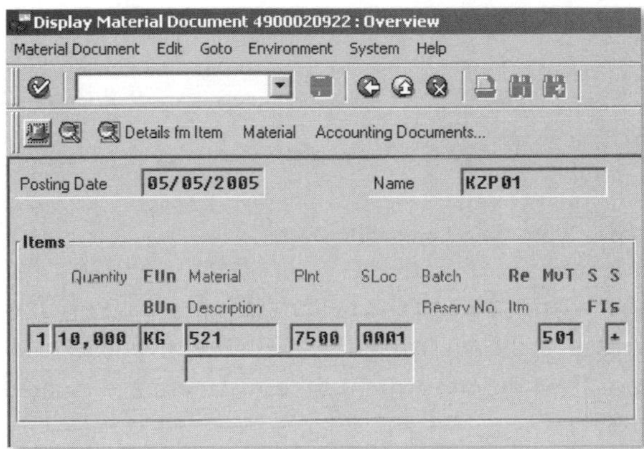

Figure 19.2 Detail of Material Document Using Transaction MB03

Changes cannot be made to the material document once it has been posted. If an error was made on the material movement, the material document cannot be changed to alter the material movement. If an error was made, then the material movement will have to be reversed and the movement correctly entered. This will produce a material document for the reversal and then a new material document for the correct movement.

19.1.2 Movement Types

The movement type is a three-character field, used to describe the type of material movement that needs to be performed. The movement type is used for all type of movements; receipts, issues, transfers, reversals.

The SAP system is delivered with pre-defined movement types between 100 and 899. Movement types 900 upwards can be used for customized movement types.

A movement type can be created with transaction OMJJ or via the path **IMG • Materials Management • Inventory Management and Physical Inventory • Movement Types • Copy, Change Movement Types**.

Copying an existing movement type and modifying the field contents can create the new movement type.

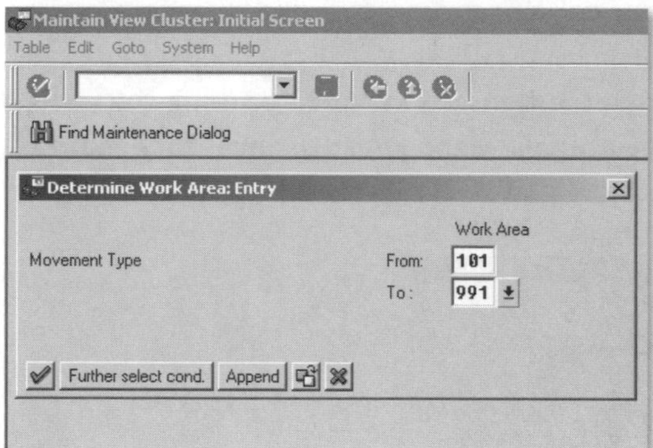

Figure 19.3 Creation of New Movement Type Using Transaction OMJJ

The new movement type number is entered and the field details from the existing movement type are copied across, as shown in Figure 19.3. The inventory user can then change the contents of the new movement type to create the desired effect of the new movement type.

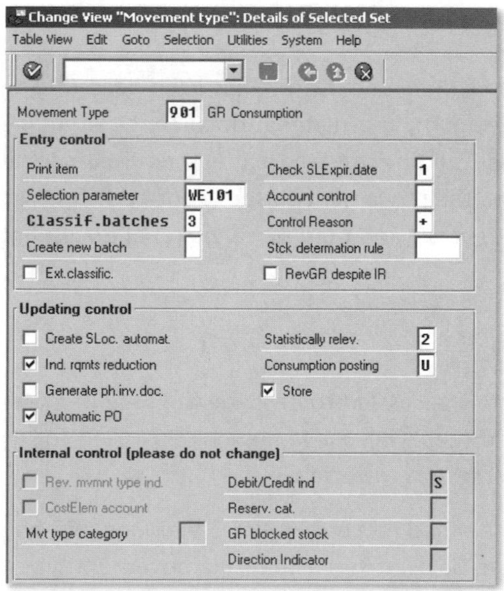

Figure 19.4 Field Contents of New Movement Type to be Configured

Existing movement types can be modified to restrict or allow certain functionality to be allowed. For instance, reasons may be required for certain movement types and this would require configuration of the **Control Reason** field as seen in Figure 19.4. The control-reason field is defaulted as optional, but this can be configured so it can be required for any movement type.

Overall the movement type is a key to the inventory management process as it controls the updating of the quantity of the stock, determines what fields are displayed and required for entry and also can update the correct account information.

19.2 Goods Issue

A goods issue is a reduction of stock triggered by one of the following:

- Shipment to a customer
- Withdrawal of stock for a production order
- Return of material
- Material required for sampling
- Material scraping

The movement types identify the various goods issues. Goods Issues will be discussed more fully in Chapter 20.

19.3 Goods Receipt

The goods receipt process allows the receipt of material from a vendor or from the in-house production process. In addition, SAP allows other types of goods receipt, including initial stock creation. A goods receipt is an increase in stock that is triggered by one of the following:

- Receipt from a production order
- Receipt from a purchase order
- Initial Entry of Inventory
- Other triggers

Goods receipts will be discussed more fully in Chapter 21.

19.4 Physical Inventory

Physical inventory is a process where a company stops all goods movements transactions, and physically counts inventory. A physical inventory may be required by financial accounting rules or tax regulations to place an accurate value on the inventory. Other reasons may include the need to count inventory so materials can be restocked.

Cycle counting is a type of physical inventory. Cycle counts have the advantage that they are less disruptive to operations, provide an ongoing measure of inventory accuracy, and can be configured to focus on higher value materials or materials with frequent movement. Physical Inventory will be discussed more fully in Chapter 22.

19.5 Returns

19.5.1 Introduction to Returns

Returns are sometimes referred to as reverse logistics. These cover activities related to returning materials, pallets, and containers. Companies also return material to vendors for disposal or recycling. Returns to a vendor may also be related to a product recall notice.

Before any material can be returned to the vendor, the agreement between the customer and vendor with regards to returns should be examined. The agreement is either part of an overall agreement between the two companies or specifically for the individual material or group of materials.

The returns clause will usually determine the valid reasons that allow material to be returned to the vendor. These will include an obvious material defect; incorrect material received, over-delivery of material, and returnable packaging material. The process may involve the customer obtaining a Return Material Authorization (RMA) number from the vendor. This will allow the vendor and customer to successfully track the return.

Material to be returned to the vendor does not need to be in a special status. Material returns can be from stock in quality inspection, blocked stock, goods-receipt blocked stock, even unrestricted stock.

19.5.2 Creating a Return

The returns process is the reverse of the goods receipt process. A return delivery is created by the transaction MIGO_GR, which is the same transaction for the goods receipt of materials. The transaction can be found using the path **SAP Menu • Logistics • Materials Management • Inventory Management • Goods Movement • Goods Receipt • For Purchase Order • Good Receipt for Purchase Order**.

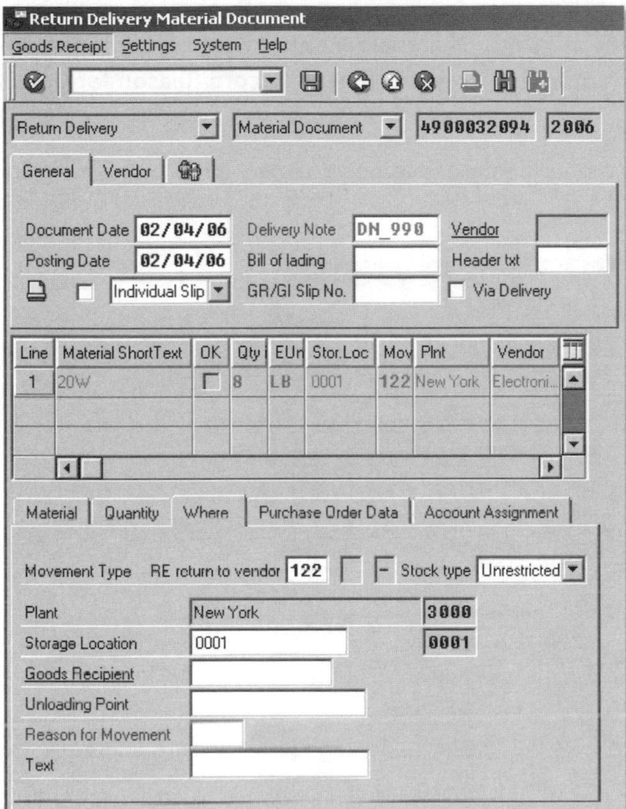

Figure 19.5 Return-material Document Created via Transaction MIGO_GR

The return delivery, shown in Figure 19.5, obtains the information from the material document created from the original goods receipt for the purchase order.

The information from the material document shows the vendor, the vendor's delivery-note number, and the item details. The line item details show the movement type for the return delivery, which is 122, and what status the material, is in, either unrestricted, quality inspection, or blocked stock. The inventory user can alter the quantity of the material to be returned and also can enter a reason for the return, if this is configured.

19.5.3 Configuring Reason for Movement

The reason for the return can be entered into the return process on the line item level. The reason can only be added if it is configured for that movement type, in this case movement type 122.

The transaction to create and change reason for movement is OMBS and can be accessed via the navigation path **IMG • Materials Management • Inventory Management and Physical Inventory • Movement Types • Record Reason for Goods Movements**.

The transaction allows a number of reasons to be added for goods movement for each movement type.

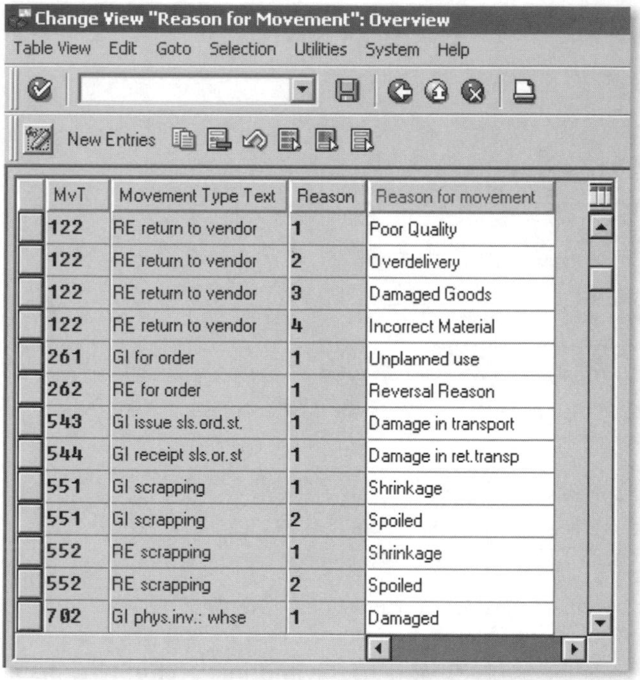

Change View "Reason for Movement": Overview

Table View Edit Goto Selection Utilities System Help

New Entries

MvT	Movement Type Text	Reason	Reason for movement
122	RE return to vendor	1	Poor Quality
122	RE return to vendor	2	Overdelivery
122	RE return to vendor	3	Damaged Goods
122	RE return to vendor	4	Incorrect Material
261	GI for order	1	Unplanned use
262	RE for order	1	Reversal Reason
543	GI issue sls.ord.st.	1	Damage in transport
544	GI receipt sls.or.st	1	Damage in ret.transp
551	GI scrapping	1	Shrinkage
551	GI scrapping	2	Spoiled
552	RE scrapping	1	Shrinkage
552	RE scrapping	2	Spoiled
702	GI phys.inv.: whse	1	Damaged

Figure 19.6 Transaction OMBS

The inventory user can add in a number of reasons for return of goods and this field can be used to monitor returns to vendors, as shown in Figure 19.6. This allows the purchasing department to identify issues with vendors or particular materials.

The reason for movement field can be configured to be suppressed, optional, or mandatory. This can be seen in Figure 19.7. This can be carried out in the same configuration transaction, OMBS. There are three options to choose from for each movement type. The inventory user can use a plus sign to represent that the field is mandatory and a minus sign to indicate that the field is suppressed. A blank field indicates that a reason is optional.

Change View "Control: Reason for Movement": Overview

Table View Edit Goto Selection Utilities System Help

MvT	Movement Type Text	Reas.	Control reason
122	RE return to vendor	+	Entry in this field is required.
123	RE rtrn vendor rev.	-	Field is suppressed.
124	GR rtrn blocked stck	+	Entry in this field is required.
125	GR rtn blkd stck rev	-	Field is suppressed.
131	Goods receipt	-	Field is suppressed.
132	Goods receipt	-	Field is suppressed.
141	GR G subseq. adjustm	-	Field is suppressed.
142	GR G subseq. adjustm	-	Field is suppressed.
161	GR returns	.	Entry in this field is optional.
162	GR rtrns reversal	-	Field is suppressed.
201	GI for cost center	-	Field is suppressed.
202	RE for cost center	.	Entry in this field is optional.
221	GI for project	-	Field is suppressed.
222	RE for project	-	Field is suppressed.
231	GI for sales order	-	Field is suppressed.
232	RE for sales order	.	Entry in this field is optional.

Figure 19.7 Control of Reason-for-Movement Field in Transaction OMBS

19.5.4 Material Documents

Once the reason for movement has been chosen and the return is posted, the SAP system will produce a material document to provide a trail of what happened.

The material document will show the material, quantity, and the original purchase order for the material, as shown in Figure 19.8. The material document can be identified as a return to a vendor, as the movement type 122 is shown at the line item. The material document can be found using transaction MB03.

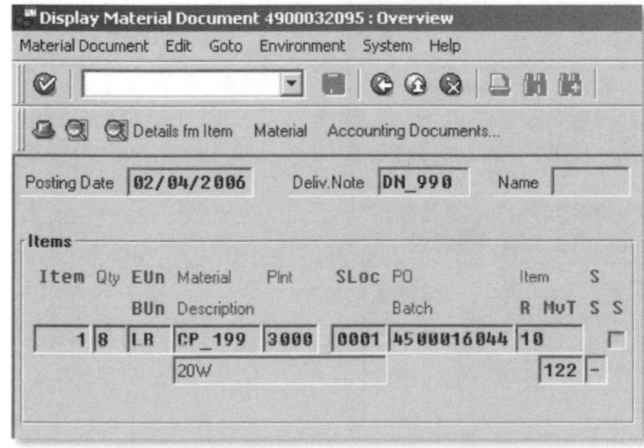

Figure 19.8 Material Document for Return to Vendor

The material documents relevant for goods receipt and return delivery can be seen by selecting the relevant line item and from the top menu on the screen select **Environment • Material Document for Material**. This is shown in Figure 19.9.

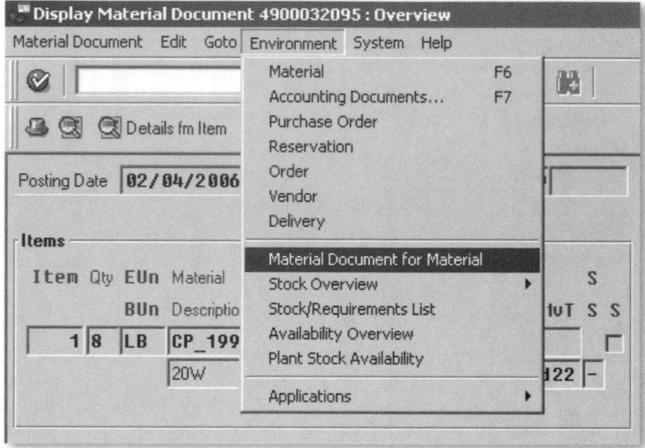

Figure 19.9 Path to Material Documents Inside Transaction MB03

This moves the inventory user into transaction MB51 with the particular material and vendor information carried over from the material documents. The detail screen of MB51 shows all the material documents relevant for the material/vendor combination. In this case, see Figure 19.10. There are four material documents: two goods receipts for the amounts 7 lbs and 8 lbs, shown by movement type 101, and two returns to vendor, shown by movement type 122 also for amounts of 7lbs and 8lbs. The latter are shown as minus figures as they are reducing the inventory.

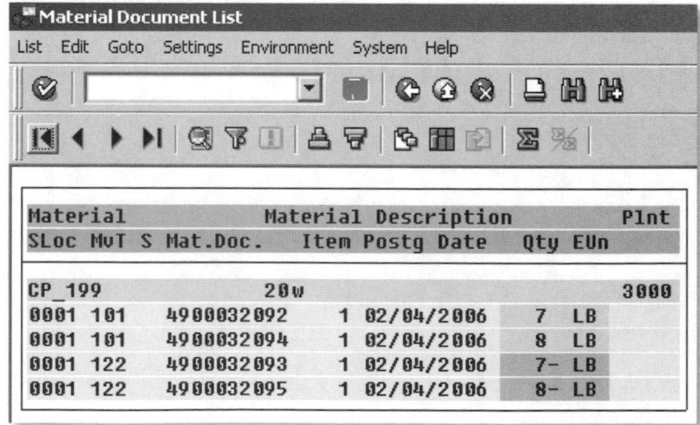

Figure 19.10 Material Documents Relevant for Particular Material and Vendor Combination

19.6 Reservations

19.6.1 Introduction to Reservations

A reservation is a request to hold material in the plant or storage location for movement to a process before that process begins. For example, if material is needed for a production order, then a reservation can be created for that material so that it is allocated for production.

Automatic reservations can be created by a process such as project or a production order that creates a reservation for the material without manual intervention. Automatic reservations can also be created at the storage-location level in situations when stock levels fall below the specified amount and a reservation for a stock transfer can be created.

After a reservation has been created, the reserved amount can be viewed using the stock overview transaction MMBE. This will show the reserved quantity for the material. However, the unrestricted stock total will not be reduced by the reserved stock amount. The reserved stock is still part of the unrestricted stock.

The reservation is treated differently within MRP. The reservation of material will lower the MRP available stock in the stock-requirements list. Therefore, it is important to realize the effect the reservation has on different parts of the system.

19.6.2 Creating a Manual Reservation

A manual reservation can be created using transaction MB21, or via the navigation path **SAP Menu • Logistics • Materials Management • Inventory Management • Reservation • Create**.

The reservation is a planned movement, so the date of the reservation cannot be in the past. Before creating a reservation, it should be decided what movement type should be referenced, because once the reservation is created, the movement type cannot be changed. However, the reservation can be deleted and re-entered if the movement type was initially entered incorrectly.

The reservation line item has detailed information on the item that the reservation is created for, as shown in Figure 19.11.

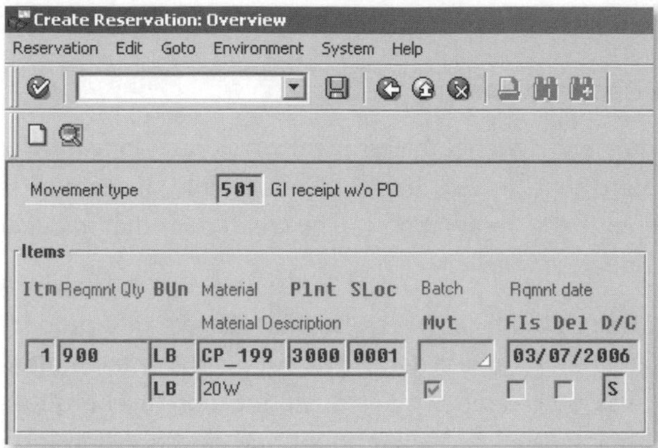

Figure 19.11 Detail Line for a Reservation Created Using Transaction MB21

Movement Type

The movement type that is entered is decided upon before the reservation is entered, as it cannot be changed. There are a number of movement types to choose from. These are:

- Consumption; such as consumption by a cost center, network, sales order
- Transfer posting; such as plant to plant or storage location to storage location
- Goods receipts; such as from production, by-product or without purchase order

Requirements Date

This is the date of the planned movement. This cannot be a date in the past and should be as accurate as possible, as this date is relevant to MRP.

Requirements Quantity

Enter a quantity that is the most accurate at the time the reservation is made. This quantity can be fixed by setting an indicator on the item detail screen.

Movement Indicator

The movement indicator is defaulted to be always on, allowing a goods movement to take place for the entered reservation. However, if the inventory user does not want to allow the goods movement to take place until a future period, he or she can uncheck this indicator, thus disallowing any goods movement.

FI Indicator

The Final Issue, or **FI**, indicator is automatically set when there has been a goods movement or a number of goods movements that have fulfilled the reservation. If the inventory user decides that after a partial goods movement the reservation cannot or should not be completed, he or she can manually set the **FI** indicator.

Deletion Indicator

The deletion indicator is used when the inventory user has decided that the reservation line item is incorrect or no longer needed.

Debit/Credit Indicator

This indicator shows whether the line item is a credit or debit. An **H** indicates a credit; an **S** indicates a debit.

19.6.3 MRP and Reservations

The reservation is relevant to MRP, and when MRP is run the reservation will be seen on the MRP list for that material.

Transaction MD05 can be used to view the MRP list for a material. The transaction can also be found using path **SAP Menu • Logistics • Materials Management • Material Requirements Planning • MRP • Evaluations • MRP List—Material**.

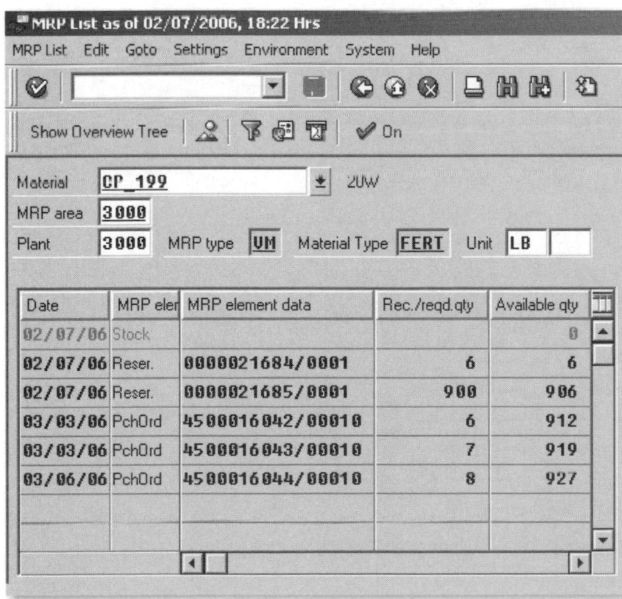

Figure 19.12 MRP List for Material

The line items in Figure 19.12 show the manual reservations with their date of expected delivery as available quantity on that date. The other line items refer to future purchase orders that need to be placed.

19.6.4 Reservations Management Program

The reservations that are created need to be managed to control old and unnecessary reservations. The transaction to perform this is MBVR. This can be accessed via **SAP Menu • Logistics • Materials Management • Inventory Management • Reservation • Administer**.

The reservation-management program will allow the inventory user to set the deletion indicator on the reservation file based on user entered selection criteria, as shown in Figure 19.13.

The main reason this management program is needed is that many goods movements do not reference the reservation that was made for that movement. In such cases the material has already been received or consumed, but the reservation will remain in the system until the management program cleans up these unnecessary reservations.

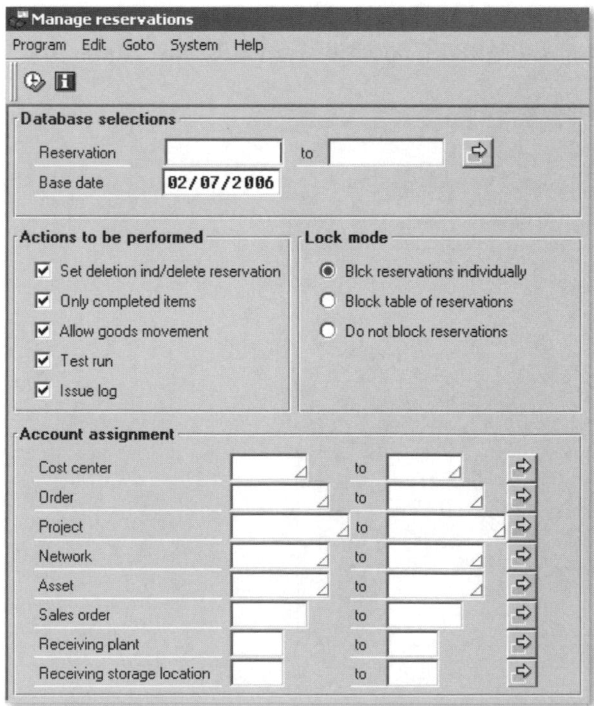

Figure 19.13 Selection Screen for Transaction MBVR

The management program will set the deletion indicator for two scenarios:

- If the final indicator has been set on the reservation, indicating that the reservation has been satisfied
- If the requirement date of the reservation is prior to a date calculated by the system. The system calculates the date using the base date entered in transaction MBVR, minus a set number of retention days. The usual number of the retention days set for this transaction is 30. However, this can be changed to the customer's needs in configuration.

To change the number of retention days for the reservation-management program, changes need to be made in configuration. Transaction OMBN allows the configurator to change the retention days for the calculation, as shown in Figure 19.14. This transaction can be found via the path **IMG • Materials Management • Inventory Management and Physical Inventory • Reservation • Define Default Values**.

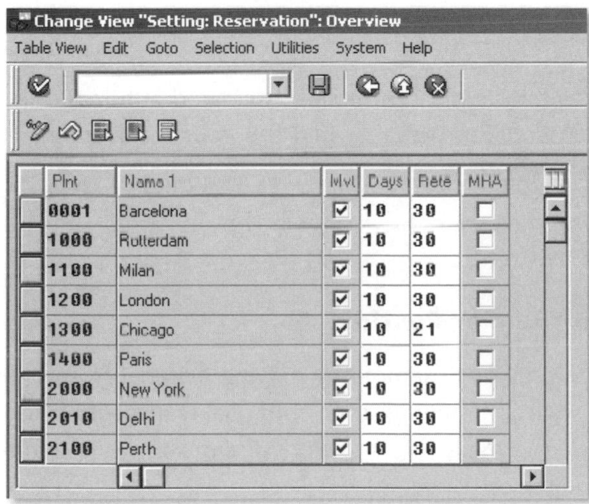

Plnt	Name 1	Mvt	Days	Rete	MHA
0001	Barcelona	☑	10	30	☐
1000	Rotterdam	☑	10	30	☐
1100	Milan	☑	10	30	☐
1200	London	☑	10	30	☐
1300	Chicago	☑	10	21	☐
1400	Paris	☑	10	30	☐
2000	New York	☑	10	30	☐
2010	Delhi	☑	10	30	☐
2100	Perth	☑	10	30	☐

Figure 19.14 Configuration Transaction OMBN

The inventory user can change a number of defaults for the reservation, based on the plant.

Movement Indicator

If the movement indicator is set, then this specifies that goods movements are allowed for the reservation item. If the indicator is not set, then this indicator needs to be set manually in each reservation line item before a goods movement can take place.

Days for Movement Default Value

This field is used when the movement indicator is not set in configuration. The reservation-management program uses this value to set the indicator on in the reservation line item, if it has not already manually been set.

If the requirement date of a reservation item is further in the future than the number of days configured in this field, the goods movement indicator is not set and no goods movements are allowed for that item.

Retention Period in Days

The inventory user can enter a value for the retention period, which is the number of days that the reservation item resides in the system before being deleted by the reservation-management program.

If the required date of a reservation item is older than the current date minus the number of retention days, the reservation-management program sets the deletion indicator in the reservation item.

MRA Indicator

If this indicator is set, the storage location information is created automatically, based on the information from the reservation, when the goods movement is made.

19.7 Stock Transfers

19.7.1 Stock Transfer and Transfer Posting

A stock transfer can occur physically, for example by moving material from one storage location to another, or logically, moving stock from quality inspection status to unrestricted. Stock transfer normally refers to a physical move, while transfer posting usually describes the logical move.

A stock transfer occurs in three distinct ways:

- Storage location to storage location
- Plant to plant
- Company code to company code

A stock transfer can be performed by a:

- One-step procedure
- Two-step procedure

19.7.2 Transfer Between Storage Locations

Movement of material between storage locations in a plant arises because of normal everyday operations. Material is moved due to storage limitations, future needs, reclassification of stock, etc. The movement of material between storage locations does not create a financial record as the material is valuated the same within a plant. The movement can be carried out by either a one-step or two-step procedure.

One-Step Procedure

This is a straightforward procedure where the material is moved in one step between storage locations. The stock levels in the different storage locations are changed in relation to the amount entered in the transaction.

The one-step storage location to storage location transfer is achieved by using transaction MB1B and can be found via the navigation path **SAP Menu • Logistics • Materials Management • Inventory Management • Goods Movement • Transfer Posting**.

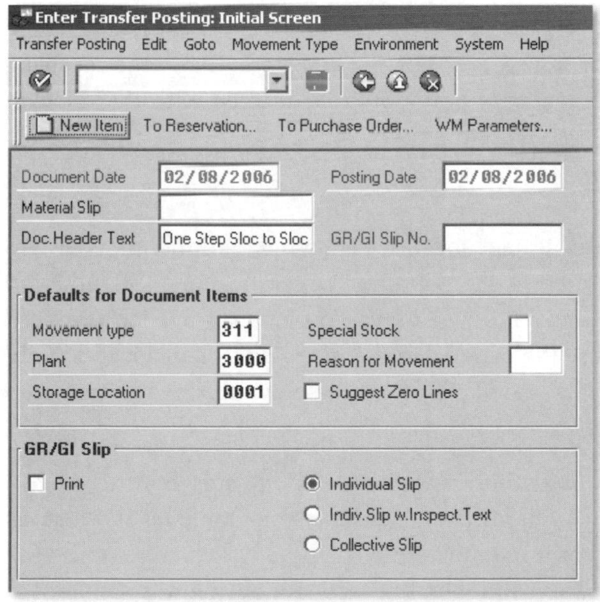

Figure 19.15 Initial Screen for Transaction MB1B

The movement type entered on the initial screen, shown in Figure 19.15, is 311, which is the movement type for a one-step move between storage locations. However, if the material to be moved is a special stock, then the special-stock indicator will need to be entered, as well, as the movement type.

Subsequent to a 311 movement, there is the possibility of reversing this movement by using the reverse movement type 312. This should be used if an error has been made.

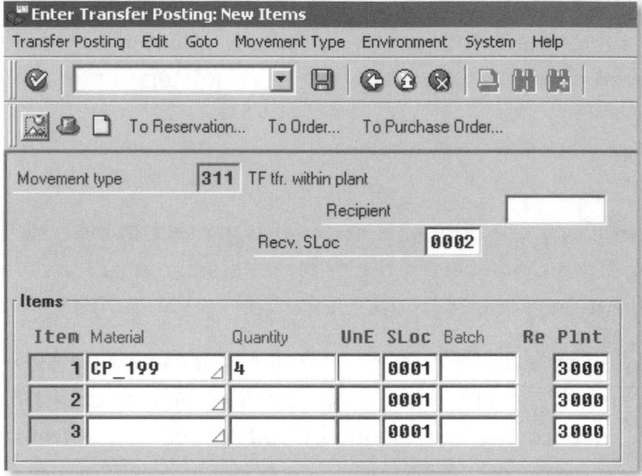

Figure 19.16 Line item for Transaction MB1B

On the item-detail screen for transaction MB1B, see Figure 19.16, the receiving storage location and the material to move should be entered with the relevant quantity and batch number, if applicable.

Two Step Procedure

The two-step transfer between storage locations is used where the materials are actually in transit, i.e. not stored in a physical or logical location. This situation occurs in the plant where material must be moved out of a storage location, but where it is not possible to store the material in the receiving storage location until a later time. However, the only material that can be moved using the two-step procedure is unrestricted stock.

The two-step procedure uses the same transaction as a one-step transfer, MB1B. In this case there are two movements to be made, a stock removal and a stock placement. The first movement is with movement type 313, which removes the material from one storage location and then the second movement is with movement type 315, which places the material into the receiving storage location.

Since the movement of material between storage locations is not instant, as with the one-step procedure, the materials are in different stock statuses as the movement progresses.

The movement type 313 produces the following:

- Originating Storage Location Unrestricted stock level is reduced
- Receiving Storage Location Stock in Transit stock level is increased
- Plant Unrestricted stock level is reduced
- Plant Unrestricted Stock in Transit stock level is increased

The movement type 315 produces the following:

- Receiving Storage Location Stock in Transit stock level is reduced
- Receiving Storage Location Unrestricted stock level is increased
- Plant Unrestricted stock level is increased
- Plant Unrestricted Stock in Transit stock level is reduced

19.7.3 Transfer Between Plants

Movement of material between plants occurs where material is moved to replenish stock levels, to deliver material from a production site to a distribution center, or move obsolete or slow moving stock, among other reasons.

Movements between plants can use a one-step or two-step procedure as with storage locations, but there will be a financial element in this transaction. Transaction MB1B is used for the plant-to-plant transfer of material.

One-Step Procedure

The one-step plant to plant transfer is similar to the one-step storage location transfer with the movement type 301 used for plant transfers. In this case the receiving plant and storage location are required by the transaction.

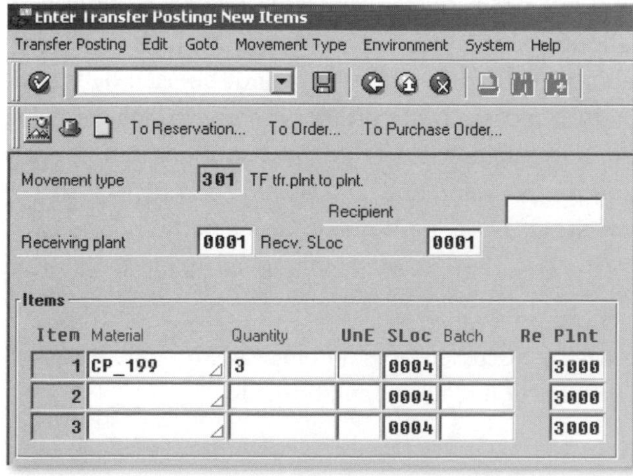

Figure 19.17 Detail item line for Transaction MB1B

In the case of the one-step transfer, as seen in Figure 19.17, the stock is reduced in the supplying plant and increased at the receiving plant simultaneously. Both material and accounting documents are produced by the system.

Two-Step Procedure

In the case of the two-step procedure the material is removed from the supplying plant and placed in the receiving plant. In the same method as with storage locations, this requires two movement types; 303 to remove the material from the supplying plant and 305 to place that material into the receiving plant.

When the movement type 303 is posted, the stock is reduced at the supplying plant and placed in the receiving plant's stock in transit. Once the material is received and placed into stock at the receiving plant using movement type 305, the material moves from stock in transit to unrestricted stock.

19.7.4 Transfer between Company Codes

The company code transfer is functionally the same as a plant-to-plant transfer. Material is moved between different plants. The differences being that the plants belong to different company codes. Additional account documents are produced for either a one-step or two-step procedure.

There is an accounting document for each of the plant movements. In addition an accounting document is created for the stock posting in the company clearing accounts.

In this chapter, the inventory management functionality was introduced. Traditional goods movements, such as issues and receipts will be discussed in detail in later chapters. However, it is important for the materials management user to understand returns, reservations and stock transfers. Returns are a part of everyday life at a company. Often material is delivered that cannot be used by the client. Knowing your clients return process is important when decisions are being made as regards the material. In addition to returns, reservations can be very important to a manufacturing company and how and when reservations are used at your client should be understood. Stock transfers occur regularly and the decision of whether to use one or two-step transfers should be made early in an implementation.

In Chapter 20, goods issue will be discussed with an emphasis on how it is used in production and for other production related operations.

20 Goods Issue

A goods issue decreases the stock levels and makes a financial posting to reduce the value of the stock. This occurs when the materials are issued. A goods issue process results in material and accounting documents being created in SAP.

The goods issues for material movements include issues to production orders, sampling, scrapping, and internal goods issues. For all of these goods issues, financial and material documents are created.

20.1 Goods Issue to a Production Order

The production order requires materials, which are identified in the bill of materials, in order to complete production of finished goods. The materials requirements planning (MRP) process plans the order and ensures the correct materials are available, and the materials management process supplies material to the order through a goods issue.

Apart from the planned issue of material to a production order, the material can be issued to a production order by an unplanned issue and also by a process known as backflushing.

20.1.1 Planned Goods Issue

When a production order is planned the system can produce a reservation for the material. The goods issue to the production order can reference a reservation if applicable.

A goods issue can be created by using transaction MB1A. This is found via the navigation path **SAP Menu • Logistics • Materials Management • Inventory Management • Goods Movement • Goods Issue**.

The goods issue initial screen, shown in Figure 20.1, requires that the inventory user enter a movement type. For goods issue of materials to a production order, the 261movement type is used.

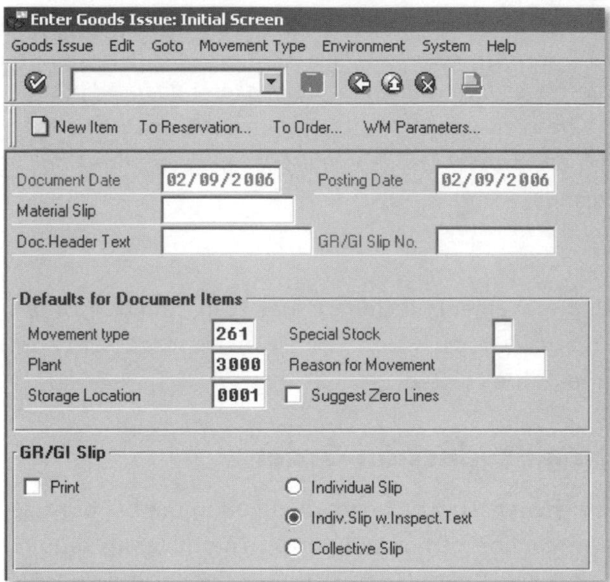

Figure 20.1 Initial Screen for Goods Issue Transaction MB1A

The goods issue to a production order requires the inventory user to enter the production order number, as well as, the material number and quantity.

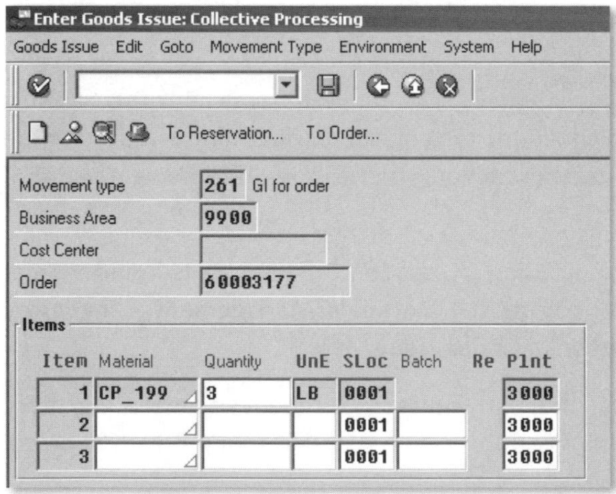

Figure 20.2 Detail Line Item Screen for Goods Issue Transaction MB1A

Once all the line items have been entered for the goods issue, as shown in figure 20.2, the transaction can be posted, producing a material and an accounting document.

20.1.2 Unplanned Goods Issue

It often becomes necessary to issue additional material to a production order that is unplanned. For instance, if a production order requires 100 Kg of raw plastic pellets and was goods issued 100 Kg, then a unplanned issue would be if the production supervisor asked the inventory department for an addition 40 Kg to be issued to that production order. There are many reasons why this would occur, including damage to the original material issued, or problems with the production process. In such cases, additional material will need to be issued on an unplanned basis.

If the inventory user has information on the production order and the material needed, the goods issue can be created with reference to the bill of materials.

The inventory user can enter the header information as usual for the goods issue, but once the relevant movement type is entered, i.e. movement type 261, the inventory user should access the header menu **Goods Issue • Create with Reference • To BOM**.

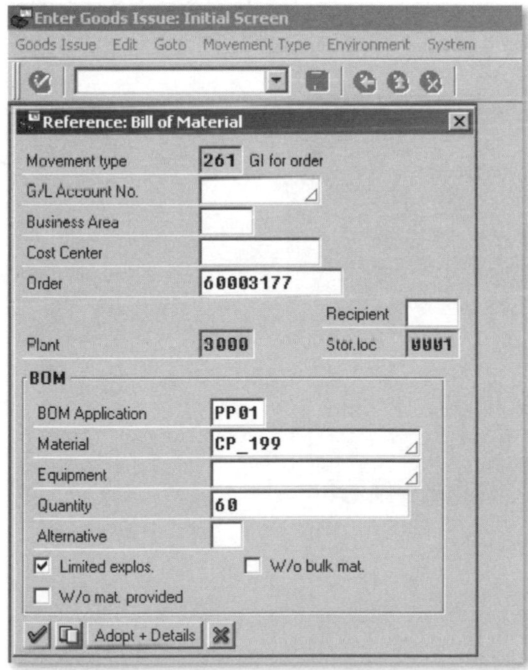

Figure 20.3 Information Required to Issue Unplanned Material to BOM

Once the information is entered for the bill of materials, as shown in Figure 20.3, the inventory user can adopt the information from the BOM for the goods issue.

20.1.3 Backflushing

Backflushing is a process that occurs after production has taken place. Materials used in the production order are not consumed in the system until the production is posted against the operation in the routing. The backflushing procedure will then process the production order using the sum of the finished products and scrap quantity to recalculate the materials required. The inventory user then will issue all the materials as one transaction, as would have done initially in a normal goods issue to a production order. At this time, there is the option of changing individual material quantities and adding individual scrap quantities to detail lines. As an example we can look at the production order from section 20.1.2, that requires 100 Kg of raw plastic pellets. If the production order was not issued the 100 Kg, but the production order was backflushed then the backflush would have one issue of 140 Kg and an added scrap line item of 40 Kg.

Backflushing occurs when either the material, production work center, or routing has been flagged as relevant for backflushing and this designation is copied to the production order (see Figure 20.4). The material can be flagged for backflushing by setting an indictor on the material master record. The backflushing indicator can be found in the MRP area of the material master record.

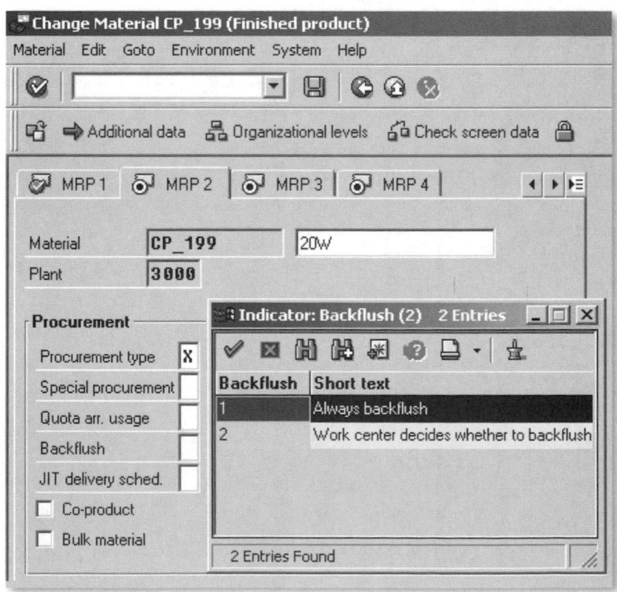

Figure 20.4 Backflushing Indicator on the Material Master Record

Backflushing can be very useful to production operations as it gives significant benefits over the normal goods issue procedure, for certain production situations:

- If a production process has a long operation time, such as days or weeks, then it may not be beneficial to the company to move material out of stock and issue to a production order, given that the material will not be recorded as consumed for a long period of time. With backflushing, this material will remain in stock until the operation is complete.
- Where a production operation involves a lot of scrap material, a complicated issuing process may ensue in which the inventory user will not know exactly how much material to issue. It is simplier to use backflushing to calculate the used material on the basis of finished product plus scrap quantity.
- Bulk materials make exact issuing very difficult, and backflushing allows a simplification of the issuing process. It is easier to allow the system to backflush the correct quantity after the operation.

20.2 Goods Issue to Scrap

Scrap material can be defined in any way that a company decides. A material that is scrap for one company may be not be scrap for another. The most useful general definition is that a material can be defined as scrap when it is no longer of any use or value to a company.

Scrap material can be:

- Material that has exceeded its expiry date
- Material that is no longer in tolerance with respect to quality
- Material that is unusable due to the production process
- Material that is damaged in the warehouse

Material that has been identified as scrap material needs to be removed from stock and the value reduced. To perform the scrapping of material, the inventory user can perform a goods issue with the relevant movement type for scrapping.

Material to be scrapped can be either in unrestricted stock, quality inspection stock, or blocked stock. Depending on the company and the scrapping procedure it uses, the material can be located in any of the three areas.

The transaction MB1A should be used for the goods issue with movement type 551, as shown in Figure 20.5. The scrapping of material reduces the inventory by the quantity entered in MB1A. The transaction also has an accounting element that will post the value of the stock to a scrapping account and post any scrapping costs to a cost center that is entered in the scrapping transaction. In many companies, the inventory user has to enter a reason for movement and the configuration has been set to allow for this. Scrapping material can be very costly and companies are always trying to reduce the level of scrap and find ways to stop scrapping material if at all possible.

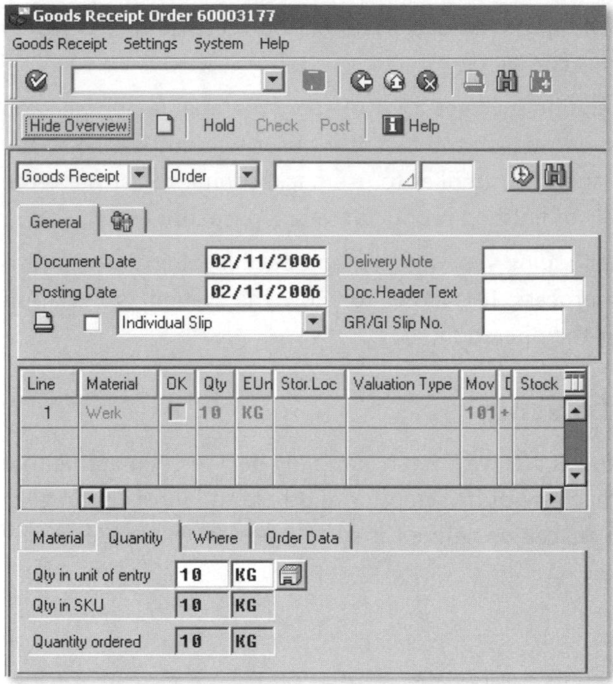

Figure 20.5 Line Iitem to be Scrapped and Relevant Cost Center for Scrapping Costs

20.3 Goods Issue for Sampling

Companies take samples of material in conjunction with testing for quality. Chemical materials can be safe to use within a range of certain tolerances. If the material changes its chemical make-up over time, e.g., then the company needs to know that information. To monitor the material, the company would instruct the quality department to test samples of the material in stock. In the majority of cases, a sample of the material is tested.

To test a sample it must be removed from stock. A goods issue is performed to issue some material for sampling. The sample can be taken from material in unrestricted, quality, or blocked stock.

Sending material for sampling reduces the inventory by the quantity entered in MB1A, as shown in Figure 20.6. The transaction has an accounting element that will post the value of the stock to a sampling account. It will post any costs involved in sampling, such as external testing labs or procedures, to a cost center that is entered in the sample transaction.

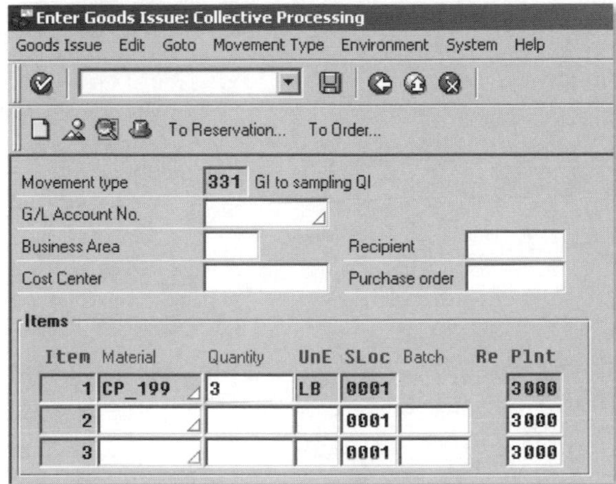

Figure 20.6 Line Item to be Issued as Sample in Transaction MB1A

20.4 Goods Issue Posting

When a goods issue is posted, e.g., to a production order, the system produces accounting and material documents, updates tables, and can trigger events in other modules.

20.4.1 Material Document

The material document is the audit document that describes the movements of the material entered in the goods issue. The material document is created during the posting of the goods issue and can be displayed using transaction MB03.

20.4.2 Accounting Document

The accounting document is created in parallel with the material document during the posting of the goods issue. The accounting document describes the financial movements associated with the material issue. The accounting document can be accessed from the material document transaction MB03.

20.4.3 Goods Issue Slip

The goods issue slip is a printed document that can be used by the warehouse to find the material and provide a physical record that the material has been picked for goods issue. The goods issue slip can be described as an IM version of a WM picking ticket.

The goods issue slip selection is made from the initial screen of a goods issue, which can be seen in Figure 20.7.

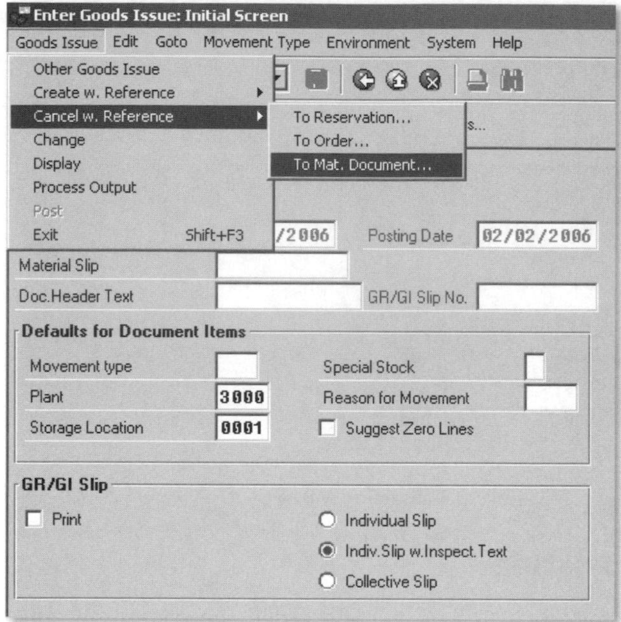

Figure 20.7 Goods Issue Reversal with Reference to Material Document.

There are three goods issue slip printed versions that can be selected in transaction MB1A:

- Individual slip. An individual goods issue slip is printed for each of the material document items
- Individual slip with inspection text. One goods issue slip is printed per material document item, but will include any quality inspection text that is contained in the material master record.
- Collective slip. This goods issue slip containing all of the items

The goods issue slip has three printed versions defined within SAP. These are WA01, WA02, and WA03. These can be modified to include the information relevant for the issuing procedure of each company.

20.4.4 Stock Changes

When a goods issue is posted, the relevant stock levels will change. The stock level will be reduced for a goods issue and increased for a goods issue reversal.

20.4.5 General Ledger Account Changes

As part of the goods issue process, the accounting module posts updates to the general ledger material accounts. When the goods issue posts, the material is valuated at the current price, whether the material is valuated at a standard price or at a moving average price. Therefore the goods issue process reduces the total value and the total quantity in relation to the price, but the price of the material does not change as a result.

20.5 Goods Issue Reversal

When material is issued to a production order, it is issued because it will be part of the bill of materials for the item that is being produced. The bill of materials is a list of materials with quantities that go into producing the finished item. Items on the bill of materials are goods issued to the production order.

In some industries, the exact issued amount will be consumed in production, e.g., in assembly operations. In other industries, such as chemicals, the exact amount of the end product is variable and therefore so is the amount of material consumed. If there is a goods issue to the production order for 500 Kg of a material and only 300 Kg were consumed, the remaining 200 Kg can be returned to stock. The inventory user will issue the material back to stock by performing a goods issue reversal.

The reversal can be entered with reference to either the material document, created on the initial goods issue, or with reference to a reservation that was made to reserve the stock for the production order.

20.5.1 Goods Issue Reversal with Reference to a Material Document

The reversal for a good issue can be made with reference to a material document. In a goods issue reversal transaction MB1A will be accessed, as saw earlier in Figure 20.7. The inventory user does not need to enter the movement type relevant to the process he or she is trying to reverse. The material document can be referenced by accessing the header menu and by following the path **Goods Issue • Cancel.w reference • To Mat. Document**.

Once the material document has been entered, the detail screen will be the next to display (Figure 20.8), and the details of the material to be reversed can be added.

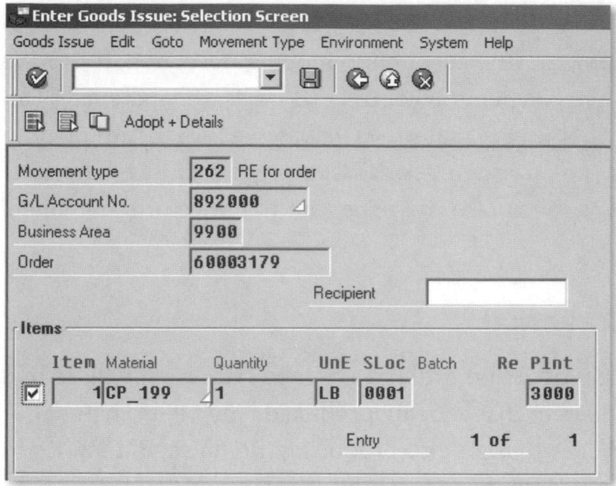

Figure 20.8 Detail Screen for Goods Issue Reversal with Reference to Material Document

20.5.2 Goods Issue Reversal with Reference to a Reservation

In addition to making a reversal against a material document, one can make a reversal against a reservation. This reversal also uses transaction MB1A, as shown in Figure 20.9. The reservation can be referenced by accessing the header menu and following the path **Goods Issue • Cancel w. reference • To reservation**.

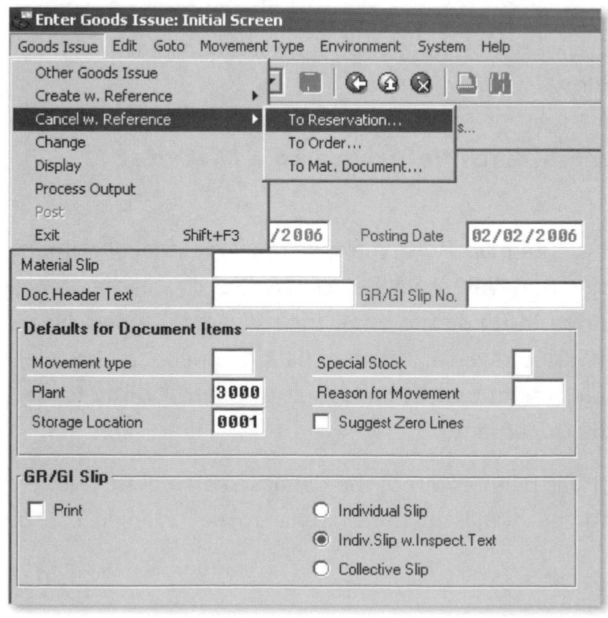

Figure 20.9 Goods Issue Reversal with Reference to Reservation

In this chapter the goods issue process was explained. Goods issue to production orders occur everyday in manufacturing plant, and production planning elements such as backflushing should be understood by the materials management user. Issuing material to scrap is a process which should be examined carefully. This process writes value from the company books, therefore any movement of this kind requires a detailed procedure with checks at several levels. Issuing material to scrap is a simple transaction to perform in SAP, but the ramifications of the transaction can have a significant financial effect.

21 Goods Receipt

A goods receipt transaction is used to receive material via a purchase order or an in-house production order. The goods receipt process can be simple or complex depending on the nature of the material being received.

Goods receipts are mainly used for receipt of stock from an external vendor via a purchase order (PO) or receipt of material from in-house production via a production order. Goods receipts are also used as the movement that initially creates inventory in the system and enters materials that were received without a purchase order. A goods receipt is important to a company as it moves the material into stock, updating the stock levels and allowing production to occur.

Every company has its own procedures for the receipt of material, and these have to be considered when using the goods receipt functionality in SAP. If the material is received into stock, either unrestricted or quality, the value of the material is posted to the plant accounts. That means that the company has spent money to have that material in the plant. Minimizing the length of time that materials spend in the goods receipt process saves the company money.

21.1 Goods Receipt for a Purchase Order

A goods receipt can be defined as a company's formal acceptance that materials were received from a vendor against a purchase order. Once the material is received and the transaction completed, the value of the material is posted to the general ledger.

21.1.1 Goods Receipt Where Purchase Order Number is Known

The goods receipt transaction is accessed through transaction MIGO. The transaction can be used whether the purchase order is known or unknown. The transaction can be accessed via the path **SAP Menu • Logistics • Materials Management • Inventory Management • Goods Receipt • For Purchase Order • PO Number Known**.

In the initial entry screen for the MIGO transaction, as shown in Figure 21.1, the **Purchase Order** number, if known should be entered. The information from the purchase order will be transposed to the goods receipt MIGO transaction, where the purchase order details can be checked and amended if necessary.

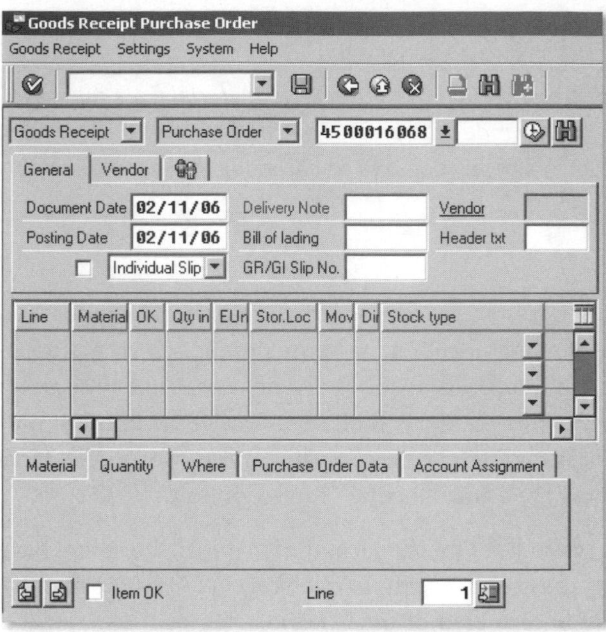

Figure 21.1 Initial Entry Screen for MIGO Transaction

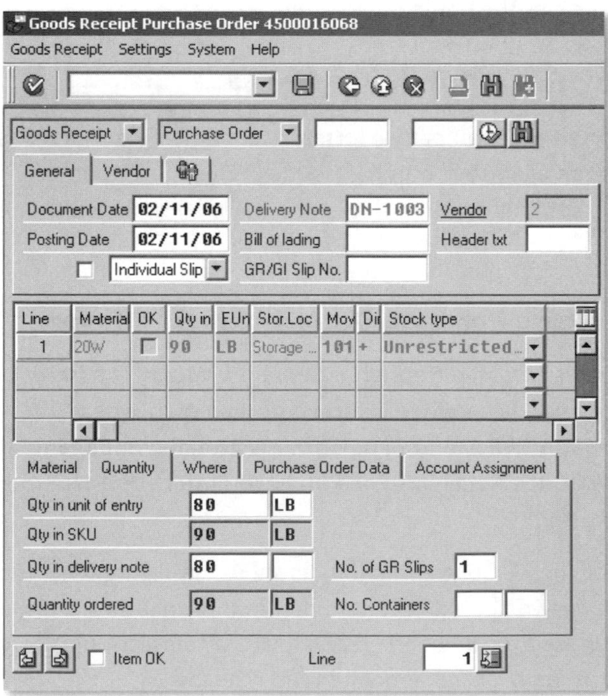

Figure 21.2 Detail Screen for Goods Receipt with Information from Purchase Order Displayed

Once the purchase order information has been transposed to the MIGO transaction, changes can be made to the delivery quantity if needed, as seen in Figure 21.2. If the delivery note from the vendor shows an amount different from that on the PO, then this can be entered into the goods receipt along with the actual amount delivered.

Once all the relevant information for the goods receipt has been entered, the goods receipt can be posted.

21.1.2 Goods Receipt Where Purchase Order Number is Unknown

On rare occasions material arrives from a vendor and the purchase order is not known because it does not appear on the documents from the vendor and no suitable purchase order number can be found in SAP. This may be due to a delay in entering the purchase order in SAP or it can be because of an error by the vendor where the material was never ordered. In any case, the company needs a procedure for handling these cases.

Some companies will not accept material without a purchase order on the documents or for which no suitable purchase order can be found in SAP. In this case, the material will be refused and the delivery not accepted. Other companies will accept delivery of the materials and keep the material in quality or blocked stock until the situation is resolved. In this case the material will need to be received and there is a movement type in SAP to perform this task.

The goods receipt for receiving material without a purchase order number uses the same goods receipt transaction MIGO. The information required for this transaction is minimal, as there are no details available from a relevant purchase order. The material and quantity information should be entered as well as storage location information.

Once all the relevant information has been entered, the goods receipt can be posted (see Figure 21.3) and the material will be part of the plant stock unless it is receipted into Goods Receipt Blocked Stock.

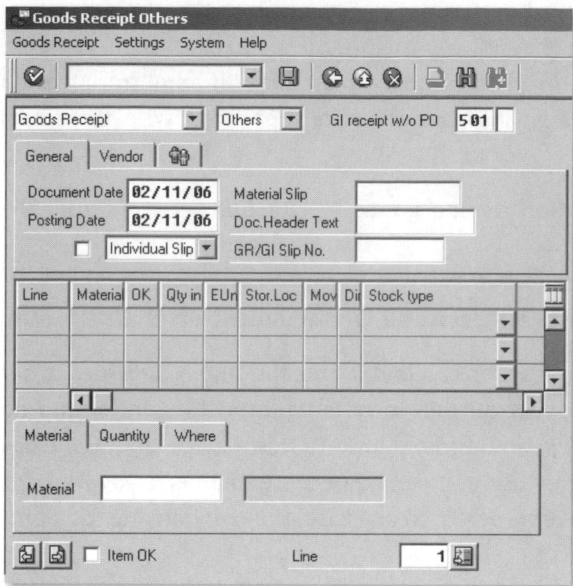

Figure 21.3 Goods Receipt Transaction for Receiving Material Without Purchase Order

21.1.3 Goods Receipt Posting

Once the goods receipt has been posted, a series of events are triggered.

Material Document

The material document is the audit that describes the movements of the material of entered in the goods receipt. The material document is created during the posting of the goods receipt and can be displayed using transaction MB03.

Accounting Document

The accounting document is created in parallel with the material document during the posting of the goods receipt. The accounting document describes the financial movements associated with material receipt. The accounting document can be accessed from the material document transaction MB03.

Goods Receipt Note

The goods receipt note is a printed document that can be used by the warehouse to store the material in the correct location.

Three goods receipt note printed versions can be selected in transaction MIGO:

- Individual GRN: An individual goods receipt note is printed for each of the material document items
- Individual GRN: With inspection text. One goods receipt note is printed per material document item, but will include any quality- inspection text that is contained in the material master record.
- Collective slip: This goods receipt note containing all of the items

The goods receipt note has three printed versions defined within SAP. These are WE01, WE02, and WE03. These can be modified to include the information relevant for the issuing procedure of each company.

Stock Changes

When a goods receipt is posted, the relevant stock levels will change. The stock level will be increased for a goods receipt and decreased for a goods receipt reversal. A goods receipt reversal may occur if the material was found to be defective or failed quality inspection. If this occurs, the inventory control department may decide to reverse the goods receipt so the material will de deducted from the plant stock level.

21.2 Goods Receipt for a Production Order

If yours is a manufacturing company then you will need to perform goods receipts for production orders to receive the finished goods into stock for use or sale.

The production order quantity can be receipted into stock by using the goods receipt transaction for orders, MIGO_GO or via **SAP Menu • Logistics • Materials Management • Inventory Management • Goods Receipt • GR for Order**.

The inventory user will be required to enter the appropriate production order number, which is found on the documents supplied from the production facility, as shown in figure 21.4.

Once the production order is entered, the material information is transposed to the goods receipt. The quantity of the finished material can be entered into the goods receipt if it varies from that on the production order.

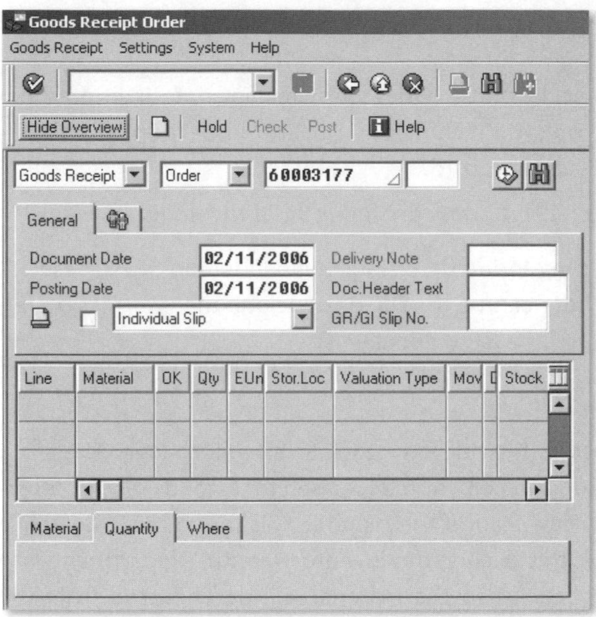

Figure 21.4 Initial Screen for a Goods Receipt from Production Order

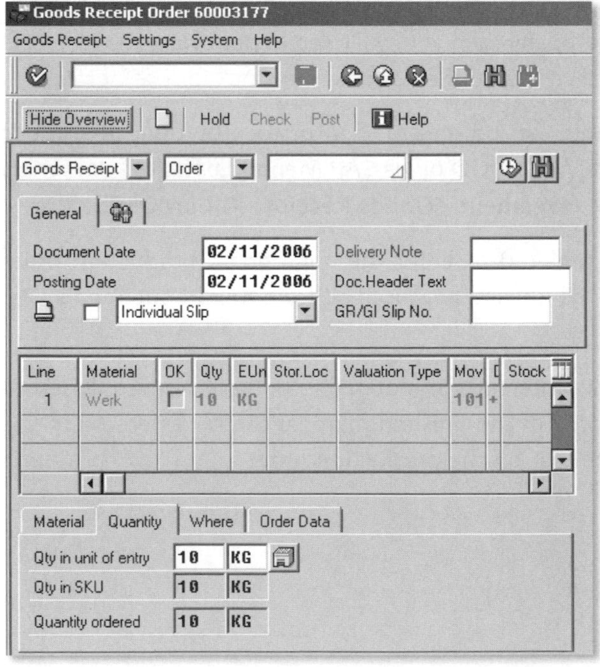

Figure 21.5 Detail Screen for Goods Receipt with Information Displayed from Production Order

Once the goods receipt is posted, the production order is determined to be fully delivered or partially delivered, providing that a partial quantity was delivered to the warehouse, as seen in Figure 21.5.

21.3 Initial Entry of Inventory

When a new SAP system is brought into production, a number of tasks need to be completed to make the transition from the legacy system to the new SAP system as seamless as possible. When replacing a legacy inventory system, the inventory on hand in the warehouse needs to be entered into the SAP system to reflect the current situation. To facilitate this, we use the goods receipt process to load the inventory via a specific movement type. This is shown in Figure 21.6.

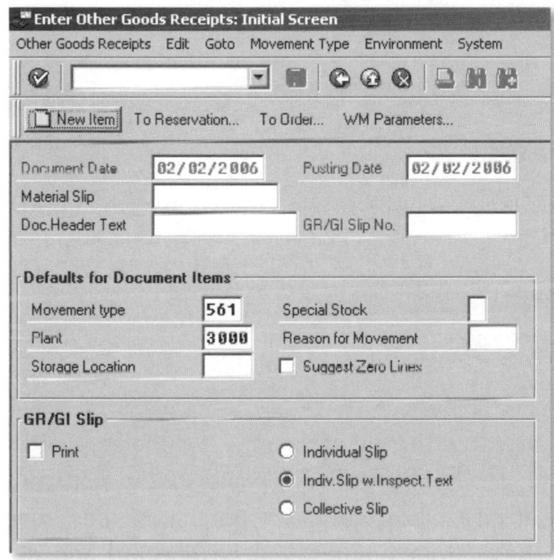

Figure 21.6 Initial Screen for Loading Initial Inventory into SAP Using Goods Receipt

The initial load of inventory uses transaction MB1C. This can be found using the navigation path **SAP Menu • Logistics • Materials Management • Inventory Management • Goods Receipt • Other**.

The transaction requires that a movement type be entered. Three of these can be used for initial inventory loads:

- 561—Goods receipt for initial entry of stock balances into unrestricted, shown in Figure 21.7
- 563—Goods receipt for initial entry of stock balances into quality inspection
- 565—Goods receipt for initial entry of stock balances into blocked stock

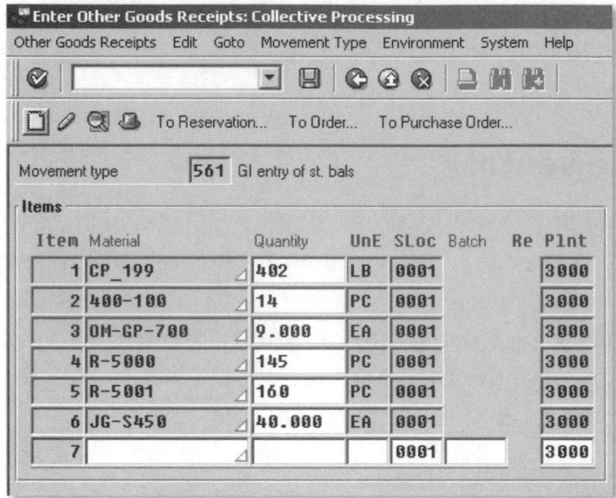

Figure 21.7 Detail Screen for Initial Inventory Load Goods Receipt.

21.4 Other Goods Receipts

There are scenarios where the material cannot be receipted by one of the normal procedures. These scenarios include:

- Goods with no Production Order
- Goods from Production that are By-Products
- Goods that are Free Goods

In these cases, the goods receipt is treated slightly differently. It is the company's decision whether and how these goods receipts take place. If the company decides that no goods receipt will take place without a purchase order, then goods that arrive without a purchase order number will be rejected and not received. However, most companies sometimes need material that arrives without appropriate documentation, and there should be procedures in place to deal with these anomalies.

21.4.1 Goods Receipt Without a Production Order

If your company has not implemented SAP Production Planning (PP), then the goods receipt of finished goods from production cannot reference a production order. In this case the material needs to be receipted into stock using a miscellaneous goods receipt.

The goods receipt of finished goods without production orders uses the same transaction as the initial load of inventory, MB1C, shown in Figure 21.8. This can be found via the path **SAP Menu • Logistics • Materials Management • Inventory Management • Goods Receipt • Other**.

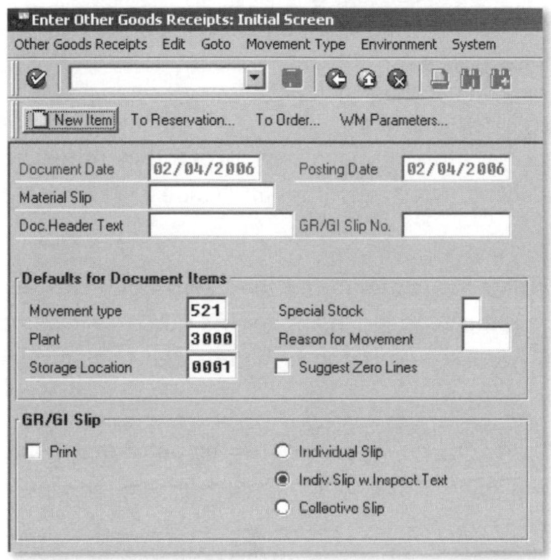

Figure 21.8 Initial Screen for Goods Receipt without Production Order

Goods receipt without a production order requires that a movement type be entered, and there are three that can be used:

- 521—Goods receipt for finished goods without a production order into unrestricted stock
- 523—Goods receipt for finished goods without a production order into quality inspection stock
- 525—Goods receipt for finished goods without a production order into blocked stock

21.4.2 Goods Receipt of By-products

A by-product is a secondary or incidental product created by the manufacturing process or from chemical reaction in a manufacturing operation. It is not the primary finished product being manufactured. In many cases, the by-product can be captured, receipted into stock, and either used again in part of the manufacturing process or sold as a finished good.

An example of the by-product scenario is the creation of lanolin from the processing of wool into textiles. The wool is processed into cloth and a by-product of that process is lanolin, also known as wool wax. Lanolin is sold as a finished good for skin ointments, waterproofing and also as a raw material for the production of shoe polish. The by-product can be received into stock using the MB1C transaction. The movement type that is used for receiving by-products is 531.

21.4.3 Goods Receipt for Free Goods

On occasion a vendor's delivery contains goods for which payment is not required. These free goods may be promotional items or sample products. Although the materials are free of charge, their quantities and value will be posted to the general ledger.

The purchasing department can create a purchase order for a zero value for free-of-charge goods if the delivery from the vendor is planned. If a purchase order is entered into the system, then the goods receipt can be referenced to that purchase order.

If no purchase order was created, then the goods receipt can be performed using the MB1C transaction with the movement type 511. This can be seen in Figure 21.9.

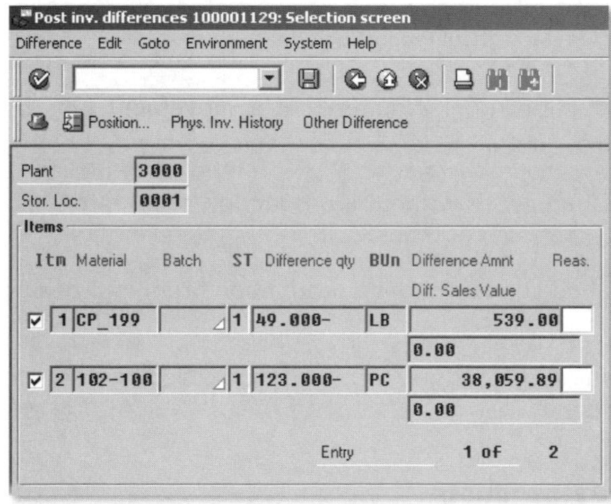

Figure 21.9 Detail Screen for Goods Receipt for Free Goods Transaction

This chapter discussed the goods receipt process that occurs in a normal manufacturing company. It is important for the material to be received, as it is imperative to keep the production line operational and to avoid stock outs. As companies move to Just-In-Time operation, goods receipt must be achieved in a timely fashion to keep operations flowing. Chapter 21 will look into the physical inventory functionality.

22 Physical Inventory

Regular physical inventories in the plant, combined with improvements in inventory accuracy are important goals for companies. Physical inventories can be customized to produce faster and more accurate results, lowering inventory costs and improving customer service levels.

A physical inventory is a count of what is currently in stock in a plant or storage location, and comparing that count to what the SAP inventory system says is in stock, and making any necessary adjustments to get the counts to match the physical warehouse counts. An inventory variance report is produced to see where your counts differed and by how much. The count can be retaken for specific variances or the variance difference can be posted to correct the differences.

Some companies perform a full physical inventory only once a year, which is the traditional method. However many companies need more accurate information more frequently. Many companies with fast-moving stock will perform cycle counting, which means that selected parts of the warehouse or specific products are counted, usually on a more frequent basis.

Physical inventory in SAP covers all aspects of the counting material at the plant. This includes the yearly inventory, cycle counting, continuous inventory, and inventory sampling.

Physical inventory can be performed on stock that is held in unrestricted, quality inspection or on blocked status. Physical inventory also can be performed on the company's own stock and special stocks, such as returnable packaging and consignment stock at customer locations.

22.1 Physical Inventory Preparation

Before the physical inventory can begin, a series of operations needs to be performed in order to prepare for the count.

In complex plants, companies may have to develop count procedures that use different approaches to counting, such as one method for finished goods, and another for raw materials. Deciding what to count is very important, as counting the wrong materials negates any count that takes place.

Companies should weigh the effects of inventory inaccuracies to determine which materials or warehouse sections are more critical than others. Small variances in the stock levels of certain materials may have little or no effect on operations, while small inaccuracies in the inventory of critical materials may shut down production. Inventory inaccuracies in finished goods will have a negative effect on customer service if deliveries are delayed or cancelled due to lack of inventory.

22.1.1 Preparations for a Physical Inventory Count

The following procedures should be followed to complete the physical inventory process:

- Process and post all transactions that will affect inventory counts: Goods Receipts, Inventory Adjustments, Transfer Postings, and Sales Orders that have been filled and shipped. These steps should be followed to keep the inventory transaction history sequenced properly.
- Put away all of the materials that are being counted in the warehouse.
- Segregate from the rest of the warehouse material stock that has been used to fill sales orders but that has not physically left the warehouse.
- Stop all stock movements within the warehouse.
- Stop all transactions in the warehouse.
- Run a Stock On-Hand report for the items you are going to count. The transaction to use for this report is MB52. This will show you the material in unrestricted, quality inspection, and block quantities for each storage location. It is a record of the inventory status before you start the physical inventory count.

22.1.2 Creating the Physical Inventory Count Document

Create the physical inventory count sheets. The physical inventory count document can be created through transaction MI01 or the menu path **SAP Menu • Logistics • Materials Management • Physical Inventory • Physical Inventory Document • Create**.

Posting Block

It is possible to set the posting block on the physical inventory count document when you create it, as you can see in Figure 22.1. As there is often a delay between a material movement and the posting of the movement, there can be a discrepancy between the physical warehouse stock and the book inventory. To ensure that there is no discrepancy during the physical inventory count, you should set the posting block indicator on the initial screen of the count document. The posting block is automatically removed when the counting results are posted for the physical inventory document.

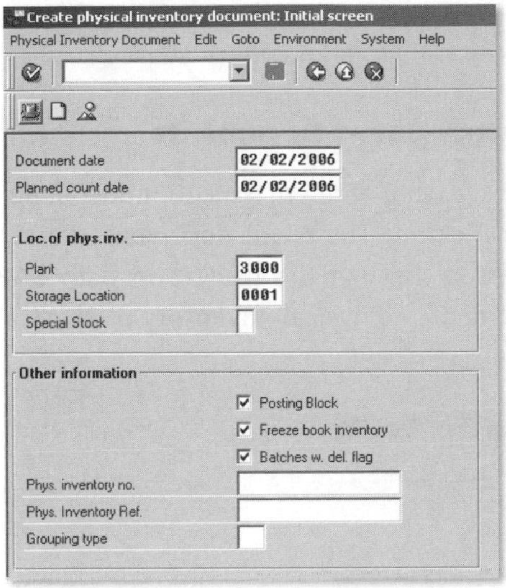

Figure 22.1 Initial Screen for Creating Physical Inventory Count Document

Freeze Book Inventory

If the inventory count has not been completed, the book inventory balance can be frozen in the physical inventory document with the freeze book inventory indicator. This is to prevent the book inventory balance from being updated by any goods movements, as this could lead to incorrect inventory differences.

Include Deleted Batches

There is an option to allow the count document to include batches of a material that has been flagged for deletion. To ensure these batches are included in the count, the indicator must be set on the initial entry screen.

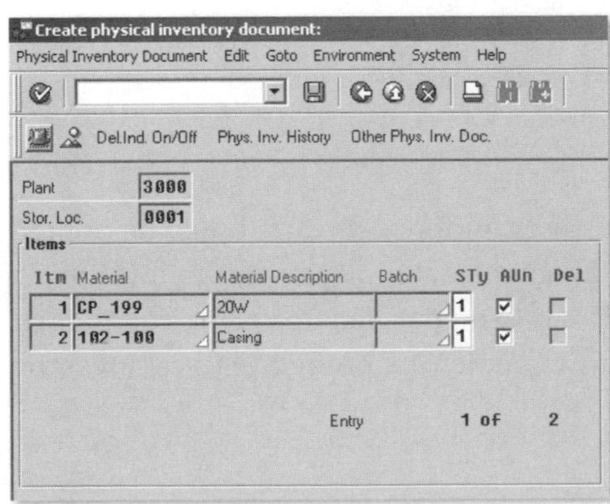

Figure 22.2 Detail Screen for Transaction

The material to be counted is added line by line for the count document as shown in Figure 22.2. The line items will not show a quantity of current stock.

22.1.3 Printing the Physical Inventory Count Documents

Once the physical inventory documents have been entered, the count documents can be printed out for the actual physical count. The count documents can be printed using transaction MI21 or accessed through the navigation path **SAP Menu • Logistics • Materials Management • Physical Inventory • Physical Inventory Document • Print**.

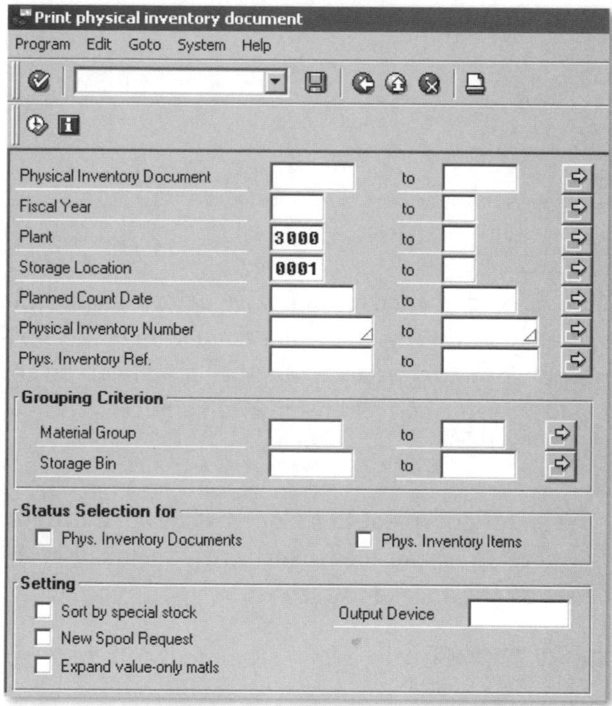

Figure 22.3 Selection Screen for Transaction MI21

The selection can be entered to decide what count documents should be printed, e.g., Figure 22.3 shows the selection by count date, plant, storage location, or document numbers. Once the selection has been decided upon, the count documents can be printed. Figure 22.4 is an example of a printed physical inventory count sheet.

```
Plant                  : 3000
Description            : New 3000
Phys. inv. doc.        : 100001127
Created by             : 1303611
Planned count date     : 02/02/2006
Phys. inv. reference:
Phys. inv. no.         :
-----------------------------------------------
Itm Material             Batch   SLoc Stor. bin
    Mat. short text              Stock type
    Status of item               Counted qty. Un
--------------------
001 CP_199                       0001
    20W                          Warehouse
    Not yet counted              ____________ LB
002 102-100                      0001
    Casing                       Warehouse
    Not yet counted              ____________ PC


                    Date         Signature
```

Figure 22.4 Version of Printed Physical Inventory Count Sheet

22.2 Counting and Recounts

Once the physical inventory count sheets are printed they can be distributed to the personnel allocated for the counting process, and the count can begin.

With more emphasis being given to accuracy of material counts, many companies now only use highly trained employees to count materials accurately. They believe that giving employees direct responsibility for counting inventory and resolving discrepancies will significantly improve the physical inventory process.

22.2.1 Entering the Count

Once the count has been completed, the physical count needs to be entered into the SAP system. The count quantities from the count sheets are transferred to their respective physical inventory documents. The inventory user will access transaction MI04 or will use the navigation path **SAP Menu • Logistics • Materials Management • Physical Inventory • Inventory Count • Enter**.

The inventory user will transfer the quantity from the inventory count sheet into the line item in transaction MI04, shown in Figure 22.5. Once all the inventory count has been entered, the transaction is posted. This will release the posting block, if one had been placed on the physical inventory document. The count can be posted and the physical count completed at that point.

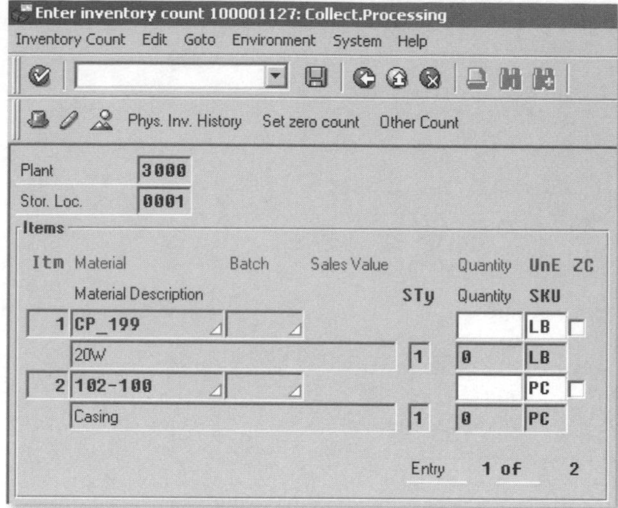

Figure 22.5 Transaction MI04.

If the inventory user made an error while entering the count document, using the transaction MI05 can change the physical count. The inventory user needs to know the physical count document in order to perform this transaction. Once the changes are made, the count can be posted if the inventory user or their supervisor is satisfied.

22.2.2 Difference List

The count can be compared against the book inventory by using transaction MI20. The transaction allows the inventory user to enter a material and the physical inventory document. The transaction can be accessed via the path **SAP Menu • Logistics • Materials Management • Physical Inventory • Difference • Difference List**.

Once the selection information has been entered the report can be run and it shows the materials from the selection. The report, shown in Figure 22.6, identifies the book quantity, the counted quantity, and the difference, if any. Once the differences have been identified, the count can be repeated to check the differences or the differences can be posted approved by management.

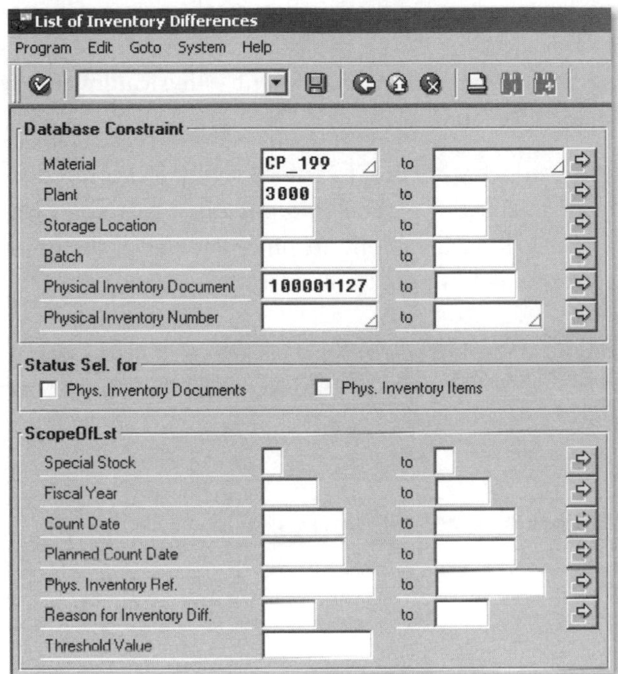

Figure 22.6 Selection Screen for Differences List for Physical Inventory Documents

22.2.3 Missing Material

Management must decide how to resolve inventory differences. The physical inventory procedures within SAP show where the material discrepancies occur, but it is the management's decision how to find the missing material. Many companies have designed an auditing process to aid the physical inventory process in investigating the discrepancies. In many instances, an adjustment is made to the book quantity of the missing product, and then an offsetting adjustment is made days later when the material is found. In this case, the changes cause additional work, disrupt the production schedule, and may lead to excess inventory of this material.

Some companies have created a variance location to move the lost and found material to and from, as a way of showing the variances without creating adjustments. A variance location must be closely monitored, and there must be an on going procedure for finding the material discrepancies.

22.2.4 Recounts

If the management does not accept the discrepancy or the discrepancy is above a certain tolerance, then those materials will need to be recounted. The recount will allow the users to recount the material in the location on the physical inventory document. The recount transaction is MI11 and can be found via the transaction path **SAP Menu • Logistics • Materials Management • Physical Inventory • Physical Inventory Document • Recount**.

The recount transaction allows the inventory user to enter the physical count document number and view the detail lines. The detail information, displayed in Figure 22.7, shows the materials relevant to the count document as well as the physical count quantity and the difference from the book quantity.

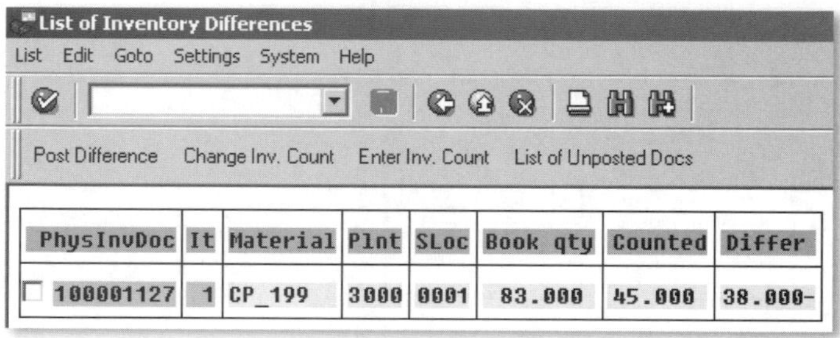

Figure 22.7 Transaction MI11

Once the recount document has been printed, the recount can be performed. When the recount is complete, the material quantities can be entered into transaction MI04. At this point, the count can be posted within the MI04 transaction, or the count can be posted through transaction MI07.

22.3 Physical Inventory Posting

22.3.1 Posting the Count Document

Once the count has been entered, the document can be posted using transaction MI07 that can found using the navigation path **SAP Menu • Logistics • Materials Management • Physical Inventory • Difference • Post**.

The physical document number has to be entered along with the posting date and threshold value. This is an optional field that holds the maximum amount to which inventory differences are allowed for the inventory document.

The detail lines of the count document shown in Figure 22.8, identifies the difference quantity and the difference value. The inventory user can post the differences unless the difference value totals more than the threshold value, assuming the threshold value was entered.

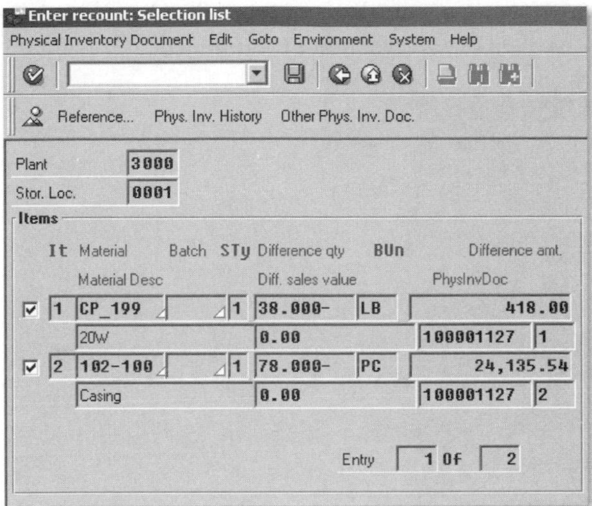

Figure 22.8 Detail Lines for Physical Count Document Before Posting in Transaction MI07

The inventory user can add a reason code for posting of the document line item, provided the reason code has been configured for the posting movement type, as seen in Figure 22.9.

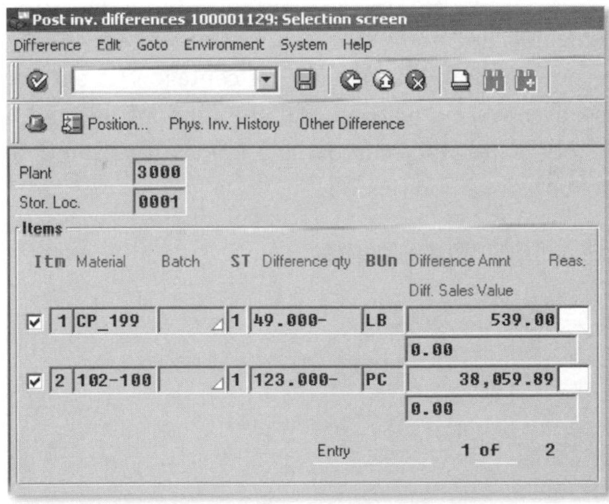

Figure 22.9 Posting of Count Document with Differences

22.3.2 Posting a Count Without a Document

If a count is made without a physical count document, an inventory user can enter the count directly into a transaction, which can be posted immediately, as shown in Figure 22.10. The transaction to be used is MI10, which can be, accessed though the path **SAP Menu • Logistics • Materials Management • Physical Inventory • Difference • Enter w/o Document Reference**.

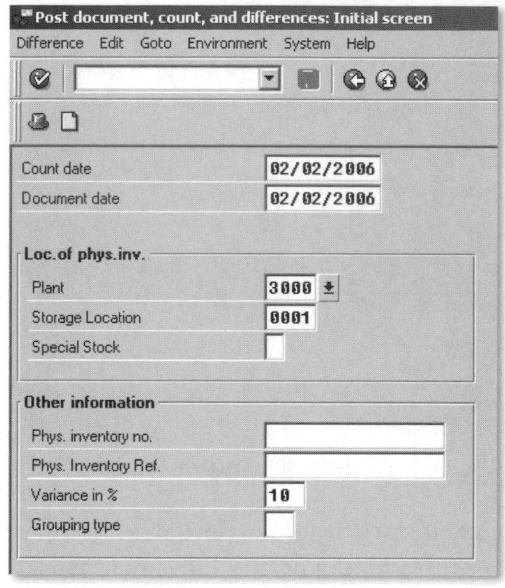

Figure 22.10 Entry screen for Transaction MI10

The inventory user can add individual line items that have been counted, and the amount can be entered for each line item. If a variance percentage was entered on the initial screen then the user will be warned that the amount entered is greater than the allowed variance. Once the material line items are entered, as shown in Figure 22.11, the document can be posted.

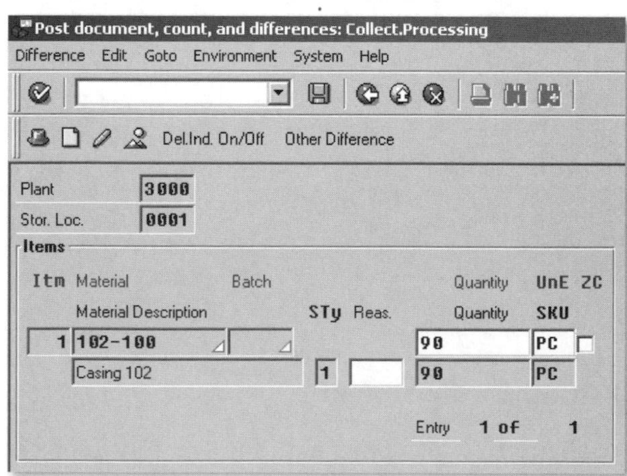

Figure 22.11 Counted Material Lineitems for Transaction MI10

22.3.3 Accounting of Inventory Differences

When the inventory differences are posted, the total stock is automatically adjusted to the counted quantity on the document. When the document is posted, the differences will correspond to either a goods receipt or goods issue.

If the counted quantity is smaller than the book inventory, the stock account is credited with the value of the inventory difference. The accounting entry is posted to the expense from physical inventory account.

Subsequently, if the counted quantity is greater than the inventory balance, the stock account is debited with the value of the inventory difference. The accounting entry is posted to the income from physical inventory account.

This chapter explained the aspects of performing a physical inventory in the traditional manner, with count sheets and recounts, and the less conventional manner of entering counts directly into the system without count sheets. Physical inventory is an important part of inventory management despite being a simple process to follow. The writing off and on of material affects other areas. These are:

- Production—is there enough stock for production orders
- Sales—is there enough stock for customers sales orders
- Accounting—total stock value goes up or down

If the physical inventory is not accurate and errors are made, then others are affected. Therefore, it is important to investigate all potential count differences to ensure that the count is accurate and the difference is not just due to a counting error.

23 Invoice Verification

Invoice verification is the procedure through which vendors will be paid for the material that they deliver to the customer. The procedure can involve a three-way matching process between the customer's purchase order, the goods-received note, and the vendor's invoice.

Invoice verification is part of the accounts-payment process in which the vendor is paid for materials or services that they have provided to the customer. The verification of the invoice is important to both the vendor and the customer as it ensures that the quantities and the pricing are all correct and that neither party has made an error. The standard method of invoice verification is the three-way match. This method uses the purchase order supplied to the vendor, the goods receipt or delivery note supplied by the vendor, and the invoice sent to the customer from the vendor. In a successful three-way match, the quantity and price of the three documents will match, and the payment to the vendor will be sent via check or bank transfer at a date agreed to by both parties.

In this chapter, we shall describe this process and a process called Evaluated Receipt Settlement (ERS), which is a two-way match between the purchase order and the delivery note, whereby the vendor is paid without an invoice being sent to the customer.

23.1 Standard Three-Way Match

23.1.1 Entering an Invoice

The receipt of an invoice at the account payable department triggers the invoice verification process. The invoice can either be in the form of a fax, hard copy, or though EDI. The invoice can be entered into the system using transaction MIRO or by following the menu path **SAP Menu • Logistics • Materials Management • Logistics Invoice Verification • Document Entry • Enter Invoice**. The initial entry screen for MIRO is shown in Figure 23.1.

The invoice entry screen requires the user to enter the details from the incoming invoice. The completed MIRO screen is shown in Figure 23.2.

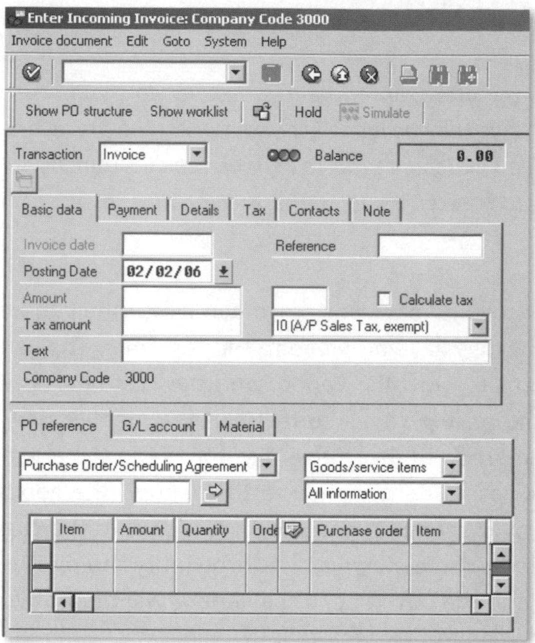

Figure 23.1 Entry Screen for Transaction MIRO

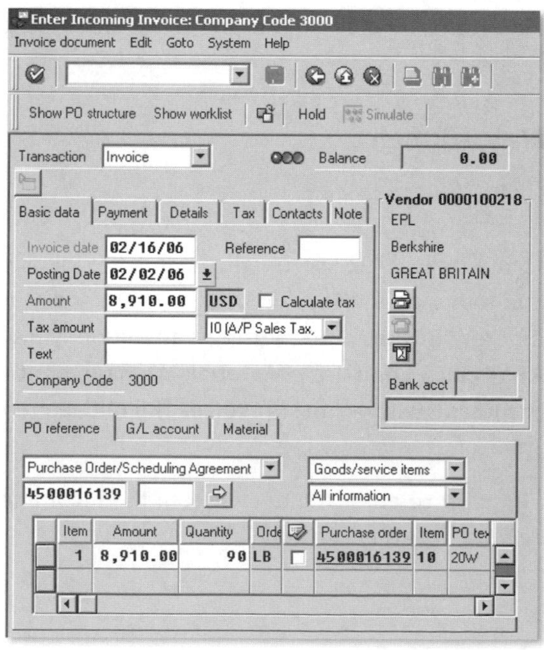

Figure 23.2 MIRO Transaction with Relevant Purchase Order Details Displayed

Invoice Date

The user is required to enter the date of the invoice. The invoice date should not be entered as a future date. The posting date is defaulted to the current date, but can be changed as necessary.

Amount

The user will enter the amount of the invoice as displayed on the vendor's invoice. The user should also enter the currency of the invoice as stated on the invoice. Invoices produced by international vendors may be in their local currencies rather than the currency entered in the purchase order.

Calculate Tax

This indicator should be set if the user would like the tax to be calculated automatically when the invoice is posted. If the vendor has entered the tax information on the invoice then this field should not be set, and the tax details entered from the invoice into the tax amount fields.

Purchase Order Number

The match can only take place when the purchase order number is entered into the MIRO transaction. Once the purchase order number is entered, the details from the purchase order will be displayed in the PO reference tab.

23.1.2 Simulate Posting

Once the details have been transferred from the purchase order to the invoice and the user believes that the invoice can be posted, the user can test the posting of the invoice by simulating the posting. The document can be simulated by accessing the header menu and selecting **Invoice Document · Simulate Document**.

The simulation is a trial posting. Even if the invoice can be posted, the simulation will not actually post the invoice. If the simulation process cannot post the invoices, messages will be posted to a message log, see Figure 23.3. The message log shows errors and warnings. The messages will indicate to the user what issues are preventing the posting.

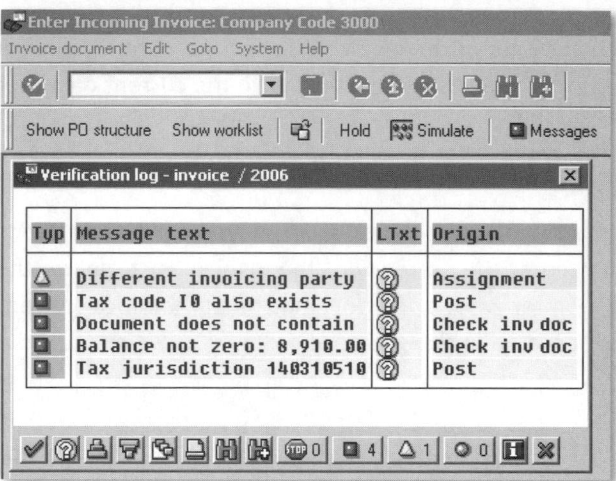

Figure 23.3 Message Log for Posting Simulation in Transaction MIRO

23.1.3 Invoice Posting

Once the message log has been cleared, there is nothing to prevent the invoice items from being posted. When the posting is complete, the information is passed through to the payment process in the Financial Accounting module. The payment process updates general ledger accounts relevant to the posted document.

The payment process is defined by a number of payment rules that can be defined in master records for the customer and vendor as well as configuration in the payment program.

The payment program can be executed by the transaction F110 in the Financial Accounting Module. It can be found via the navigation path **SAP Menu • Accounting • Financial Accounting • Accounts Payable • Periodic Processing • Payments**.

The payments processing can be scheduled using the Schedule Manager; transaction SCMA.

23.2 Evaluated Receipt Settlement (ERS)

23.2.1 Benefits of ERS

ERS is the process whereby the goods receipt and the purchase order are matched and posted without any invoice, in other words, a two-way match. The vendor does not send an invoice for materials that are defined for evaluated settlement. This process is not standard for most companies, as the evaluated-receipt process requires a significant level of co-operation and trust between customer and vendor. However, this method is of particular benefit to companies that purchase materials between different parts of the organization. The evaluated receipt process reduces the need for sending and matching invoices between departments.

The benefits of evaluated receipt settlement include:

- No quantity or price variances with invoices
- Purchasing process completed sooner
- Vendors are paid on receipt of goods at customer
- Favorable material prices from vendor

The ERS indicator can be found on the vendor master record, as shown in Figure 23.4. The ERS indicator on the vendor file is passed through to the purchase order by way of the purchase information record or the vendor file. It is possible to remove the ERS indicator in the purchase order if normal invoice verification is required.

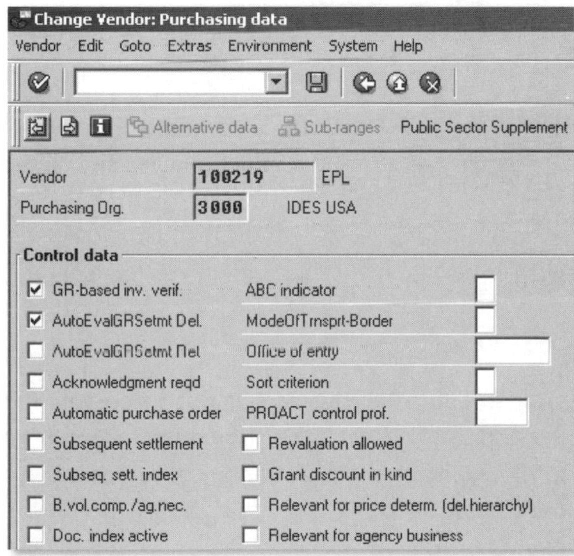

Figure 23.4 ERS Indicator on Vendor Master Record.

23.2.2 Running the Evaluated Receipt Settlement

The ERS process can be run on a schedule or on an ad-hoc basis. The ERS transaction is MRRL and can be found by the path **SAP Menu • Logistics • Materials Management • Logistics Invoice Verification • Automatic Settlement • Evaluated Receipt Settlement**.

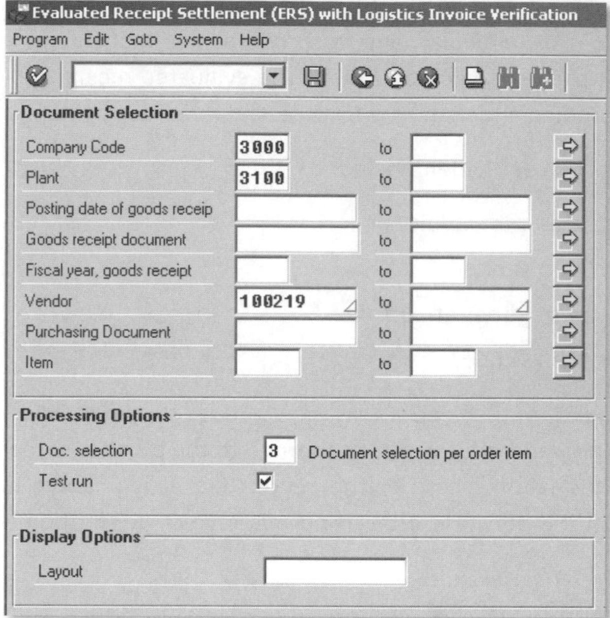

Figure 23.5 Selection Screen for Transaction MRRL

The selection screen, as shown in Figure 23.5, allows the user to restrict the program to a certain plant, vendor, or date range. Once the selection has been made, the program can be executed.

23.3 Document Parking

23.3.1 Document Parking Overview

Document parking allows the user to enter the invoice but not to post it. The invoice document can be defined as parked. The invoice should be parked if the invoice is not ready for posting. This can happen for a number of reasons: if the invoice needs changes to ensure successful posting, e.g., or if the balance of the invoice is other than zero.

23.3.2 Benefits of Document Parking

The main reason that documents are parked and not simply placed on hold is that the invoice in a parked status can be modified, while the invoice that is just held remains in its current state.

23.3.3 Parking an Invoice

The invoice can be parked using transaction MIR7, this can be found using the path **SAP Menu • Logistics • Materials Management • Logistics Invoice Verification • Document Entry • Park Invoice**.

The transaction is similar to the MIRO transaction for entering an invoice. The main difference is that when you are parking an invoice the document does not need to be correct or to balance to zero, as the invoice is not going to be posted. The document is parked and can be modified as needed.

If, after entering the information into the MIR7 transaction, the user decides that the invoice does not need to be parked or that all the information needed to post the invoice is now entered, the invoice can be posted. The user can go to the header menu and select **Invoice Document • Save as Completed (Ctrl + F8)**.

If you are entering an invoice into the transaction MIRO and decide that the information is not sufficient for posting the invoice, the user can make the decision to park the invoice and not post it. This can be performed in MIRO by selecting from the header menu **Edit • Switch to Document Parking**.

23.4 Variances and Blocking Invoices

23.4.1 Variances

An invoice has a variance if there are values, such as quantity or value that are different between the invoice and the other documents. There are four types of variances associated with invoices:

- Quantity Variance—where there are differences in the quantity delivered and the invoice quantity.
- Price Variance—where there are prices differences between the purchase order and the invoice.
- Quantity and Price Variance—where there are differences in price and quantity.
- Order Price Quantity Variance—where the price per ordered quantity is different, i.e. $3 per Kg in the purchase order, but an invoice of $3.25 per Kg in the invoice.

Variances occur when the invoice is entered and the matching finds one of the four scenarios stated above.

23.4.2 Tolerance Limits

The invoice can be posted if the variance is within the stated tolerance limits. The tolerance limit can be an absolute limit or a percentage limit. If the user does not want to block an invoice on the basis of a particular variance, the tolerance limit indicator should be set to "Do not check."

The different types of tolerances are called tolerance keys, and these are predefined in SAP. Each tolerance key describes a variance between the invoice and the goods receipt or purchase order. The tolerance limits are assigned to each tolerance key. Each tolerance key can be defined for each separate plant. The tolerance limits can vary for each plant for the same tolerance key.

The tolerance keys defined in the SAP system are:

- **AN**: Amount for item without order reference
- **AP**: Amount for item with order reference
- **BD**: Form small differences automatically
- **BR**: Percentage order price quantity unit variance (Invoice Receipt before Goods Receipt)
- **BW**: Percentage order price quantity unit variance (Goods Receipt before Invoice Receipt)
- **DQ**: Exceed amount: quantity variance
- **DW**: Quantity variance when Goods Receipt quantity equals zero
- **KW**: Variance from condition value
- **LA**: Amount of blanket purchase order
- **LD**: Blanket purchase order time limit is exceeded
- **PP**: Price variance
- **PS**: Price variance of the estimated price
- **ST**: Date variance
- **VP**: Moving average price variance

The configuration to define the tolerance limits can be found in transaction OMR6 or by using the navigation path **IMG • Materials Management • Logistics Invoice Verification • Invoice Block • Set Tolerance Limits**.

The tolerance limits for each company code are defined in transaction OMR6. Once the tolerance key is established, the tolerance limits can be entered, as shown in Figure 23.6.

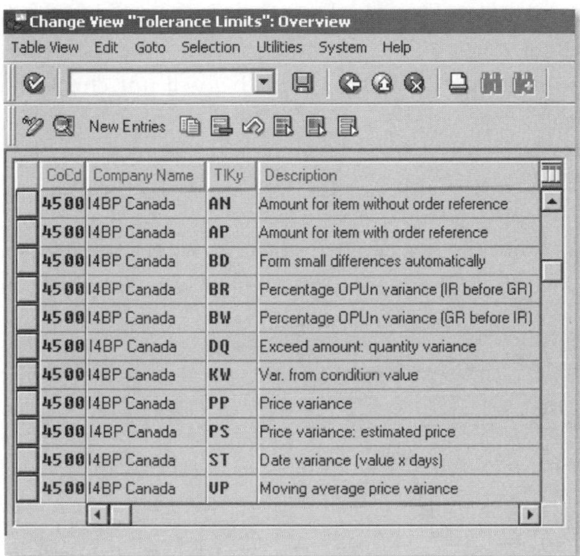
Change View "Tolerance Limits": Overview

Table View Edit Goto Selection Utilities System Help

New Entries

CoCd	Company Name	TlKy	Description
4500	I4BP Canada	AN	Amount for item without order reference
4500	I4BP Canada	AP	Amount for item with order reference
4500	I4BP Canada	BD	Form small differences automatically
4500	I4BP Canada	BR	Percentage OPUn variance (IR before GR)
4500	I4BP Canada	BW	Percentage OPUn variance (GR before IR)
4500	I4BP Canada	DQ	Exceed amount: quantity variance
4500	I4BP Canada	KW	Var. from condition value
4500	I4BP Canada	PP	Price variance
4500	I4BP Canada	PS	Price variance: estimated price
4500	I4BP Canada	ST	Date variance (value x days)
4500	I4BP Canada	VP	Moving average price variance

Figure 23.6 Transaction OMR6

Figure 23.7 shows the details for each company code/tolerance key. These are found by selecting from the header menu **Goto • Details**.

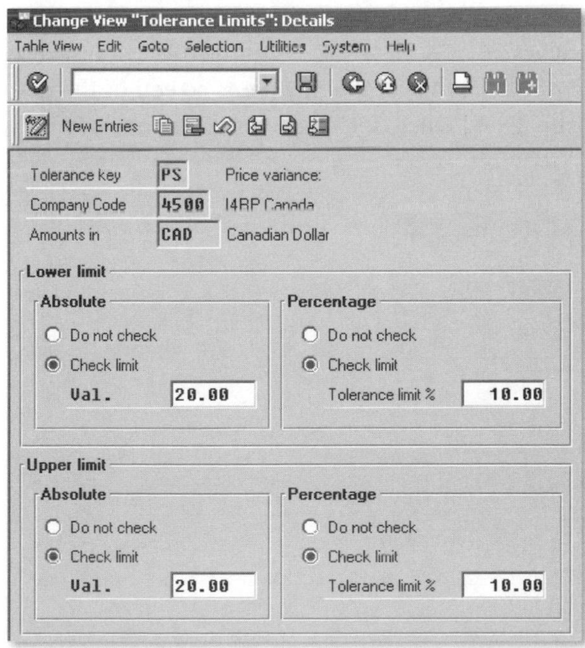

Figure 23.7 Tolerance Details for Tolerance Key in Transaction OMR6

Figure 23.7 shows the upper and lower tolerances that can be configured for both a price value (in the specified currency) and a percentage value. The user does have the option to set the **Do not check** indicator, and this will not check the invoice for this type of variance.

23.4.3 Blocking Invoices

When the invoice has been blocked, the invoice is in a status where the invoice amount cannot be paid to the vendor. There are a number of ways in which an invoice can be blocked:

- Manual Block
- Stochastic or Random Block
- Block due to Amount of an Invoice Item
- Block due to Variance of an Invoice Item

Once an invoice is blocked, then all the individual line items are blocked. This is problematic when there are many line items and only one item is causing a variance. It is then up to the finance department to investigate the variance and to unblock the invoice for payment.

23.4.4 Manual Block

The user can set the manual block during the entry of the invoice, transaction MIRO. The manual block field can be found on the payments screen of the document header, shown in Figure 23.8. Once set, the whole of the invoice is blocked for payment.

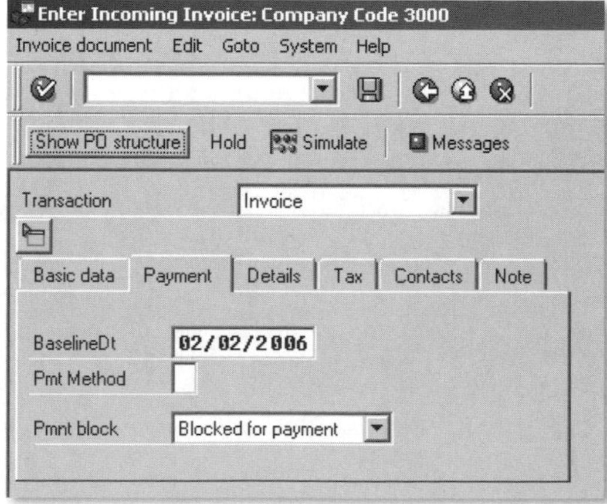

Figure 23.8 Manual Block Field of Iinvoice Header in Transaction MIRO

The user can also set the manual block indicator in the appropriate line item, as shown in Figure 23.9. This will not just block that line item, but will block the whole invoice from payment. Note that the line item will show the blocked indicator, but the manual block field will not be changed until after posting.

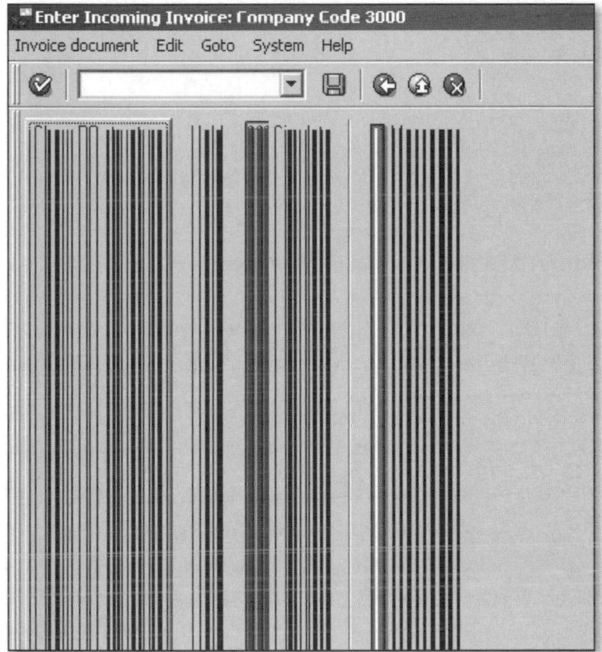

Figure 23.9 Manual Block Field of Invoice Detail Line in Transaction MIRO

23.4.5 Stochastic or Random Block

The stochastic or random block allows the company to check invoices at random or above a threshold value defined in configuration. Setting the stochastic block is a two-step process in configuration. First, the stochastic block has to be activated at the plant level. Second, a threshold can be set for each plant, as well as a percentage that represents the degree of possibility of the invoice being checked.

The configuration for the activation of the stochastic block is shown in Figure 23.10. The configuration transaction can be found using the navigation path **IMG • Materials Management • Logistics Invoice Verification • Invoice Block • Stochastic Block • Activate Stochastic Block**.

When the threshold value and probability are being configured, users have to realize how the stochastic block works. If the total value of the invoice is larger or the same as the configured threshold value, the probability of that invoice being blocked is configured.

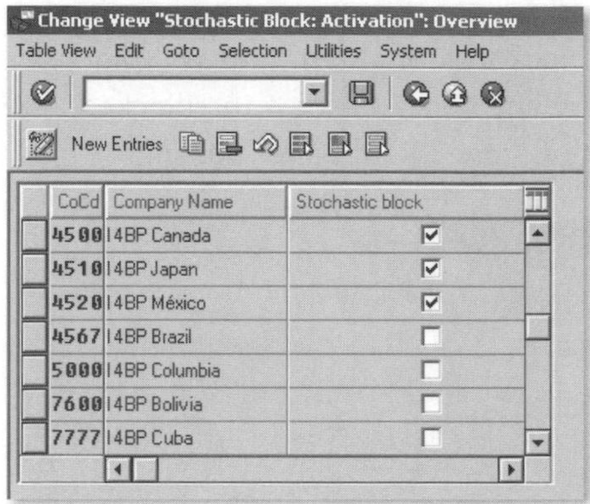

CoCd	Company Name	Stochastic block
4500	I4BP Canada	☑
4510	I4BP Japan	☑
4520	I4BP México	☑
4567	I4BP Brazil	☐
5000	I4BP Columbia	☐
7600	I4BP Bolivia	☐
7777	I4BP Cuba	☐

Figure 23.10 Activation of Stochastic Block at Plant Level in Configuration

However, if the total value of the invoice is smaller than the threshold amount, the probability that the invoice will be blocked is calculated proportionally to the percentage configured.

Therefore, if the user configures the threshold value for company code 4500 to be CAD 3,000 and configures the percentage to be 50%, each invoice entered over CAD 3,000 would have a 50% probability of being blocked, as shown in Figure 23.11. If an invoice of CAD 1500 was entered, then this would have a 25% change of being blocked, as it is half the value of the threshold value. If the users require the degree of probability to be the same for all invoices, the threshold value should be configured to zero.

The configuration for the threshold values of the stochastic block can be found using the navigation path **IMG • Materials Management • Logistics Invoice Verification • Invoice Block • Stochastic Block • Set Stochastic Block**.

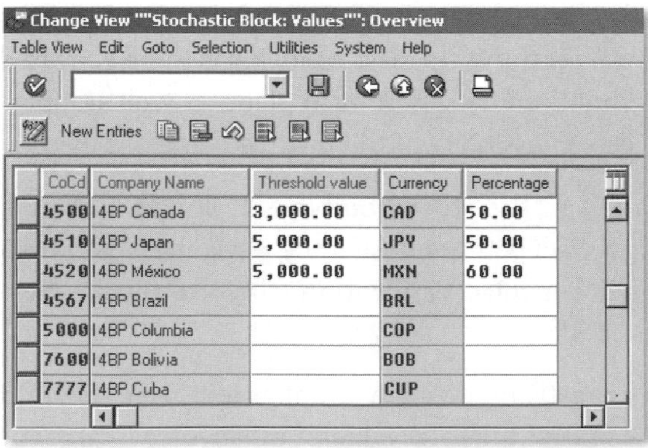

CoCd	Company Name	Threshold value	Currency	Percentage
4500	I4BP Canada	3,000.00	CAD	50.00
4510	I4BP Japan	5,000.00	JPY	50.00
4520	I4BP México	5,000.00	MXN	60.00
4567	I4BP Brazil		BRL	
5000	I4BP Columbia		COP	
7600	I4BP Bolivia		BOB	
7777	I4BP Cuba		CUP	

Figure 23.11 Threshold Value and Percentage Probability Value for Stochastic-Block Configuration

23.4.6 Block due to Amount of an Invoice Item

Sometimes companies decide to block all invoices that have line items with larger values. This is a safety feature to ensure that vendors are not paid on invoices that have incorrectly been sent by the vendor or incorrectly entered by the finance clerks.

The first step in configuring this particular block is to activate the block due to item amount in the IMG, as shown in Figure 23.12. The configuration can be found using the path **IMG · Materials Management · Logistics Invoice Verification · Invoice Block · Item Amount Check · Activate Item Amount Check**.

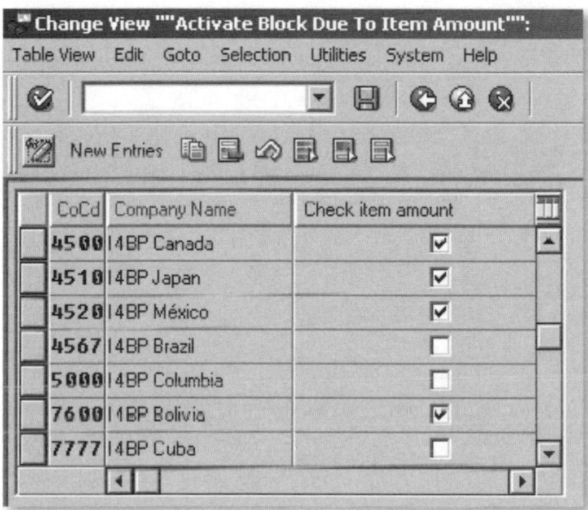

Figure 23.12 Configuration of Activation Flag for Each Company Code.

Once the indicator has been activated for the item amount check for a company code, the detailed configuration of the item amount can commence. The first part of the configuration can be found using the navigation path **IMG · Materials Management · Logistics Invoice Verification · Invoice Block · Item Amount Check · Set Item Amount Check**.

This configuration, shown in Figure 23.13, allows the user to determine which invoice line items are checked by the system. The item amounts for invoice items are checked on the basis of the item category and the goods-receipt indicator, depending on the configuration.

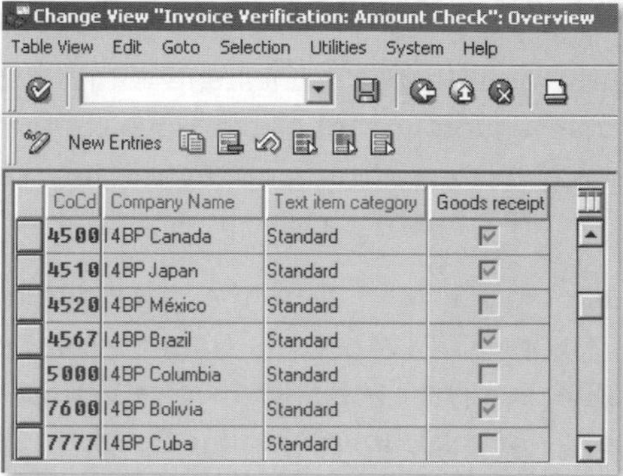

Figure 23.13 Configuration for Checking Item Amount for Item Category and Goods Receipt Indicator

The final step of the configuration is to set the amount at which the invoice is blocked, as shown in Figure 23.14. The amount is dependant on the company code and the tolerance key.

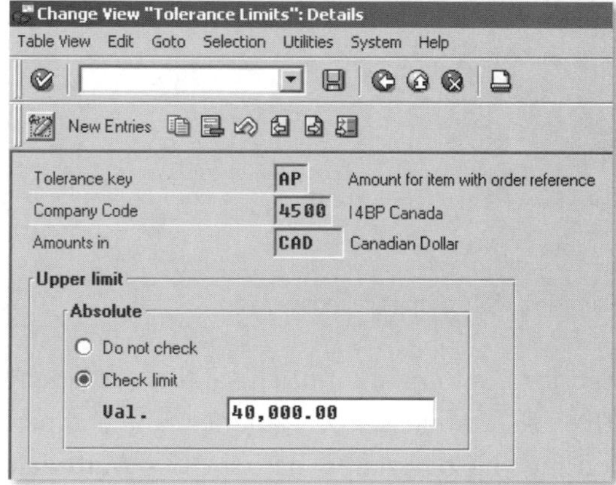

Figure 23.14 Upper-limit Configuration for Block due to Amount of Invoice Item

23.4.7 Block due to Variance of an Invoice Item

A number of blocks can be set due to the variance in an invoice item. These are:

- Quantity Variance (**Q**), where the block is due to a variance between purchase order quantity, delivered quantity and invoiced quantity.
- Price Variance (**P**), where the price of the item in the purchase order does not match the price of the item in the invoice.
- Schedule Variance (**D**), where the delivery of the items has occurred before the scheduled date.

- Quality Inspection (I), where the block is due to an issue with the quality of the items at or after goods receipt.

In case of blocking due to a variance, the invoice may still be blocked even though the blocking reason is no longer valid. The block must be released either automatically or manually for the invoice to be paid.

23.5 Releasing Invoices

After the invoice has been blocked, a procedure needs to be set up to ensure that the invoices are released when the reason for the block is no longer valid. The whole invoice is blocked despite the fact that only one line item may be causing the block. Therefore, before the invoice can be paid for all the line items, the invoice must be released. We do this by canceling the blocking indicator that was set when the invoice was originally posted.

23.5.1 Releasing Invoices Automatically

The automatic release of blocked invoices deletes all blocks that no longer apply to the invoices the user has selected to be reviewed by the program.

To release the invoices automatically, the user can use the transaction MRBR, which is shown in Figure 23.15. The transaction can be found using the navigation path **SAP Menu · Logistics · Materials Management · Logistics Invoice Verification · Further Processing · Release Blocked Invoices**.

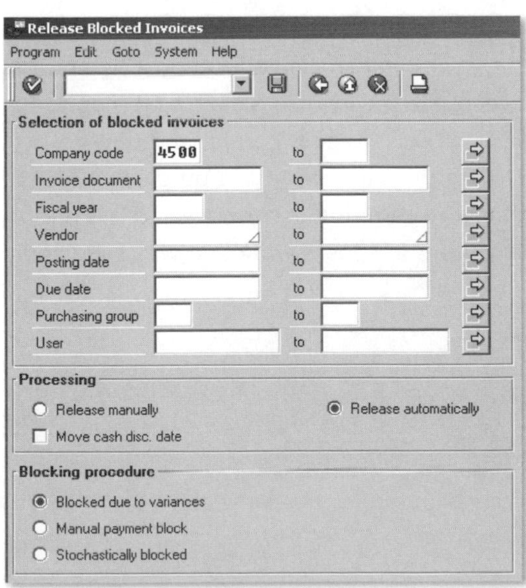

Figure 23.15 Selection Screen for Transaction MRBR

If the accounts payable department decides that it wants to review all invoices before release, then the transaction MRBR allows the user to flag that the release of the invoices will be made manually. In this case, the program will display all the relevant blocked invoices for the selection criteria entered.

The detailed display for the invoices shows the reasons for the blocked invoices and will highlight those where the block is still in place but no longer valid. The user can then release manually those they choose, as shown in Figure 23.16.

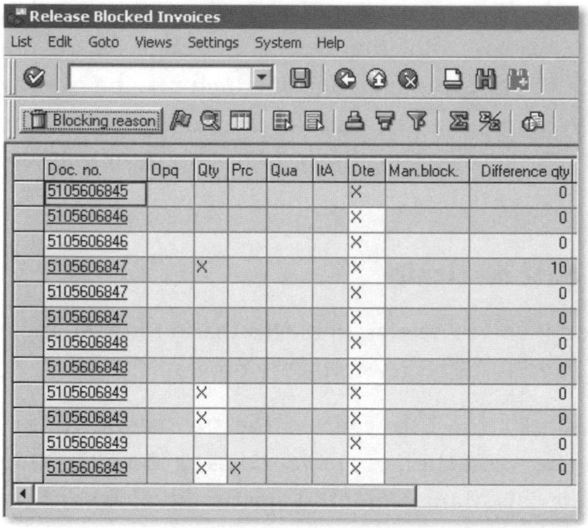

Release Blocked Invoices

List Edit Goto Views Settings System Help

Blocking reason

Doc. no.	Opq	Qty	Prc	Qua	ItA	Dte	Man.block.	Difference qty
5105606845						X		0
5105606846						X		0
5105606846						X		0
5105606847		X				X		10
5105606847						X		0
5105606847						X		0
5105606848						X		0
5105606848						X		0
5105606849		X				X		0
5105606849		X				X		0
5105606849						X		0
5105606849		X	X			X		0

Figure 23.16 Output from Transaction MRBR

This chapter described the processes involved in invoice verification. The entry of the invoice is a simple process. However, once the invoice is entered it is up to the accounts payable department to decide if the invoice is correct and how to proceed if the invoice does not match the information from the purchase order or the goods receipt. Blocking invoices is a very common occurrence and it is important to understand how these different types of blocks work and why they are in place.

24 Balance Sheet Valuation

Balance sheet valuation is the calculation of the material value for use in balance sheets. The method employed may depend on country-specific tax regulations, state and federal legal requirements, corporate financial practices, and internal accounting policy procedures.

A balance sheet is a financial statement of a business at a specific point in time. The balance sheet reports on the source of funds to a business and how those funds have been used or invested. Within the use of funds section of the balance sheet, there are two areas, fixed assets, and working capital. Fixed assets are those that can be depreciated, such as machines and buildings. Working capital is defined as the funds used to provide the flow of material and services to achieve sales and satisfy the customer. Working capital can be two areas: current assets and current liabilities. Current assets are cash, payables, receivables, and the material in the warehouse. The material includes raw material, work in process, and finished goods. The stock value is the lowest cost or the net realizable, or saleable, value.

24.1 LIFO Valuation

Last-in, first-out (LIFO) valuation is based on the principle that the last deliveries of a material to be received are the first to be used. If this is true, then no value change occurs for older material when new materials are received. Because of the LIFO method, the older material is not affected by the higher prices of the new deliveries of material. If the older material is not affected, that means it is not valuated at the new material price. If the older material value is not increased, this stops any false valuation of current inventory.

LIFO valuation enables the increased amount of material stock per fiscal year to be valuated separately from the rest of the material stock. This is important as it ensures that the new material is valuated at the correct amount, while old stock remains valuated without being affected by the new material price. A positive variance between the opening and closing material balances of a fiscal year is known as a layer for LIFO valuation. The layer is valuated as a separate item. The total of a material is the sum of all layers.

A layer is dissolved if there is a negative difference between the opening and closing stock balances at the end of a fiscal year. This would happen, e.g., if all the new stock was consumed plus some of the existing stock.

24.1.1 Configuration for LIFO

The first step in configuration is to ensure that LIFO is active. The transaction is OMWE and can be found via the navigation path **IMG • Materials Management • Valuation and Account Assignment • Balance Sheet Valuation Procedures • Configure LIFO/FIFO Methods • General Information • Activate/Deactivate LIFO/FIFO Valuation**.

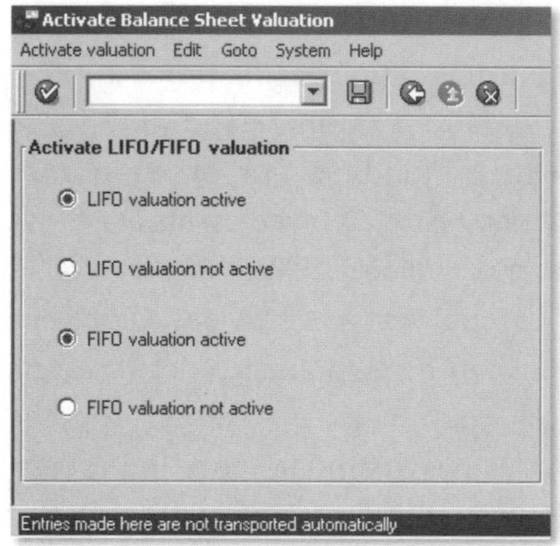

Figure 24.1 Transaction OMWE

Once the LIFO valuation has been activated, as shown in Figure 24.1, the LIFO valuation can be configured for each company code or valuation area. This configuration can be completed using transaction MRLH and is shown in Figure 24.2.

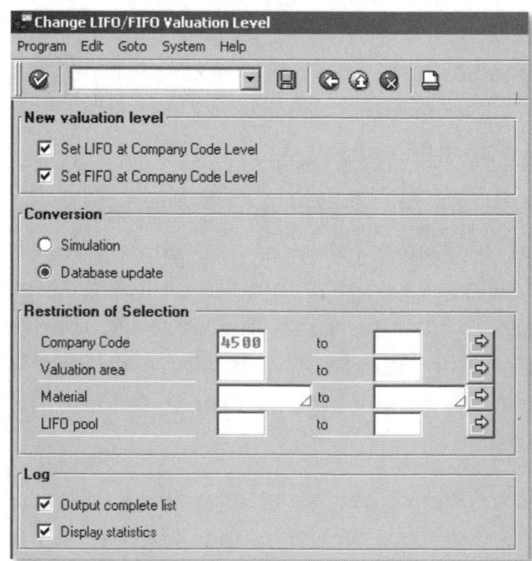

Figure 24.2 Configuration for LIFO and FIFO at Plant or Valuation Area Level

The LIFO method also depends on the movement types being set up to be relevant for LIFO. The configuration is shown in Figure 24.3. It can be found using transaction OMW4 or via the path **IMG • Materials Management • Valuation and Account Assignment • Balance Sheet Valuation Procedures • Configure LIFO/FIFO Methods • General Information • Define LIFO/FIFO Relevant Movement Types**.

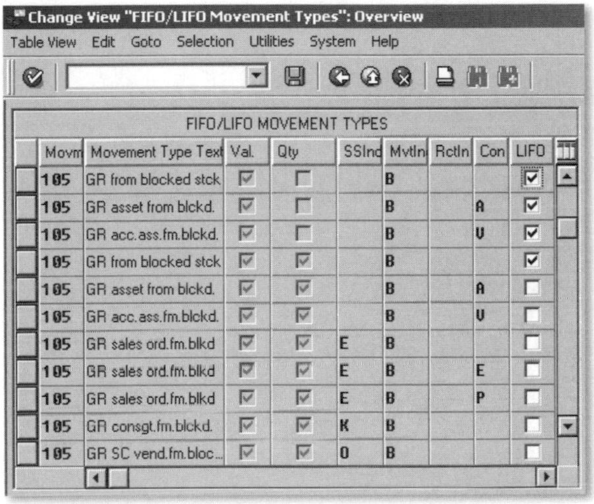

Change View "FIFO/LIFO Movement Types": Overview

Table View Edit Goto Selection Utilities System Help

FIFO/LIFO MOVEMENT TYPES

Movm	Movement Type Text	Val.	Qty	SSInd	MvtIn	RctIn	Con	LIFO
105	GR from blocked stck	☑	☐		B			☑
105	GR asset from blckd.	☑	☐		B		A	☑
105	GR acc.ass.fm.blckd.	☑	☐		B		V	☑
105	GR from blocked stck	☑	☑		B			☑
105	GR asset from blckd.	☑	☑		B		A	☐
105	GR acc.ass.fm.blckd.	☑	☑		B		V	☐
105	GR sales ord.fm.blkd	☑	☑	E	B			☐
105	GR sales ord.fm.blkd	☑	☑	E	B		E	☐
105	GR sales ord.fm.blkd	☑	☑	E	B		P	☐
105	GR consgt.fm.blckd.	☑	☑	K	B			☐
105	GR SC vend.fm.bloc...	☑	☑	O	B			☐

Figure 24.3 Movement Types Configured as Relevant for LIFO Valuation

24.1.2 Preparation for LIFO

Material Master Records

To prepare for LIFO valuation, you must make sure that the materials you want to value are flagged for LIFO. The flag is located within the material master on the accounting screen. This flag needs to be set for LIFO.

You can use the transaction MRL6 to update the LIFO flag for a selection of materials, material types, plants, etc. This transaction can be found using the navigation path **SAP Menu • Logistics • Materials Management • Valuation • Balance Sheet Valuation • LIFO Valuation • Prepare • Select Materials**.

Base Layers

As discussed above, the measurement of material value changes are based on comparing different layers. Before LIFO can be started, the base layer should be created from information in the older existing material.

The base layer can be seen in Figure 24.4. The base layer can be created using transaction MRL8, or by using the navigation path **SAP Menu • Logistics • Mate-**

rials Management • Valuation • Balance Sheet Valuation • LIFO Valuation • Prepare • Create Base Layer.

Once in transaction MRL8, the user needs to enter the materials for which to create the base layer and enter the LIFO method that is to be used.

Users should select the values that are to be used to determine the layer value. The choices include: from previous month, month before last, previous year, and year before last.

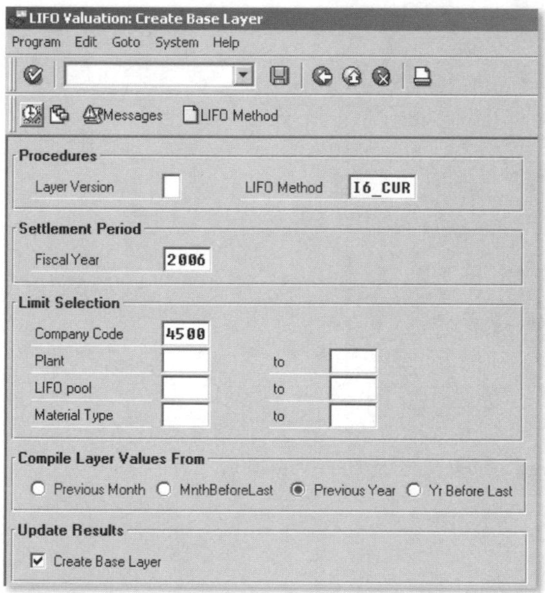

Figure 24.4 Transaction MRL8

Determination of Basis for Comparison

Before running a LIFO valuation, a basis for comparison needs to be determined. During LIFO valuation, the stocks are compared at a particular point in time with the total of the layer quantities. These are the periods that are defined in SAP:

- GJE—where the stock at the end of the previous fiscal year is compared with the total quantities in the existing layers.
- VOM—where the stock at the end of the previous period is compared with the total quantities in the existing layers.
- VVM—where the stock at the end of the period before last is compared with the total quantities in the existing layers.
- CUR—where the current stock is compared with the total quantities in the existing layers.

24.1.3 Running a LIFO Valuation

Once the configuration and preparation is completed for the LIFO valuation, the transaction can be executed to run the valuation. The transactions that can be run are:

- MRL1 for Single Material Level
- MRL2 for the Pool Level
- MRL3 for Comparison of Lowest Values

The navigation path to find these transactions is **SAP Menu • Logistics • Materials Management • Valuation • Balance Sheet Valuation • LIFO Valuation • Perform Check**.

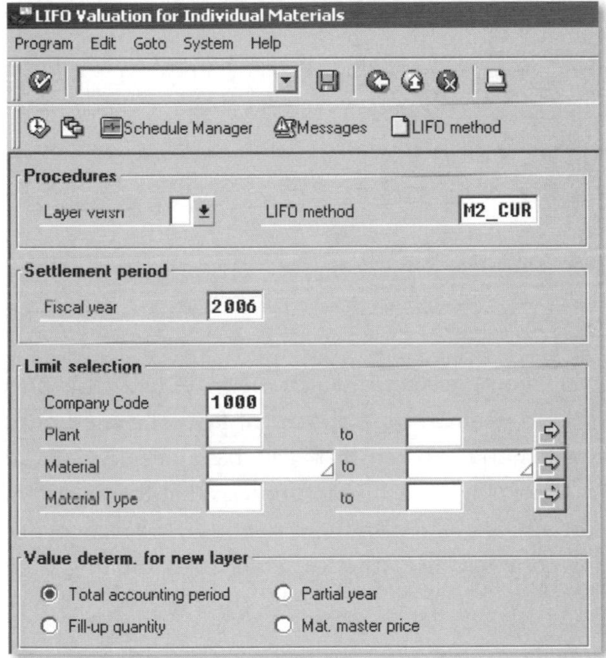

Figure 24.5 Selection Screen for LIFO Valuation Transaction MRL1

In transaction MRL1, shown in Figure 24.5, the user can choose the LIFO method, the selection criteria, and the value determination for the new layer. Once these have been entered, the transaction can be executed and the result can be seen in Figure 24.6.

LIFO Valuation for Individual Materials

List Edit Goto System Help

LIFO Valuation for Individual Materials

Material	Year	Old qty	New qty	Old value	New value
500-120	2001	400	400	306.78	306.78
	2002	350	350	276.86	276.86
	2003	1,730	1,730	1,578.86	1,578.86
	2004	385	385	425.27	425.27
	2005	3,610	3,610	4,230.07	4,230.07
	2006	0	3,550	0.00	4,649.45
500-130	2001	400	400	204.52	204.52
	2002	1,000	1,000	539.41	539.41
	2003	1,585	1,585	946.25	946.25
	2004	200	200	281.21	281.21
	2005	3,635	3,635	5,380.60	5,380.60
	2006	0	3,400	0.00	5,449.21
500-140	2001	300	300	76.69	76.69
	2002	300	300	79.15	79.15
	2003	2,060	2,060	679.86	679.86
	2004	130	130	59.82	59.82
	2005	4,430	4,430	2,313.26	2,313.26
	2006	0	3,550	0.00	2,397.51
500-150	2001	200	200	127.82	127.82
	2002	450	450	299.16	299.16
	2003	1,789	1,789	1,316.34	1,316.34
	2004	120	120	106.14	106.14
	2005	4,150	4,150	3,943.84	3,943.84
	2006	0	2,900	0.00	3,145.04

Figure 24.6 Result of LIFO Valuation Transaction MRL1

24.2 FIFO Valuation

First-in, first-out (FIFO) is a valuation method in which the material that is purchased or produced first is sold, consumed, or disposed of first. This method is employed by companies whose material is batch-managed, has an expiry date, or degrades in quality with time. Use of this method presupposes that the next item to be shipped will be the oldest of that material in the warehouse. In practice, this usually reflects the underlying commercial method of companies rotating their inventory.

It is common for newer companies to use FIFO for reporting the value of merchandise, in order to bolster their balance sheets. As the older and cheaper materials are sold, the newer and more expensive materials remain as assets on the balance sheet. However, as the company grows it may switch to LIFO to reduce the amount of taxes it pays to the government.

24.2.1 Configuration for FIFO

The configuration steps for FIFO are very similar to those of configuring the LIFO valuation. The first step in configuration is to ensure that FIFO is active. The transaction is OMWE and can be found via the navigation path **IMG • Materials Man-**

agement · Valuation and Account Assignment · Balance Sheet Valuation Procedures · Configure LIFO/FIFO Methods · General Information · Activate/Deactivate LIFO/FIFO Valuation.

After FIFO valuation has been activated, FIFO valuation can be configured for each company code or valuation area. This configuration can be completed using transaction MRLH.

Lastly, configure the movement types being set up to be relevant for FIFO. The configuration can be found using transaction OMW4 or via the navigation path **IMG · Materials Management · Valuation and Account Assignment · Balance Sheet Valuation Procedures · Configure LIFO/FIFO Methods · General Information · Define LIFO/FIFO Relevant Movement Types**.

24.2.2 Preparation for FIFO

After configuration for FIFO, the materials relevant for FIFO need to be selected. This can be performed using transaction MRF4, as shown in Figure 24.7. It can be found using the navigation path **SAP Menu · Logistics · Materials Management · Valuation · Balance Sheet Valuation · FIFO Valuation · Prepare · Select Materials**.

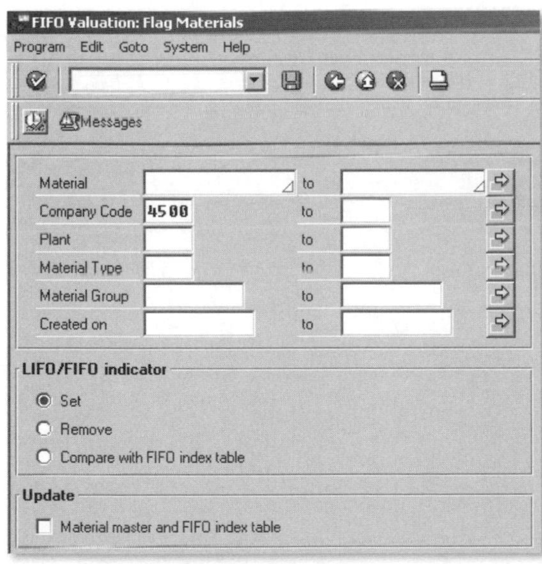

Figure 24.7 Material Selection for FIFO Valuation Method

24.2.3 Running a FIFO Valuation

Once all the configuration and preparation has been completed for the FIFO valuation, the transaction MRF1 can be executed to run the valuation as shown in

Figure 24.8. The transaction can be found using the navigation path **SAP Menu • Logistics • Materials Management • Valuation • Balance Sheet Valuation • FIFO Valuation • Perform Check**.

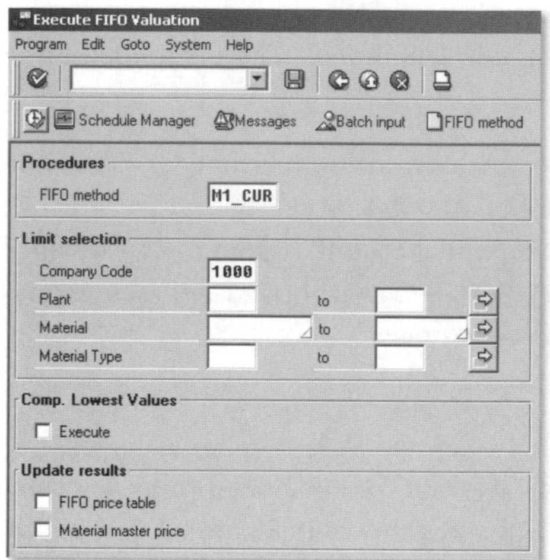

Figure 24.8 Selection Screen for MRF1Transaction

Once the transaction has been executed, the FIFO valuation will be formed for the selected materials, plant, etc., and a report will be displayed, Figure 24.9 shows the results.

Execute FIFO Valuation

List Edit Goto System Help

Execute FIFO Valuation

Material	Stock		Stk val	FIFO val.	difference	
500-110	0	L	0.00	0.00	0.00	%
500-120	10,025	KG	13,129.79	13,311.03	1.38	%
500-130	10,220	KG	16,379.68	16,553.43	1.06	%
500-140	10,770	KG	7,273.57	7,491.91	3.00	%
500-150	9,609	KG	10,420.94	10,598.32	1.70	%
500-160	8,528	KG	5,873.02	6,026.95	2.62	%
500-170	8,585	KG	7,051.09	7,241.78	2.70	%
500-180	5,415	KG	5,218.16	5,321.69	1.98	%
500-190	5,195	KG	4,616.78	4,726.44	2.38	%
500-200	4,760	KG	2,604.67	2,693.71	3.42	%
500-210	1,765	KG	924.85	938.53	1.48	%
500-220	5,346	KG	2,916.34	3,011.64	3.27	%
500-230	0	L	0.00	0.00	0.00	%
M-310	10	KG	8.50	8.50	0.00	%
Y-510	2,000	KG	9,748.90	9,748.90	0.00	%

Execute FIFO Valuation

Totals for company code 1000

Book value	FIFO net val	Difference	FIFO gross val
246,166.29 EUR	247,672.83	0.61 %	247,672.83
246,166.29 EUR	247,672.83	0.61 %	247,672.83
246,166.29 EUR	247,672.83	0.61 %	247,672.83

Figure 24.9 Result of FIFO Valuation Transaction MRF1

24.3 Lowest Value Determination

Lowest value determination uses the valuation method of the lowest value principle (LVP). This method is used widely in industry in many countries. Simply put, LVP indicates where the material is valued at the lowest value held on the system.

Three types of value determination can be used to calculate the material value. These are:

- Based On Market Prices
- Based On Range of Coverage
- Based On Movement Rate

24.3.1 Lowest Value Determination Based on Market Prices

To determine the lowest value on market prices, the SAP system searches for the lowest price from the different prices stored for each material. The procedure looks at the material price from the following:

- Purchase Orders
- Scheduling Agreements
- Goods Receipts for Purchase Orders
- Invoices for Purchase Orders
- Purchasing Information Records

The transaction to run the lowest value based on market price is MRNO and can found via the path **SAP Menu • Logistics • Materials Management • Valuation • Balance Sheet Valuation • Determination of Lowest Value • Market Price**.

The selection screen, shown in Figure 24.10, allows the user to enter a range of materials, plant, material type, or valuation class.

Once the selection criteria have been entered, the transaction can be executed. The resulting display, Figure 24.11, shows the new price and the percentage change.

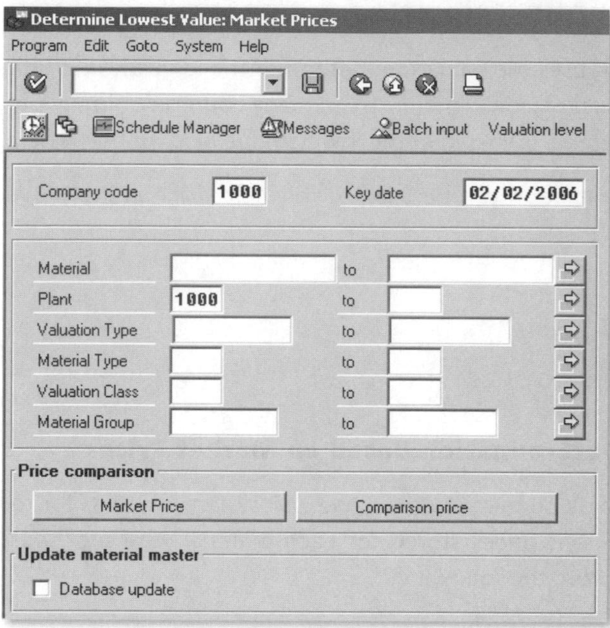

Figure 24.10 Selection Screen for Transaction MRNO

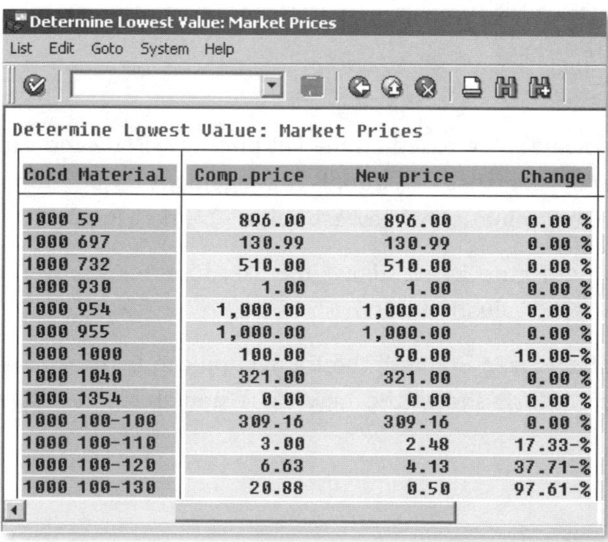

Determine Lowest Value: Market Prices

CoCd Material	Comp.price	New price	Change
1000 59	896.00	896.00	0.00 %
1000 697	130.99	130.99	0.00 %
1000 732	510.00	510.00	0.00 %
1000 930	1.00	1.00	0.00 %
1000 954	1,000.00	1,000.00	0.00 %
1000 955	1,000.00	1,000.00	0.00 %
1000 1000	100.00	90.00	10.00-%
1000 1040	321.00	321.00	0.00 %
1000 1354	0.00	0.00	0.00 %
1000 100-100	309.16	309.16	0.00 %
1000 100-110	3.00	2.48	17.33-%
1000 100-120	6.63	4.13	37.71-%
1000 100-130	20.88	0.50	97.61-%

Figure 24.11 Results from Transaction MRNO

24.3.2 Lowest Value Determination Based on Range of Coverage

With this method, the SAP system checks whether the price for a material should be devaluated because it has a high range of coverage. The system defines the range of coverage as the average stock divided by the average consumption.

The user can configure the percentage discount for devaluating materials by company code. The configuration to define the devaluation is found in transaction OMW5, shown in Figure 24.12, or via the navigation path **IMG • Materials Management • Valuation and Account Assignment • Balance Sheet Valuation Procedures • Configure Lowest Value Methods • Price Deductions by Range of Coverage • Maintain Devaluation by Range of Coverage by Company Code**.

The configuration allows the user to enter a range of coverage value; average stock divided by the average consumption, and a devaluation percentage for each company code.

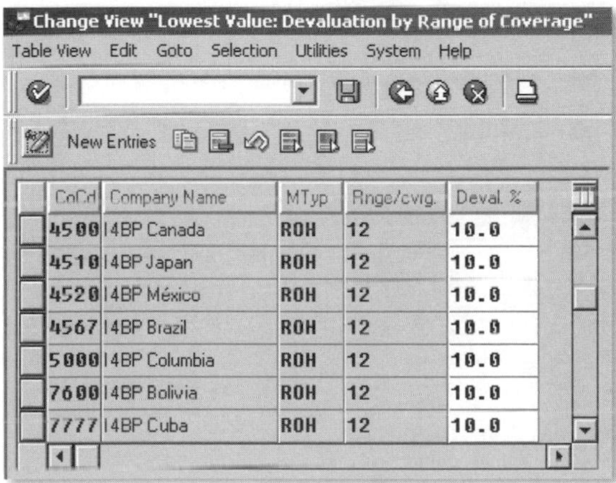

CoCd	Company Name	MTyp	Rnge/cvrg.	Deval. %
4500	I4BP Canada	ROH	12	10.0
4510	I4BP Japan	ROH	12	10.0
4520	I4BP México	ROH	12	10.0
4567	I4BP Brazil	ROH	12	10.0
5000	I4BP Columbia	ROH	12	10.0
7600	I4BP Bolivia	ROH	12	10.0
7777	I4BP Cuba	ROH	12	10.0

Figure 24.12 Configuration in Transaction OMW5

The transaction to run the lowest value based on range of coverage is MRN1 and can be found via **SAP Menu • Logistics • Materials Management • Valuation • Balance Sheet Valuation • Determination of Lowest Value • Range of Coverage**.

The selection screen, shown in Figure 24.13, allows the user to enter a range of materials, plant, material type, or valuation class.

Once the selection criteria have been entered, the transaction can be executed. The resulting display, as shown in Figure 24.14 shows the range of coverage, which determines the devaluation percentage and the calculated new value.

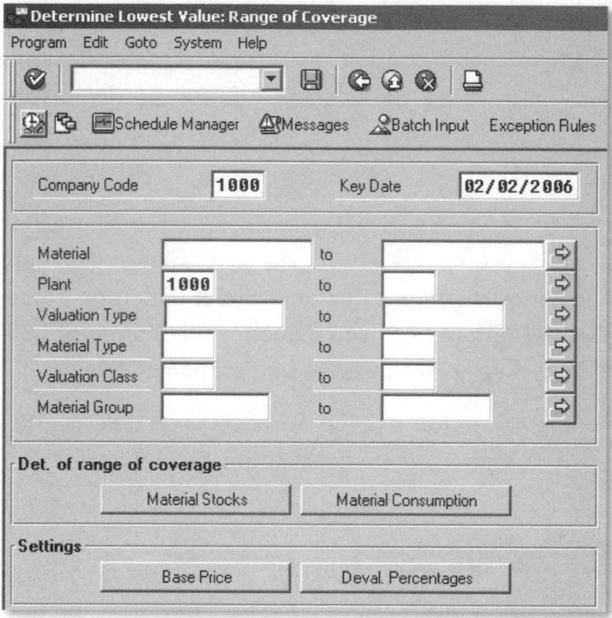

Figure 24.13 Selection Screen for Transaction MRN1

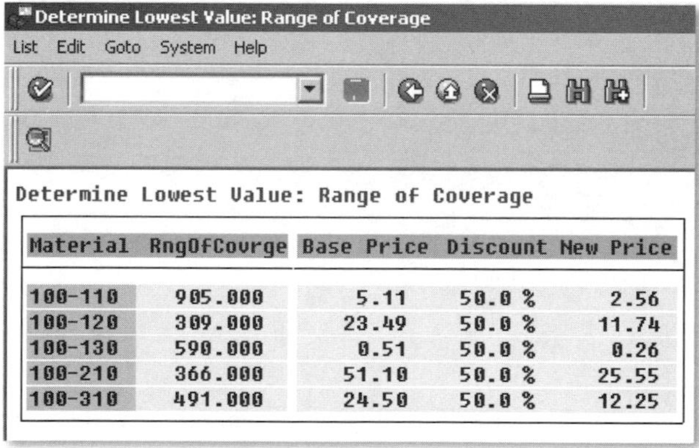
Determine Lowest Value: Range of Coverage

Material	RngOfCovrge	Base Price	Discount	New Price
100-110	905.000	5.11	50.0 %	2.56
100-120	309.000	23.49	50.0 %	11.74
100-130	590.000	0.51	50.0 %	0.26
100-210	366.000	51.10	50.0 %	25.55
100-310	491.000	24.50	50.0 %	12.25

Figure 24.14 Results from Transaction MRN1

24.3.3 Lowest Value Determination Based on Movement Rate

In using the lowest value based on movement rate, we determine the value of the material based on the slow movement or non-movement of a material. The system defines the movement rate as a percentage, where the total quantity of receipts is divided by the material in stock and then multiplied by 100 to give the figure as a percentage.

Therefore, if a company has stock of 400 units of material ABC in a valuation area and the number of movements has been only 40 in the period, then the movement rate is movements divided by the stock, i.e. 40/100, multiplied by 100 to calculate the percentage, which in this case is 10%.

The devaluation percentage is configured in transaction OMW6, in a similar manner as transaction OMW5 for range of coverage, where a percentage is configured per company code. Using the example above, if a decision was made that a slow-moving material is anything with a movement rate of below 15%, then the material ABC would be a slow-moving stock. This would mean the stock is devalued.

The transaction to run the lowest value based on movement rate is MRN2, shown in Figure 24.15. It can found in the navigation path **SAP Menu • Logistics • Materials Management • Valuation • Balance Sheet Valuation • Determination of Lowest Value • Movement Rate**.

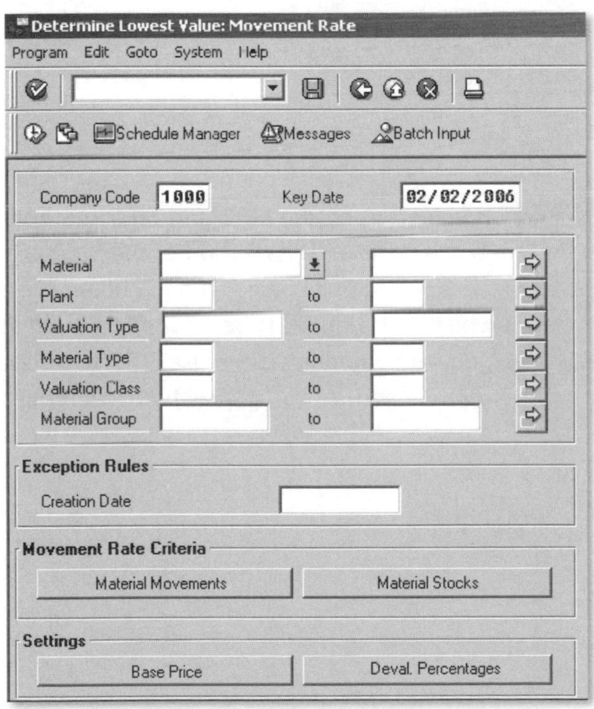

Figure 24.15 Selection Screen for Transaction MRN

Once the selection criteria have been entered the transaction can be executed. The resulting display, shown in Figure 24.16, shows the indicator with the corresponding percentage discount. This discount is then applied to the base price to calculate the new lowest price.

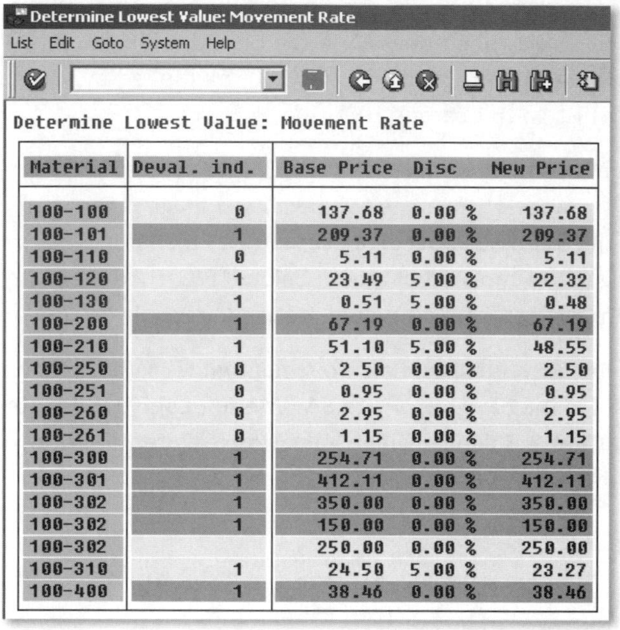

Determine Lowest Value: Movement Rate

List Edit Goto System Help

Determine Lowest Value: Movement Rate

Material	Deval. ind.	Base Price	Disc	New Price
100-100	0	137.68	0.00 %	137.68
100-101	1	209.37	0.00 %	209.37
100-110	0	5.11	0.00 %	5.11
100-120	1	23.49	5.00 %	22.32
100-130	1	0.51	5.00 %	0.48
100-200	1	67.19	0.00 %	67.19
100-210	1	51.10	5.00 %	48.55
100-250	0	2.50	0.00 %	2.50
100-251	0	0.95	0.00 %	0.95
100-260	0	2.95	0.00 %	2.95
100-261	0	1.15	0.00 %	1.15
100-300	1	254.71	0.00 %	254.71
100-301	1	412.11	0.00 %	412.11
100-302	1	350.00	0.00 %	350.00
100-302	1	150.00	0.00 %	150.00
100-302		250.00	0.00 %	250.00
100-310	1	24.50	5.00 %	23.27
100-400	1	38.46	0.00 %	38.46

Figure 24.16 Results from Transaction MRN2

This chapter explained how material is valued using the LIFO and FIFO methods and lowest value determination. Companies refer to the method of their material valuation in annual reports and all of these methods are used. There is no one correct method and companies choose whichever method is best suited to them at the time. As described in this chapter, newer companies often use FIFO to inflate their stock value, while LIFO can be used by mature companies trying to reduce their tax payments.

25 Material Ledger

The benefits of the material ledger include keeping inventory records in up to three currencies, thus facilitating consolidation for companies belonging to multinational groups. It also includes calculating the actual costs for procured material or material from production.

25.1 Material Ledger Overview

The material ledger serves two purposes. First, it records actual costs of materials and at the same time considers and records all the factors behind price fluctuation. This functionality of material ledger enables faster and more effective decision-making regarding materials management, controlling, and production.

Second, the material ledger can hold values in three currencies simultaneously, which is a major benefit for companies that need to report valuation in different currencies. In addition, the material ledger makes it possible to revaluate stock on the basis of real calculation, which is legally required in some countries.

Using actual costing, all goods movements within a period are valuated at the standard price. In parallel, all price and exchange rate differences for the material are collected in the material ledger.

Within the material ledger at the end of the period, an actual price is calculated for each material. This is based on the actual costs for that particular period. The actual calculated price is called the periodic unit price and can be used to revaluate the inventory for the period to be closed. This calculated actual price is the standard price for the next period.

25.1.1 Activating the Material Ledger and Actual Costing

To use the material ledger the functionality must be activated. The transaction in configuration is shown in Figure 25.1. The configuration to activate it is transaction OMX1 or can be found via the navigation path **IMG • Controlling • Product Cost Controlling • Actual Costing/Material Ledger • Activate Valuation Areas for Material Ledger**.

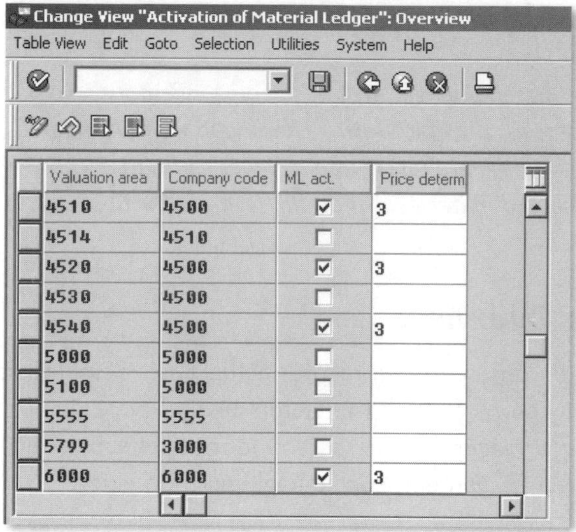

Figure 25.1 Configuration for Activation of Material Ledger for Certain Valuation Areas

In addition, the configuration to activate actual costing can be found via the path **IMG • Controlling • Product Cost Controlling • Actual Costing/Material Ledger • Actual Costing • Activate Actual Costing**.

25.2 Material Ledger Data

25.2.1 Material Master Record

Several items must be checked before a material can be used in the material ledger:

- The material ledger indicator must be set in the material
- The material must be assigned to a valuation class
- The material type must allow the material's valuation to be updated

The material master record contains the flag that determines whether a material is relevant for the material ledger. The flag is on the accounting screen and should be set for material ledger, as shown in Figure 25.2. Once this is set, data is collected about this material for the material ledger.

The material type can be checked to see if the material valuation can be updated by viewing the configuration transaction, Figure 25.3, which can be found via the navigation path **IMG • Controlling • Product Cost Controlling • Actual Costing/Material Ledger • Actual Costing • Activate**.

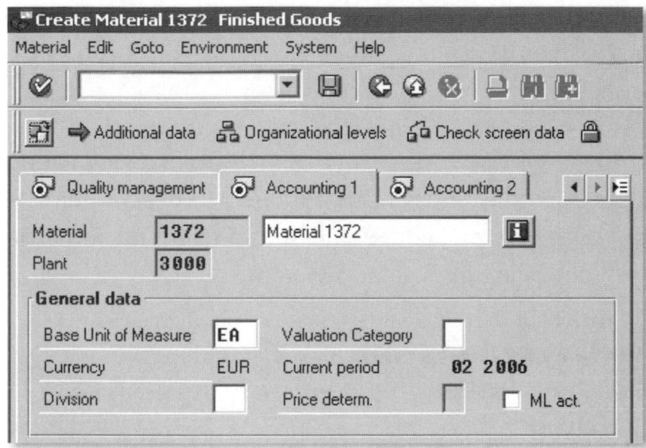

Figure 25.2 Material Ledger Indicator and Valuation Class in Material Master Record Accounting Screen

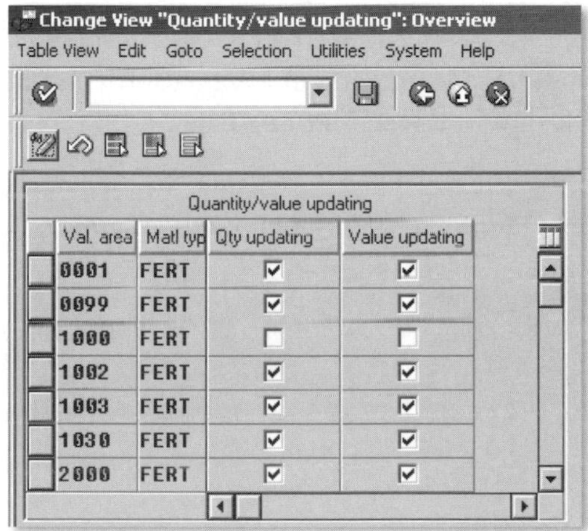

Val. area	Matl typ	Qty updating	Value updating
0001	FERT	☑	☑
0099	FERT	☑	☑
1000	FERT	☐	☐
1002	FERT	☑	☑
1003	FERT	☑	☑
1030	FERT	☑	☑
2000	FERT	☑	☑

Figure 25.3 Quantity and Value Updating Indicators on Material Type Configuration

25.2.2 Data for the Material Ledger

For materials that have been activated for the material ledger, the system automatically collects information on valuation-relevant transactions. Information is also collected on account postings from inventory management, invoice verification, and order settlement. This collected data is used during material price determination.

The transaction variances or differences are posted to the material ledger. Three types of differences are collected:

- Price Differences
- Exchange Rate Differences
- Differences caused by revaluation

Transactions that cause an inward flow of data to the material ledger include, Inventory Management, Invoice Verification, and Production Order Settlement. The outward flow of data out of the material ledger includes data for the Financial Accounting module and the Controlling information system.

25.3 Material Price Determination

25.3.1 Material Price Analysis

The material price analysis shows the valuated transactions. It also displays the results of material price determination, with price and exchange rate differences for a given material in a plant in a specific period.

The transaction to run the material price analysis is CKM3. This can be found via the path **SAP Menu • Logistics • Materials Management • Valuation • Actual Costing/Material Ledger • Material Ledger • Material Price Analysis**.

Once the transaction is run, a report will be displayed showing the Beginning inventory, goods receipts, goods issued, Invoice, etc. This is shown in Figure 25.4.

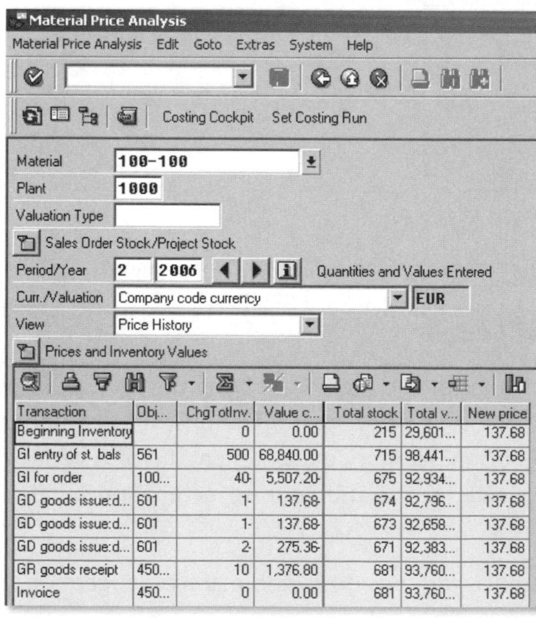

Transaction	Obj...	ChgTotInv.	Value c...	Total stock	Total v...	New price
Beginning Inventory		0	0.00	215	29,601...	137.68
GI entry of st. bals	561	500	68,840.00	715	98,441...	137.68
GI for order	100...	40-	5,507.20-	675	92,934...	137.68
GD goods issue:d...	601	1-	137.68-	674	92,796...	137.68
GD goods issue:d...	601	1-	137.68-	673	92,658...	137.68
GD goods issue:d...	601	2-	275.36-	671	92,383...	137.68
GR goods receipt	450...	10	1,376.80	681	93,760...	137.68
Invoice	450...	0	0.00	681	93,760...	137.68

Figure 25.4 Detailed Report for Material Price Analysis Transaction, CKM3

25.3.2 Single-Level Material Price Determination

Single-level material price determination calculates a unit price for a material for a specific previous period. The actual costing for single-level price determination calculations are made for the previous period and do not affect the current period. The single-level calculation is valid only for materials that are flagged for standard price control and for which the price determination field is set to 3 for single- and multi-level price determination. Both these indicators are found on the accounting screen of the material master record. The single-level refers to the fact that the price differences are only for one level, and no other material price differences are examined. Other price differences occur for materials used in making this material. Where these price differences are taken into account, we refer to multi-level price determination.

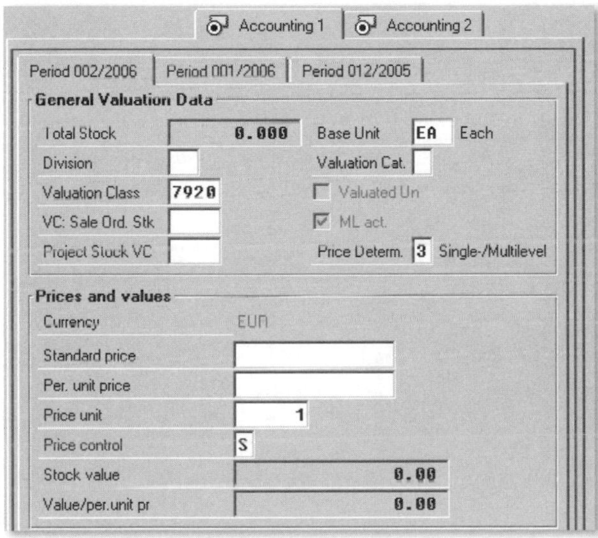

Figure 25.5 Material Valid for Single-Level Price Determination

The price determined by the single-level calculation, shown in Figure 25.5, is the standard price of the material, plus or minus any price differences and exchange-rate differences. Price differences can occur for the following reasons:

- Goods receipts for a purchase order
- Invoice receipts
- Settlement of production orders
- Transfer postings
- Initial entry of stock balances (movement type 561)

- Free delivery of goods for a purchase order
- Inward movements from consignment

The differences between the standard price of the material and the price determined by this calculation are updated in the material ledger.

The single-level price determination, as shown in Figure 25.6, can be accessed through transaction CKMH or through the path **SAP Menu • Logistics • Materials Management • Valuation • Actual Costing/Material Ledger • Periodic Material Valuation • Determine Material Prices (Single Level)**.

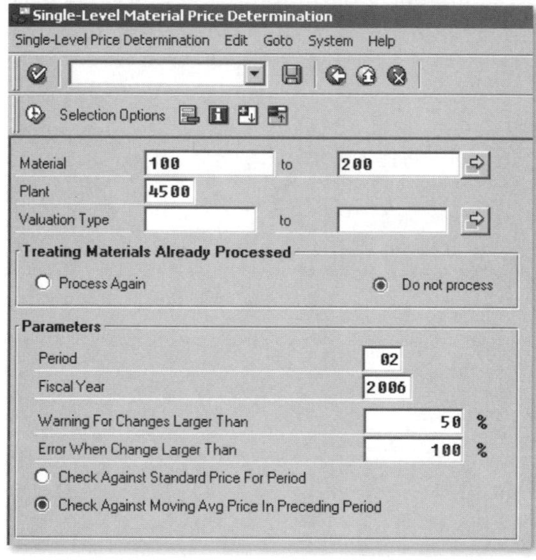

Figure 25.6 Selection Screen for Calculating Single-Level Price Determination

25.3.3 Multi-Level Material Price Determination

While a single-level price determination looks at the material in isolation, the multi-level price determination looks at all price determinations of the materials that go into making the final material. All of these price determinations roll up to produce a price determination. For a multi-level price determination to be calculated, a single-level calculation has to be complete for all the component materials.

25.3.4 Transaction-Based Material Price Determination

This price determination allows the moving average price to be calculated after every goods movement that is relevant to the material. This type of price determination does not need the material ledger to be active. If the material ledger is not active, then the moving average price is calculated in one currency, as determined on the material master. If the material ledger is active, then the price is calculated in up to three currencies on the material ledger.

To have the material activated for transaction-based material price determination, the material should be flagged for moving-average price control and the price determination field set to **2** for transaction-based price determination, as shown in Figure 25.7.

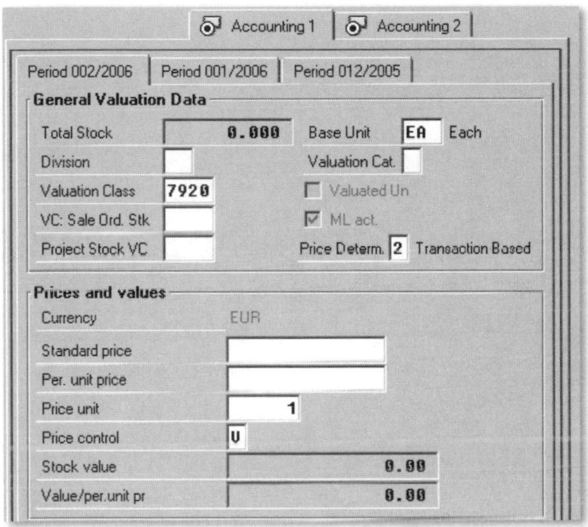

Figure 25.7 Material Valid for Transaction-Based Price Determination

This chapter dealt with the material ledger, which is sometimes not clearly understood by those working with materials management. The material ledger retains the actual costs of materials and at the same time considers and records all the factors behind price fluctuation. It can also hold values in three currencies at the same time, which is needed by companies frequently using or reporting in different currencies. It is important that decisions are made on the material ledger so that information needed on the material master can be decided upon at an early stage of the implementation.

26 Classification System

The classification system is a powerful tool that allows objects in SAP to be described by characteristic values. These characteristics are used for the same group of objects, i.e., vendors, materials. The classification system uses these values to perform powerful searches.

26.1 Classification Overview

26.1.1 What is a Classification System?

Classification systems occur everywhere. The Dewey Decimal system used in libraries is a classification system, zoologists use the Linnaean system for animal classification, and the U.S. Government uses the Standard Occupation Classification System (SOC) for classifying workers into occupational categories. There are many more examples.

A definition of a classification system by the Public Work and Government Services Department of Canada states, "a classification system is a structured scheme for categorizing entities or objects to improve access, created according to alphabetical, associative, hierarchical, numerical, ideological, spatial, chronological, or other criteria."

The classification system in SAP fits this definition, as it too is a structured framework primarily used for the searching of objects based on a series of characteristics that describe the object. The object can be a material, a vendor, a batch, etc.

The classification system can be an extremely powerful tool if it is constructed in a strategic manner with a significant amount of planning. Classification systems that are ignored by companies are those that have evolved over time with no planning and that are cumbersome and difficult to maintain. The more planning is put into creating a classification system, the more likely it is to become a worthwhile tool.

Some companies employ outside consultants to review the materials they have and develop a structured naming and classification framework based on the description and use of the material. Although this can be an expensive and time-consuming project, it can allow the company to start implementation of the classification system with rules and procedures already in place.

26.1.2 Describing an Object

In developing the classification system, three areas need to be addressed. These are:

- Object
- Characteristics
- Class

The object to be described needs to be examined and a set of standard descriptions or characteristics defined. For instance, for an object such as a vendor, characteristics that may be used to describe it could include: how many employees does the vendor have, is the vendor a minority owned company, how many products does the vendor sell, is the vendor a registered small business, etc.

These descriptions are called characteristics, and the characteristic will have values or a range of values valid for each characteristic. For example, if we again consider the vendor as an object again and look at the characteristic "how many employees the vendor has," a valid value could be 20,000. The value can be an exact figure or the value can be configured to be a range, if required.

The characteristics are grouped together in a class. The class contains a number of characteristics that are of similar values. The class is the entity that is assigned to the material in the material master.

A class is associated with a class type. The class type is the key to which object the class can be assigned. For example, if a class is assigned to class type 010, then the class can only be assigned to those objects relevant for class type 010, i.e. vendors.

26.2 Characteristics

26.2.1 Create Characteristics

Once the company has decided upon a set of descriptive characteristics for an object, the next step is to create the characteristic. The transaction to create the characteristic is CT04. The transaction can be found via the path **SAP Menu • Cross-Application Components • Classification System • Master Data • Characteristics**.

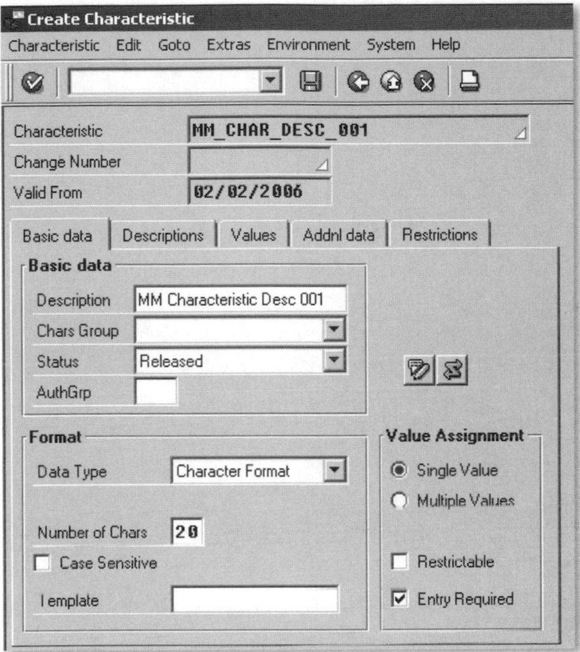

Figure 26.1 Basic Data Screen for Transaction CT04

On the basic data screen, shown in Figure 26.1, the following can be included:

- Description for the characteristic
- Data type—which can be a numeric, date, currency, time or character
- Format of the data type, number of characters, etc.
- Template, if necessary
- Single or Multiple values
- Entry required flag

Once the data has been entered for the basic screen, allowed values for the characteristics can be entered.

In the value screen, shown in Figure 26.2, the values that have been determined for the characteristic can be entered. One of these values can be made a default value by setting the **D** flag on the value line. If no defined values are entered, then any value will be allowed.

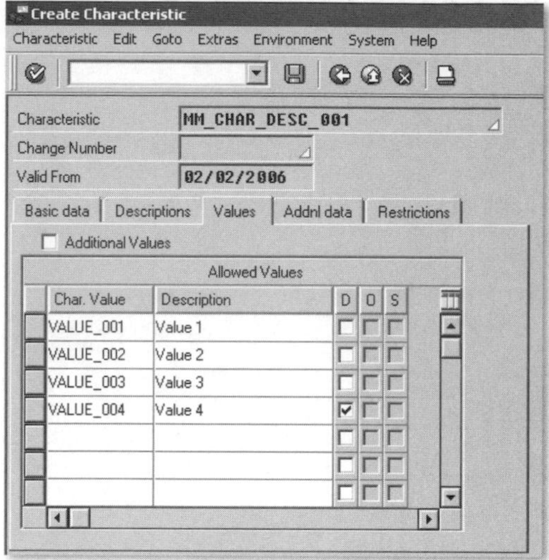

Figure 26.2 Values Screen for Transaction CT04

26.2.2 Configuring Characteristics

Characteristic Defaults

A number of configuration steps can be performed to allow characteristics to operate in the manner the user wishes. The first of these is to set default settings for the characteristic. If the end users always requires a certain field to be set in one particular manner, this can be configured so that it defaulted each time a characteristic is created. The configuration for the defaults can be seen in Figure 26.3.

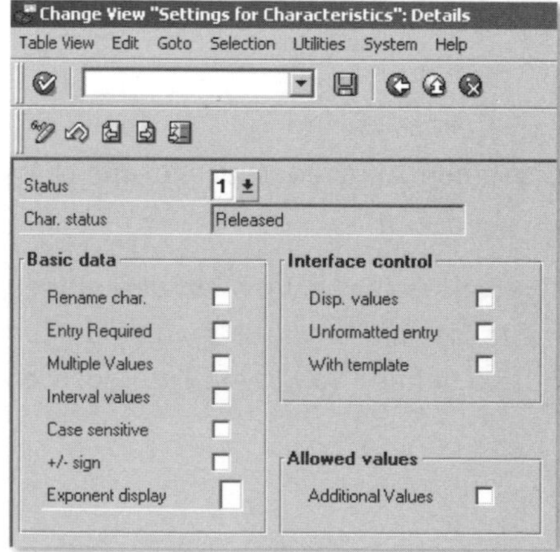

Figure 26.3 Configuration Screen in which Users set Characteristic Defaults

Accessing the transaction using the path **IMG • Cross-Application Components • Classification System • Characteristics • Define Default Settings** can configure the default settings for a characteristic.

Characteristic Status

The characteristic can be set to different statuses. These are pre-defined in SAP as either released, in preparation, or locked. There is a configuration transaction, shown in Figure 26.4, which allows the configurator to create new statuses that may be needed by the client. For example, a status may be required that allows for review, and this can be configured.

Accessing the transaction using the navigation path **IMG • Cross-Application Components • Classification System • Characteristics • Define Characteristic Statuses** allows the configuration of the characteristic status.

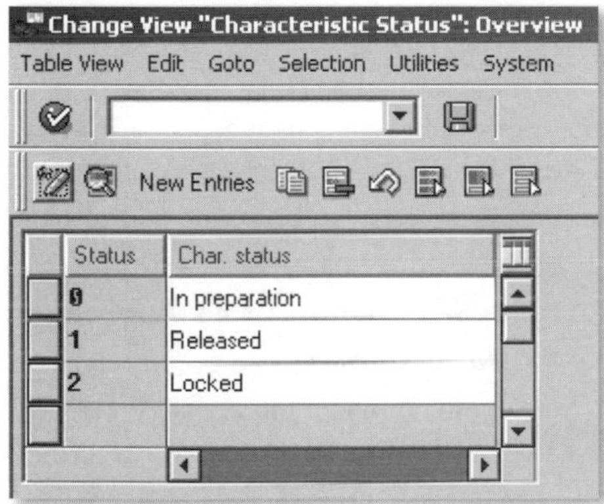

Figure 26.4 Configuration Screen in which Users can create New Characteristic Statuses

Value Templates

The SAP system is delivered with a number of templates that can be used for the entry of information into the characteristic values. If the end user requires a new template for a specific characteristic value, then this can be configured, as shown in Figure 26.5.

Accessing the transaction using the path **IMG • Cross-Application Components • Classification System • Characteristics • Define Templates**, allows the user to configure new characteristic value templates or to modify existing templates.

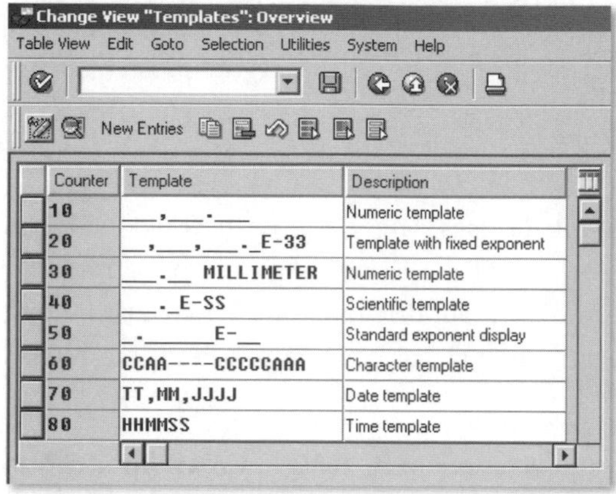

Figure 26.5 Configuration Screen That Allows Creation and Modification of New Characteristic Value Templates

26.3 Classes

26.3.1 Create Classes

Once the relevant characteristics have been created, they can be grouped together by assigning them to a class. The class can be created by using transaction CL02, see Figure 26.6, or by using the navigation path **SAP Menu · Cross-Application Components · Classification System · Master Data · Classes**.

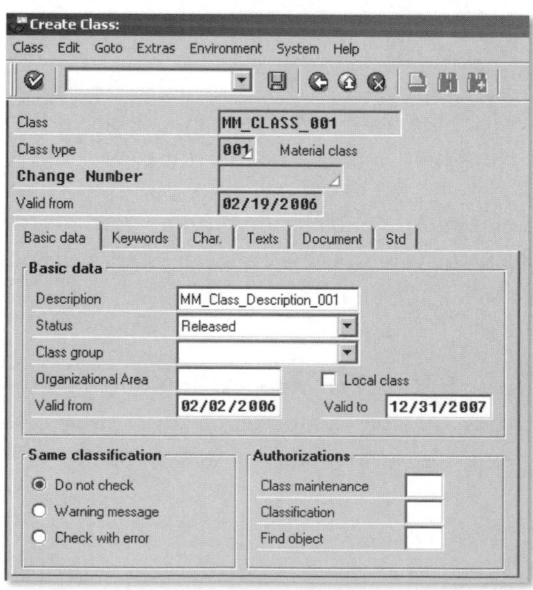

Figure 26.6 Basic Data Screen for Transaction CL02

The basic data screen will require a class type to be entered. The class type will be discussed later in this chapter. There is the option of entering keywords that can be used to search for the specific class. The keywords can be entered on a separate screen within transaction CL02. Once the basic data has been entered, the specific characteristics that should be assigned to this class can be entered as shown in Figure 26.7.

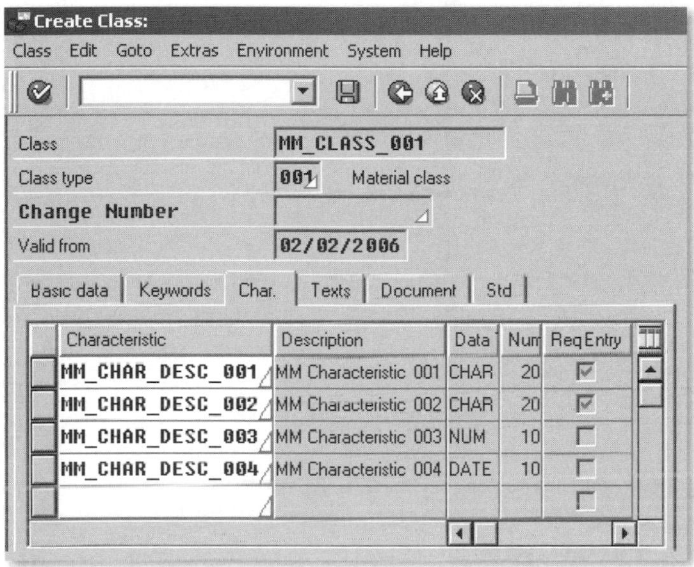

Figure 26.7 Characteristics Assigned to Class in Transaction CL02

26.4 Class Type

26.4.1 Class Type Overview

As mentioned in the previous section, when creating a class, the class must belong to a class type. The class type represents the type of objects the class is being created for. In Figure 26.6, the class has been assigned to class type 001, which is the class type for the material. This means that the characteristics in the class will pertain to a material. If the user creating the class had entered class type 022, this would have meant that the characteristics were describing a batch, as the batch is the object for class type 022. Figure 26.8 shows some of the class types available when creating a class.

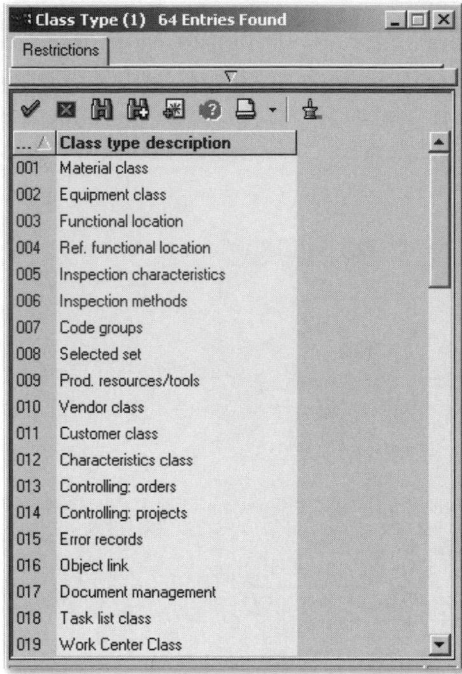

Figure 26.8 Some Class Types and Objects Assigned to Class Types

26.4.2 Configuring a Class Type

Many class types already are defined within SAP. However, on occasion the user might need to create a new class type. This may be an instance where the client has a unique combination of objects, i.e., a vendor/equipment combination that has no defined class type. If the client needed to describe this combination of objects then the class would require a new class type so that it accesses the correct tables.

The class type refers to an object. When starting to create a new class type, the correct object must be selected. If the object is not currently listed in configuration, this can be added.

The configuration for object types and class types can be found using the path **IMG · Cross-Application Components · Classification System · Classes · Maintain Object Types and Material Types**.

A new object can be added in this transaction, as shown in Figure 26.9, by accessing the header menu, selecting **Edit · New Entries** and selecting a new object to include. Most SAP objects are already included in this transaction.

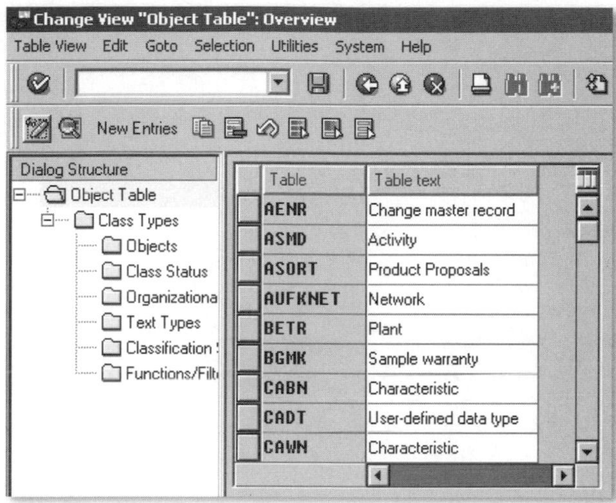

Figure 26.9 Partial Object List for the Class Type

To create a new class type, the user should select the object, which will be linked to the class type. Once the object is selected, the configurator can click on class types in the dialog structure. This will display current class types for that object, as shown in Figure 26.10.

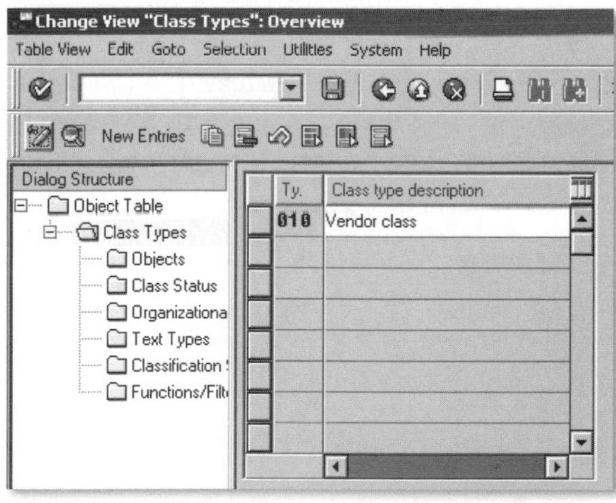

Figure 26.10 Class Types Currently Assigned to the Object

A new class type can be created for this object by selecting from the header menu, **Edit · New Entries**, or by using the F5 function key. This will display a screen, as shown in Figure 26.11, for the new class type information to be entered.

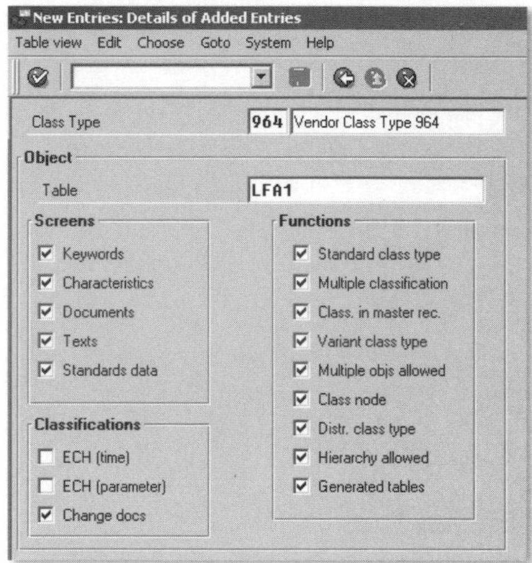

Figure 26.11 New Class-Type Entry Screen

26.5 Class Hierarchies

26.5.1 Creating a Class Hierarchy

As with other classification systems, the SAP classification system contains the ability to create a hierarchy within the class structure.

A class can be assigned to another class creating a class hierarchy. This can be created by using transaction CL24N, or by using the navigation path **SAP Menu • Cross-Application Components • Classification System • Assignment • Assign Objects/Classes to Class**.

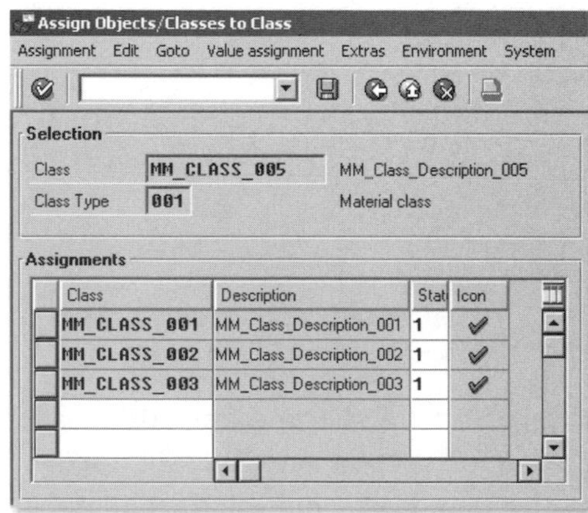

Figure 26.12 Assignment of Classes to a Class using Transaction CL24N

In Figure 26.12, the following are assigned classes, MM_Class_001, MM_Class_002 and MM_Class_003 to be subordinate classes of MM_Class_005.

If the class MM_Class_05 is assigned to be a subordinate of MM_Class_04, the following class hierarchy structure will occur.

The class hierarchy can be seen using the transaction CL6C, or through the navigation path **SAP Menu • Cross-Application Components • Classification System • Environment • Reporting • Class Hierarchy**.

Transaction CL6C allows the user to enter a class and have the system display the class hierarchy either graphically or in text, and Figure 26.13 shows the graphical representation of this hierarchy.

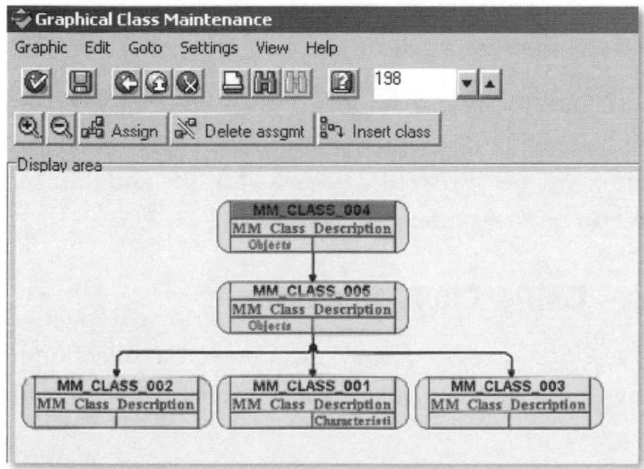

Figure 26.13 Graphical Representation of the Class Hierarchy Using Transaction CL6C.

26.5.2 Inherited Characteristics

A characteristic is inherited when a characteristic and its value is passed from a superior class in the class hierarchy to the subordinate classes. The main advantage of inheritance is that the end user does not need to enter the characteristic in the subordinate classes, as it has been entered once in the superior class and then inherited.

26.6 Object Dependencies

26.6.1 Object Dependency Overview

The object dependency in classification refers to the limitations that can be placed on objects to ensure that the correct classification occurs. Dependencies can force values for characteristics to be allowed only if a certain value for another characteristic as been selected. For instance, if the characteristic called **Color** has values **Red**, **Blue**, and **Green**, and another characteristic called **Finish** has values **Matte**, **Gloss**, or **Semi-Gloss**, then the user can define a dependency that states that only **Gloss** can be selected for characteristic **Finish** if the value **Green** is selected for **Color**. This prevents incorrect characteristic values to be chosen.

26.6.2 Dependency Creation

The method of creating a dependency is as follows. Within the class transaction CL02, display the characteristics. To create a dependency between characteristics, select the characteristic required and using the header menu select **Environment · Change Characteristic**.

The display will show the change characteristic transaction. The following should be selected **Extras · Object Dependencies · Editor**.

A dialog box will appear that allows the user to choose a Precondition, Selection Condition, Action, or Procedure. Once the appropriate object dependency is selected, the dependency editor will be displayed. In this editor, the end user can create the dependency based on normal syntax.

26.7 Finding Objects Using Classification

The standard feature of the classification system is that can make the selection of objects easier, as they can be found by using values that have been entered for that specific material.

26.7.1 Classifying Materials

In materials management, the most common function through which classification is seen is in the creation of the material master. When a material is created, one of the creation screens is for assigning classes to the material.

In the material master creation transaction, MM01, the classification screen allows a class or classes to be assigned to the material, as shown in Figure 26.14.

A class can be selected and then assign the values for the characteristics, as seen in Figure 26.15. The material can be assigned to any number of classes.

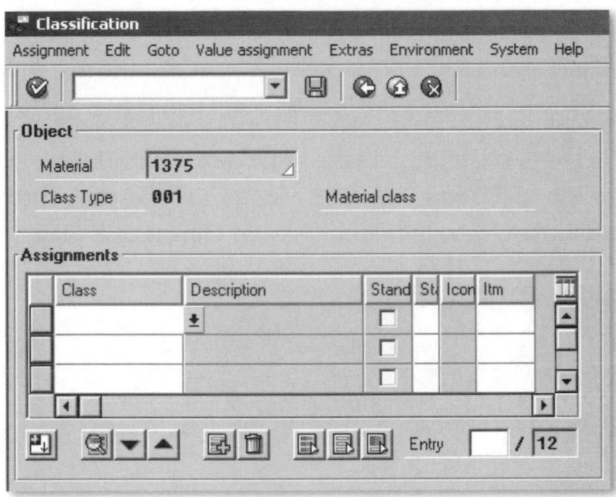

Figure 26.14 Assignment of Classes for a Material in Material Master Creation Transaction MM01

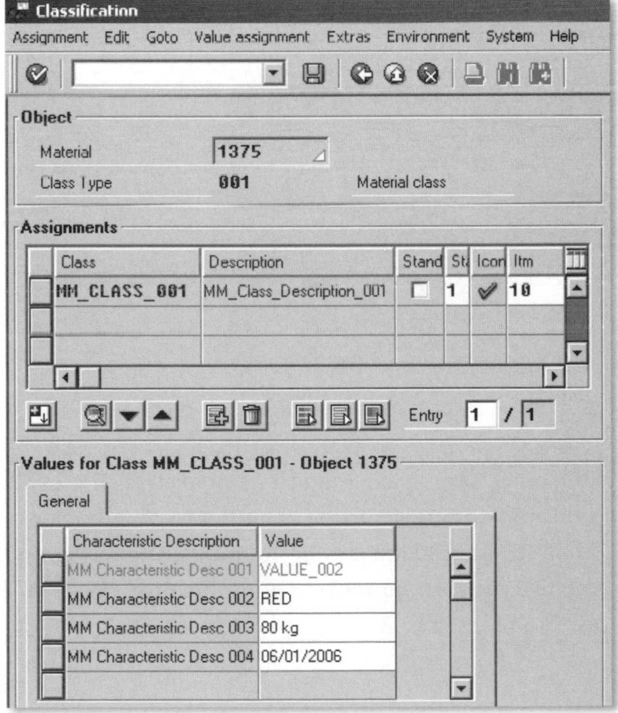

Figure 26.15 Selection of Characteristic Values Associated with Class Assigned to Material

26.7.2 Classifying Objects

An object can be assigned to a class or classes. This method is used in the material master creation or to assign many objects to a single class as seen in Figure 16.16..

Transaction CL20N allows the many classes to be assigned to an object. This transaction can be found through the navigation path **SAP Menu • Cross-Application Components • Classification System • Assignment • Assign Object to a Class**.

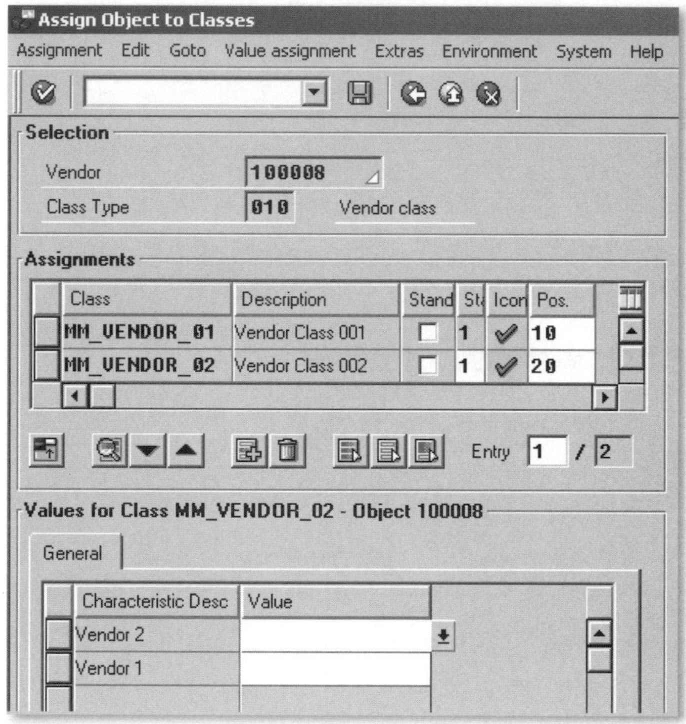

Figure 26.16 Assignment of Classes to a Single Object Using Transaction CL20N

Transaction CL24N allows many objects to be assigned to a single class. This saves time if a new class has been created and needs to be assigned to many objects, which is shown in Figure 26.17. This transaction can be found via the navigation path **SAP Menu • Cross-Application Components • Classification System • Assignment • Assign Objects/Classes to a Class**.

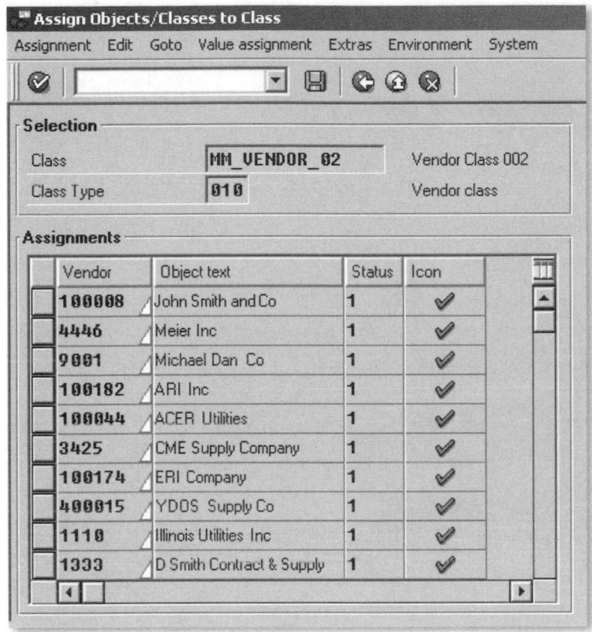

Figure 26.17 Assignment of Objects to a Single Class Using Transaction CL24N

26.7.3 Finding Objects

After implementing the classification system by creating characteristics and classes, assigning classes to objects and assigning values for the objects, the system can be used to find objects.

The key to finding an object is to use the characteristic values to find the object or objects that fit the value. The search criteria the end user enters, and the characteristics and the values assigned, are compared with the characteristic values assigned to the objects.

Transaction CL30N can be used to find objects using characteristic values. This transaction can be found using the path **SAP Menu • Cross-Application Components • Classification System • Find • Find Objects in Classes**.

The initial screen will ask the end user to enter a specific class and class type. There is a matchcode selection if the end user is unclear about the class name. The detail screen will show the characteristics for the class that was chosen and values can be entered against those characteristics. The transaction is then executed by selecting from the header menu **Find • Find in Initial Class** or by using the F8 function key.

The transaction will return all objects that have the characteristic value that was entered as can be seen in Figure 26.18.

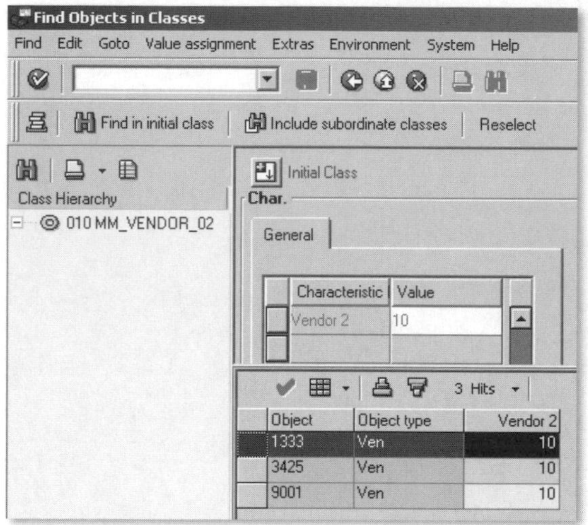

Figure 26.18 Objects Found Using Characteristic Value Entered in Transaction CL30N

This chapter described the classification system in SAP in detail. End users should learn that the classification system is a great tool for finding material that may appear to be similar to other materials but can be found easily using the characteristic value that has been assigned to it via the classification of the object. Classification is a long-term process. It requires a significant level of commitment from the client and then on-going maintenance to ensure that new materials or vendors or equipment or whatever objects are classified when entered into SAP. If the classification system is correctly defined and implemented, it offers a powerful and comprehensive search tool.

27 Document Management

Document management is a powerful tool within SAP that enables a company to link important documents to objects within the SAP system. Not having to duplicate or move the original document saves both time and effort.

27.1 Document Management Overview

The Document Management System (DMS) allows the user to link external documents to objects within the SAP system. Company documents such as CAD drawings, technical specifications, MSDS files, and photographs are often found on different computer systems, different locations, and different applications. The DMS allows a company to link these documents to the appropriate object within SAP.

Document management is important for companies that are pre-certified or certified ISO 9000. Also, the strict requirements of the new HIPAA (Health Insurance Portability and Accountability Act of 1996) and Sarbanes-Oxley Act of 2002 require businesses to manage documents more carefully. The DMS gives auditors and administrators documented evidence of internal controls that communicate, store, and protect documents. DMS allows unalterable logs or databases showing who has accessed which pieces of information, where and when.

The SAP DMS system uses a document information record to link the document to the object in SAP.

27.2 Document Information Record

The document information record is the master record in SAP that describes the information pertaining to the external document. The document information record contains the external file name and location of the file on the network.

27.2.1 Document Number

The document number can be defined in an identifier with up to 25-alphanumeric characters. The identifier can be internally or externally defined and the number assignment can be configured in the IMG.

27.2.2 Document Type

The document type is used to categorize the type of document. The document type is defined as a three-character field, as shown in Figure 27.1. For instance, DRW is defined as the document type for an engineering drawing, EBR is the document type for a batch record, and SB is the document type for a service bulletin.

The document type can be configured in the IMG. The navigation path to reach the transaction is **IMG • Cross-Application Components • Document Management • Control Data • Define Document Types**.

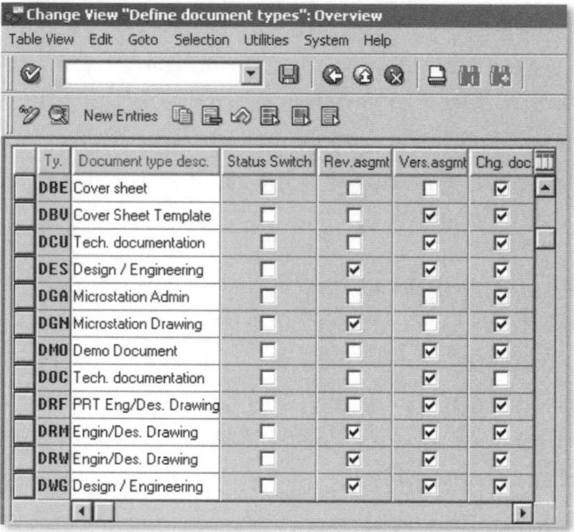

Ty.	Document type desc.	Status Switch	Rev.asgmt	Vers.asgmt	Chg. doc
DBE	Cover sheet	☐	☐	☐	☑
DBU	Cover Sheet Template	☐	☐	☑	☑
DCU	Tech. documentation	☐	☐	☑	☑
DES	Design / Engineering	☐	☑	☑	☑
DGA	Microstation Admin	☐	☐	☐	☑
DGN	Microstation Drawing	☐	☑	☐	☑
DMO	Demo Document	☐	☐	☑	☑
DOC	Tech. documentation	☐	☐	☑	☐
DRF	PRT Eng/Des. Drawing	☐	☐	☑	☑
DRM	Engin/Des. Drawing	☐	☑	☑	☑
DRW	Engin/Des. Drawing	☐	☑	☑	☑
DWG	Design / Engineering	☐	☑	☑	☑

Figure 27.1 Document Types Configured for Document Management System

Status Switch

The status-switch indicator shows that the status must change when a field is changed in the document information record, once this indicator is set.

Revision Level Assignment

If this indicator is set, then a revision level is automatically assigned to a document with reference to a change number, if used.

Version Assigned Automatically

If this indicator is set, a new version number is assigned automatically when the DMS user creates a new version of a document,

Change Document

If the indicator is set, then a change document is created when the document is changed.

27.2.3 Document Part

A document part is defined as part of a document that is maintained as a separate document. This may be needed if the original document is large and can be divided into relevant sections. For instance, if a large specification document has relevant information for many different materials, the specification can be divided into part for the relevant materials.

27.2.4 Document Version

The document version describes the version number of the document. This is particularly important in keeping the document current in situations where modifications may have been made to specifications, engineering drawings, etc.

27.2.5 Document Status

The document can be given a status depending where it resides within the process. A status may be **Released**, **In Approval**, **Rejected**, **Locked**, etc. The status can defined in configuration and is shown in Figure 27.2.

The status can be configured using the path **IMG • Cross-Application Components • Document Management • Control Data • Define Document Types**.

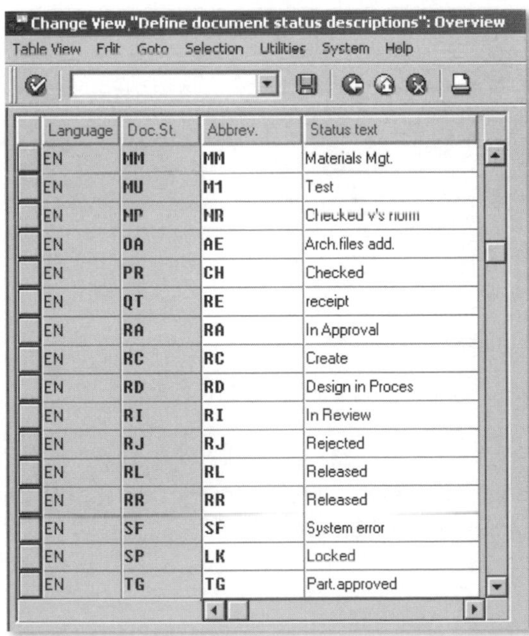

Language	Doc.St.	Abbrev.	Status text
EN	MM	MM	Materials Mgt.
EN	MU	M1	Test
EN	NP	NR	Checked v's norm
EN	OA	AE	Arch.files add.
EN	PR	CH	Checked
EN	QT	RE	receipt
EN	RA	RA	In Approval
EN	RC	RC	Create
EN	RD	RD	Design in Proces
EN	RI	RI	In Review
EN	RJ	RJ	Rejected
EN	RL	RL	Released
EN	RR	RR	Released
EN	SF	SF	System error
EN	SP	LK	Locked
EN	TG	TG	Part.approved

Figure 27.2 Document Statuses Configured in the DMS

27.3 Creating a Document

27.3.1 Create a Document

To create a document record, the transaction CV01N is used, see Figure 27.3. The transaction can be found using the navigation path **SAP Menu • Logistics • Central Functions • Document Management • Document • Create**.

The initial screen allows a document number to be entered if it is externally assigned or to leave a blank for an internal number assignment. The document type can be added as well as the document part and version if applicable.

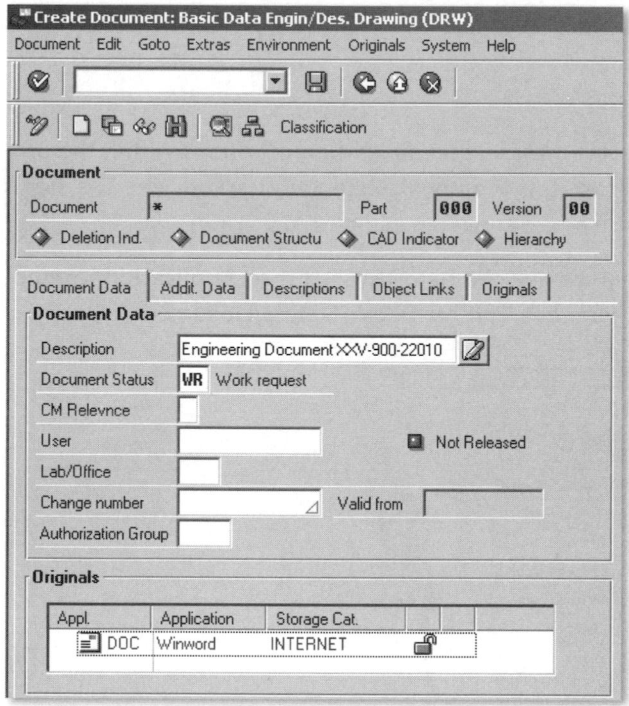

Figure 27.3 Detail Screen for Document Creation Using Transaction CV01N

Description

Once in the detail screen for creating a document, a long description should be added, which can be the title of the external document.

Document Status

The document status describes if the document is in its primary stage, initial stage, locked, or temporary.

Change Number

The document can be linked to a change number that links together documents for the change.

27.4 Linking an Object to a Document

27.4.1 Configuration for Linking Documents

Once the document record has been created, it can be linked to the object that it relates to. For instance, a Master Safety Data Sheet (MSDS) can be assigned to the material it was produced for.

The document type has to be configured to allow links between the document type and the object, as seen in Figure 27.4. If a drawing is involved, document type DRW needs to be assigned to WBS element. The link then must be created between DRW and the object PRPS. This configuration can be found using the using the navigation path **IMG · Cross-Application Components · Document Management · Control Data · Define Document Types**.

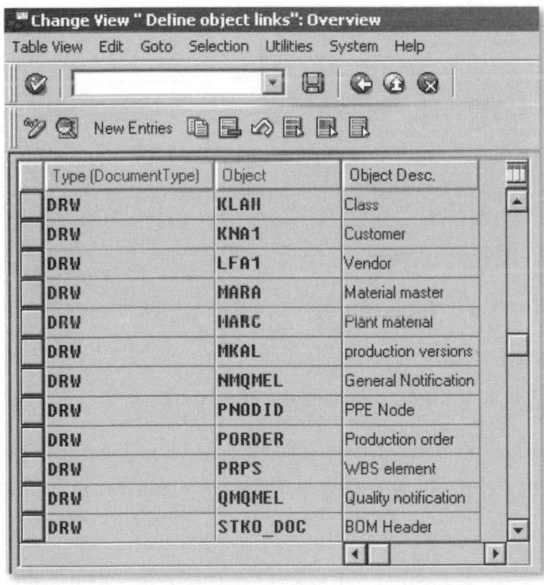

Type (DocumentType)	Object	Object Desc.
DRW	KLAH	Class
DRW	KNA1	Customer
DRW	LFA1	Vendor
DRW	MARA	Material master
DRW	MARC	Plant material
DRW	MKAL	production versions
DRW	NMQMEL	General Notification
DRW	PNODID	PPE Node
DRW	PORDER	Production order
DRW	PRPS	WBS element
DRW	QMQMEL	Quality notification
DRW	STKO_DOC	BOM Header

Figure 27.4 Configuration of Document Types and Links to Objects within SAP

27.4.2 Linking a Document to a Material Master Record

The most common link is between documents and the material master record. The material master has a built-in link process, and documents can be linked quickly.

Using transaction MM01 for material master record creation, the DMS user can access the links to document management from the Basic data screen. The DMS user should access the header menu and select the **Additional Data** icon. This will display the additional data tabs for descriptions, unit of measure, European Article Numbers, (EAN), inspection text and document data.

The documents tab can be selected, and a screen will be displayed where linked documents can be entered, as shown in Figure 27.5.

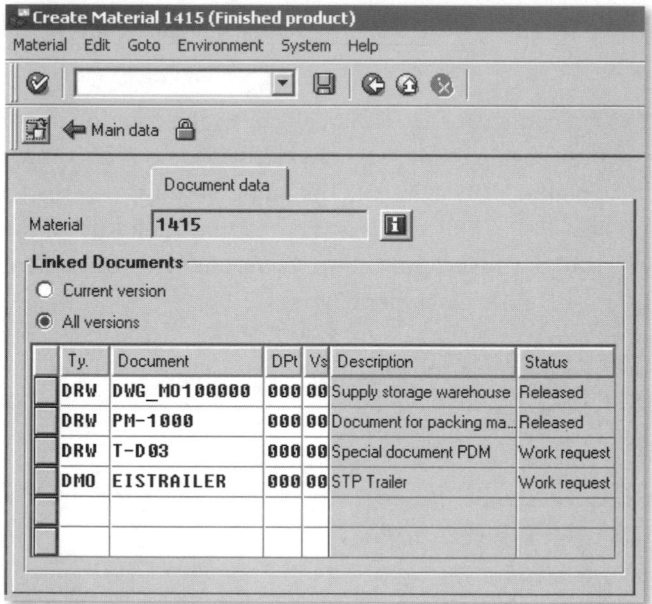

Figure 27.5 Entry screen for Linked Documents for Material Master Record Using Transaction MM01

27.4.3 Linking a Document to a Vendor Master Record

Another common object to have in linked documents is the vendor master. The vendor can have documents linked to it via the vendor master creation transaction, XK01, as shown in Figure 27.6.

The document links can be added to the vendor master record when the DMS user accesses the option through the header menu **Extras · Documents**.

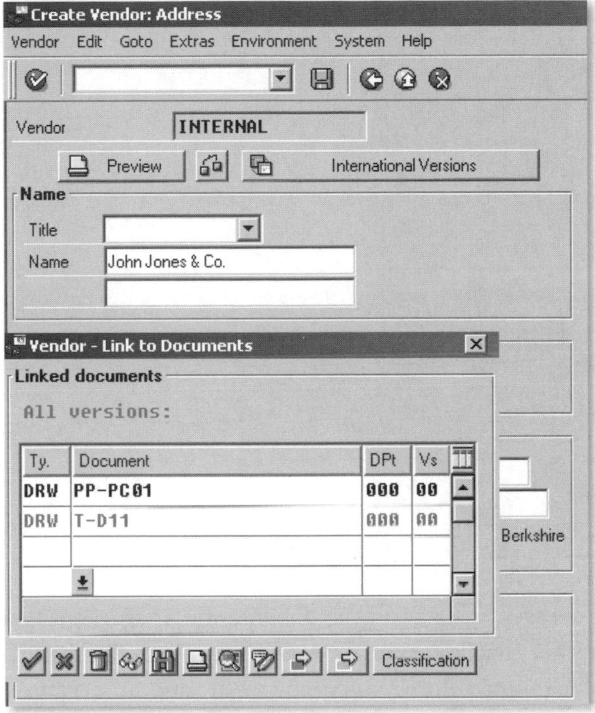

Figure 27.6 Linked Documents to Vendor Created Using Transaction XK01

27.5 Documents and Classification

27.5.1 Using Classification for Documents

Using the classification system, characteristics can be used to describe a document. This will be increasingly more important as more and more document records are loaded into the DMS and finding the correct document becomes more difficult.

In standard SAP, class type 017 has been pre-defined for documents. Therefore, to create a classification of documents, a set of characteristics can be created to combine into a class that can be assigned to a document, in the same way classification is set up for any other object. This can be seen in Figure 27.7.

Using transaction CL24N, the class can have any number of objects—in this case that would mean documents—assigned to it. The values for the characteristics can then be added. This will aid the end user when he or she is trying to find specific documents.

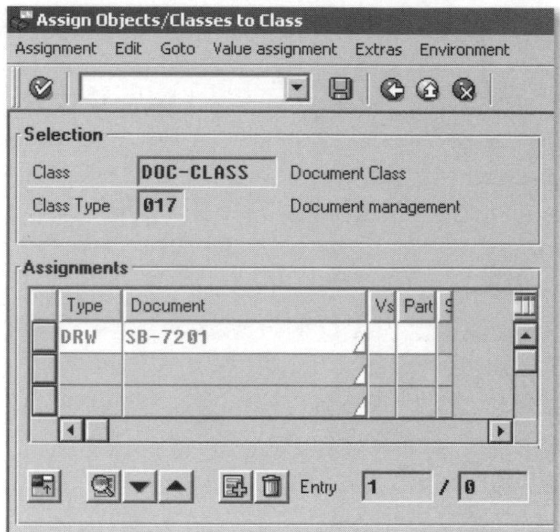

Figure 27.7 Assignment of Document to Specific Class in Transaction CL24N

This chapter described the processes included in the document management system (DMS). Most companies have developed or are developing strategies regarding their documents. Having hard-copy documents moving around an organization can cause delays, errors and miscommunications. The scanning of documents on receipt, e.g., invoices from vendors, is one way in which companies can reduce time between approvals and payment to vendors. Knowledge of the DMS in SAP is key when advising clients on best practices for purchasing and other areas where document management can be an issue.

A Bibliography

Douglas M. Lambert: *Supply Chain Management: What Does It Involve?* Supply Chain & Logistics Journal, Fall 2001.

Oracle Corporation, Cap Gemini Ernst & Young U.S. LLC and APICS: *The Adaptive Supply Chain: Postponement for Profitability.* APICS International Conference and Exposition, October 2003.

Warren H. Hausman: *Financial Flows and Supply Chain Efficiency.* Visa Commercial Solutions, March 8, 2005.

European Agency for the Evaluation of Medical Products (EMEA), Inspection Sector: *Mutual Recognition Agreement between Australia and the EU*, July 6, 2001.

Pennsylvania Department of Environmental Protection: *The Beneficial Use of Municipal and Residual Waste*, 2005.

Michael L. George: *Lean Six Sigma: Combining Six Sigma Quality with Lean Production Speed*, McGraw-Hill, First Edition, April 2002.

National Motor Freight Traffic Association: *Directory of Standard Carrier Alpha Codes*, February 2005.

European Committee on Banking Standards: *Annual Report of the ECBS, 2004.* April 2005.

Virginia Polytechnic Institute and State University: *Program for Participation by Small Businesses and Businesses Owned by Women and Minorities.* September 2004.

Ellen Fussell: *The Yoga of Batch.* Instrument Society of America, April 2003.

Nicholas Sheble and D.A. Coggan: *A Batch of Rules and Regulations.* Instrument Society of America, December 2004.

Glenn Restivo: *Standard Goes Live for Life Sciences: A New Approach to Navigating Regulatory Requirements*, Instrument Society of America, November 2004.

Bruce R. Parker and J. Gregory Lahr: *Pharmaceutical Recalls: Strategies for Minimizing the Damage*, Drug Information Journal, April—June 1999.

Stephen N. Chapman: *The Fundamentals of Production Planning and Control*, Prentice Hall, March 2005.

Michael K. Evans: *Practical Business Forecasting*, Blackwell Publishers, March 2002.

James A. Brimson: *Activity Accounting: An Activity-Based Costing Approach*, John Wiley and Sons, February 1991.

B Glossary

Account Assignment When creating an SAP requisition, charging the goods and/or services to a specific cost object and general-ledger account on the Account Assignment screen.

Account Assignment Category Determines which account assignment details are required for the purchase order item (e.g., cost center or account number).

Account Determination A system function that determines automatically the accounts in financial accounting to which the amount(s) in question should be posted for the user during any posting transaction.

Alpha Factor Smoothing function in forecasting

Assembly Products that are combined. An assembly can be used as a component in another assembly.

ASAP (AcceleratedSAP) Standardized methodology for R/3 implementations.

Authorizations Access to a transaction in the SAP system is based on a set of authorized values for each of the fields in the system. Users are given access to the appropriate fields, screens, and data using the authorization or security programs.

Authorization Check Check performed to determine whether a user is authorized to execute a particular function.

Automatic Reorder Point Planning In consumption-based planning, if a material falls below its reorder point, a purchase requisition is created during the MRP run.

Availability Check Check that is run as part of a goods movement to ensure the material stock balance does not go negative.

Backflushing Automatic issue of materials after they have been used in a production order or physically moved.

Base Unit of Measure The unit of measure for a material from which all other units of measure for the material are converted.

Batch An amount of material that is unique and managed separately from others.

Batch Determination Function that allows a program (e.g., a sales order) to select a batch based on selection criteria.

Blanket Order Standing purchase order (contract) with fixed start and end dates for repetitive purchases from a single vendor. Requisitioners can purchase against the order until the amount of the blanket order is depleted or the blanket order expires.

Bill of Materials (BOM) List of all of the items, including quantity and unit of measure, that make up a finished product or assembly.

Blocked Stock Valuated stock of a material that cannot be used. In the availability check, blocked stock is "not available".

Change and Transport System (CTS) A tool for managing and transporting configuration changes from the development and quality systems to the production system.

Change Management The change involved in implementing an SAP system with new processes and procedures requires a level of change management to assist employees and management with the effects of change.

Characteristic Description of a material that is defined by the user, such as color, viscosity, etc.

Characteristic Value The value that is assigned to a characteristic when it is used to describe a material, e.g., the characteristic Color, the value may be entered as blue.

Chart of Accounts Consists of a group of general ledger accounts. For each G/L account, the chart of accounts contains the account number, name, and any technical information.

Class Grouping of characteristics that in total describe an object.

Client A self-contained unit in the SAP system with its own separate master records and set of tables.

Company Code Used to represent an organizational unit with its own complete, self-contained set of cost objects for reporting purposes.

Condition Used to calculate prices, discounts, taxes, etc., according to the selection of vendor, customer, material, etc.

Configuration The formal process of establishing the SAP settings to support a company's specific business rules, validations, and default values.

Consumption-Based Planning A generic term for the procedure in materials resource planning (MRP) for which stock requirements and past consumption values are critical.

Contract Long-term outline purchase agreement against which materials or services are released according to user requirements over a specified period of time.

Cost Center Organizational unit within a controlling area that represents a separate location of cost incurred. Cost centers can be set up based on functional requirements, allocation criteria, activities or services provided, location, or area of responsibility.

Customer A business partner with whom a relationship exists that involves the issue of goods or services.

Customizing The process of configuring the SAP system to meet the business needs of the company.

Cycle Counting The physical inventory that is performed on materials several times during the year, unlike a yearly physical inventory.

Dialog Box Part of the GUI. It is a window that is called for by the main transaction and is displayed in the main window.

Document The electronic record of a transaction, entered in SAP. Examples include a material document or an accounting document.

Document Management System (DMS) The system that captures and manages documents within an organization.

Dunning Notifying vendors to ensure the resubmission of vendor declarations that are about to reach their expiration dates.

Electronic Data Interchange (EDI) Electronic communication of business transactions, such as orders, confirmations, and invoices, between organizations.

EnjoySAP A design of user interfaces that are visual, interactive, and personal, developed by SAP. It has new visual aesthetics, a new interaction model, and a role-based personal user interface.

Factory Calendar Defined on the basis of a public holiday calendar. Shows the work days for the client.

FIFO—first in, first out Materials and products are withdrawn from stock for sale or use in the order of their acquisition.

Financial Accounting The SAP module that monitors real-time values from financially relevant transactions and maintains a consistent, reconciled, and auditable set of books for statutory reporting and management support.

Forecast Estimation of the future values in a time series.

G/L Account—general ledger account A six-digit code that records value movements in a company code and represents the G/L account items in a chart of accounts.

Gamma Factor A smoothing factor for the seasonal index.

Goods Issue A reduction in warehouse stock due to a withdrawal for consumption in-house or the delivery of goods to a customer.

Handling Unit (HU) A physical item consisting of a material and packaging material. A handling unit has an identification number that can be used to recall the data on the HU.

IDoc (Intermediate Document) data container for data exchange between SAP systems or between an SAP system and an external system.

Implementation Guide (IMG) Explains the steps in the implementation process. The structure of the IMG is based on the application-component hierarchy and lists all the documentation that is relevant to implementing the SAP System.

Inventory Adjustment Correction to the material stock level due to physical inventory or goods movements.

Inventory Valuation Process of calculating the value of the material in the plant.

Invoice Bill sent to the client from a vendor for goods and/or services delivered.

Item Category Indicator that identifies whether certain fields are allowed for a material.

Kanban A procedure for controlling production and material flow based on a chain of operations in production.

LIFO—last in, first out Materials and products are withdrawn from stock for sale or use in the order of the most recent purchase.

Lot Size A defined quantity to purchase or produce.

Manufacturer Part Number (MPN) A material number that the vendor uses to identify their material.

Material Group A group that classifies materials by commodity or service type and is used by the purchasing department for reporting purposes.

Material Type A grouping of materials with the same basic attributes such as raw materials, semi-finished products, or finished products.

Material Valuation The determination of the value of the material in stock.

Movement Type Indicates the type of goods movement. It enables the system to use predefined posting rules determining how the accounts are to be posted and how the material master record is to be updated.

Material Requirements Planning (MRP) A term for procedures in production planning that take into account and plan future requirement during the creation of order proposals.

MRP Controller The person responsible for a group of materials in MRP at a plant.

MRP List A document in SAP that shows an overview of the result of the MRP run.

MRP Type A key that controls the MRP process for a material.

Navigation Path Transactions are organized into folders in a directory structure in the navigation area. A navigation path is the series of folders you access in order to find and launch an SAP transaction.

Negative Inventory A logical situation where the inventory is below zero due to a goods issue being performed before the goods receipt has been entered.

One-Step Stock Transfer Issue of material one step where the material is issued and received simultaneously.

One-Time Vendor A term for a vendor master record used for processing transactions with vendors who are not normally or have never been used.

Operation A manufacturing activity step in a routing. Used in Production Planning.

Output Device The name of the printer to which your SAP printouts will be sent, e.g., LPT1 or US99. Many SAP printers are labeled with the output device name.

Park Saving a document, such as invoice, so that changes can be made at a later time.

Physical Inventory The recording of actual stock levels of materials by counting, weighing, or measuring at a given location at a specific time.

Pipeline Material A material that flows directly into the production process such as electricity from power lines, water from a pipe, etc.

Plant An organizational unit within the company code where material is produced, purchased, and planned.

Procurement Card An item issued by a company to employees who purchase material from selected vendors.

Purchase Order Document generated by the purchasing department. A purchase order is an official order sent from the client to a vendor requesting goods and services.

Purchase Requisition A request by a user or a process to the purchasing department to purchase certain material at a specific time.

Purchasing Group A person or group of people in the purchasing department responsible for purchasing a type of good or service.

Purchasing Information Record An information record that defines the specific details for a vendor/material combination.

Purchasing Organization An organizational unit that procures materials or services and negotiates the conditions of purchase with vendors.

Putaway Used in warehouse management to describe the physical movement of the material into the bin locations.

Quota Arrangement A purchasing concept that allows the source of supply for a material to be determined via quotas decided upon with a number of vendors: Vendor A supplies 40%, vendor B supplies 35% and Vendor C supplies 25%.

Quotation A reply to a request for quotation from a vendor specifying its terms and conditions for the materials or servers required by the purchasing department.

Release To approve a purchase requisition or a purchasing document.

Release Strategy A set of business rules used to evaluate a purchase document or line item to determine the type of approvals needed before it can be released.

Request for Quotation (RFQ) A request to a vendor or number of vendors for a quotation to supply materials or services.

Reservation A request to the warehouse to ensure that certain materials are available on a certain date.

Routing Defines one or more sequences of operations for the production of a material

Safety Stock The level of material in stock below which a material shortage may occur.

Scheduling Agreement A purchasing agreement with a vendor where they supply material to the customer at agreed upon days and times.

Serial Number An unique number assigned to a single item. Each item will have a unique number. For example, each vacuum cleaner produced at a plant has its own serial number.

Subcontracting A form of outsourcing, where an external vendor produces material for the customer.

Tolerance The dollar amount or percentage by which a document may exceed specification. For example a tolerance for a purchase order could be no more than 10% per line item and no more than $500 for the total of the purchase order.

Transaction Code An unique command that is a shortcut to run an SAP transaction. A transaction code can contain letters or a combination of letters and numbers; e.g., ME21 for creating a purchase order, or MMBE for stock overview report.

Transfer Order A warehouse management term that describes the request to move material to or from a storage bin.

Transport Request A method of organizing changes to an R/3 system. The transport request records changes made to the system and controls what is transported to other systems in the landscape: e.g., development to quality then to production.

Two-Step Stock Transfer A procedure whereby the stock is issued from one plant and then received at the receiving plant. This is the same for transfers between storage locations.

Unit of Measure Defines the amount or size of the material or service such as bottle (BT), each (EA), hour (Hr), etc.

Universal Product Code (UPC) Standardized number used in the U.S. to uniquely identify a material. The EAN number is used in Europe.

Valuation The process of estimating the value of the company's stock.

Vendor A business partner from whom materials and services are purchased.

Vendor Evaluation The functionality that allows the vendors to be evaluated based on price, quality, service, and delivery reliability. The evaluation can determine how a material is sourced.

Warehouse An organizational structure that resides within the Warehouse Management functionality. It can be linked to materials management via the storage location.

Work Center A location used in Production Planning where a manufacturing operation is performed.

Workflow A routing tool in SAP that forwards documents for review or approval. For instance, a requisition that needs to be approved is sent to the appropriate approver's inbox.

C About the Author

A native of London, Martin Murray joined the computer industry in 1986. In 1981, he began working with SAP R/2 in MM for a London—based beverage company. He moved to the United States in 1994 to work as an SAP MM consultant. Martin has implemented MM and WM projects worldwide. He now works for IBM and lives with his wife in Orange County, California.

Acknowledgements

The author would like to specially thank Jawahara Saidullah of SAP PRESS for her faith in the author and her tireless efforts in getting this book completed. Thanks also go out to John Parker for his editing of the final drafts.

Index

C

D

E

F

M

N

O

S

U

V

W

Y

Z

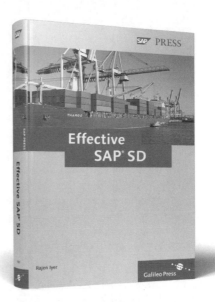

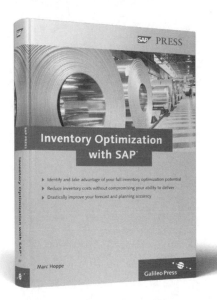

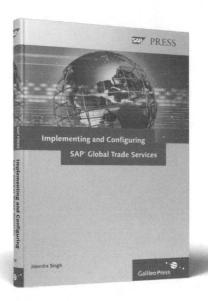

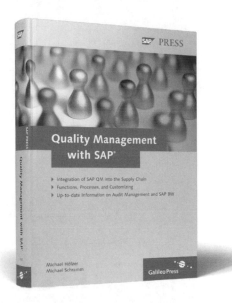